Yon-Gyong Kwon

Eschatology in Galatians

Rethinking Paul's Response
to the Crisis in Galatia

Mohr Siebeck

YON-GYONG KWON, born 1965; BA at Seoul National University; M.Div. at Fuller Theological Seminary; STM at Yale Divinity School; 2001 Ph. D. at King's College London; 2001-2003 Pastoral ministry for Korean Americans in NY; Professor of New Testament at Westminster Graduate School of Theology in Seoul.

ISBN 3-16-148438-X
ISSN 0340-9570 (Wissenschaftliche Untersuchungen zum Neuen Testament 2. Reihe)

Die Deutsche Bibliothek lists this publication in the Deutsche Nationalbibliographie; detailed bibliographic data is available in the Internet at *http://dnb.ddb.de*.

The book was printed by Druckpartner Rübelmann GmbH in Hemsbach on non-aging paper and bound by Buchbinderei Schaumann in Darmstadt.

Printed in Germany.

Wissenschaftliche Untersuchungen zum Neuen Testament · 2. Reihe

Herausgeber/Editor
Jörg Frey

Mitherausgeber / Associate Editors
Friedrich Avemarie · Judith Gundry-Volf
Martin Hengel · Otfried Hofius · Hans-Josef Klauck

183

To my wife Inhwa
Sine qua non

Preface

The present study represents a slightly revised and updated version of my Ph. D. thesis submitted to King's College, University of London, in September 2000 and accepted in January 2001. The work consists mostly of exegesis of Galatians in the traditional sense of the word. There are some important methodological suggestions, but its focus throughout is to explicate the meaning of Paul's argument itself. Readers who look for a 'novel' approach or a 'groundbreaking' methodology will be disappointed; its contribution lies in challenging the traditional reading of the letter by looking at it from a different perspective.

Scholarly interest in Galatians does not show any sign of abating, and many interesting studies have appeared since the completion of my dissertation. On the whole, however, I have not come across many studies that either seriously challenge my thesis or are directly relevant to it. On those salient points proposed in this book, most studies still seem to follow the 'consensus' that I take issue with. For this reason, I do not feel it necessary to undertake a major revision of my original thesis; therefore, the extent of updating and revision is fairly limited.

I have incurred a huge debt of gratitude during the years of my research for this thesis. My first and special thanks go to Professor Graham Stanton, who supervised my work throughout, even after his move to Cambridge. I cannot thank him enough for his ready help, careful criticism, warm encouragement and particularly his patience with my raw materials, without which my research would have been much more torturous. I also thank him for encouraging me to seek publication of this work. I also offer my sincere thanks to Dr. Douglas Campbell, now at Duke University, who acted as another supervisor at the latter stage of my research, whose careful readings of my earlier drafts have greatly enhanced the quality of my work. I also thank Dr. Edward Adams who also read my draft and offered many helpful suggestions.

My doctoral research would not have been possible without the financial assistance of many institutions, to all of which I offer my sincere gratitude: the British Committee of Vice-Chancellors and Principals for the granting of an ORS award for the years 1997-2000; the KCL Theological Trust for the 'small' grants; the DooRae research foundation for financial support. I also thank Ulsan Presbyterian Church and DooRe Presbyterian Church in Korea for their prayers and financial assistance.

I also send my thanks and affection to my parents and my mother-in-law for their unfailing love and support which has always been a precious part of my life.

A warm word of thanks is also due to my colleagues here at Westminster Graduate School of Theology in Seoul for their support and encouragement. I also thank Dr. Joseph S. Park and Mr. Sang Lee, both of whom read part of the material and offered me many helpful suggestions in stylistic matters.

I am grateful to Professor Dr. Jörg Frey for accepting this work into the WUNT series, as well as for his comments and suggestions. I also thank the staff at Mohr for their kind and swift help, in particular Mr. Matthias Spitzner.

Needless to say, my deepest gratitude goes to my wonderful wife, Inhwa Choi. Throughout our years together she has been a cheerful imitator of the self-sacrificing love of Christ, of which I am a most fortunate and most grateful beneficiary. It is she who made my research possible in the first place, and by dedicating this published version to her, I am thus merely repeating what I did with the original thesis version, namely, getting the work back to its rightful owner.

The biggest change since the completion of the thesis is, of course, the birth of my daughter, Sarah, who was conceived around the time I submitted my thesis. Her birth put an end to our ten years of anxious waiting, but I am sure she will protest that it was she who had had to wait all those years to allow daddy to complete his project. During the time of revision she would come and sit on my lap, duly promising that she would keep 'quiet', and I loved her breaking her promises as much as she did herself. Both my wife and I, together with our parents and friends, are grateful for no other reason than her just being here with us, knowing that that is the very dream our Father in heaven is still dreaming (Rom 8:29). So, as always, my final words remain: SOLI DEO GLORIA.

June 2004

Yon-Gyong Kwon

Table of Contents

Chapter 3

Justification as an End-Time Gift 51

Chapter 4

Son, Seed and Heir: Paul's Sonship Language 78

Chapter 5

Chapter 6

Chapter 9

Conclusion 213

Notes

The abbreviations used in this work follow the convention of *Journal of Biblical Literature*, *New Testament Studies*, and *Catholic Biblical Quarterly*. In the notes, a short title and year are given; full titles are available in the bibliography at the end. Where the name of an author is given without a short title, the reference is to that author's commentary on Galatians. For commentaries on the other books of the Scripture both author and a short title are given. For an author who shares the same name with another, the initial of that person's first name is also given to avoid confusion.

Chapter 1

Introduction

1.1 The Task

Paul's letter to the Galatians continues to attract lively scholarly interest.[1] This is hardly surprising since this relatively short letter contains much valuable information about Paul and the early church and presents many fascinating issues both for historians and for theologians. It is thus not surprising to see that this letter often provides a crucial test case for students of earliest Christianity. It is not an exaggeration to say that one cannot speak with any degree of confidence about Paul and early Christianity without first making one's mind up about Galatians.[2] So the stakes are high and discussion is intensive. This being so, it is also quite rare to find a happy consensus on most issues that concern the letter.

There is, however, one glaring exception: most scholars accept that there is 'a structure of realized eschatology' in Galatians.[3] Here two claims are involved. First, Paul's logic is an 'eschatological' one; to understand Paul is to grasp this fundamentally eschatological way of thinking undergirding his argument in the letter.[4] Secondly, it is a 'realized' eschatology. In Galatians it

---

[1] Recent major studies include Dunn, *Theology* (1993) and *Galatians* (1993); Hong, *Law* (1993); Hansen, *Galatians* (1994); Eckstein, *Verheißung* (1996); Williams, *Galatians* (1997); Martyn, *Issues* (1997) and *Galatians* (1997); Witherington, *Grace* (1998, commentary); Esler, *Galatians* (1998); B. Longenecker, *Triumph* (1998); Smiles, *Gospel* (1998); Kern, *Rhetoric* (1998); Choi, 'Spirit' (1998, Ph. D. thesis, Denver-Iliff); Nanos, *Irony* (2002). See also Nanos ed., *Debate* (2002).

[2] Good illustrations can be found in the theories of Beker, Martyn, Sanders and Dunn.

[3] Beker, *Paul* (1980) 98–99. See e.g., Marshall, 'Eschatology' (1997) 49; R. Longenecker lxxxvii–lxxxviii; Barclay, *Truth* (1988) 100; Meeks, 'Apocalyptic' (1982) 695.

Unlike the more technical use of the term 'realized eschatology' in the work of C. H. Dodd, in the present study we use it loosely to denote *an emphasis on the realized aspect of salvation*. In contrast to this, we shall use the term 'future eschatology' to describe Paul's perspective in Galatians, in which he understands the meaning of the present (and the past) as it pertains to the future hope of final salvation.

[4] One thinks of such influential studies as Schweitzer, *Mysticism* (1930); Vos, *Eschatology* (1930); Cullmann, *Time* (1950) and *Salvation* (1967); Schoeps, *Paul* (1961); Davies, *Rabbinic Judaism* (1948); Ridderbos, *Outline* (1975); Furnish, *Theology* (1968).

is this aspect of 'already' that carries the sharpest edge of his contextual polemic.[5] To exaggerate a little, to understand Paul's argument in Galatians is to grasp its realized eschatological structure.[6]

Is this consensus, which seems so obvious to most interpreters, well-founded? Or is it possible that it is merely the result of repeated assertion which nevertheless lacks hard evidence? Indeed, when scholars agree on a certain issue, they usually do so because the relevant data is so clear as not to allow any other interpretation. Unfortunately, however, this is not always the case. Not infrequently, scholarly consensus may involve more than disinterested exegesis, as the story of the emperor's 'new clothes' reminds us. It is for this reason that once in a while we need to hear the cry of a boy who clearly *sees* the naked body of the king, but not the wonderful robe he *is supposed to see*. The present study is our attempt to express such a boyish surprise at the 'transparent robe' of 'realized eschatology' in Galatians, with the conviction that there is indeed good reason to question its reality.

1.2 Ways of Reading the Galatian Eschatology

Let us begin the discussion with a simple but crucial question: granted, for the time being, a realized eschatology in chapters 3 and 4 of the letter, what do we do with the strong future eschatology in chapters 5 and 6 where Paul issues solemn ethical instructions and warnings (5:5, 21b; 6:7–9)? If his emphasis is indeed on realized eschatology, why does he, as he rounds up his argument, confuse his readers by saying things which almost seem to bring his earlier words to naught? What then should we do with these troublesome chapters? Is there a satisfactory answer to this question–namely, an interpretation of Paul's argument which shows a level of self-consistency as one might expect in such a highly polemical writing as Galatians?[7]

We begin our study with a brief overview of the scholarly treatment of the subject, with the goal of demonstrating that *Paul's eschatology in Galatians has not yet been adequately accounted for*. Being a virtual consensus, eschatology has seldom been a major topic in scholarly discussion, which renders a systematic review of the subject difficult. We divide our survey into three major groups: 1) a fully realized eschatology; 2) the eschatological tension between 'already and not yet'; 3) future eschatology. In addition to

---

[5] Scholars disagree over the nature and extent of this 'fulfillment'.

[6] Even those who take Paul's main concern to be the 'ongoing' aspect of Christian life think that the 'already' of the 'getting in' forms the essential ground for Paul's thesis.

[7] We do not, of course, mean the kind of rigid systematic consistency in which every single detail logically fits together. What we mean is a sharply focused *perspective* which shapes the contour of Paul's argument as a whole. Cf. the helpful discussion in Silva, *Galatians* (2001) 143–150.

these, we shall also take a look at the view of Betz about future eschatological justification. This grouping is, of course, somewhat artificial, but our purpose is not so much to discuss who says what as to discern major ways of construing Paul's eschatology in Galatians. This will pave the way for the presentation of our own reading of the letter in the subsequent chapters. Since eschatology is intrinsically related to ethics, and in turn, to the larger issue of the structure of the letter, we will also be paying some attention to how successful each approach is in making a coherent case out of Paul's argument as a whole.

1.2.1 Fully Realized Eschatology: Traditional Approach

Many scholars discern what we may call a 'fully realized eschatology' in Galatians. Overall, the view is presented in unambiguous terms, which renders a long discussion unnecessary. What follows is thus a brief analysis of some major lines of approach within this position, with special reference to their implications for understanding the eschatological structure of the letter.

An obvious starting point is the 'traditional' reading of the letter in which Paul's doctrine of justification is understood as his attempt to thwart the 'legalistic' attitude of 'justification by works of the law'. Burton[8] provides a good account of this view. For him, the letter concerns whether the Gentiles should receive circumcision or not in order to gain 'membership' in the covenant people and salvation (lvii). Paul rejects this legalistic view of his opponents by claiming that justification is only in Christ and by faith. Paul's main contention is, of course, that legalistic 'works of the law' can never be the proper ground for God's acceptance.

What concerns us here is Burton's claim that Paul's refutation of such 'legalism' carries a strong *a posteriori* polemic in it. In other words, Paul falsifies the legalistic notion of justification on the basis of the factual reality[9] of justification by faith: the undeniable fact that Christ actually died (2:21), which marked the revelation of God's righteousness, requires that faith in the crucified Christ has to be the only way of justification and that the law-righteousness is a blind alley which flies in the face of what has actually happened (141).

Paul's scriptural argument is also read in the same light. What is crucial for Burton is, of course, the Galatians' actual experience of the Spirit by faith and without the law. Taking 'the promise of the Spirit' (3:14) as the fulfillment of the Abrahamic promise which dominates much of Paul's discussion in chapters 3 and 4, he suggests that Paul makes his claim of 'by faith' on the ground that the promised inheritance is already realized in the form of the

---

[8] Burton, *Galatians* (1921).

[9] This reality is interpreted either forensically or ethically. For the more recent 'apocalyptic' approach, see 1.2.3 below.

Spirit, namely, the Spirit that the Galatians received by faith. Paul renders pointless the demand of circumcision as the condition of becoming children of Abraham by pointing out the fact that the Galatians are already sons of Abraham by their faith in Christ. By stressing the 'realized' nature of Christian life, then, '[t]he appeal of the apostle is to retain the status they already possess' (225). Throughout, Paul's thought is 'concentrated on the way of acceptance with God in the *present* life', and naturally, 'eschatological references are few and indirect' (15, emphasis added).

This does not mean that the element of 'not yet' is completely denied.[10] The trouble is, however, that, though acknowledged, it simply remains *inconsequential* for Paul's *main* argument. We are not told how it can be understood as part of Paul's response to the crisis without letting it hamper its otherwise neat realized eschatological framework.[11] Given this rather disruptive nature of future eschatological references, it is not surprising that some scholars, such as Eckstein,[12] come up with a much neater version of realized eschatology, denying *any* relevance of future eschatology for Paul's argument in the letter. For him, even the 'hope of righteousness' (5:5) does not refer to future justification but to the hope *present* justification bestows on those justified (247). He too acknowledges that believers' perseverance will prove 'meaningful in the end' and 'surely be rewarded'. As it becomes immediately clear from the way he puts the matter, however, the sharp teleological edge in Paul's words is carefully blunted so as not to disrupt the emphatically realized thrust (251). '[D]ie eschatologische Spannung', Eckstein unequivocally concludes, 'spielt in der konkreten galatischen Kontroverse keine Rolle' (118).

1.2.2 Fully Realized Eschatology: Sociological Readings

The traditional reading of the letter has presently been under heavy attack, especially since the publication in 1977 of E. P. Sanders's major book.[13] Many scholars, with various degrees of modification, still continue to hold the traditional view of Judaism and Paul,[14] but different ways of resolving the tension are vigorously sought, most noticeably in terms of sociology and

---

[10] Burton acknowledges future justification and the necessity of proper obedience. Compare pp. 471 and 278, 311–312. Duncan's more Lutheran reading also allows the element of 'not yet'.

[11] Such silence is typical of many scholarly interpretations, e.g., Hendriksen; Guthrie; Bruce; Hübner, *Law* (1984); Smiles, *Gospel* (1998); Schreiner, *Law* (1993).

[12] Eckstein, *Verheißung* (1996).

[13] Sanders, *Palestinian Judaism* (1977); *Law* (1983). For some reviews, see Neusner, 'Comparing' (1978) 177–191; Best, 'E. P. Sanders' (1982) 65–74. One should not forget that Sanders joins an already growing momentum detected, e.g., in Stendahl, *Paul* (1976).

[14] See, e.g., Hübner, *Law* (1984); Kim, *Origin* (1984); Westerholm, *Law* (1988); Thielman, *Plight* (1989); idem, *Law* (1994); Laato, *Law* (1995); Hagner, 'Jewish Matrix' (1993); Gundry, 'Grace' (1985); Stanton, 'Law' (1996).

eschatology. Without doubt, one of the mounting concerns since the work of Sanders has been how to relate Paul's criticisms of the law to the 'covenantal nomism' that Sanders so forcefully describes. What is relevant for us here is the fact that these newer trends do not seem to help us to appreciate the future eschatological thrust in Galatians. While the notion of 'legalism' is seriously questioned, its basic, realized eschatological framework goes almost unchallenged.

In recent years, the sociological dimension of Paul's argument attracts growing scholarly interest. [15] Being sociological, attention is necessarily focused on the *present*, allowing little room for the future eschatological dimension of Paul's polemic to stand on its own. Watson[16] provides a good example. Failing to find any 'theological' ground for Paul's rejection of the law (64), he takes it to be a sociological call for 'separation from the Jewish community'. 'Paul's use of an antithesis asserts the separation of church from synagogue, but does not explain theologically why such a separation is necessary' (69). For the Gentiles, justification by works of the law means 'entry into the Jewish people', which is wrong 'for that reason alone' (69).[17] Paul's polemic in Galatians is manifestly a *sociological* one on which his theological conviction has no bearing at all. Naturally, Watson practically passes over the issues of eschatology and ethics, together with the role of the Spirit which forms the spine of Paul's argument (3:2–5; 4:21–31; 5:16–26; 6:7–9).

Barclay[18] does view ethics as an integral part of Paul's polemic. With the convenient scheme of 'identity' and 'pattern of behavior', he competently demonstrates how Paul's theological argument 'points toward and requires the moral instruction at the end of the letter' (77–105, here 105) which, as the 'necessary consequence' of identity, describes 'how the members of God's people should live' (217). What is puzzling for us here is that, while ethics is well anticipated by Paul's discussion of identity, its futuristic framework is neither 'anticipated' nor 'necessitated' by it. This is inevitable, since Barclay takes Paul's theological argument to be about 'realized identity' and explain ethics in that particular light rather than the 'not yet' of future salvation.[19]

---

[15] The prevalence of such motifs as 'identity', 'inclusion', 'unity', 'equality', 'openness', 'separation' and 'boundary' illustrates this trend.

[16] Sanders, *Paul* (1986).

[17] Italic is removed in the last quote. Here he cites the frequently cited words of Sanders in *Palestinian Judaism* (1977) 552: 'In short, this is what Paul finds wrong with Judaism: it is not Christianity'.

[18] Barclay, *Truth* (1988). Unlike Watson, his *main* concern is theological. R. Longenecker's 'legalism and libertinism' resembles Barclay's scheme. See also Matera, 'Culmination' (1988) 85; Gaventa, 'Singularity' (1991) 149: 'a new identity in Christ' and 'new life in the Spirit'; Hong, *Law* (1993); Fee, *Presence* (1995) 367–471.

[19] See pp. 90, 91–92, 95, 96–97. This is much more explicit in Esler. See below.

After all, he too agrees with Beker and Martyn that 'Galatians does not match the other apocalyptic Pauline letters' in its lack of 'the near-expectation of the end' (100). Ethics is well integrated into the scheme, but future eschatology still does not find any role to play, even in what is arguably one of the most successful attempts to interpret the letter as a unified argument.

Esler's reading of Galatians in terms of a social anthropological theory of identity[20] seems more successful in accounting for the role of ethics and eschatology, in that both elements are now taken up as 'aspects of a much larger reality called identity' (172, 217). Esler reminds us, quite legitimately, that 'a group's sense of their destiny, of where they are headed, can constitute an important part of their sense of who they are', since 'identity' has 'both a present and future dimension' (175, 233). From this he further claims that such an identity-generating function is the *main* purpose behind Paul's talk of future salvation (233).[21] Here the domestication of *future* eschatology into the concept of *present* identity, already visible in Barclay, becomes quite explicit. However, one cannot help feeling that this is the answer Esler gets from the theory with which he began and not a conclusion gained from his actual reading of Paul's argument.[22]

By saying this, we do not mean that these interpreters argue for a realized eschatology. They explicitly affirm the future eschatological dimension of Paul's theology, as well as the necessity of proper conduct for end-time salvation (6:7–8).[23] The point is, however, that as in Burton this recognition is *irrelevant* for their readings of Paul's polemic itself, which is the inevitable consequence of their sociological orientation. But the future eschatological thrust is clearly there in the letter (5:5, 21b; 6:7–9), and one cannot help wondering if too much is not left unexplained for their sociological readings to be convincing.

---

[20] Esler, *Galatians* (1998). See his own summary in 'Social Identity' (1998). See also 'Reading' (1996) 215–240 and 'Family Imagery' (1997) 121–149.

[21] Meeks, 'Apocalyptic' (1982), speaking of the function of the motif, anticipates the full-blown study of Esler.

[22] Through the methodological glasses of 'identity', Esler seems to see *everything* in Galatians in that particular light, thereby creating the impression that Galatians is about identity. What really happens, however, is that from the start Galatians is approached from the particular angle of 'identity'. Although we do not thereby deny the dimension of identity altogether, claiming that such an identity-forming function is the *main* purpose of Paul's theological argument is pushing this otherwise valuable insight a bit too far. For a telling criticism of Esler's work, see the review by Bonnington (1999), especially pp. 144–145.

[23] See, e.g., Watson, *Paul* (1986) 64–65; cf. pp. 119–121, 148, 159; Barclay, *Truth* (1988) 165, 227, 230: 'it was not just a matter of what God *had* done...but what he *continued to do* in and for the believer' (227, italics his). Here we observe a 'theological' turn in his language, which becomes strategic for an 'eschatological' or 'apocalyptic' reading of Paul. See the next section.

Sanders, very instructively, reveals the problem future eschatological motifs cause for these sociological readings.[24] Calling Paul's justification language a 'transfer terminology',[25] he claims that the issue in Galatians is not the condition the Gentiles must meet to be 'saved' or 'justified' at the Judgment but to enter the people of God,[26] namely, to become true 'sons of Abraham'. 'Justification', 'freedom from the law' and 'receiving the Spirit' all deal with this issue of 'getting in'.[27] Paul's case is clear: by believing in Christ, Gentile converts have already become proper members of God's people. This does not mean that Sanders denies future salvation in Paul.[28] It simply is not the issue in Galatians which is only about the *initial entry*.[29] Naturally, 'Galatians is remarkable for the relative absence of end-time language, but the ruling topic of chapter 3 is how to become a descendant of Abraham'.[30]

Sanders *does* notice the motifs of future salvation (5:5), however. He explains that in the end initial entry matters, because it is the 'precondition of end-time salvation'. And behind this lies 'the unspoken assumption that the true descendants of Abraham will be saved'. Ultimately, then, Galatians is about 'how to enter the body of those who would be saved'.[31] The strategic split between 'getting in' and 'staying in' has then proved rather artificial from the first,[32] as well as his suggestion of 'entry' as the subject of the letter.

1.2.3 Fully Realized Eschatology: Eschatological Readings

Another important way of explaining Paul's polemic against the law is to seize upon the alleged realized eschatological convictions of Paul: the coming of Christ has established a new era and thereby rendered the law obsolete. Not surprisingly, this approach is often combined with a strong christological[33] or

---

[24] Sanders, *Law* (1983), which is an exegetical substantiation of his view suggested in *Palestinian Judaism* (1977) and *Paul* (1991). With varied nuances, the term 'identity' is currently in vogue among Pauline scholars. Cf. Wilckens, *Rechtfertigung* (1974) 132; Davies, 'People of Israel' (1977) 10.

[25] Sanders, *Palestinian Judaism* (1977) 470–472, 501, 544. Cf. pp. 491–495; *Law* (1983) 5–10.

[26] Sanders, *Law* (1983) 18, 20; *Paul* (1991) 50. The point is, no doubt, to eliminate the theological, more specifically, *soteriological* connotation.

[27] Sanders, *Law* (1983) 52, n. 20. The intention of Sanders is clear: since Paul's polemic is not against 'works-righteousness', 'the quality and character of Judaism are not in view' (19). Throughout his discussion, Sanders takes issue with Hübner.

[28] Sanders, *Palestinian Judaism* (1979) 441–442, 515–518; *Paul* (1991) 21–22, 26–33.

[29] Sanders, *Law* (1983) 20 (emphasis original).

[30] Sanders, *Law* (1983) 46.

[31] Sanders, *Law* (1983) 45–46; *Paul* (1991) 59.

[32] Moo, 'Law' (1987) 292; Stanton, 'Law' (1996) 105.

[33] The 'sacramental' reading of Brinsmead, *Response* (1982) is a prominent case in point (e.g., p. 197). See also Campbell, 'Coming' (1999).

theocentric[34] orientation. An obvious merit of this perspective is that, like the sociological one, it provides an attractive way out from the difficulty of explaining Paul's polemic against the law. By focusing on the eschatological decisiveness of Christ, one can render the law 'obsolete' without actually having to criticize it.[35]

Beker[36] provides an ironic example of this approach. Despite his emphasis on 'future apocalyptic'[37] as the core of Paul's gospel, Beker fails to make Galatians support his case and admits that the letter 'almost presents us with a "realized eschatology", since the fullness of eschatological reality coincides with the Christ-event' (98–99).

> Indeed the eschatological present dominates the letter, for the crisis situation demands the either/or of bondage under the law or freedom in Christ. And this either/or is so centrally grounded in the death of Christ as the annulment of slavery under the Torah (Gal 2.19–21; 3:1, 12–14; 4:5; 6:14) that the apocalyptic future with its basis in the resurrection of Christ does not receive its proper emphasis…. Indeed, *if we ignore the future apocalyptic hints in Galatians*, the letter can be easily interpreted as a document of realized eschatology' (58).[38]

---

[34] B. Longenecker, *Triumph* (1998) gives a 'realized eschatological' reading in which he combines a strong theocentric perspective (35–67) with an equally strong emphasis on morality (69–88; 147–171).

[35] See McLean, *Curse* (1996) 113–119; Davies, 'Pitfall' (1982) 4–16; Barclay, *Truth* (1988) 240. The solution is, however, more apparent than real since eschatological logic alone is in reality nothing but a chronological variant of Sanders; 'because it is *not* Christianity' is now phrased 'because it is *before* Christianity'.

[36] Beker, *Paul* (1980).

[37] After Schweitzer, Käsemann has been most influential in spreading the 'apocalyptic' Paul. 'Apocalyptic' in *Questions* (1969) 108–137. Cf. *Perspectives* (1971).

Despite its popularity, the term 'apocalyptic' is fraught with ambiguity. Inevitably, each interpreter gives the term his/her own definition. Using the same term does not prevent interpreters from subscribing to widely different views (cf. the 'future apocalyptic' of Käsemann and Beker vs. Martyn's 'realized, cruciform apocalyptic') and using different terms does not necessarily mean that their views differ (e.g., B. Longenecker's 'eschatological' view shares much of the 'apocalyptic' views of Beker and Martyn). This state of affairs renders the value of the term questionable. See Stanton's review of Martyn's commentary. An excellent critical review of the ways in which major interpreters use the term for their own theological programs is available in Matlock, *Unveiling* (1996).

[38] Italics added. For Beker, the dictation of the situation makes Galatians 'a first-level polemical response' and not 'a second-level dogmatic proposition': Paul's logic is 'cryptic, intuitive, and often inconsistent', with no 'fundamentally consistent picture' emerging. Since 'the Christocentric focus of Galatians pushes Paul's theocentric apocalyptic theme to the periphery', 'Galatians cannot serve as the central and normative guide for all Paul's letters and theology', because it is utterly 'contingent'. Thus, by exaggerating the contingency of Galatians Beker minimizes its negative impact for his thesis of (future) 'apocalyptic Paul'. Here we see how his hermeneutical scheme of 'coherence and contingency' serves his case. We shall see that, ironically, Galatians

The point is clear, but a question immediately pops up: how can a fundamentally realized eschatological perspective accommodate at the same time an equally unambiguous note of future eschatology in the letter?

An easy way out is to excise the disturbing part. So Beker says that Galatians will present a neatly realized eschatology 'if we ignore the future apocalyptic hints in Galatians'. B. Longenecker, like many others,[39] takes this route. His silence on future eschatology is made more poignant by his uncompromising emphasis on morality as part of salvation itself.[40] As with Barclay, morality is understood as a 'demonstration' of God's established triumph in Christ rather than as the precondition of God's future salvation. As in the sociological approach, however, the problem of expurgation is too obvious to ignore.

There is another difficulty here, however, namely, the problem of confusing the categories of theology or christology and anthropology. How does the announcement of God's accomplished triumph relate to the contingency of human life which is far from complete? More specifically, how does the talk of *God's* triumph serve as an effective response to the problem of *human* backsliding? Martyn, who puts a strong emphasis on the realized eschatological thrust of Galatians, illustrates this problem most acutely: 'Paul speaks of our redemption as an accomplished fact, giving no indication that any aspect of it is as yet incomplete' (90). This note of 'already' concerns God's victory, which is, of course, grounded on the cross of Christ, the 'centerpiece' of God's rectifying apocalypse.[41] The thrust of Paul's argument is thus clear:

> There was a "before," the time when we were confined, imprisoned; and there is an "after," the time of our deliverance. And the difference between the two is caused…by the coming of Christ and his Spirit. … In a significant sense, the time of

---

provides one of the strongest pieces of evidence for Beker's 'future apocalyptic' interpretation of Paul.

[39] See e.g., Barclay, *Truth* (1988) 102–103; Keck, *Letters* (1988) 72–73; Hong, *Law* (1993) 27, 76–78, 88–89; *idem*, 'Perspective' (1991) 1–16; Wright, 'Gospel' (1994); Smiles, *Gospel* (1998) 73–74, 142–146, 182, 217.

[40] B. Longenecker, *Triumph* (1998). A case in point is his heavy use of 5:6 ('faith active through love') which stands in stark contrast to his complete silence on 5:5, despite the explicit connection between the two.

[41] This notion of *cruciform* apocalyptic constitutes one of the most crucial aspects of Martyn's 'apocalyptic' reading of Paul, generating a framework of realized eschatology with the note of absolute disjuncture from the past. For his view of 'apocalyptic' see Martyn 38–39, 97–105, 163–167, 263–275; *Issues* (1997) 77–84, 141–156, 279–297. See also his 'Events' (1991) 166, n. 2, 179. Also see the evaluation in B. Longenecker, *Triumph* (1998) 5–8.

cosmic enslavement is now past, and *its being past is a central motif of the entire letter* (99).[42]

With God's redemptive work already accomplished, 'the turn of the ages is no longer ... an event in the future' (101). What Paul proclaims in Galatians then is the indicative truth of 'God has done it!' (103).[43]
Martyn is not, however, oblivious to the consummation in the future. He is, as Sanders, sensitive enough to be surprised at the futuristic note Paul frequently strikes (550). He even says that 'Christian life is essentially oriented to the future, being determined by Christ's future no less than by his past' (*Issues* 65). How then can God's 'already' produce a meaningful combination with future 'consummation'? Is it just a matter of time, with no human contingency whatsoever, not even apostasy, ever affecting the final result? Martyn sums up the matter in this way: 'God's rectification in Christ is *accomplished*' but still '*remains under attack*' by the enslaving flesh. 'God's rectification is therefore consistently *to be lived out*', continuously '*finding its concrete form* in the daily life of the church' (478–479).

Here Martyn becomes quite dialectical, even paradoxical. A rectification at once accomplished and yet to be lived out, already accomplished but still to find its concrete form, does not go down the throat smoothly. Further still, God's 'powerful' rectification that is at once completed and yet still under attack also puzzles us.[44] His point is that *God's* accomplished rectification expresses itself in the life of *believers*. It is precisely at this *anthropological* turn that his *theo*logical and *christo*logical affirmation of 'already' falters, since the contingency of human obedience, as well as God's judgment, still remains (498, 479). Of course, God's triumph is never doubted, but the Galatians' participation in it, which has a lot to do with their obedience, remains an open question. Indeed, it seems to be this anthropological (ethical) problem that reduces Paul to such desperate measures as we see in Galatians.[45]

Hence one-sided focus on God's or Christ's faithfulness does not seem to take us to the bottom of the matter. After all, Martyn seems to end up with the

---

[42] Emphasis added. Similarly, Bornkamm, 'Revelation' (1974) 95.

[43] See also pp. 104, 275, 475; *Issues* (1997) 64–65; cf. pp. 279–297.

[44] Cf. B. Longenecker, *Triumph* (1998) 77: 'To promote "works of law" is to incorporate matters of the flesh into the gospel, thereby *stripping it of the power of the sovereign God* who brings into existence a united community transformed into the image of the self-giving Christ' (italics added). If one turns Paul's talk of human behavior into the theocentric talk about God's victory, the Galatians' present disobedience is also elevated to an effective threat to God's powerful activity, damaging 'God's reputation' (cf. 46). Would Paul approve such a statement?

[45] This is pointed out by Engberg-Pedersen in 'Response to Martyn' (2002), which is his response to Martyn's criticism in 'De-apocalypticizing Paul: An Essay focused on Paul and the Stoics by Troels Engberg-Pedersen' (2002).

very position he himself criticizes: justification is 'to be had on earth only as a pledged gift, always subject to attack, always to be authenticated in practice – a matter of *promise* and *expectation*' (479).[46] 'God has done it!' turns out to be 'God has given the promise!' This is a practical recantation of his earlier, accentuated, affirmations. Once we take future eschatology into account, there does not seem to be an adequate way of construing Paul's argument within the structure of realized eschatology.

There is still one more problem to be dealt with: given such a realized eschatological logic as proposed by these interpreters, it becomes very difficult, if not impossible, to explain the sense of urgency and distress Paul's argument so visibly bears out. A recent major study by Nanos, for example, claims that Paul's argument is based on an inherently eschatological conviction that 'because of Christ the age to come has begun in the midst of the present age', requiring Paul to modify the way 'the traditions of the Father' are applied, namely, 'from expectation to implementation, from an awaited future to the dawn of the age to come'. Because of this change of the ages, the Galatians 'can participate in this eschatological reality *as Gentiles*', and that constitutes 'the truth of the gospel' Paul has set out to defend ('Context', 403). According to Nanos, Paul's gospel

> has uniquely maintained that they are already honored righteous ones in the present age without completing the ritual process of proselyte conversion, because it claims that the age to come has dawned, thus modifying the terms of identification (*Irony*, 12).

If the Galatians have already, albeit unwittingly, attained to the goal they are mistakenly trying to reach, there is no real need for Paul to make such a fuss, since in that case he could just remind them of that unalterable eschatological reality, saying that Christ has come and thus circumcision has now become *superfluous*.

As far as we can tell from the way Paul responds, however, his position does not seem to be so relaxed. Unless we conclude that Paul is unduly overreacting, both the explicit meaning and the urgent tone of Paul's argument require one to suppose that there is real danger involved in the current development in Galatia with actual damage being done to the faith of the Galatians. As Nanos himself repeatedly notes, Paul views his converts' behavior as an action that 'necessarily entails defection from the grace of God toward themselves in Christ while yet Gentiles'. 'It will in effect nullify the purpose of Christ's death for themselves' (52–53) and 'subvert the very foundation of their faith' (12). The real point of Paul, then, is not the eschatological decisiveness of Christ, but that the effect of the Christ event is

---

[46] He is quoting Käsemann, 'Righteousness' in *Questions* (1969) 168–182 (170). See his critique of Käsemann's *futuristic* definition of 'apocalyptic' in *Issues* (1997) 112.

being effectively undone by the foolish behavior of the Galatians. But then, their willingness to concede to the demands of the 'influencers' shows that the Galatians have not understood this thus far.[47] If so, what we should expect from Paul is a clear explanation about why circumcision has to be *harmful*, instead of being merely unnecessary. Cleary, the Galatians are of a different opinion, and will not be convinced by Paul unless it is made crystal clear *why* the seemingly harmless addition of circumcision to their already righteous status should be taken as 'so dangerously undermining the good news message of Paul about Jesus' (312). Yet on this most critical point we find Paul completely silent. We only hear Paul repeat, 'Circumcision is nothing'. He seems to be playing a different note.

Nanos himself suggests that circumcision of Gentile believers violates the conviction which he considers to be the essence of Paul's gospel–that in view of the age to come already present, the Gentiles should come into the people of Israel as *Gentiles* ('Context' 403). But, as Nanos himself identifies as Paul's major theological point, as far as Paul is concerned, the Gentiles are already part of God's people. In other words, the Galatians, regardless of their status *vis-à-vis* the local Jewish synagogues, are *already* in the community of God's people as Gentiles by believing the gospel and receiving the Spirit, even though the 'influencers' dispute that claim. If that is the case, what then is so wrong about adding circumcision, clearly an *adiaphoron*, now that the membership issue has long been settled? To put it differently, as far as Paul is concerned, the question is not about membership in God's people but about membership in the Jewish synagogue, since they are already God's people anyway. Why does the latter nullify the former for the Gentiles?[48] For this question, as already noted, one does not hear any clear answer from Nanos.

This only shows that merely appealing to the realized eschatological logic cannot explain the threat Paul detects in the current situation in Galatia. A realized eschatological reading can make circumcision *superfluous* but never *harmful*.[49] That is, an answer has to be provided for the *danger* Paul feels about his converts' circumcision. As we have seen above, mere appeal to God's faithfulness or the eschatological decisiveness of the Christ event does

---

[47] This is another problem of Nanos's reconstruction: Until the writing of Galatians, Paul did not feel it necessary to make this point clear to the Galatians, a point Nanos claims to be 'the purpose of Christ's death for them' and 'the foundation of their faith'.

[48] The artificiality of such a position is also visible in his view that the Gentiles already converted to Judaism can be Christ-followers but those Gentiles who have become believers cannot now be Jews without losing their membership as God's people. How can we apply this 'rule' to a half-Jew like Timothy, Paul's co-worker, or an uncircumcised Jew who, having previously become a Christian, now wishes to be circumcised and become a true Jew?

[49] Also see our discussion in 7.2 below where we make the same point in regard to the law.

not in itself explain the crisis as Paul perceives it. As Boyarin says 'it is not just that the fulfillment of time has come but more to the point is that Paul understands it *in a certain, specific way*'.[50] The key is finding out what that 'specific way' is.

1.2.4 Eschatological 'Already and Not Yet'

The future eschatological thrust of Paul's argument fares much better in the widely held scheme of the eschatological 'already and not yet'.[51] Dunn is an eloquent voice for this position. Informed by Sanders's view of Judaism yet critical of his failure to relate it adequately to Paul, Dunn[52] proposes that the issue in Galatians is 'staying in' – whether the Gentiles, having already claimed a share in God's covenant, still need the law in order to *sustain* that claim.[53] The 'works of the law' are not entrance requirements but 'the first act of covenantal nomism'.[54] Naturally, justification, the central theme of the letter, does not mean 'initial acceptance into the covenant' (*pace* Sanders) but 'God's acknowledgement that someone is in the covenant', whether 'initial', 'repeated' or 'final',[55] covering 'a sustained relationship with God'. By 'justification by faith' Paul then means that 'as their initial acceptance by God was through faith, so is their continuation and their final acceptance (Gal 5.5)'.[56]

---

[50] Boyarin, *Jew* (1994) 35 (italics added). His is a version of realized eschatological reading set within the larger hermeneutical framework of 'flesh-spirit' dualism. According to him, the problem of the Galatians 'is not that they suddenly are becoming proud and self-righteous but they are abandoning the higher condition of being "in the spirit" for a lower one of observance of circumcision in the flesh' (70). To these Galatians Paul is basically saying that 'they have already achieved a higher state, which is the purpose of the Law and should not wish now to regress to a lower state' (70). Such an act signifies a regression, since it implies thereby 'that only physical descent or physical adoption into the Jewish family saves' and if so, 'Christ died on the cross in vain' (144). Once again, it is not clear *why* mere addition of circumcision has to be interpreted as a regression into a lower state. Observing Paul's treatment of the issue, is it also not possible to argue that it is Paul who is still bound to the lower level of the flesh, in that he is unable to leave circumcision alone as an *adiaphoron*?

[51] To various degrees, this seems the most widespread way of reading Paul's eschatology. Hester, *Inheritance* (1968); 'Heilsgeschichte' (1967) presents such a view with the concept of inheritance and Byrne, *Sons* (1978) 141–190 with sonship and freedom.

[52] Useful reviews of Dunn's view of Paul include Silva, 'Synthesis' (1991) 339–353; Hagner, 'Jewish Matrix' (1993) 111–130.

[53] Dunn, 'Theology' (1991) 130. Cf. Gundry, 'Grace' (1985); Smiles, *Gospel* (1998) 24.

[54] Dunn, 'Theology' (1991) 130–131; *Theology* (1993) 103.

[55] Dunn 134–145, 148; *Law* (1990) 190. Here Dunn depends heavily on his view of the Antioch incident. See *Law* (1990) 129–182, 183–214.

[56] Dunn 139–140, 155–158; 264–272; *Law* (1990) 208, 209.

Into this framework of 'covenantal nomism' Dunn gathers both 'already' and 'not yet'.[57] On the one hand, having 'already experienced' the Spirit, the eschatological fulfillment of the promise and hope (3:14), the Galatians have been 'fully accepted by God and did not fall short in any degree in their standing before him' (154, 156). Having begun 'by faith', the status of the Galatians is complete and sufficient. Yet, the 'already' of faith is not intended to press a 'realized eschatology' but to show how to work out such a beginning in the ongoing life of 'not yet' until the day of final justification, the full realization of the 'promise' and 'inheritance'. Of course, 'how they began' continues to be determinative also for their ongoing life. '"By the Spirit, from faith" continued to be the basis, primary and sufficient, so long as that hope lay before them yet to be fully realized; to think that this hope could be realized or made more certain in terms of the flesh was to destroy that whole basis' (269–70). Paul's *main* concern is this 'second', ongoing and eschatological phase. Paul's statement in 3:3 sums up the whole point: since they have begun with the Spirit, they also have to finish with the Spirit (3:3).

The thrust of 'not yet' becomes even stronger in Witherington.[58] Like Dunn, he too takes the issue in Galatians not to be 'getting in' but 'going on',[59] making 'life in the Spirit' in chapters 5 and 6 the main subject of the letter. Of course, for Witherington too chapters 3 and 4 deal with initial entry, with unequivocal emphasis on the fulfilled promise and realized inheritance in the form of the Spirit. As in Dunn, however, this is only a preliminary step. Paul's real point is that 'precisely because they did not come to be in Christ by obeying the law…, they should not now add obedience to the law to their faith in Christ' (174).[60]

In Witherington, together with his emphasis on ethics, the future eschatological thrust takes on much greater prominence, for the simple reason that life in the Spirit necessarily 'affects their eternal status and reward' (432).[61] Chapters 3 and 4 are still read in terms of a realized eschatology but now the real issue becomes whether they should live by works of law or by faith 'in order to gain the final salvation or acquittal of God in the future'. The question of final justification thus 'gets at the heart of the problem in Galatia'. Paul's point is that obedience to the law is 'neither necessary nor

---

[57] This works on two levels: within individual concepts (such as justification and inheritance) and within the structure of the letter.

[58] Witherington, *Grace* (1998).

[59] Instead of redefining justification in terms of covenantal nomism, he relegates it to a subsidiary place as Cosgrove, *Cross* (1988) does. See n. 1 in chapter 3.

[60] The ethical section, building upon the 'theological rationale' in chapters 3 and 4, forms 'a crucial part of the argument'. See pp. 25, 193, 217, 360–361. Cf. Fee, *Presence* (1995) 385.

[61] At this point, he takes part with Barclay and B. Longenecker who deal with ethics in the light of 'realized identity'.

beneficial...if the goal is justification before God or at the final judgment' (184, 369).

Clearly, this position has its own merit: at least we do not have the problem of undue selectivity; Paul's ethical emphasis and its future eschatological thrust have both been fully appreciated. Is this then the way we should interpret the letter? There are, however, questions to be answered.

An inevitable problem is that the covenantal nomistic logic suggested by Dunn and Witherington is not as plausible as it first seems: *as* you have begun with faith and the Spirit, *so* you have to go on in the same way.[62] For one thing, Paul never presses this point; it has to be *inferred* by the Galatians.[63] Yet, persuaded by the agitators, the Galatians are presently drawing precisely the opposite inference: as you have begun well by faith, now you need to continue by works of the law! Of course, Paul brands such a decision as 'foolish', but we are not told why it has to be so. Does it mean then that Paul just keeps asserting his own position without ever getting at his disputed point?[64]

In addition, it also strikes us as very strange that Paul spends no less than two closely argued chapters (3 and 4) just to make a preliminary point. Paul's tone in these chapters seems too final and definitive to be merely preparatory. In a way, this consideration alone should prove compelling enough to have these interpreters reconsider their covenantal nomistic logic.

A more serious problem of this position, however, is the juxtaposition of an emphatic 'already' and an equally strong 'not yet' within a single argument. For example, Dunn says that with the coming of the Spirit, 'the hope of Israel' is already fulfilled and thus, the promised inheritance is already given. The Galatians are '*fully* accepted' by God. Nevertheless, there is a hope 'yet to be *fully* realized', a belief which constitutes a 'common ground' in Galatia (269). But how can an emphatic 'already' go hand in hand with an equally unequivocal 'not yet'? If justification is still outstanding with ongoing obedience as its condition, the claim of full acceptance is certainly claiming too much in the first place.

We have to remember that in Galatians we are not dealing with a *summa theologiae* of Paul himself in which he presents a comprehensive synthesis of his eschatology but a polemic designed to deal with a specific problem. And it is very difficult, if not impossible, to imagine that Paul utters both 'already' and 'not yet' in the same breath in such a polemical letter as Galatians. An

---

[62] If one construes chapters 3 and 4 as concerning the 'beginning', while taking the main issue as the 'ongoing', this seems to be the only way of connecting the two.

[63] 3:3 is the only possible evidence for such logic, but, as 3:5 suggests, the intended contrast is between 'works of the law' and 'faith', not between 'beginning' and 'ongoing'. See our discussion of the passage in 2.3.2 below.

[64] Here we have exactly the same problem that we have spotted in those solutions based on realized eschatological reasoning.

emphatic 'already' works precisely on the basis of its denial of 'not yet'. By the same token, an unequivocal recognition of 'not yet' necessarily renders any claim of 'already' illusory. The framework of 'already and not yet', which may be appropriate as a synthetic scheme devised to gather diverse materials in Paul's letters into a comprehensive whole, falls short of an adequate explanation of a polemical argument tailored to a specific context. The urgent situation in Galatia seems to require a more unified perspective.[65]

1.2.5 *Libertinism and Paul's Future Eschatology*

A few scholars have paid special attention to chapters 5 and 6 taking them as the key to Paul's response to the Galatian crisis. Lütgert and Ropes proposed the well-known 'two-front' theory.[66] Schmithals went further and suggested a 'Gnostics' theory, dismissing chapters 3 and 4 as irrelevant to the Galatian crisis.[67] Crownfield proposed a sort of compromise describing the agitators as 'Jewish syncretists'.[68] Yet for these scholars the clearly future eschatological thrust of Paul's ethical talk does not make any contribution to reconstructing Paul's argument. It is Jewett[69] who, building on these earlier studies, takes the eschatological 'not yet' fully into account.

Jewett, acknowledging both the nomistic threat (3:6–4:30) and the libertinistic problems (5:13–6:10), tries to explain them in relation to the Galatians' 'Hellenistic assumptions' which are 'as susceptible to the propaganda of the agitators as to the lures of libertinism' (209). Concerning the former, however, the judaizers did not sell their nomism as it really was but under the disguised name of Hellenistic religiosity. That is, promoting circumcision and cultic calendar as means of gaining 'the final level of perfection', the agitators exploited the Galatians' propensity for mystery and perfection which is 'not nomistic at all' (212). They used such 'cunningly devised tactics' which are 'far from orthodox' (206–208) since they needed 'quick and observable results' to thwart persecution by the Zealots. It is *Paul* who construes the crisis in terms of 'nomism'.

The Galatians' Hellenistic religiosity is also crucial for Paul's anti-libertinistic polemic in chapters 5 and 6. Apart from the nomistic threat, the Galatians are from the first 'pneumatic libertinists', sharing a typical

---

[65] Cf. the remark of Sänger, 'Argumentationsstrategie' (2002) 388: 'Trotz wechselnder Tonlage (1.8–9; 3.1, 15; 4.12–20; 5:4; 6:1–2), abrupter Übergänge (3.1; 4.21) und gedanklicher Sprünge (4.25–26) präsentieren sie sich als eine konzeptionelle Einheit mit dem Ziel, die Galater von der Wahrheit des paulinischen Evangeliums zu überzeugen (1.6–9; vgl. 2.5, 14) und sie vor der Annahme eines in Wahrheit gar nicht existenten (1.6–7) zu bewahren'.

[66] Lütgert, *Gesetz* (1919); Ropes, *Singular Problem* (1929).
[67] Schmithals, *Gnostics* (1972) 13–64.
[68] Crownfield, 'Problem' (1945) 491–500.
[69] Jewett, 'Agitators' (1971).

enthusiastic misunderstanding of the Spirit. They took the Spirit as a 'self-sufficient circle' granting immediate immortality and salvation 'rather than a path leading to the *parousia'* (3:2–5, 14). This led them into 'a disregard for ethical distinctions' and 'the scornful rejection of the impending future judgment', coupled with 'an intensely proud spiritual self-consciousness'. Countering such a tendency, in 5:13–6:10 Paul emphasizes the 'normative function of the Spirit' and utters solemn warnings about the last judgment and individuals' moral accountability before God (5:10; 6:7–8) (210–212). In sum, it is the Galatians' 'Hellenistic assumption' that lies behind both problems of Jewish nomism and their libertinism.

The merit of Jewett's reading is that he takes Paul's ethical discourse seriously as a major part of Paul's response to the crisis. Considering the 'libertine' problem as the heart of the matter, he sensitively follows the relentless thrust of Paul's moral warnings. The explicitly future eschatological thrust of Paul's argument, which is all too often neglected or put into interpreters' procrustean beds of various sorts, exerts its full force.

Nevertheless, Jewett's claim that the Galatians' libertinism is based on their mistaken experience of the Spirit fails to be convincing. Paul's discussion of the Spirit throughout chapters 3 and 4 does not show any hint that he is correcting such a mistaken view of the Spirit.[70] Such an assumption also flies in the face of Paul's highly positive view of the Galatians' 'life in the Spirit' before the arrival of the agitators (3:3; 5:7). His view that the Galatians repudiated the Judgment also reads too much into Paul's polemic (cf. 1 Thess 1:9–10; 1 Cor 1:7–8).[71] Paul may well be correcting their mistaken sense of security which neglects the importance of believers' moral accountability.

Moreover, by relating the 'libertinistic' problem only to the 'Hellenistic assumptions' *inherent* in the Galatians themselves from the first, Jewett practically denies any real connection of it with the problem of nomism. In fact, Jewett seems aware of a sort of relation between the two, since he says at one point that Paul's 'ethic arrayed against libertinism was phrased *as a replacement of the law*'. Yet, his concern is only to prove that Paul's polemics against both problems are 'directed to the congregation as a whole' (210), without succeeding in relating nomism and libertinism as inter-related phenomena. After all, despite his recognition that 'some connection with nomism' is indispensable in explaining the Galatian crisis, (198–199), in practice, Jewett does not go much beyond the proposal of Schmithals.[72]

---

[70] Rightly, Matera, 'Culmination' (1988) 82.

[71] Rightly, Watson, *Paul* (1988) 198, n. 75.

[72] R. Martin, *Foundations* (1986) 152–158 offers a similar reading, connecting 'realized eschatology' both to the Galatians and to the agitators. But he too fails to relate the misguided experience of the Spirit with the propaganda of circumcision. Both contribute to the problem of libertinism, but how do they relate to each other?

1.2.6 Future Eschatological Justification

Finally, we shall comment briefly on the view of Betz that justification in Galatians is future-eschatological, throughout the letter.[73] As we shall argue later, this is in fact the view we are proposing as the only coherent interpretation of the data.

Unfortunately, however, Betz's view of end-time justification creates a blatant contradiction in his exposition of Paul's argument as a whole. Commenting on Paul's argument of 'blessing' in 3:8, he rightly says that Paul 'simply identifies the blessing with God's "grace" and his "justification by faith"' (142). Yet, in 3:14, following most other interpreters, he identifies 'the promise of the Spirit' with 'the promise God made to Abraham'. Further, he identifies the content of the Abrahamic promise as the 'blessing' mentioned in 3:8 ff., and infers that the Spirit should therefore be the promised blessing (3:14). With the coming of the Spirit, this promised blessing has therefore been fulfilled (152–153, 175). If so, it necessarily means that justification has also been realized, since, as noted above, he explicitly identifies 'blessing' with 'justification'.

Betz does not seem to be aware of the problem, but this interpretation flatly contradicts his claim that justification in Galatians is a future blessing to be given at the Last Judgment. The problem is, of course, that his future eschatological interpretation of justification does not cohere with his exposition of other parts of the letter which follows the line of 'realized eschatology'. Since various themes in Paul's argument are clearly inter-related, he should have done more to substantiate his claim of future justification in its relation to other themes such as 'blessing' and 'promise'. In view of Paul's clear statement in 5:5, Betz' suggestion of 'future justification' is perhaps the most promising option to take. Nevertheless, subsequent interpreters have mostly ignored his suggestion, which is unfortunate but also understandable, considering his failure to relate it to Paul's argument as a whole.

1.3 Thesis

Our survey above shows that, despite intense scholarly interest in the letter, Galatians still awaits an adequate account of its eschatological structure. In 1965 MacGorman[74] argued that 'the structure of a *parousia*-eschatology is never abandoned; neither does it fade into a meaningless background' (331). Yet he too, without being able to integrate it into Paul's *main* argument, concedes that the evidence is incidental, probably due to the historical

---

[73] See his discussion of the theme, e.g., pp. 116–119.

[74] Jewett, 'Analysis' (1965).

circumstances of the letter (253). Our survey confirms that this is indeed the situation in which most interpreters find themselves. For this reason the future eschatological motifs in Galatians are easily ignored or superficially treated, perpetuating the impression that Galatians is a document of 'realized eschatology'.

We cannot, however, follow the advice of Beker to 'ignore the future apocalyptic hints in Galatians'[75] since, however annoying they may be to us, they are certainly part of Paul's argument in which he is as serious as anywhere else in the letter. We have to lend due weight to the unequivocally future eschatological tone of Paul's statements in such passages as 5:5, 21b and 6:7–9. We have also rejected as unrealistic the attempt to hold both the 'already' and the 'not yet' together as Paul's response to the Galatian crisis. We are then left with only one, albeit radical, possibility to consider: does Paul's theological argument in chapters 3 and 4 really show a realized eschatology? Is the structure of realized eschatology in the 'central' section of his argument, which has almost become a 'fact' beyond the burden of proof, as obvious as so many assume? Is it possible that the consensus reading of Paul's theological argument is a projection of scholarly idea into Paul's language which in fact runs in quite a different direction?

The present study attempts to demonstrate that the structure of realized eschatology in Galatians is more assumed than actually proved, and that Paul's argument in Galatians is in fact set within a distinctively future eschatological framework. By saying this, of course, we do not mean that the letter does not have any interest in the past or the present. Galatians does speak frequently of what happened in the past as well as the believers' present privileges. Our contention is that Paul's immediate intention in bringing them out, however, is not to impress their realized nature on his readers, but to make them see the meaning of the present within a fundamentally future eschatological point of view. This will then provide a coherent connection to Paul's ethical discourse in chapters 5 and 6.

1.4 Context and Method

Before we turn to detailed examination of the letter, however, a methodological discussion is in order. Interpretation, to a certain degree, is a subjective business, since interpreters necessarily bring their own presuppositions to the text with their distorting effects.[76] As S. Garrett

---

[75] Beker, *Paul* (1980) 58.

[76] Stanton, 'Presuppositions' (1977) 60–71 (61): 'the philosophical and theological starting point which an interpreter takes and which he usually shares with some others'.

reminds us,[77] interpreters of an ancient text do not have the 'advantage' of ethnographers, who have both the living author and the original context of the 'social text' they are studying. Bewilderingly divergent, and often mutually contradictory, interpretations are proffered for a single text, all with their own claims and grounds but with the jury always out. That is, the text is 'malleable';[78] interpreters have to actively 'construe' its meaning. And it is because of this malleability of the text that the question of context takes on special importance. Establishing the 'context' of the text in effect means gaining an 'expectation' of how the text should be, and in actual reading, it is this expectation or interpretive context that critically determines the way we 'construe' the text.[79]

1.4.1 Historical Reconstruction and Mirror-Reading

In Galatians the dominant way of establishing a context is historical reconstruction through 'mirror-reading'. Here scholarly interest usually centers on the identity and teaching of Paul's opponents. Since Galatians is thought to be Paul's *response* to his opponents and their propaganda, it is a matter of 'extraordinary importance' for us, says Mußner, to 'grasp the physiognomy of the opponents as precisely as possible'.[80] Or, in Barclay's words, 'we will not understand the true import' of Paul's statements 'until we have critically reconstructed the main issues in the dispute and allowed ourselves to enter into the debate from *both* sides'.[81]

The logic of mirror-reading is simple. Paul's statements are examined with a view to 'determine Paul's specific answers to charges and to opposing teachings'. Since 'in most cases, the charge can be seen by taking the negative

---

[77] Garrett, *Demise* (1989) 7–8.

[78] Cosgrove, *Cross* (1988) 6.

[79] For the importance of 'genre expectation', see Hirsh, *Validity* (1967) 68–126 and Longman, *Literary Approach* (1987) 76–83. Here we are speaking in more general terms, not strictly 'literary genre'. Boers, *Justification* (1994) 1–41 discusses the issue in terms of 'macro-structure'.

[80] Mußner 29. Sampley, 'Text' (1991) 7 is more emphatic: 'Because Paul focuses so frequently on the position of his opponents, our capacity to understand Paul is *directly proportionate* to our ability to understand Paul's opponents.' See also Dunn, *Theology* (1993) xv.

Naturally, most studies of Paul begin by asking about the identity of the agitators. E.g., Howard, *Crisis* (1991) 1–19; Barclay, *Truth* (1988) 36–74; Smiles, *Gospel* (1998) 4–29; Martyn, *Issues* (1997) 1–36; B. Longenecker, *Triumph* (1998) 25–34. For some interpreters, this question forms their main concern, as in Schmithals, *Gnostics* (1972) 13–64, Munck, *Paul* (1954) 87–134, and now, Nanos, *Irony* (2002), who is a most recent addition to the list.

[81] Barclay, 'Mirror-reading' (1987) 73. See also Roetzel, *Letters* (1991) 83.

of the defense' or 'by reversing the defensive statements',[82] with caution, the teachings of the opponents against whom Paul fights can be reconstructed. In this way, one gains a broad understanding of what transpires among those involved, which in turn gives an idea about the subject of the letter. Then, by reading Paul's argument anew in this newly reconstructed context, one may hope to have a better understanding of what Paul really means.

Lyons has already exposed the fundamental problems of this 'widely practiced art', with the radical conclusion that it is 'arbitrary, inconsistently applied, and unworkable'. [83] Since the reconstruction comes 'only as implications from some very brief and unclear statements', the interpreter has first to select relevant statements, and this process can be nothing but 'almost totally arbitrary'. [84] And since the textual data is also 'meager', other 'background sources' are needed to complete the picture. And selecting presumably relevant material is a very precarious process.[85] Lyons' main point is that the method inevitably involves too high a degree of arbitrariness, and there is no way of avoiding it. Mirror-reading is, he insists, 'the fruitless cultivation of an unsown field'.[86]

Most relevant for our purpose is Lyons' comment that Paul's depiction of the opponents is 'obviously one-sided, probably exaggerated, even distorted'.[87] This observation about the inherently subjective nature of Paul's letter is extremely important, since it reminds us of the crucial point that indiscriminate talk of a 'historical context' is epistemologically misleading in the first place. There is no such thing as *the* situation; it has to be *constructed* by somebody, as researchers of human perception teach us.[88] In Watson's word, 'in its textual embodiment reality is inevitably shaped and reconstructed out of a heterogeneous mass of raw material; it is not simply transcribed or repeated'.[89] Then what we have in Galatians is Paul's 'construction of the

---

[82] The quotes are from Tyson, 'Opponents' (1968) 241–254 (246, 244, 249). His statements seem somewhat mechanical but nevertheless depict the gist of the method concisely.

[83] Lyons, *Autobiography* (1985) 119, 95.

[84] Lyons, *Autobiography* (1985) 95, quoting Howard, *Crisis* (1991) 7.

[85] Lyons, *Autobiography* (1985) 120.

[86] Lyons, *Autobiography* (1985) 120. Most interpreters simply ignore or brush aside his criticism as too pessimistic without properly answering the criticism he offers. E.g., Murphy-O'Connor, *Paul* (1997) 195; Esler, *Galatians* (1998) 64–68. Closer to the truth is probably that we do not know where to cultivate since we do not know what is sown. It is to be noted that Lyons's own 'rhetorical' approach too is based on *historical* analogy.

[87] We do not endorse, however, his uncalled-for value judgment.

[88] See Berger/Luckmann, *Construction* (1966); Geertz, *Culture* (1973); Ornstein, *Consciousness* (1986). Morgan/Barton, *Interpretation* (1988) 1–43 highlights the importance of an interpreter's 'interests' and 'aim' as crucial factors in interpretation.

[89] Watson, *Text* (1994) 2. 'A certain opacity and resistance to penetration attend the phenomenon of the text' (3). Thus, as Geertz, *Culture* (1973) 9 reminds us, 'what we call

reality'. Paul, as an interpreter, actively constructs the situation, defining the problem in the light of his own theological presuppositions and his own apostolic purpose.[90] We can, of course, speak of the 'situation' as the Galatians or the agitators would perceive it from their own, probably quite different, perspectives. But, then, the data we have in front of us is hopelessly inadequate for that purpose.[91]

As noted before, scholarly efforts to get to the bottom of the situation means attempts to reconstruct the agitators' point of view, namely, the agitators' construction of the situation, which involves recovering the data Paul has rejected as inconsequential but are crucial for his opponents.[92] However, this audacious double jump from Paul's perspective to the agitators' viewpoint and back to Paul himself is not only impossible but also *unnecessary*, and even *detrimental*, if what we are after is Paul himself. In our effort to draw a more comprehensive and 'balanced' picture of the situation, we in fact run the risk of impairing the 'zone of lucidity'[93] Paul has constructed from his own particular viewpoint. If we are to learn the view of the Galatians or the agitators, we will have to venture a mirror-reading after all, making up for the 'distortion' with other external sources that our 'poetic fantasy' happens to consider as 'relevant'.[94] If we are to understand *Paul's perspective*, however, such measures will only confuse us, since what we now have before us is the best possible source of what we are looking for. The conclusion seems inevitable: if our aim is to understand *Paul's argument*, we have to take *Paul's own perspective* as our interpretive framework.[95] Beginning with Paul's opponents is beginning from the wrong end.

---

our data are really our own constructions of other people's constructions of what they and their compatriots are up to'. This is quoted by Garrett, *Demise* (1989) 8–9.

[90] This is what Beker ignores when he speaks of the situation *dictating* Paul's argument. *Paul* (1980) 23–36, 37–108 (45, 53). His 'coherence-contingency' scheme is based on an unrealistic and outmoded 'stimulus-response' model of human perception. See also his 'Recasting' (1991) and the response by Achtemeier, 'Finding' (1991), especially p. 32 (on Sampley).

[91] So Schmithals excises 3:6–4:20 as reflecting only 'Pauline interpretation of the situation'. *Gnostics* (1972) 41–42.

[92] Martyn's articulate reconstruction of the agitators' sermon provides an excellent example of this focus on the agitators. *Issues* (1998) 7–24.

[93] Berger/Luckmann, *Construction* (1966) 44: 'the reality of everyday life always appears as a zone of lucidity behind which there is a background of darkness'.

[94] Martyn, *Issues* (1998) 12, n. 10 says that historical reconstruction requires both 'scientific control' and 'poetic fantasy'. For example, the recent study by Nanos, *Irony* (2002), focuses on this very thing (see his statement in p. 31). He cuts his path through Paul's language by appealing to its rhetorical character, taking Paul's argument as a whole to be an 'ironic rebuke'. See our criticism of his reconstruction in the next chapter.

[95] The importance of Paul's perspective is noted by Schlier 24; Westerholm, *Law* (1988) 150. See also Cosgrove's criticism of Schlier in *Cross* (1988) 22.

Cosgrove[96] perceives this problem, when he says that since Galatians is not an objective record of the Galatian crisis, the necessary presupposition for proper exegesis is not the historical 'reconstruction of the opponents' position' but 'what Paul sees as the real issue', namely, 'the apostle's viewpoint'.[97] Despite this insight, however, his actual discussion fails to gain sufficient clarity, since he still operates under the notion of the historical situation. This is revealed by his tacit, but clear identification of the 'epistolary perspective' with the 'situational context' of the debate. Raising the right question of *Pauline* perspective, Cosgrove still considers it to be determined not by Paul but by the situation, rendering his hard-won insight into 'Pauline perspective' rather hollow.[98] He manages to produce the criteria of 'directness' and 'specificity' for the reconstruction, but it is Cosgrove himself who determines what is 'direct' and 'specific' and what is not.[99]

Also noteworthy is Stanley's discussion.[100] He is quite explicit about the subjective nature of interpretation. Rightly noting the 'obscure' nature of Paul's references to 'the situation', he says that Paul's letters 'stand as *primary* sources regarding Paul's *perception* of the situations in the churches he addressed, but only as *secondary* sources regarding their *actual* condition.'[101] Here, he is much closer to the mark, though he still speaks of 'actual' situation out there. This time too, however, the promise fails to substantiate itself, since Stanley resorts to the notion of 'implied readers' as a way of grasping Paul's perspective.[102] Obviously, we do not have the 'implied reader' before us; it has to be reconstructed by somebody. After all, it is Stanley himself who assumes the role of the implied reader informing us (and Paul) how his intended readers would respond to his argument.[103]

1.4.2 Rhetorical Criticism and the Context of Paul's Letters

Rhetorical criticism also requires some consideration. Since Betz first cleared the way with his landmark studies,[104] a vast amount of literature has been produced, exploiting all the possible avenues available in this area.[105] Once

---

[96] Cosgrove, *Cross* (1988) 6–23.

[97] His term is 'epistolary perspective'. Cf. Smiles, *Gospel* (1998) 6.

[98] Thus, Cosgrove does carry out a reconstruction in his next chapter.

[99] Cosgrove, *Cross* (1988) 23–38.

[100] Stanley, 'Curse' (1990) 481–511.

[101] Stanley, 'Curse' (1990) 486, 496 (original emphases).

[102] Stanley, 'Curse' (1990) 497.

[103] As in Cosgrove, here the interpreter's subjective decision replaces external sources as the basis for reconstruction.

[104] Betz, 'Literary Composition' (1975) and *Galatians* (1979).

[105] Well-informed surveys are found in Anderson, *Theory* (1996) 111–123 and Kern, *Rhetoric* (1998) 43–56. For a collection of a few important studies, see now Nanos, *Debate* (2002) 3–196.

again, the sheer diversity of proposed solutions indicates that Galatians does not display obvious marks of any particular rhetorical genre.[106] It has to be imposed on the text by the interpreter who approaches the text with a prior 'expectation' about its rhetorical genre. Then, it is in fact this expectation that determines the purpose of Paul's 'speech-act' in Galatians. 'Once Galatians is expected to look like an example of classical rhetoric', Kern rightly complains, 'it does not seem to matter how far the text deviates from the handbook descriptions'.[107]

Here, the fundamental problem is ignoring the fact that classical rhetoric functioned within its own specific social contexts which are quite different from that of Paul's letters. It is such disregard for the different social contexts and the consequent neglect of the contextual particularity of Paul's writings that constitute Kern's main critique of scholarly practice of this method. Paul's writings, including Galatians, differ from other ancient writings and this difference is 'conditioned by the fact that they were composed from a different point of view and for different people'.[108] Kern puts the matter succinctly.

> If the epistle is recognized to be a persuasive, purposive text, then it should be analysed as such, and within the rhetorical world that created it. The constraints of that world shape the text; and, if the text and its shape can reveal the intent of the author (as Muilenburg maintained), then that social world with its particular constraints may be properly brought in.[109]

This is a perfectly sensible demand: Galatians written by Paul should be interpreted according to 'the apostle's values and cultural outlook' instead of being 'determined from outside'.[110] Of course, it is not to deny the value of rhetorical consideration altogether; Paul does use many rhetorical devices and proper examination of these will enhance our understanding of his argument significantly.[111] The point is that it is dangerous to appeal to rhetorical genre

---

[106] See Anderson, *Theory* (1996) 124, 166–167.

[107] Kern, *Rhetoric* (1998) 257.

[108] Auerbach, *Mimesis*, (1953) 45, quoted in Kern, *Rhetoric* (1998) 257.

[109] Kern, *Rhetoric* (1998) 55. As Dunn 20 says, it is 'the theological issues and logic which are likely to have determined the main line and structure of the argument'. Martyn 23 (20–23, 145–146) even suggests 'a moratorium of some length in this branch of research' (21). Also see Stanton's 'Review' (2000) and Dunn's earlier study, 'Prolegomena' (1994) 414.

[110] Kern, *Rhetoric* (1998) 260. See also Weima, 'Aristotle' (1997) 458–468.

[111] Kern, *Rhetoric* (1998) 260 acknowledges the value of investigating rhetorical 'commonplaces', various rhetorical 'devices', and the 'communicative forces' of the letters' shape. Anderson, *Theory* (1996) 249–257 reaches a similar conclusion. A good case in point is the study of oral patterning by Harvey, *Listening* (1998). Also see the comments in more recent studies such as Nikolakopoulos, 'Aspekte' (2001) 194–195 and Sänger, 'Argumentationsstrategie' (2002) 386–389.

as a way of determining the *context* and *function* of the letter as a whole. Once again, we are back to Paul himself.[112]

1.5 Outline of the Study

Naturally, we shall begin our study by examining the letter with a goal of ascertaining the context of Paul's argument. Abstaining from hazarding yet another hypothetical reconstruction of the situation, we will focus our attention on Paul's own statements about the situation, demonstrating that he provides a very clear picture of the crisis, no doubt, from his own particular perspective. This is chapter 2. Chapter 3 concerns justification, the central theme of Paul's argument. In this chapter we shall argue that in Galatians justification is a future hope, not a present reality, as it is the case in Romans. The following three chapters deal with Paul's exegesis of the Abrahamic tradition: sonship (chapter 4), promise (chapter 5) and inheritance (chapter 6). Here we shall attempt to show that the realized eschatological reading is based on ill-advised exegetical decisions and that Paul's perspective is fundamentally future eschatological. This concludes our argument concerning the future eschatological nature of Paul's theological discussion. Chapter 7 examines Paul's interpretation of the Christ event which allegedly sustains his realized eschatological perspective. By highlighting the contextual purpose of Paul's interpretation, we will try to refute the claims of realized eschatology, bringing out at the same time the centrality of the Spirit in his christological argument. In the last chapter (chapter 8), explicating the moral thrust of Paul's future eschatological argument, we shall see how the whole letter coheres as a single, well-unified, polemic against what Paul perceives to be the problem in Galatia. In the conclusion we shall summarize the result of our study with some reflections on its implications for future study of Galatians and Paul's letters in general.

---

[112] In the following chapters, we shall emphasize the importance of the letter's 'pastoral context' for proper interpretation of Paul's words.

Chapter 2

The Context of Paul's Argument

This chapter concerns the context of Paul's argument. As we have seen in the preceding chapter, this discussion is unavoidable because no clear description of the context of the original communication is available to us modern readers and thus Paul's words are open to diverse interpretations. Building on our discussion in the previous chapter, we shall here attempt a reconstruction of the proper context in which to interpret Paul's argument. As already noted, the moment we begin the reconstruction of the context, we are already well into the process of exegesis itself. So it is hoped that the findings produced in this chapter will provide a helpful preview of what will follow in the rest of the study.

2.1 The Majority View

Scholars have long debated over the destination and date of Galatians without having reached any firm conclusion. It is also very unlikely that a happy consensus will emerge in the near future.[1] Fortunately, however, our ignorance on such external matters does not necessarily hamper our understanding of the letter since the issues dealt with in the letter are mostly theological in nature. Even if the veil over these questions is somehow removed, it is unlikely that it will affect the way we understand Paul's argument to any significant degree.

2.1.1 Typical Features of the Majority View

More crucial for the proper interpretation of Paul's argument is the *immediate* situation which prompted him to write this letter. As already noted, for most interpreters the question of 'situation' mainly concerns Paul's opponents. Numerous attempts have been made to identify the nature of these agitators, only to produce the 'welter of opposing opinions and conflicting theories'.[2] Despite such diversity, however, a survey of

---

[1] These questions are frequently rehearsed in major commentaries.

[2] R. Longenecker lxxix.

major proposals reveals a substantial family resemblance in the general
contours of the situation behind the letter and the basic thrust of Paul's
response to this crisis.[3]

First of all, in focusing on Paul's opponents, it is normally *assumed* that
Galatians is a résumé of the conflict between Paul and his (Jewish
Christian) opponents. Thus Paul's real dialogue partners are the agitators
and not the Galatians.[4] Though being actual recipients of the letter, the
interpretive role of the Galatians remains secondary. It is the agitators, not
the helpless Galatians, that Paul's theological polemic primarily takes
issue with.

Secondly, as far as Paul's central theological argument is concerned, the
crisis is primarily dogmatic in nature. For Paul it is the 'false doctrine' of
his opponents that constitutes the heart of the crisis. Naturally, his
response too is fundamentally doctrinal, refuting their false theology by
reaffirming the validity of his own, especially through a reinterpretation of
the Christ event. As Betz puts it, Galatians represents 'the first systematic
apology of Christianity' over against 'the first radical questioning of the
Pauline gospel'.[5] That is, Galatians is read primarily as the record of a
'theological debate'.[6]

Thirdly, these two contextual assumptions determine the thrust of Paul's
polemic: since the agitators attack Paul's gospel by *questioning* the status
of the Galatians founded on his law-free gospel, Paul *defends* his Galatian
converts by affirming the validity of his gospel. Paul polemicizes against
the Galatians too, but he does so by *reminding* and *reassuring* them of the

---

[3] Eckert, *Verkündigung* (1971) 31–71, 229–238; Beker, *Paul* (1980) 43–44; Mußner
11–29; Lull, *Spirit* (1980) 29–52; Brinsmead, *Response* (1982); Barrett, *Freedom* (1985);
Barclay, *Truth* (1988) 36–74; R. Longenecker lxxxviii–c; Hong, *Law* (1993) 97–120; B.
Longenecker, *Triumph* (1998) 25–34; Martyn, *Issues* (1997) 7–24; Betz 6–9, 28–33; *idem*,
'Defense' (1976) 99–114.

[4] Hence the title of Brinsmead's study, *Galatians: A Dialogical Response to
Opponents.* See also, e.g., Donaldson, 'Curse' (1989) 97; Murphy-O'Connor, *Paul* (1997)
200; Weima, 'Gal 6:11–18' (1993) 90–107; Kertelge, 'Rechtfertigungslehre' (1968) 212;
Dunn 275.
    Thus, Galatians is usually read in the context of the Jew-Gentile problem. Mußner
11–29; Sanders, *Law* (1983) 19, 51 n. 18; Martyn 40–42; *idem*, *Issues* (1998) 71–84, 47–
75, 191–208 stress that the conflict is intra-Christian, but it still remains that Paul's
criticism falls on the *Jewish* side of the Jewish Christians, as Hübner, *Law* (1984) 152
rightly reminds us.

[5] Betz 28.

[6] It is somewhat ironic to note that *historical* reconstruction often means one of a
dogmatic dispute. Both in taking the letter in the context of the conflict between Pauline
and Jewish forms of Christianity and as an expression of a theological conflict (ideas), F.
C. Baur still seems to be carrying the day. Cf. Baur, *Paul (1875).* See also Kümmel,
History (1972) 132.

privileges they already possess in Christ and not by questioning them as the agitators do.

Finally, intent on authenticating the present status of his Gentile converts, Paul's argument naturally carries a strong note of *realized* eschatology. This is done by the strategic christological focus he gives to his argument. By faith in Christ the Galatians have already been justified. The only seed of Abraham is Christ; the Galatians who by faith are now in Christ share the same identity as the seed of Abraham. Since Christ also represents the fulfillment of God's promise, in Christ the Galatians already enjoy the benefit of this fulfilled promise, i.e., the realized inheritance. Inevitably, a strong emphasis also falls on the Galatians' experience of the Spirit, which functions as the proof *par excellence* for the present reality of such contested blessings.[7] It is the present reality of justification and the promised inheritance, and the eschatological superfluity of the law that forms the heartbeat of Paul's polemic in Galatians.

This widely subscribed view of the epistolary situation sketched above reveals one very striking fact about the usual practice of historical reconstruction: *interpreters attempt to reconstruct the context of Paul's polemic mostly from his theological argument in which the situation in Galatia is less visible, while leaving out of account those passages in which he speaks of it directly and explicitly.*[8] This neglect is due to the implicit decision that Paul's confrontations with the Galatians are not immediately relevant for reconstructing the context of his argument, since the situation is assumed to be his doctrinal debate with the Jewish Christian rival missionaries rather than the Galatians themselves. This is, however, begging the question. Of course, it is a possible way of reading Paul's heavily 'theological' response, but the problem is that it does not cohere well with what he actually says of the situation in Galatia.

As we have suggested above, the proper step to take first is to listen carefully to what Paul himself says about the 'problem' he deals with and to try to follow his argument accordingly, instead of trying to read between his lines in the light (or darkness) of a hypothetically imagined context. To be sure, many think that one has to run the risk of reading Paul's slippery lines after all, since he says so little about it. This is true, if one means by the 'situation' the Galatian crisis from the *agitators'* point of view. Paul's interest in the teaching of his opponents remains superficial; even the little

---

[7] Hence one often hears of 'defense of the Spirit'. See n. 27 in chapter 8.

[8] The problem is detected by Schmithals who claims that Paul's argument in chapters 3 and 4 do not reflect the situation in Galatia since it is 'traditional' and 'relatively timeless'. 'Judaisten' (1983) 27–58 (49–50). In our opinion, however, his exclusive focus on chapters 5 and 6 is equally problematic, in that he too ignores those passages where Paul is most explicit about the nature of the problem he deals with.

he says about them is not necessarily objective. This should not, however, blind us to the equally true fact that throughout the letter Paul does provide a substantial amount of information about what *he* perceives to be the 'crisis' in the Galatian churches (1:6–10; 3:3; 4:8–11, 12–20, 21; 5:1–4, 7–12; 6: 12–13).

2.1.2 Recent Developments

Indeed there seems to be a growing acknowledgement of this point among recent scholars. For example, Mitternacht suggests that in ascertaining the context we should first look at those 'discourse units with direct pertinence for the situation of the addressees', and comes up with the basically the same list of passages as the one we gave in the previous paragraph.[9]

The recent suggestion of Mark Nanos[10] merits some lengthy comments. He divides the letter into two distinct categories: the 'situational' discourse and the 'narrative' one. The situational discourse materials are those 'directly written to the addressees' and thus 'contain the primary rhetorical information from which we may derive details of the exigencies in Galatia' (62). On the other hand, the 'narrative discourse' is to be analyzed only 'for the salient rhetorical connections' (63, 67), since 'with respect to the details of the exigency in Galatia, they provided secondary data' (63). His suggestion that in establishing the context one should begin with the direct 'situational discourse' is a welcome confirmation of the point we are making here, representing a significant advance.

Problems remain, however. First, although he rightly beings with the 'situational discourse' but he goes on to the other extreme, and more or less ignores the other parts of the letter. While it would not be totally amiss to say that the 'details of this narrative material is not necessarily relevant for construction of the situations or players in Galatia', nevertheless one should exercise caution, since the 'situation' we are dealing with involves central theological points and not just ecclesiological or sociological agendas.[11] Thus, while agreeing with Nanos in giving priority to the 'situational' discourse, we find him a bit puzzling when he claims that 'the most important details' for reconstructing the situation 'are contained specifically within the sections of the letter wherein Paul expresses ironic

---

[9] Mitternacht, 'Assessment' (2002). The list is found on p. 417. His exclusive focus on the theme of persecution, however, seems too narrow to cover what Paul means by 'faith working itself out through love'. On his hypothesis, one cannot help wondering why Paul does not say more straightforwardly: 'Do not avoid persecution!' A comparison with 1 Thessalonians, where the theme of persecution stands out quite prominently renders his reading of Galatians very unlikely (1:6; 2:2, 14; 3:3–4, 7).

[10] Nanos, *Irony* (2002) and 'Context' (2002).

[11] Cf. the comment of Barclay, *Truth* (1988) 60: 'These social factors are not at all easily teased out of Paul's letter, since Paul focuses so much on the theological issues'.

rebuke' (10) and that the narrative material matters only for its 'rhetorical points as they support the situational discourse' (62).

Nanos's claim that the context is one of an intra- and inter-Jewish conflict deserves serious attention. At the same time, however, it is not to be ignored that his picture stands on rather flimsy grounds exegetically – that is, on a few ambiguous statements and words in the letter rather than on a reading of the letter as a whole. Apart from scattered references here and there, most of Paul's argument, especially those parts identified by him as the 'narrative discourse', remain unaccounted for with nothing to contribute to the picture. While he acknowledges the value of these 'narrative' material as providing the testing material for the hypothesis drawn up from the situational material, he does not make any attempt to put his own picture to test with Paul's theological argument. Instead, one finds that his discussion of the exigencies is heavily informed by extra-textual materials, most notably rhetorical theories both ancient and modern and historical works on c ontemporary Judaism. In contrast to this rich extrapolation, his reluctance to consider the data found in the letter itself is quite glaring. The only major point he sees in this heavily theological section is the simple eschatological point that the coming of Christ, marking the dawn of the age to come, has modified the application of the tradition *vis-à-vis* the Gentiles and that now the Gentiles have to enter the community of God's people as Gentiles. And that, one has to note, is the assumption he begins with from the start, not the result of serious engagement with Paul's argument.[12]

In this respect, one telling case in point is Nanos's silence about what Paul says in 5:6, a verse generally considered to be crucial in grasping Paul's perspective in the letter. One would think that this passage would surely pose a serious challenge to his view of 'the good message of inclusion by circumcision versus the good message of inclusion apart from circumcision' as competing in the addressee's situations' (58) and, therefore, the view that for Paul circumcision itself is considered as necessarily nullifying the meaning of Christ's death for the Gentiles (52–53, 54, 109, *passim*). However, although the parallel passage in 6:15 is referred to a couple of times, the crucial phrase 'neither circumcision nor uncircumcision' escapes his attention completely.

After all, if, as Nanos asserts, most of what Paul says in the letter does not have any direct bearing on the conflict at hand, why would Paul spend so much time and space to say it? Just to say that he does so for 'rhetorical effect' sounds far from convincing, especially considering the heavily theological nature of the material. Paul's theological argument is certainly ambiguous *to us*, for which reason we propose to begin with the clearer

---

[12] In his article, 'Context', he makes this point by referring to Krister Stendahl.

data. This call is, however, never to be mistaken as implying that it is therefore largely irrelevant to the situation.

Nanos's failure to relate his reconstruction to the actual theological argument of Paul in the letter seems to have to do with his preoccupation with the perspectives of the 'influencers'. His choice of the 'situational discourse' materials is apt, but he looks at them not to understand Paul but to decipher the identity of Paul's opponents hidden behind Paul's 'rhetorical' language. Namely, his agenda is different in the first place. As we argued in the previous chapter, however, that is putting a wrong question to the text before us. Our purpose is not to decide how Paul's theological argument can be used to reconstruct the exigencies of the letter but to establish the proper interpretive context for Paul's theological argument itself. Our question is about how Paul perceives the situation. And this *Pauline* portrait of the situation is, after all, what we need to know since *his argument in the letter is his response to what he considers to be the problem*; not a reflexive reaction to an agenda set by his opponents.[13]

2.2 Pauline Context

The purpose of this section is to ascertain the context of Paul's polemic by examining his statements about the crisis to which he is responding. Two main questions will be discussed: 1) What exactly is the problem Paul perceives in Galatia? 2) Given the way he perceives the problem in Galatia, is the view of 'realized eschatology' plausible?

2.2.1 The Galatian Apostasy as the Heart of the Problem

What is the problem in Galatia? That is, what problem does the letter respond to? Once again, it should be clear that we are asking about the problem Paul perceives, not about what seems to be the problem for the Galatians or the agitators.

(a) Abandoning God (1:6–10). Right from the beginning of the letter, Paul does not leave his readers in any doubt: 'I am astonished that you are defecting from the One who called you in the grace (of Christ)' (v. 6). Since καλέσαντος most probably refers to God,[14] Paul's depiction of the Galatians' behavior as a 'turning away' (μετατίθεσθε)[15] from God forms an

---

[13] Rightly, Gundry, 'Grace' (1985) 9.

[14] Cf. 5:8; Rom 4:17; 8:30; 9:12, 24; 11:29; 1 Cor 1:9, 26; 7:15; Phil 3:15; 1 Thess 2:12; 4:7; 5:24.

[15] The word frequently refers to 'conversion'. Schlier 36, n. 1; Betz 47, n. 41 and references there.

unmistakable charge of apostasy. [16] His perspective is radical but unambiguous: the Galatians are defecting from God; it is a clear case of apostasy. Perhaps, it may not have been fair to the Galatians since, as Paul's reference to 'another gospel' [17] implies, they may have had no intention of leaving God at all. For him, however, there is no such thing as 'another gospel', which in reality is nothing but a 'perversion' (μεταστρέψαι) of the true gospel he had himself proclaimed to the Galatians. As far as Paul himself is concerned, the Galatians are really turning away from God, and that is the heart of the problem that provoked this bitter response on his side.

It is widely noted that this is the place where Paul normally announces the central theme of the letter in the form of 'thanksgiving' and 'intercessory prayer' (cf. Rom 1:8; 1 Cor 1:4–8; Phil 1:3; 1 Thess 1:2–10; cf. Col 1:3; 1 Tim 1:12; 2 Tim 1:3; Philem 4). [18] Instructively, in Galatians a severe 'rebuke' [19] replaces the usual, appreciative, 'thanksgiving'. This move, hardly abnormal in terms of epistolary convention, [20] is nevertheless exceptional for Paul. [21] That is, by dropping the usual thanksgiving and throwing in a stern rebuke instead, Paul deliberately 'signals the mood and purpose of the letter', providing a forecast of what is to follow. [22] If we take

---

[16] Hübner, *Law* (1984) 20. Mußner 53 suggests a possible allusion to Israel's apostasies in LXX Ex 32:8, Deut 9:16A and Judg 2:17.

[17] This is not a slip of tongue immediately corrected by Paul himself but an intended case of irony whose true intent is clarified by the following phrase as Nikolakopoulos, 'Aspekte' (2001) 201 aptly observes. Nanos, *Irony* (2001) seems to push his case a bit too far when he denies the Christian character of this 'gospel'. He is certainly right to say that the word could have a more general application, but the weight of evidence, especially in Paul, seems to lend support to the majority interpretation. Even 1 Thessalonians 3:6, which Nanos adduces as Pauline evidence for his non-Christian reading of the term, does not support him at all, insofar as this 'good news' of 'faith and love' reported by Timothy, just as the earlier and fuller depiction of the Thessalonians' triadic steadfastness in 1:3 (faith-love-perseverance), is described as the evidence for the effective outworking of the gospel Paul has proclaimed to them.

[18] Schubert, *Thanksgivings* (1939) 180; Funk, *Language* (1966) 257. As Stowers, *Letter Writing* (1986) 21–22 reminds us, this too is 'a genuine Hellenistic epistolary form' but this recognition does not diminish the importance of Paul's creative use of thanksgiving.

[19] θαυμάζω is a formula of rebuke. See Mullins, 'Formulas' (1972) 380–390. Cf. Nanos, *Irony* (2002) 39–61 who, based on this verse, defines Paul's argument as a whole as an 'ironic rebuke'.

[20] So White, *Greek Letter* (1972) 18, 49; Hansen, *Abraham* (1988) 33–43; Anderson, *Rhetorical* (1996) 126.

[21] Dunn 39 rightly criticizes the overly rhetorical approach of Betz 47 and Hansen, *Abraham* (1988) 44.

[22] Rightly, Stowers, *Letter Writing* (1986) 22; Duncan 15–16; Bruce 80; Becker, *Paulus* (1998) 289; Fung 43.

this cue seriously, then, the *major* target of his polemic is the apostatizing behavior of the Galatians and not the 'theology' of the agitators. The 'truth of the gospel' is at the center of the matter, but the immediate focus does not seem to be discussing is theological content but denouncing the Galatians' defection from it.[23] Of course, he is fully aware of certain (τινες) 'trouble makers' (ταράσσοντες) behind them (v. 7), on whom he does not hesitate to pour divine curse (v. 9).[24] Yet, it is the defecting behavior of the Galatians rather than the false teaching of the agitators that receives the direct brunt of his rebuke. It is the Galatians who are abandoning God's calling; it is they who Paul takes issue with.[25]

(b) Abandoning the Spirit for the Flesh (3:1–5). The next place where Paul speaks directly of the Galatian problem is 3:1–5. His definition of the problem is succinct: the Galatians, despite having begun with the Spirit, are now ending with the flesh (v. 3). This is, of course, not to say that they are 'adding' the flesh onto the Spirit just for good measure. Within his deliberate and strict antithesis of Spirit and flesh (4:21–31; 5:16–26; 6:7–9), his point is that the Galatians, now allied with the flesh, are giving up the Spirit, the very foundation of their Christian existence. The point is not the theological meaning of the Spirit or flesh;[26] Paul's concern is the Galatians' act of abandoning the Spirit in favor of the flesh.[27]

Here too, Paul is not oblivious to the presence of τίς behind their defection, 'casting an evil eye' (ἐβάσκανεν)[28] on the Galatians (v. 1). However, the primary target of his indignation is the Galatians:῏Ω ἀνόητοι Γαλάται! (v. 1); οὕτως ἀνόητοί ἐστε; (v. 3).[29] Bewitched or not, it is still the Galatians themselves, not the obscure τίς, who are most responsible for the crisis; *they* should have known better.

---

[23] *Contra* most interpreters, e.g., Cousar 19; R. Longenecker 19.

[24] Even this curse aimed at the agitators carries a paraenetic (warning) function for the Galatians, as Wiles, *Intercessory* (1974) 134 and Mußner 62 note.

[25] See Hartmann, 'Gal 3.15–4.11' (1993) 130: 'The meta-propositional base "I am surprised that"/"I urge you (not) to" is an indicator that the theme is not directly a theoretical, theological one, but one concerning behavior'. Cf. Hydahl, 'Gerechtigkeit' (2000) 428–429.

[26] *Contra* Lull, *Spirit* (1980) 38, 42–43, 103. Cf. Duncan 81.

[27] Martyn 285 perceives this: 'the Spirit and the flesh primarily as *means* that enable the human being to accomplish something' (emphasis added).

[28] It is not clear how literally Paul speaks at this point. See especially B. Longenecker, 'Christ' (1999) 93–100 and *Triumph* (1998) 150–155; Witherington 201–204; Neyrey, 'Bewitched' (1988) 72–100. Anyway, Paul's distress is effectively expressed.

[29] This expresses 'indignant astonishment'. Zerwick, *Greek* (1963) 12. Cf. *BDF* § 146. See Schlier 118; Anderson, *Theory* (1996) 142: 'However, the nature of this letter as primarily a *rebuke* explains the high degree of πάθος throughout' (emphasis original).

(c) Reversing the Conversion (4:8–20). In 4:8–11 the problem is described as the observance of the Jewish[30] calendar (v. 10). Again, Paul's criticism is radical but straightforward: in so doing, they are 'converting' (ἐπιστρέφετε) back to their former slavery under 'the elements of the world' (v. 9).[31] In Paul's view, this is a denial of their knowledge of God, or of God's act of knowing them. This is precisely the same charge as that in 1:6. Here, the agitators do not come into the picture at all; the issue is strictly between the angry apostle and his wayward converts caught in the act of backsliding.[32]

Gal 4:12–20 is particularly instructive for grasping Paul's perception of the problem in Galatia. Scholarly embarrassment over this 'not-quite-theological' talk in the midst of highly theological argument is well known. Why an abrupt 'emotional' appeal in the middle of serious 'theological' arguments? When Burton states that at this point Paul, 'dropping argument', 'turns to appeal begging the Galatians',[33] he speaks for the majority of interpreters.[34] Betz's appeal to rhetorical function may explain the presence of an 'emotional' piece in the midst of theological argument, but otherwise it still does not carry the discussion any further.[35] R. Longenecker thinks that at this point Paul begins the second, 'request section' 'by recalling his past relations with his converts and contrasting their past and present attitudes to him'.[36] Yet, it is still not clear how an appeal to the once amiable relationship helps to get down to the real business of 'requesting' them to stop their nomistic enthusiasm and Spirit-less life.[37]

---

[30] So Vielhauer, 'Gesetzesdienst' (1975) 552; Thornton, 'New Moon' (1989) 97–100. *Contra* T. Martin, 'Apostasy' (1995) 437–461, who suggests a reference to 'pagan' idol worship.

[31] The meaning of the phrase is debated. Bandstra, *Elements* (1964) 31–72; Reike, 'Law' (1951) 259–276; Vielhauer, 'Gesetzesdienst' (1975) 543–555; Martyn 393–406 = *Issues* (1997) 125–140. A good review is available in Arnold, 'Stoicheia' (1996) 55–76.

[32] According to Hartmann, 'Gal 3.15–4.11' (1993) 134, 4:8–11 rounds off the unit 3:1–4:11 by returning to the main, practical theme, thereby producing a ring-composition.

[33] Burton 235.

[34] Mußner 304–305 advises us to exercise 'intuitive grasping of the meaning and supplementing what is missing'. According to Schlier 208, the passage is 'an argument of the heart', revealing not just 'strong pathos' but also an 'erratic train of thought'.

[35] Betz 220–221. For him, the passage is based on the Hellenistic *topos* of 'friendship' (περὶ φιλίας).

[36] R. Longenecker 188.

[37] R. Longenecker 184–188. The scheme of 'rebuke-request', first articulated by Hansen, *Abraham* (1988) and 'Paradigm' (1994), is artificial. A rebuke is by definition a rebuke of something, and thus automatically carries hortatory function within it, and *vice versa*. Are 4:12b–18, 20, 5:2–5, 7–10 rebukes or requests? For a critique of this scheme, see the review of his book by Stanton (1992).

This seems as far as one can get up this particular alley.[38] If one sets aside one's preoccupation with 'theology', however, it is not difficult to see that this is exactly the same kind of response Paul has been making to his defecting converts (1:6; 3:1–5; 4:8–11). In fact, what one has to explain is not the presence of this passage in the middle of his 'theological' argument, but the role of the theological argument which backs up his rebuking appeals to the backsliding Galatians.

Now with the aching sense of estrangement, the immediate issue seems to be a personal relationship between Paul and the Galatians. Since Paul himself is the embodiment of the truth, [39] however, this relational breakdown also involves their deviation from the gospel itself (cf. 1 Cor 4:16; 11:1; 1 Thess 1:6). Paul's focus is still on the Galatians' defection from the gospel.

More concretely, the change of attitude by the Galatians and their loss of 'blessing' are evidence of their losing sight of the Spirit of Christ mediated by Paul's ministry (cf. 3:3). That this is not an overinterpretation is confirmed by Paul's agony-stricken cry that he now undergoes the pain of child-birth until Christ should be formed among the Galatians (v. 19).[40] His remark that he does this 'again' reflects his fear that Christ is not visible any more in the Galatian churches, and thus he has to convert them all over again. His focus remains consistent: 'I am perplexed about *you*!' (v. 20).[41] His 'almost sarcastic and bitter tone' renders even his calling them τέχνα μου polemical.[42]

(d) Aborting the Race (5:7). The same charge appears again in 5:7. The Galatians were running well, but someone cut in on their race (ἐνέχοψεν) with the result that they are not obeying the truth any more. Inasmuch as the 'truth' refers to the truth of the gospel (2:5, 14),[43] this is yet another variation of the same charge of apostasy. Paul's remark that the agitators' propaganda is not 'from the one who calls you' confirms this (5:8; 1:6). Here, as in 3:1, Paul is not just reminding the Galatians of the obvious

---

[38] Martyn 418–419; Dunn 231.

[39] Note the words of Kelber quoted in Thiselton, *New Horizons* (1992) 70–71: 'The teacher lives a life that is paradigmatic in terms of his message. Because in oral hermeneutics words have no existence apart from persons, participation in the message is inseparable from imitation of the speaker: "We decided to share with you not only the Gospel of God but also ourselves" (1 Thess 2:8, 9)'.

[40] The 'formation of Christ' means more than restoration of relationship. Cf. Betz, 'Spirit' (1974) 158.

[41] ἀπορούμαι is not so much an expression of uncertainty as of perplexity. Paul has no shred of doubt about the present condition in Galatia (1:6; 3:1; 4:15, 16, 21; 5:2–5, 7; 6:12–13). Rightly, Betz 236.

[42] Mußner 312.

[43] Hübner, *EDNT* 1:59.

cause of the trouble; by way of a rhetorical question, he in fact rebukes the Galatians who have allowed themselves to be carried away by these agitators.[44] Once again, his concern is the conduct of the Galatians: *they* have stopped obeying the truth. And this is the crisis Paul perceives in Galatia.

Paul's problem is thus clear: the apostasy of his Galatian converts.[45] Though he is fully aware of the influence of the agitators, it is the Galatians' following them that he takes to be the real problem. As he sees it, the Galatians are the main culprits of the crisis, and not helpless victims of conflicting theologies. Accordingly, they form the major target of Paul's angry polemic in the letter. That is, the primary purpose of the whole letter, *including his theological argument*, is to upbraid the Galatians for their apostatizing behavior with a view to restoring them to the truth of his gospel.[46] The proper subject of the letter is not the theological content of Paul's gospel but *the Galatians' disposition in relation to that gospel*.

Thus, Galatians is not a résumé of Paul's theological altercation with his rival theologians but his pastoral engagement with his backsliding converts. It is crucial to bear this *pastoral* context in mind, especially when we interpret the function of his theological argument which is open to diverse interpretations. To be sure, the Galatians' apostasy is caused by the 'bad theology' promoted by the agitators; Paul's polemic too is thoroughly grounded on his own gospel. But his immediate burden is not to expound his theology, either Christology or pneumatology, since the problem at hand is not these *theological* issues *per se* but the *anthropological* one of the Galatians' disobedience (5:7).[47] His talk of the Christ event and the Spirit is guided by the immediate purpose of dealing with the Galatians who are presently *deviating* from Christ and the Spirit.[48]

---

[44] Rightly, Williams 139; Martyn 474; Betz 264; Mußner 355. Anderson, *Theory* (1996) 160 sees here an example of ἔμφασις, 'implying ... the stupidity of the Galatians in allowing themselves to be seduced away from the *truth'* (emphasis original).

[45] We do not need to discuss the precise nature of this apostasy at this point, which we will do in chapter 8. What we need to confirm here is that this apostasy of the Galatians, whatever it may be, is Paul's main concern.

[46] Cf. Anderson, *Theory* (1996) 164–165: 'Paul's forthright critique of the Galatians'.

[47] Scholars' own interest in Paul's 'thought-world' or 'theology' often obscures Paul's more practical concern. E.g., Patte, *Paul's Faith* (1983); Boers, *Justification* (1994) 50, 65. Paul's pastoral concern is based on his theological convictions but it does not mean that the latter are his main reason for writing this letter.

[48] So Stanley, 'Curse' (1990) 486–492. In a recent study of irony in Galatians (1:6–9; 2:16; 5:12), Nikolakopoulos concludes: 'Die rhetorische Ironie an den drei behandelten Stellen richtet sich *erstens* an die irregeführten Christen von Galatien (Gal 1,6), um sie in drastischer Weise aufzurütteln, damit sie einer bestimmten Sicht des jüdischen Gesetzes entkommen'. 'Aspekte' (2001) 207 (Emphasis original).

2.2.2 'Then and Now': Paul's Polemical Depiction of the Present

Paul's identification of the present crisis as a case of apostasy has a critical bearing on the thrust of his polemic: if Paul is criticizing the apostatizing Galatians, it would scarcely occur to him to make his case by endorsing the sufficiency of their present status. On the contrary, a natural way of dealing with the problem would be to show them the serious nature of their present behavior and its consequences. This is precisely what he does in Galatians. Indeed, one of the most prominent devices he employs in his polemic is *the deliberate contrast between the terrible situation in the present and the desirable condition in the past.*[49]

The first contrast is between the Galatians' *present* defection (μετατίθεσθε, present) and God's calling in the past (καλέσαντος).[50] The present time is that of apostasy in which agitation and perversion of the gospel hold sway (v. 7). Both θαυμάζω and οὕτως ταχέως[51] effectively express the complete change of situation Paul perceives in Galatia. Now he cannot simply celebrate the reality of God's calling (cf. 1 Thess 1:3–4); it will not do either to invoke God's faithfulness, as he often does elsewhere (cf. 1 Cor 1:9; 1 Thess 5:24). Not that he doubts the authenticity of God's calling, which was indeed 'a compelling summons they had been unable to deny' 'calling into being the new creation, the eschatological community of the church'.[52] His frustration, however, is that the Galatians themselves are abandoning this call of God, namely, their conversion itself.[53] Under the circumstances his evocation of God's calling/conversion in the past, instead of being an affirmation of the adequacy of their present status, functions as a polemic designed to awaken the Galatians to the gravity of their present deviation.[54]

In 3:1–5 too we observe the same contrast. Once again, Paul reminds the Galatians of their laudable life since conversion. The aorist

---

[49] This has not been sufficiently noted, partly due to scholarly preoccupation with the eschatological 'then-now' contrast. Cf. Tachau, *Einst* (1972). See Martyn 411; R. Longenecker 180; Fung 189. A rare exception is Suhl, 'Galaterbrief' (1987) 3129–3132: 'Mit dieser positiven Vergangenheit kontrastiert nun aufs schärfste die Gegenwart' (3130). See the diagram in p. 3131. Also Smiles, *Gospel* (1998) 157–158, who, however, still gives a realized eschatological interpretation.

[50] Cf. Mußner 54, n. 58.

[51] Whether referring to the interval between Paul's ministry and the crisis or the swiftness of their apostasy, Paul's 'astonishment' remains the same. So Ebeling, *Truth* (1981) 45.

[52] Dunn 40 and Martyn 109, respectively.

[53] Cf. Burton 20.

[54] Cf. Ebeling, *Truth* (1985) 46–47.

προεγράφη[55] in v. 1 refers to Paul's initial ministry in Galatia, through which the Christ *was* 'publicly displayed' as the crucified Messiah.[56] The same goes for the receiving the Spirit occasioned by their ἀκοὴ πίστεως (vv. 2, 5).[57] Some argue that ἐπιχορηγῶν (present) in v. 5 denotes God's continuing outpouring of the Spirit.[58] This is unlikely, since it merely resumes the question in v. 2 without any implication of continuance.[59] While Paul presupposes the ongoing presence of the Spirit (5:16–26; 6:7–9), his charge that the Galatians are abandoning the Spirit (v. 3) further renders such an intention improbable.[60]

Though not explicit, the remarks that the crucified Christ was *previously* real may imply that He is *presently* not visible in the midst of their attraction to circumcision (cf. 4:19).[61] In any case, Paul's criticism in v. 3 brings this contrast between 'then' and 'now' to telling clarity: 'having begun by the Spirit, are you now ending with the flesh?' The wonderful 'beginning with the Spirit' *in the past* (ἐναρξάμενοι, aorist participle) is brought into a stark contrast to *their present* (νῦν) in which they are ending (ἐπιτελεῖσθε, present indicative) with the flesh at the complete cost of the Spirit. In all probability, their life in the Spirit must have continued until recently, namely, until the intrusion of the agitators (5:7).[62] Yet their allegiance to the Spirit has now become a thing in the past; they are now allied with the flesh. Paul, referring the Galatians back to their happy days in the past (the crucified Christ displayed, their hearing with faith, the subsequent coming of the Spirit), brings the deplorable poverty in the

[55] Davis, 'ΠΡΟΕΓΡΑΦΗ' (1999) explores the possibility that Paul presented the Christ crucified by his own personal disposition, which makes good sense in the light of 2:19–20 and 6:14–16. Similarly, Stuhlmacher, *Reconciliation* (1986) 159–160.

[56] προεγράφη, qualified by κατ' ὀφθαλμούς, is better taken as locative, as most commentators agree.

[57] See our discussion of the passage in 7.4.2 below and footnotes there.

[58] E.g., Mußner 211; Bruce 151; Fee, *Presence* (1995) 388; Witherington 215; Cosgrove, *Cross* (1988) 47–48.

[59] E.g., Dunn, *Baptism* (1970) 108; Stott 71; Bligh, *Greek* (1966) 129.

[60] Cf. Burton 152.

[61] Now compare Mitternacht, 'Assessment' (2002) 424: 'And there is the contrast between then and now focusing on right and wrong cognition: *then* they had perceived Christ within the paradox; *now* they are foolish for not appreciating the implications for their own lives' (italics his). As the aorist προεγράφη suggests, the vivid display of the crucified Christ does not apply to the *present* of the Galatian believers (4:19!; 5:4). *Contra* R. Longenecker 101.

[62] Martyn's association (123) of the Spirit with the work of the agitators is puzzling. If so, Paul's whole case based on the fact of 'the Spirit by faith' falls to the ground. Rightly Bruce 152: 'It is a natural inference from Paul's rhetorical questions that the 'other gospel' which was being presented to the Galatian Christians took no notice of the Spirit'. See also Hays, 'Review' (2000) 376.

present, their association with the flesh, into sharp relief. In other words, Paul speaks of the Spirit not to remind them of what they already possess but to make them realize what they have lost due to their apostatizing disposition.

The same perspective keeps occurring whenever Paul turns to the situation in Galatia. 4:8–11 is particularly interesting in that now the comparison is threefold: before and after Christ; before and after the coming of the agitators; the Galatians' pre-conversion life and their present backsliding which Paul depicts as an act of counter-conversion. 'Formerly' (τότε), that is, before they knew God, they were enslaved to mere idols (v. 9). Then comes the contrasting 'but now' (νῦν δέ). The contrast should have ended here but, tragically, another set of contrast has become necessary. The reference to 'having known God' (γνόντες) and 'having been known by God' (γνωσθέντες) clearly points to their conversion.[63] Yet, these two aorist participles[64] are subordinate to the main question led by πῶς. In this way, the immediate force of νῦν falls on the main verb ἐπιστρέφετε with the result that it stands in a stark contrast to their knowledge of God gained at the time of their conversion. Of course, the aorist participles are 'ingressive',[65] but the syntax suggests that Paul's immediate intention is not to affirm their knowledge of God in the present[66] but to accentuate their present behavior of abandoning it against the backdrop of their previous experience of receiving it.[67]

The tragic irony of the Galatian crisis is that there is now an incredible disjuncture where there should be continuity, namely, between their conversion/'knowledge of God' (past) and their defection (present). The inevitable result is that an ominous continuity now emerges where there should have been an absolute disjuncture; the νῦν of their second 'conversion' (ἐπιστρέφετε) to the agitators turns out to be a reversion to the τότε of the pre-conversion slavery![68] Paul's incredulity at such a 'foolish' retreat (3:3) is borne out forcefully by the structure of the sentence: πῶς ... πάλιν ... πάλιν ... ἄνωθεν.

Paul's point is not that taking up the suggestion of the agitators 'in their quest for salvation, the Galatians are behaving as though Christ had not

---

[63] With Dunn 225.

[64] For the tense of the aorist participle, see Fanning, *Verbal Aspect* (1990) 408–416.

[65] Bruce 202.

[66] *Contra* Dunn 225. The judgment of Tachau, *Einst* (1972) 128 that the τότε–νῦν contrast is designed to awaken the Galatians to their present status of freedom from the law is off the mark.

[67] The frequently found 'But now, knowing God' is therefore misleading. *Contra* Martyn 411; R. Longenecker 180; Fung 189; Mußner 298.

[68] See Bruce 203; Fung 192; Betz 216; and especially, Byron, *Slavery* (2003) 191. Martyn is somewhat confusing here. Compare pp. 411 and 418.

come, thereby showing that they do not know what time it is'[69]. The mere forgetfulness of time would not have been a serious problem, since they can 'wake up to the real world' at any time without any real damage done. The truth is that their present behavior actually *transfers* them back to the time of τότε, thereby putting them back under the control of 'the elements of the world'. Once again, the issue is not the eschatological decisiveness of Christ but the gravity of the Galatians' behavior which renders it meaningless and all 'in vain'.[70] No wonder Paul's agony is so great: φοβοῦμαι ὑμᾶς μή πως εἰκῆ κεκοπίακα εἰς ὑμᾶς (v. 11).[71]

In 4:12–20 too Paul creates the same contrast between the wonderful 'then' and the terrible 'now'. When he first proclaimed the gospel, the Galatians, against the odds, received him 'as an angel of God', or even 'as Christ Jesus' (v. 14), willing to do anything for him (v. 15). Then the agitators slipped in, which has changed the situation completely. He continues to tell the truth, but the Galatians have turned their back on him; he is now (γέγονα, perfect) treated as their 'enemy' (v. 16). This radical change from 'angel of God' and 'Christ Jesus' to 'enemy' is succinctly depicted by the rhetorical demand: ποῦ οὖν ὁ μακαρισμὸς ὑμῶν; (v. 15a; cf. 3:1), which accentuates the painful absence of the 'blessing' *in the present* which used to be so vivid among them *in the past* (τὸ πρότερον).[72]

As in 4:8–11 Paul describes this change as a reversion to their pre-conversion life. By saying that he is now undergoing the 'birth pang' *again* (πάλιν), he in effect says that the deviation from him and his gospel means nothing but the *reversal* of the birth of the Galatian community itself mediated through his ministry.[73] Burton sums up Paul's point aptly: 'The reactionary step which the Galatians are in danger of taking, forces upon the apostle the painful repetition of that process by which he first brought them into the world of faith in Christ, and his pain, he declares, must continue till they have really entered into vital fellowship with Christ'.[74]

---

[69] *Contra* Witherington 302; Parsons, 'Being' (1988) 241.

[70] As noted in the previous chapter, it is confusing the categories to gloss over the problem of human apostasy by appealing to God's faithfulness. See 1.2.2 above.

[71] Paul has already toiled for the Galatians. Seeing what is happening in Galatia, he now worries about the possibility of his past toil becoming in vain. For the force of μή πως + indicative construction, see *BDF* 188; Zerwick, *Greek* (1963) 118.

[72] Bruce 209 notes the connection between v. 13 and v. 16.

[73] Rightly, Martyn 429; Cousar 101. *Contra* Cosgrove, *Cross* (1988) 78 who takes the reference to be to 'maturation' rather than to 'reconversion'. The 'apocalyptic' readings found in Käsemann, *Perspectives* (1971) 31; Gaventa, 'Maternity' (1990) 189–201; Martyn 426–431; Witherington 315–316 confuse the issue, loading too much onto Paul's imagery.

[74] Burton 249. If this is true, does a realized eschatological logic cohere with this?

Paul makes the same point in 5:1. He demands that the Galatians should not become subject to the yoke of slavery *again* (πάλιν). The point is clear: if they indeed go on with their present behavior, they will end up in slavery which is in fact the same as their pre-conversion slavery under idols.[75] His reminder of the liberating work of Christ, like his reminder of their conversion, makes his warning all the more poignant, highlighting the enormity of their present deviation: following the agitators, they will lose the very thing Christ died for, their freedom in the Spirit (5:13).

Paul's charge in 5:7 reveals the same contrast. Referring to the time before the intrusion of the agitators, he says that the Galatians were running (ἐτρέχετε) very well. The use of the imperfect clearly implies that this 'running well' does not apply to their lives in the present time.[76] They have allowed the agitators to cut in, with the result[77] that they are not obeying the truth any more.

Paul's description of the Galatian situation reveals a consistent and very *negative* picture of the 'now' in Galatia: apostasy from God, absence of Christ, loss of the Spirit, return to slavery, and disobedience to the truth of the gospel. The wonderful state of affairs established by his proclamation of the crucified Messiah and his mediation of the Spirit has now been pushed back to a time in the past. The present condition in Galatia, forming an appalling contrast with the halcyon days in the past, is not something to endorse or celebrate but only to denounce and rectify. It is not that the work of Christ is insufficient or their experience of the Spirit is inadequate. That is not the issue here. The real point is that the Galatians themselves are departing from such eschatological realization, making it all 'in vain'. Paul invokes what happened in the beginning over and over again, but he does not do so to affirm the sufficiency of the Galatians' present.[78]

On the contrary, Paul's painful and contrasting reminder turns out to be a polemical device with which to impress on them the cost and consequences of their 'present deviation'. Particularly instructive in this respect is his deliberate equation of the Galatians' present with the time before their conversion, a most telling criticism of what it means to follow the lead of the agitators. This, then, falsifies the popular construal of his argument as a positive *affirmation* of the present status of the Galatians. This supposition may be able to hold water within the 'theological'

---

[75] Burton 271; Sanders, *Law* (1983) 69; Gundry-Volf, *Perseverance* (1990) 208–209.

[76] Burton 281–282.

[77] Taking μὴ πειθεσθαι as result rather than purpose. So Mußner 355.

[78] This is the function of Paul's 'reminders' in 1 Thessalonians and Philippians (where Paul is quite happy with his converts' performance), but *not* in Galatians.

argument itself but it flies in the face of Paul's own construal of the 'situation' in Galatia.

The fact that Paul depicts the present condition of the Galatians as that of apostasy in contrast to the desirable state of affairs in the past shows how shaky a foundation the assumption of 'realized eschatology' stands on. It is true that many of his statements in the theological argument may be interpreted as divulging such intent. Frequently, however, the purpose of such theological talk is not immediately clear; its function changes drastically as its context changes. As he looks at the matter, then, it is not his intention at all to solve the crisis (apostasy) by affirming the sufficiency of the divine indicative established by the cross of Christ. Such a move would be meaningless anyway in the face of the fact that the Galatians themselves are now *discarding* this very benefit.[79] His claim is not that the Galatians have already possessed enough by their faith but that their present deviation from the truth is destroying everything they have attained thus far, *re*turning them to the time before conversion/Christ. Hence Paul's reminders of their wonderful, normative beginning in the past, far from being expressions of his 'realized eschatological' outlook, function as polemical backdrop against which to accentuate the gravity of their present deviation.[80]

2.3 Future in Jeopardy: Paul's Future Eschatological Perception of the Crisis

Our last point was that Paul's depiction of the present situation in Galatia renders a realized eschatological outlook in his argument quite unlikely. In this section we make a more positive point: Paul perceives the present crisis from an essentially future-oriented perspective. Namely, he considers the Galatians' deviation perilous precisely because it is an act of putting the future in jeopardy, not only for themselves but also for Paul.

2.3.1 Paul's Ministry Becoming in Vain (4:11)

Since the ultimate aim of Paul's ministry is to convert the Gentiles so that they may participate in God's eschatological salvation, their failure in reaching this goal necessarily means that his ministry has also been 'in vain'. In 4:11 he expresses this fear of a possible failure of his ministry. In

---

[79] In Galatians, unlike in Romans, Paul does not appeal to the precedence of Abraham's justification to circumcision which would have been an effective evidence for the 'already' of justification. In the situation in which circumcision is making everything 'in vain' (4:8–11; 5:2–4), the talk of 'already' would have hardly been enough.

[80] The polemical nature of Paul's theological talk will be discussed in chapter 7.

the context, his fear of his 'apostolic toil'[81] being 'in vain' is quite apt, since the present backsliding of the Galatians is nothing but returning to their original state of slavery under the elements of the world from which he had converted them.

Here Paul's fear concerns his own ministry and not the well-being of his converts. Unlike most commentators who understand this as Paul's fear for his converts ('I am afraid for you'),[82] Gundry-Volf has shown that 'in the NT, the accusative object of φοβεῖσθαι never denotes the one for whose sake one fears, but always what or who inspires fear'. Here 'Paul expresses his concern for himself', his 'fear of personal loss, which is the primary aspect in the statements about laboring in vain'.[83] Thus, what the statement shows is not 'the note of love'[84] but his personal apprehension.

Paul's fear of his ministry becoming 'in vain' is a clear reflection of his eschatological outlook. When he says his ministry is 'in vain', he speaks 'from the perspective of the eschaton', pointing to 'the lack of divine commendation for service at the last day'.[85] In this respect, the expression, 'toil in vain' merges with 'running in vain' in 2:2, μή πως εἰς κενὸν τρέχω ἢ ἔδραμον (cf. *2 Bar.* 44:10).[86] This way of speaking of his own ministry accords very well with Paul's own apostolic self-consciousness.

Most illuminating in this respect is Philippians 2:14–16: 'It is by your holding fast to the word of life that *I can boast on the day of Christ that I did not run in vain or labor in vain* (εἰς καύχημα ἐμοὶ εἰς ἡμέραν Χριστοῦ, ὅτι οὐκ εἰς κενὸν ἔδραμον οὐδὲ εἰς κενὸν ἐκοπίασα)'. Combining both 'running' and 'toiling' images, Paul depicts his ministry from a distinctively eschatological perspective (cf. 1 Tim 4:10).[87] Since his Christian existence itself is grounded on God's will that he should preach the gospel (1:16), it is his performance as the apostle to the Gentiles that will be the criterion of his judgment on the Day of Christ (1 Thess 2:19–20; 1 Cor 3:10–15; 9:16–17; 2 Cor 1:14). Thus the performance of his Gentile converts has a direct bearing on his own future: if they manage to stand 'blameless' before God, it will mean that he has not performed his ministry

---

[81] For κοπιάω as referring to Paul's apostolic ministry see Rom 16:6, 12; 1 Cor 4:12; 15:10; 16:16; Phil 2:16; 1 Thess 5:12; Col 1:29; Eph 4:28; 1 Tim 4:10; 5:17; 2 Tim 2:6. For the usage in LXX see Deut 32:47; Isa 49:4, 8; 45:18; 65:23. These passages are listed in Bjerkelund, 'Vergeblich' (1977) 179–182.

[82] *Contra* Witherington 302; Betz 219; Mußner 304; Bruce 207; Martyn 411 and most others.

[83] Gundry-Volf, *Perseverance* (1990) 266 and n. 33 there.

[84] Ebeling, *Truth* (1985) 224.

[85] Gundry-Volf, *Perseverance*, (1990) 263–264. She fruitfully builds on the study of Bjerkelund noted in n. 81 above.

[86] The difference between εἰς κενόν and εἰκῆ is immaterial.

[87] So Lattke, *EDNT* 2:281.

in vain, which will then be to him εἰς καύχημα (cf. 2 Cor 1:14; 1 Thess 2:19).[88] If he fails to carry out his ministry properly, the result will be inevitably εἰς κενόν (cf. 1 Cor 9:16, 27).

Paul's talk of his working 'in vain' makes immediate sense in the Galatian context in which the possibility of such failure is more tangible than ever. The unavoidable result of the present apostasy of the Galatians will be that he has 'run in vain'. That is, it is not just for the Galatians that he is so anxious about the present situation. In a real sense, he also has his personal stake in the present crisis, which may partly explain the unusual vehemence of his reaction.[89] In any case, here his anxiety is about the future, the inescapable eschatological implication of the Galatians' deviation in the present. Their 'foolishness' lies not so much in their lack of appreciation of the 'already' as in their forsaking the proper path towards the Day of Christ.

Addressed to the Galatians, the implication of this statement for them is also clear. As Gundry-Volf notes, 'the eschatological nature of the implications of ineffective labor for Paul shows that the implications for his converts are also eschatological: they may be excluded from final salvation'.[90] Indeed this seems to be what he means when Paul applies the same motif of 'in vain' to the Galatians: 'have you suffered so much in vain?' (3:4) Combined with the eschatological motif of 'beginning and ending', the statement, as in the case of his 'laboring in vain' (4:11), is to be taken in a future eschatological sense: 'failing to reach the intended goal'.[91] If the Galatians resort to the flesh and stop living with the Spirit, they will certainly be unable to attain the goal for which they have come to Christ, the hope of righteousness and eternal life. For the simple reason that they do not achieve the goal of their coming to Christ, their suffering thus far is rendered 'in vain'. Paul's point then is that 'abandonment of the Spirit excludes the possibility of ending'.[92] It is precisely for this reason that this statement can function as a warning exhortation for the defecting Galatians.[93]

---

[88] So Gundry-Volf, *Perseverance*, (1990) 264.

[89] Cf. Hooker, *Adam* (1990) 49 on Phil 3:12–16 and 1 Cor 9:24–27.

[90] Gundry-Volf, *Perseverance* (1990) 267. She then tries to explain away this implication, asserting that Paul implies the possibility 'for the sake of argument only'. Her theological concern is understandable, but it should not override the plain meaning of Paul's statement. See Satake, 'Apostolat' (1968/69) 96–107; Betz 219.

[91] Mußner 210: 'ohne Erfolg'.

[92] Guthrie 93.

[93] Some interpreters read the ambiguous εἰ γε καὶ εἰκῇ as a word of encouragement rather than an exclamation of despair. E.g., Martyn 285; Dunn 157. Encouragement is, however, clearly out of place in the context of an unmitigated rebuke; the formulation itself is also odd for an encouragement. Its main function is certainly hortatory but its

2.3.2 Beginning and Ending (3:3)

According to Paul's own statement in 3:3, arguably the most succinct depiction of the Galatian problem in the letter, the essence of the present crisis concerns the Spirit. The Galatians, having begun very well with the Spirit, are presently ending with the flesh. This pithy depiction of the situation provides a clear glimpse of Paul's perspective in the letter.

First of all, Paul's depiction of the Spirit-led life of the Galatians as a 'beginning' falsifies the supposition that his interest in the Spirit in Galatians is motivated by his desire to stress the eschatological fulfillment the Spirit allegedly signifies.[94] If he had intended so, he would probably have avoided such an ineffective word 'beginning', and said instead, 'having been justified' (cf. Rom 5:1), or 'having received the inheritance through the Spirit'. The reception of the Spirit is surely important, indeed eschatological in a certain sense. Nevertheless, it is only a beginning, which should be continued until the end of the process.

More decisive is the motif of 'beginning/ending'. Paul's use of ἐπιτελέω has generated some debate. Some think that despite the intended contrast, Paul's concern is the continuing present status.[95] The point is well taken; there is no denying that Paul is speaking of the present behavior of the Galatian believers. The contrasting force, however, cannot be explained away that easily since, juxtaposed with ἐναρξάμενοι, ἐπιτελεῖσθε necessarily delivers a clear sense of 'ending'. Some speculate that Paul is here borrowing from the 'cultic terms' of Hellenistic mystery religions.[96] Such an origin would be interesting if proved true, but it does not tell us much since we cannot assume that he uses the motif in the same way as it is used in the mystery cults.

Jewett, with many others, mirror-reads here the agitators' claim that they are to 'complete' the basic and rather inadequate message of Paul by supplementing the law.[97] This makes Paul's remark a sarcastic reference to the empty promise of the agitators.[98] It is not easy, however, to see how circumcision can be demanded in such a way. Circumcision was not a

---

bleak implication still remains. Burton 151 and others (Duncan 82; Schlier 125) advise us that we should read this 'without implication as to its fulfillment' but it certainly goes against the thrust of the passage. Paul is hopeful (Lightfoot 135–136; Hansen 82; Witherington 215), but this does not gloss over the grim reality he is facing (1:6; 3:3!).

[94] See 6.3 below.

[95] E.g., Mahoney, *EDNT* 2:42.

[96] E.g., Lightfoot 135; Schlier 124; Betz 133, n. 57 and 'Spirit' (1974) 147 and nn. 6–7; Brinsmead, *Response* (1982) 79; Lull, *Spirit* (1980) 76, n. 13, 135, n. 7; Hume 46.

[97] Jewett, 'Agitators' (1971) 206–207; Betz 136; R. Longenecker xcv, 104, 106; Martyn 285; Lull, *Spirit* (1980) 103; Barrett, *Freedom* (1985) 22; Keck, *Letters* (1989) 70–71; B. Longenecker, *Triumph* (1998) 17.

[98] So Kertelge, 'Gesetz' (1984) 384.

mark of the highest accomplishment but the *sine qua non* of the covenant membership; without it one does not become a second-rate Israelite but simply remains outside the covenant.[99] It is not possible to discover the theology of Paul's opponents at this point.[100]

Another view is to take it as a sort of 'covenantal nomistic' logic: 'just as you have begun with the Spirit (getting in), so you have to continue in the Spirit' (staying in; going on).[101] The statement itself is perfectly acceptable; it is doubtful though that this is the idea expressed here. As is implied in vv. 4–5,[102] this 'beginning' covers the extended, albeit brief (1:6), period of the Spirit-filled life until the outbreak of the crisis (5:7). The intended contrast then is not a theological one between 'getting in' and 'continuing' but a historical one between the before and the after of the outbreak of the crisis.

Most probably, Paul's language of 'beginning/ending' is the reflection of his deep-rooted eschatological perspective, as is confirmed by the parallel in Philippians 1:6 where the Day of Christ is specified as the day of 'ending': 'I am confident of this, that the one who began (ἐναρξάμενος) a good work among you will bring it to completion (ἐπιτελέσει) by the day of Jesus Christ' (NRSV).[103] The Galatians have begun very well with the Spirit. This does not mean, however, that they have reached the final goal of their calling. It is the *parousia* of Christ that marks the real ending of the story, with their hope of righteousness still outstanding.[104] So their disposition in the present time takes on an eschatological significance, affecting their eternal destiny. In this sense, the Galatians' present behavior becomes an act of 'ending', that is, *an act which entails a necessary eschatological consequence.*[105]

Having begun effectively with the Spirit, they are to 'be ending' (ἐπιτελεῖσθε, present) with the same Spirit so as to reach the final goal of

---

[99] Fredriksen, 'Judaism' (1991) 536, 546. As Barclay, *Truth* (1988) 49–50 (49) points out, 'we never find this "perfection" motif in the context of Hellenistic Jewish apologetic, where we would most expect it on Jewett's thesis'. Circumcision was the *sine qua non* of Jewishness, see Jos. *Ant.* 13.257–258, 318–319 and the famous conversion story of Izates in 20. 17–96. Cf. *Mid. Rab.* Genesis 46.11. See also Feldman/Reinhold, *Jewish Life* (1996) 124–135. Cf. Mußner 208, n. 21; and Eckstein, *Verheißung* (1996) 88–89.

[100] Rightly, Hübner, *Law* (1984) 42, n. 1; Eckstein, *Verheißung* (1996) 89.

[101] See, e.g., Dunn 155–156; Barclays, *Truth* (1988) 85; R. Longenecker 103–104; Witherington 214. See 1.2.4 above.

[102] This is pointed out by Dunn himself (157) and by Witherington 215.

[103] This parallel is frequently noted but with its eschatological thrust missed out. E.g. Dunn, *Baptism* (1970) 108; Bruce 149. See also 1 Cor 1:8: 'God will strengthen you until the end, so that you may be blameless on the day of our Lord Jesus Christ'.

[104] See Chapter 3.

[105] Thus, this statement anticipates 6:7–10, where Paul employs the imagery of sowing and reaping in relation to the Spirit to emphasize the necessary relation between the two.

eschatological salvation, [106] of course, not for the reason of mere consistency[107] but for the simple reason that the Spirit is the only way of attaining to that hope. Yet, they are resorting to the law, and thereby falling to the realm of the flesh, the end of which will be destruction (6:8a). Either way, their present behavior has a necessary implication for the final outcome, and in this sense, their present life is an act of ending. [108] According to Paul's statement here, the problem of the Galatians then concerns their future: by allowing themselves to be persuaded by the circumcision propaganda, the Galatians are putting their eternal destiny at stake.

2.3.3 Benefit from Christ and the Future (5:2–5)

Paul's futuristic perspective emerges again in 5:2–5. The way he begins this warning is very impressive: 'Look, I, Paul, say to you'. The effect is, of course, 'to give to what he is about to say all the weight of his personal influence'.[109] That Paul is here thinking of justification becomes clear in v. 4, where δικαιοῦσθε is related to the Galatians' willingness to receive circumcision: the Galatians are willing to be circumcised 'in order to be justified'. His warning is that if they actually go ahead and do so, Christ will be of no use at all 'for their justification'. In v. 5 the alternative to this 'justification in the law' is presented: 'waiting for the hope of righteousness through the Spirit that comes from faith'. Thus, what we have here is a starkly contrastive, and mutually exclusive presentation of 'the two methods of obtaining righteousness'.[110]

The consequence of the Galatians' present defection is unambiguous: if the Galatians attempt to be justified in the law by receiving circumcision, they are then 'estranged from Christ' and 'cut off from grace' (v. 4). Using aorist verbs, Paul proleptically[111] visualizes the terrible consequences of their behavior. Of course, this does not mean that 'the divine grace has been taken away from them…, but that they have abandoned it'.[112] Having chosen to be under the law-covenant by way of circumcision, their relationship with Christ has become inoperative; they are now outside the

---

[106] Rightly, Witherington 214.

[107] *Contra* R. Longenecker 103. The problem is not just that the Galatians are inconsistent but that their new policy is a wrong one, since only the Spirit is able to sustain them to the end.

[108] NIV is better than others: 'Are you now trying to *attain your goal* by human effort?'

[109] Burton 273. See also Schlier 231; Bruce 229.

[110] Burton 275; Gundry-Volf, *Perseverance* (1990) 210.

[111] So Bruce 231; Witherington 369.

[112] Burton 277. See also Gundry-Volf, *Perseverance* (1990) 212 and n. 51 there.

realm of Christ and grace. It follows that for these 'Christ *will* be of no
benefit (ὠφελήσει)!'

While most interpreters simply ignore the future tense of this warning,
some do take it as a reference to the final Judgment:[113] for those who are
circumcised *now* Christ will not be of any help at the Last Judgment. This
is, however, unlikely, especially since the idea of Christ interceding for
believers at the Judgment is an idea otherwise missing in Paul (cf. Rom
8:27; Jn 17; 1 Jn 2:1; Heb 7:25). When Paul speaks of the Judgment, Christ
performs the role of the Judge, and not the mediator for believers (Rom
2:16; 2 Cor 5:10). It is also not to be ignored that for Paul God's Judgment
is always in relation to human works (5:21b; 6:7–9; Romans 2:6–11;
14:10–12; 2 Cor 5:10).

In the context, the most likely reference is to 'the immediate
consequences of receiving circumcision'.[114] 'If you are circumcised, *from
now on* Christ will be of no benefit'. The point of Paul's warning is clear.
Circumcision severs one's relation to Christ.[115] Being outside Christ, one
will receive no benefit from Christ in one's pursuit of justification; the
only option left for them is the (illusory) justification in the law (v. 3).
Those who receive circumcision, unlike 'us'[116] who resort to the Spirit,
will forfeit their hope for future righteousness.

This passage provides further evidence for Paul's futuristic perspective
from which he looks at the problem in Galatia. His worry is not that the
Galatians, by receiving circumcision, may forfeit all the benefit from
Christ that they have thus far received.[117] His concern is that the Galatians
will lose the benefit of Christ, that is, their freedom in the Spirit which
comes from the work of Christ, and thereby be unable to adopt the proper
way of 'waiting for the hope of righteousness', with the inevitable result of
eternal destruction (6:8).

2.3.4 An Aborted Race (5:7)

Paul's futuristic and teleological thinking emerges quite clearly in 5:7 too.
Using his favorite footrace motif, he now compares the Galatians to
'runners in the stadium':[118] 'you were running well'. With 'running'

---

[113] E.g., Schlier 231; Betz 259; Martyn 469.

[114] Gundry-Volf, *Perseverance* (1990) 209. See also Burton 273; R. Longenecker 226,
though his talk of 'Christ's guidance for one's life' ignores the context of justification.

[115] In view of 5:6, 6:15 and 1 Cor 7:19, Paul's warning here should not be taken as a
doctrinal statement. See our discussion of the passage in 8.2.1 below.

[116] Martyn 103 perceives this polemical contrast.

[117] Esler, *Galatians* (1998) 180 renders the statement in this way: '...if they become
circumcised, Christ has been of no use to them', which would require an aorist or a
perfect.

[118] Betz 264.

denoting 'lifestyle' and 'conduct',[119] this remark is a clear reference to their life of 'obeying the truth' prior to the intrusion of the agitators, namely, their 'beginning with the Spirit' (3:3).

As it becomes impressively clear in Paul's use of the imagery for his apostolic ministry in Philippians 3, the picture is that of runners pressing forward towards the goal still outstanding.[120] Paul demands, 'Who got in your path so that you might not obey the truth'? The reference is clearly to the agitators with a possible allusion to satanic force (3:1; 1 Thess 2:18). As Pfitzner notes, here ἐγκόπτειν suggests 'a breaking into or obstruction of the Galatian Christians in their course of following the "truth"'.[121] The resultant picture is then that of 'the runner who has allowed his progress to be blocked, or who is still running, but on the wrong course'.[122] Long before they reach the goal, the Galatians have stopped their race of 'obeying the truth'; they are running in the completely wrong direction (cf. 1 Cor 9:24–26).[123]

Obviously, basic to the race imagery are a start *and* a finish or a goal. Conversion marks the beginning; the finish line is the Day of Christ. After their Spirit-filled conversion, the Galatians had been running this race fairly well until the agitators caused them to falter. Now they have stopped running their course to Paul's agony. No doubt, the tragedy of aborting a race does not lie in stopping itself but in falling short of the goal (σκοπός) and thereby losing the prize for which they have been running (1 Cor 9:24). Paul's point is clear: if you follow the agitators, you will never finish the race and get the prize! It is not that the Galatians are ignoring the prize they already have in Christ. If it were so, Paul's use of the footrace motif would be simply confusing. For Paul the present deviation constitutes a serious danger because it means giving up the race that will lead the Galatians to the ultimate prize of final salvation.[124]

---

[119] Dunn 273.

[120] So Ebel, *NIDNTT* 3:947. As in Philippians 3:12–14, this inherently teleological image nicely captures Paul's future eschatological perspective from which to look at the situation.

[121] Pfitzner, *Agon* (1967) 136. See also Stählin, *TDNT* 3:857–860; DeVries, 'Cutting' (1975) 115–120; Betz 264; R. Longenecker 230; Bruce 234; Dunn 274.

[122] Pfitzner, *Agon* (1967) 137.

[123] So in *2 Clement* we read: 'Let us run in the straight course...' (20:2–3; cf. 7:1) to earn the 'crown' of 'salvation' and 'eternal life' (8:2–4).

[124] This motif is also related to Paul's exhortation in 6:9. There the image used in the immediate context is that of 'sowing and reaping', but the difference between the two is insignificant, in that both highlight the teleological perspective and the importance of perseverance.

2.4 Conclusion

How Paul looks at the problem in Galatia has become clear. First, the
problem concerns the disposition of the Galatians, specifically, their
apostatizing behavior. Secondly, he reveals a very negative view of the
present state of the Galatian converts, considering their behavior as a
degeneration to their pre-conversion status. This renders a 'realized
eschatology' not only very unlikely but also ineffective as a solution to the
problem at hand. Thirdly, Paul assesses the significance of the present
deviation in the light of their future: the Galatians, by deviating from the
truth of the gospel, are jeopardizing their future hope.

The significance of these points for proper interpretation of Paul's
theological argument is clear. If Paul perceives the situation from a future
eschatological perspective, it is also highly likely that his theological
argument too, which is part of his attempt to deal with the crisis, is framed
in the same future eschatological perspective rather than that of realized
eschatology as is usually thought. To demonstrate that this is indeed the
case is the burden of the following chapters. By carefully following Paul's
argument concerning justification, sonship, promise and inheritance, and
eliminating many unfounded assumptions usually made in reading it, we
shall be able to uncover the distinctively future eschatological thrust of
Paul's argument in the letter.

Chapter 3

Justification as an End-Time Gift

3.1 Justification as the Central Issue in Galatians

Despite a few dissenting voices,[1] the centrality of justification in Galatians cannot be denied. Throughout the letter, in which diverse themes and motifs intermingle, the thesis of 'justification by faith' remains a major concern of Paul's argument. Wrapping up his autobiographical narrative, Paul begins his next major section of the letter with the thesis of justification by faith (2:15–21). It is also with the theme of 'the hope of righteousness' (5:2–6) that Paul moves on to his appeal in more concrete terms. Within this section, with a view to impressing the truth of justification by faith he introduces the figure of Abraham into his argument (3:6–7), which develops further in terms of the 'blessing of Abraham' (3:8–9), and then, more polemically, of the 'curse of the law' (3:10–14). In 3:15–29, the twin themes of 'promise-inheritance', key concepts in Paul's biblical exegesis, turn out to be biblical terms Paul utilizes to supplement his argument about justification (3:21, 24). As far as Paul himself is concerned, it is with respect to the question of justification that the present crisis takes on such critical importance: how does one attain to the 'hope of righteousness' – by law or by faith?[2]

It is often claimed that 'justification by faith' forms a common ground between Paul and his dialogue partners.[3] This is not the case. The emphatic affirmation of the point coupled with a repeated denial of justification by the law necessitates the supposition that he is polemicizing against the

---

[1] E.g., Cosgrove, *Cross* (1988) 143: 'an important sub-theme' to show 'the impotence of the law', forming 'a building block in his argument that works of the law do not bring the Spirit'. See also Stanley, 'Curse' (1990) 492–495; Fee, *Presence* (1995) 368–369; Witherington 175, 184. They cannot, however, explain properly the pervasiveness of justification language.

[2] So most interpreters, e.g., Becker, *Paulus* (1991) 294; Brinsmead, *Response* (1982) 75, 87, 188; Patte, *Faith* (1983) 94, 209; Dunn, *Theology* (1993) 15. Cf. Schmithals, 'Judaisten' (1983) 47, 50.

[3] E.g., Cosgrove, *Cross* (1988) 68, 133, 143; Dunn, *Theology* (1993) 39, 55; Brinsmead, *Response* (1982) 71.

false claim of 'justification by works of the law'. The conviction of justification by faith is certainly shared among the Jewish Christians in Antioch (2:16)[4] and the Jerusalem 'pillars' (2:7–9). We should not, however, confuse these with the 'false brothers' (2:4) and the agitators in Galatia, the perverters of this very gospel (1:6–7), as, for example, Boyarin does.[5] To be sure, 'justification by works of the law' does not seem to go along with 'covenantal nomism'. Given the diversity within early Judaism,[6] however, why should the agitators necessarily be the same kind of Jews Sanders describes? Justification is *not* a common ground between Paul and his opponents.[7]

Since justification stands at the center of Paul's argument, one's position on the subject determines one's understanding of Paul's argument as a whole. It is, therefore, not surprising that much scholarly discussion revolves around Paul's justification language. For example, is the concept forensic or ethical?[8] Or is it 'apocalyptic'[9]? Is its primary thrust individual or ecclesial/social?[10] Is its function theological or sociological?[11] Does the noun δικαιοσύνη have the same meaning as the verb δικαιοῦν?[12] Discussion has been intensive.[13] It is not our aim to join the discussion at this point. The sheer diversity of the scholarly proposals suggests that the

---

[4] Eckstein, *Verheißung* (1996) 15 doubts even this.

[5] Boyarin, *Jew* (1994) 117.

[6] Now see Carson *et al.* eds., *Variegated Nomism* (2001). I thank Professor Jörg Frey for drawing my attention to this work.

[7] Hong, 'Jewish Law' (1994) 182 ends up conceding that the agitators consider 'works of the law' as 'extra entrance requirements' for the Gentiles. For this reason Räisänen, *Law* (1983) 178–90 accuses Paul of distorting or misrepresenting the position of his opponents. But note the sober warning of Barrett, *Paul* (1994) 78; Kim, *Origin* (1984) 345. Many scholars resolve the tension by redefining the concept to suit their argument. E.g., Sanders (transfer terminology); Dunn (covenantal nomism). Brinsmead, *Response* (1982) 71–72 divides the concept: initial justification (common ground) and justification of life (disputed).

[8] For example, Luther and Bultmann think it forensic, while Schlier argues for the 'ethical'. Ziesler, *Righteousness* (1972) attempts a synthesis of both.

[9] This view is associated with such scholars as Käsemann, 'Righteousness' (1969); Stuhlmacher, *Gerechtigkeit* (1966); Beker, *Paul* (1980); Keck, *Paul* (1988) 111–116; Martyn, *Issues* (1998) 141–156 and his *Galatians* (1998) 263–275; Campbell, *Rhetoric* (1992) 156–176 (Romans) and 'Coming' (1999).

[10] Fung, Eckstein, Schlier and Mußner take it as a synonym of 'salvation', while Sanders, Räisänen and Hansen speak of 'inclusion' or 'transfer'.

[11] For such scholars as Stendahl, *Paul* (1976); Sanders, *Law* (1983); Howard, *Crisis* (1991); Wolter, 'Ethos' (1997) 430–444; Theissen, *Reality* (1992) 222 it is a 'unity' language, while for Watson, *Paul* (1986) it is a call for 'separation'. Esler, *Galatians* (1998) is closer to Watson, though his concern with identity is distinct.

[12] E.g., Ziesler, *Righteousness* (1972) 147, 212; Eckstein, *Verheißung* (1996) 16–17.

[13] See Campbell, *Rhetoric* (1992) 138–156 and bibliography there.

actual data is not unambiguous. In fact, these are not the questions Paul sets out to answer, at least not explicitly, which explains why his statements are 'ambiguous', allowing diverse inferences according to the perspective one employs.

Under such circumstances, simply taking sides on these issues does not take us very far. We believe, however, that there is one crucial aspect of the subject to which scholars have hitherto paid insufficient attention: the conspicuously future-oriented nature of justification in Galatians. The question we ask in the present chapter is thus simple: is justification in Galatians realized or future? A proper answer to this question, we believe, will in fact obviate many of the thorny questions surrounding the subject, and thereby simplify our discussion to a significant degree, at least for the interpretation of Galatians.

3. 2 The Majority View

In Galatians, as in Romans, scholars detect the distinctiveness of Paul's view of justification in two respects. One obvious point is that it is only 'by faith' and never 'by works of the law'. This is immediately clear from the surface of Paul's discussion and need not detain us. The problem we are interested in is the second 'novelty' that scholars 'detect': the present reality of justification. In view of its strong nomistic connection, it seems that the Galatians, and the agitators behind them, are espousing the 'traditional' view of justification as an end-time event: at the final judgment God will justify or vindicate those who have been faithful to the law of Moses. Thus, for them justification is strictly a matter of future hope, inseparably bound up with the necessity of proper observance of the law (cf. 4QMMT 21.7; *b. Qid* 30b).[14] Then, it is as the *sine qua non* for this future justification that they demanded 'works of the law' of the Galatians (cf. 5:4).

Over against this future eschatological justification predicated on circumcision/law, the argument runs, Paul's insistence that justification is 'by faith' (2:16) and 'in Christ' (2:17, 21) also involves an important corollary. Since faith focuses on the cross and resurrection of Christ in the

---

[14] For Jewish understanding of justification, see Stuhlmacher, *Reconciliation* (1986) 72; *idem, Theologie I* (1992) 330; Kertelge, *Rechtfertigung* (1966) 41; *idem, EDNT* 1:331; Becker, *Paulus* (1998) 49–53; Dunn 267–268; Käsemann, *Romans* (1980) 56–57; Wilckens, *Römer* (1978) 212–222. For the eschatological orientation of the time, see Byrne, *Sons* (1979) 89–91, 232. Even in Paul future justification remains strong. Rom 2:1–16; 5:19; 1 Cor 4:4; Gal 5:5; Phil 3:12 (P[46] and some Western witnesses). Cf. Jas 2:14–26.

past, and since believers are already 'in Christ' by faith, saying that justification is 'by faith' amounts to claiming that 'believers' have already been justified by their 'faith'. For those in Christ, then, the hoped-for gift of justification has already become a present reality.[15]

This is indeed a bold claim to make. Naturally, for many interpreters, it is this claim of the *present* reality of justification that carries the sharpest edge in Paul's polemical exposition of the theme. By pointing to the present reality of justification gained through faith, Paul pulls the rug from under the feet of his opponents who are holding this gift back from the Galatians on condition of circumcision. In effect, then, his question to the Galatians is: 'having already been justified by faith without any help from the law, why are you still trying to be justified by the law?' The brunt of Paul's criticism then falls on the absurdity of Galatian believers' *gratuitous* attempt to be justified by the law after having already been justified by faith.[16]

The purpose of this chapter is to show that this interpretation is unfounded. To be sure, this widespread view certainly has a *prima facie* plausibility. One gains this impression, however, not from Galatians itself but from Romans where the 'now' of justification is explicitly and repeatedly affirmed. It seems that one simply carries this impression over to Galatians, assuming that Paul speaks of justification in the same vein.[17]

---

[15] With respect to Paul's teaching on justification in general, see A. Scott, *Christianity* (1961) 56–59; Bultmann, *Theology* (1951) 270; Conzelmann, *Outline* (1969) 217; Ridderbos, *Paul* (1975) 161–166; Ladd, *Theology* (1974) 437–447; Schrenk, *TDNT* 2:205; Byrne, *Sons* (1979) 232–233. Käsemann, while insisting on the context of future eschatology, nevertheless concedes that Paul does put a strong stress on the present nature of justification. 'Righteousness of God' (1961) 168–182. For those who posit a pre-Pauline, Jewish-Christian view of justification, this innovation precedes Paul. E.g., Vielhauer, 'Gesetzesdienst' (1975) 51–55; Reumann, *Righteousness* (1982) 55; Martyn, *Issues* (1997) 141–156. Less polemical as it may be, however, the present reality of justification in Paul remains the same.

Paul's view of 'justification as a present reality' is often traced back to Paul's Damascus experience. E.g., Bornkamm, 'Revelation' (1974) 90–103; Kim, *Origin* (1984) 269–311; Stuhlmacher, *Reconciliation* (1986) 68–93, 134–168. See 9.2.4 below.

[16] So, Fung 225; Kruse, *Law* (1996) 75; Smiles, *Gospel* (1998) 139–140. Emphatic or not, the present reality of justification forms a consensus. Most scholars connect justification with the Spirit, which in turn marks the realization of the promised inheritance.

[17] Frequently, scholarly discussion of justification in Galatians is heavily assisted by the data in Romans. E.g., Schlier; Eckstein, *Verheißung* (1996); Smiles, *Gospel* (1998). Becker, *Paulus* (1998) 228 calls Galatians the 'Vorbote des Römerbriefes' and 'die kleine Römerbrief'. See also Martyn, *Issues* (1998) 37–45.

This, however, runs the risk of distorting the specific contextual message Paul intends to make in Galatians.[18]

The present chapter consists of three levels of argument. The grammatical and exegetical analysis (section 3) examines Paul's actual statements on the theme, focusing on the question of the 'when' of justification. This will be followed by a broader consideration designed to see how the theme functions within Paul's overall argument (section 4). At this point, we shall conduct a brief comparison with the data in Romans. Then, we shall evaluate the significance of the result of our investigation within the broader context of the Galatians crisis (section 5).

3.3 Grammatical and Exegetical Considerations

Instead of assuming, as is often the case, the present nature of justification in Galatians, we will first examine Paul's statements in detail with a view to ascertaining what he actually does and does not say about the theme.

3.3.1 Not by Works of the Law but by Faith (2:15–21)

We begin with 2:15–21, the first, and programmatic, statement of the theme.[19] Our purpose is not to provide a detailed exegesis[20] but to examine Paul's justification language with special attention to its temporal aspect.

Paul's statement in v. 16 sums up the gist of his argument, repeating the verb δικαιοῦν no less than three times. V. 16a provides the ground for the statement in v. 16b: εἰδότες [δὲ] ὅτι οὐ δικαιοῦται ἄνθρωπος ἐξ ἔργων νόμου ἐάν μή[21] διὰ πίστεως Ἰησοῦ Χριστοῦ.[22] Paul uses here the

---

[18] The contextual nature of Galatians is a popular menu on scholarly discussion of Paul, but 'justification' seems to fail to receive its due share. But see Hübner, *Law* (1984) 124–137. Even Beker, who is most eloquent on this, fails to discuss it in his comparison of Romans and Galatians. If he had done so, he would have found that it falsifies his reading of Galatians as a document of 'realized eschatology'.

[19] Schlier 87–88; Betz 114; R. Longenecker 80–81; Fung 112.

[20] Beside commentaries, see Bultmann, 'Auslegung' (1967) 394–399; Klein, 'Individualgeschichte' (1969) 181–202; U. Wilckens, *Rechtfertigung* (1974) 77–109 (84–94); Kümmel, 'Individualgeschichte' (1978) 130–142; Eckstein, *Verheißung* (1996) 3–81; Smiles, *Gospel* (1998).

[21] Dunn's attempt to reconstruct the process from initial 'qualification' to outright 'denial' is far-fetched. Dunn 135–138 and *Law* (1990) 195–196. Rightly, Martyn, *Issues* (1997) 141–142, n. 3.

[22] This is another issue of lively debate. See the bibliography in Bruce 138–139. With Bruce, Dunn and Hansen, we take the 'objective genitive' position. See, most recently, Matlock, 'De-theologizing' (2000) 1–23. The 'subjective' reading is proposed by Hays, *Faith* (1983); B. Longenecker, *Triumph* (1998) 95–115; D. Campbell, 'Coming' (1999) and commentaries such as R. Longenecker, Williams, Martyn and Witherington.

present indicative passive form of δικαιοῦν. Without any specific time
indicator, the statement makes a general and 'timeless' theological claim
about the means of justification: justification is not 'by works of the law'
but 'by faith in Jesus Christ'.[23] The present δικαιοῦται is, then, clearly
gnomic, as the intentionally general ἄνθρωπος makes clear. The participle
εἰδότες,[24] specifying the statement as the motivating 'belief' of Jewish
Christians, further strengthens its gnomic thrust. Thus, one cannot take this
statement as giving evidence of the present nature of justification.[25] Paul's
express purpose in this statement is to define the terms of justification
('how'); other aspects of justification are not in view here.

So 'we' knew the truth and believed in Jesus accordingly. The purpose
of this believing is already clear but Paul now brings it to the surface: ἵνα
δικαιωθῶμεν ἐκ πίστεως Χριστοῦ καὶ οὐκ ἐξ ἔργων νόμου[26] (v. 16b).
The verb δικαιωθῶμεν, being an (aorist) subjunctive, does not in itself
have any tense value. The matter is not so simple, however. This purpose
statement, coupled with the aorist ἐπιστεύσαμεν which supposedly governs
the purpose clause too, is frequently taken to imply the realized nature of
justification. The logic runs: one is justified by faith; we already believed,
and therefore we have been justified.[27]

This reasoning would be legitimate if believing is a punctiliar action
completed in the past. For Paul, however, believing typically refers to a
life disposition with which believers maintain their life toward God: 'And
the life I now live in the flesh I *live by faith* in the Son of God' (2:20).[28]
The idea that faith works itself out through love (5:6) also conveys the

---

[23] So Bultmann, *Theology* (1951) 274; Mußner 170. Cf. Ziesler, *Righteousness* (1972)
172. NEB makes this gnomic thrust clearer by adding 'ever'.

[24] Historically problematic as it may be, Jewish Christians' 'recognition' precedes
their believing Christ. *Contra* Eckstein, *Verheißung* (1996) 13.

[25] *Contra* Eckstein, *Verheißung* (1996) 17, who, based on the present tense of
δικαιοῦν, insists that 'der Gegenwartscharacter der Rechtfertigungsaussagen ist
unbestreitbar'. For this, instructively, he resorts to Rom 3:28. But even there the same
generalizing ἄνθρωπος suggests a gnomic use.

[26] The meaning of this phrase is debated. See the survey in Hansen, *Abraham* (1989)
117–119. This is the *crux interpretum* of Dunn's 'New Perspective'. See his 'New
Perspective' and 'Works of the Law' in his *Law* (1990) 183–214 and 215–241.Cf. Smiles,
Gospel (1998) 119–128. But see Moo, 'Law' (1983) 73–100 (91–96); Räisänen, 'Break'
(1985) 544, 548. In view of Paul's relentless moral demand together with the obvious
abolition of such aspects as circumcision, food laws, and calendar regulations, we find
the traditional distinction between moral and ceremonial close to Paul's intention. So,
Augustine, Marius Victorinus in Edwards 36, 40. Cf. Boyarin, *Jew* (1994) 130–135.

[27] So Räisänen, 'Break' (1985) 545; Martyn 271; Kertelge, *Rechtfertigung* (1966) 128.
R. Longenecker 85: 'For while the aorist ἐπιστεύσαμεν ("we believed") of v. 16 refers to
a once-for-all response that results in a transfer of status (ἵνα δικαιωθῶμεν)'.

[28] Keck, *Letters* (1988) 51 says that faith as trust has 'a moral quality' to it.

same point. [29] Hence the aorist ἐπιστεύσαμεν should be ingressive, denoting the inception of one's life in faith: 'began to believe' or 'decided to believe'.[30] Faith in Christ still continues; we cannot assume that the purpose of believing, i.e., justification, has already been fulfilled unless Paul explicitly affirms it.

In contrast to most interpreters, Betz thinks that Paul has a definite eschatological justification in view here: 'The clause also indicates that justification remains a matter of hope, and is not in any way a present guarantee'.[31] While agreeing with his overall view of future justification, we nevertheless maintain that the idea is not explicit in the present statement.

V. 16c reiterates the idea in v. 16a, now in the negative terms: ὅτι ἐξ ἔργων νόμου οὐ δικαιωθήσεται πᾶσα σάρξ. Paul's use of the future indicative (δικαιωθήσεται) prompts many interpreters to find future eschatological justification in this clause.[32] Though this reading certainly confirms our view, there is reason to be cautious here. The clause is a quotation from Ps 143:2 (LXX 142:2). It is possible that Paul, with other Jews, acknowledged the future justification expressed in the Psalm, but it is difficult to prove that he actually has this in mind at this particular point. Paul also cites the same passage in Rom 3:20 with the same future verb, but now to describe the justification which most probably refers to a reality already revealed (3:21, 24; cf. 19–20). This makes us wary of loading too much on the future tense of the verb.[33]

Taken together, this densely packed statement in v. 16 does not provide any explicit indication about the temporal aspect of justification. As the threefold repetition of 'by works of the law' and 'by faith in Christ' indicates, Paul's manifest purpose here is to clarify the 'how' of justification and nothing else.

Having stated the common ground of justification by faith in v. 16, Paul now goes on to criticize Peter's violation of this 'truth of the gospel'.[34] 'But if, seeking to be justified (ζητοῦντες δικαιωθῆναι) in Christ, we ourselves have been found to be sinners, is Christ then a servant of sin? Certainly not!' (v. 17). Interestingly enough, Paul here combines

---

[29] So Cousar 117.

[30] Rightly, Suhl, 'Galaterbrief' (1987) 3099; Smiles, *Gospel* (1998) 129; Eckstein, *Verheißung* (1996) 20. *Contra* Schlier 94: 'das einmalige und fixierbare Ereignis des Gläubigwerden, das mit der Taufe zusammenfällt'.

[31] Betz 118.

[32] So Martyn 254; Betz 119; Silva, 'Eschatological Structures' (1994) 148; Witherington 183–184.

[33] So Esler 142. The comment of Hill, *Greek Words* (1967) 141 is not justified: 'What is a matter of hope for the Jews becomes for Paul a present possibility and reality'.

[34] The structure of the whole passage is debated. See also 7.3 below.

justification with the idea of 'seeking'. This present participle ζητοῦντες, connected to εὑρέθημεν ('were found sinners'), seems to distinguish itself from the aorist ἐπιστεύσαμεν in v.16 which traces back to the time of conversion.[35] As Tannehill rightly maintains, 'being found sinners' most probably refers to the situation in Antioch, and thus, the 'seeking' here must be a reference to 'the life of faith which Paul, and those with him, have been leading'.[36] Even if the 'seeking' is connected to ἐπιστεύσαμεν, the idea of 'being found sinners' makes clear that the reference is to the situation *after* conversion, that is, their situation in Christ. Paul considers Jewish Christians in Christ including himself as seeking to be justified, i.e., yet to be justified.[37] If justification is what believers still seek to attain in Christ, this means that justification remains a future eschatological gift. 'Paul has come to faith, and as a believer he *awaits* justification by faith in Christ'.[38]

Paul's description of 'life in faith' in vv. 19–20 is mostly taken as evidence for the present reality of justification.[39] Some, assuming that v. 17 is a sort of Jewish Christian objection to the Pauline version of justification, consider it as Paul's rebuttal designed to demonstrate the moral character of 'justified life'.[40] Assuming a realized justification, however, is certainly begging the question. In this case, scholars are frequently misled by the false analogy in Romans, where Paul actually answers a (possible) charge posed against him by defining the *present*

---

[35] Paul never says that believing Christ makes one a sinner. *Contra* Burton 125, 127; Schlier 95; Eckstein, *Verheißung* (1996) 32; Lambrecht, 'Reasoning' (1996) 58; Klein, 'Individualgeschichte' (1969) 190. Cf. Wilckens, *Rechtfertigung* (1974) 90.

[36] Tannehill, *Dying* (1967) 56. See also Soards, 'Seeking' (1989) 237–254, who notices this but reads an unnecessary negative note into Paul's words.

[37] Otherwise, we may speculate, he would probably have said: 'But, if, having been justified in Christ, we ourselves have been found to be sinners....'

[38] Kertelge, *EDNT* 1:331 (emphasis added). Also Betz 119; Tannehill, *Dying* (1967) 56; Dunn 141. Even Martyn 254 acknowledges that this phrase, together with the future verb in 2:16c, refers to 'the sure hope of ultimate rectification'. It is particularly instructive to note that both Feld, 'Diener' (1973) 126 and Bouwman, 'Diener' (1979) 17, recognizing the futuristic force of this sentence, have to brand v. 17 as 'unpaulinisch'.

[39] This is the consensus. See e.g., Ziesler, *Righteousness* (1972) 174; J. Vos, *Pneumatologie* (19) 28, 90 and *passim*; Brinsmead, *Response* (1982) 67; Esler, *Galatians* (1998) 172.

[40] This is the majority view. E.g., Schlier 95–104; Wengst, *Formeln* (1972) 80; Smiles, *Gospel* (1998) 146–154, 163–185; Esler, *Galatians* (1998) 171–172, 186; B. Longenecker, *Triumph* (1998) 113–115; Silva, 'Eschatological Structure' (1994) 149. R. Longenecker 80–96 speaks of vv. 15–16 as showing the 'forensic' and vv. 19–20 the 'ethical' aspect of justification, with v. 21 taking both up. This is reminiscent of Ziesler, *Righteousness* (1972) 173–174. Cf. Bultmann, 'Auslegung' (1967) 394–399; Dahl, *Studies* (1977) 109.

justification in terms of 'death in relation to sin' (6:2, 11) and 'life in relation to God' (6:4, 11, 13).[41] But the issue in Galatians is certainly different from that in Romans; the former speaks of 'death to the law' and the latter 'death to sin'.[42] Most of all, we should note, it would be really strange if Paul was forced to defend his doctrine against a possible criticism even *before* he has established it properly.[43] And the lack of any such concern in his later discussion of the subject (3:6–9, 10–14, 23–24) also renders the postulation of 'defense' quite spurious.

Others, objecting to the 'ethical' interpretation, take it to be a 'christological-soteriological' affirmation depicting the 'eschatological life as such'.[44] 'Resurrection life'[45] and the life of the 'new age'[46] are also frequently invoked. Again, these are ideas not found in the text itself. Paul's interest in Christ is sharply focused on his death rather than his resurrection.[47] He also says that 'Christ living in me' means his living ἐν σαρκί,[48] with the contrast being between two different ways of living one's 'fleshly life': ἐν τῷ Ἰουδαϊσμῷ (1:13) or ἐν Χριστῷ. His use of similar language in other letters also confirms this (Phil 1:20–23; 2 Cor 4:10–11; 5:14–15).

The concluding verse in v. 21 also suggests that vv. 19–20 too are part of Paul's argument about the means of justification rather than its follow-up, supposedly explaining the ethical nature of justification. Furthermore, vv. 19–20 are not intended as an objective 'christological' or 'eschatological' statement but as Paul's personal, and polemical for that matter, manifesto of his life-disposition now oriented to Christ.[49] Within the context, it polemically depicts Paul's unwavering disposition of 'seeking to be justified in Christ' over against Peter's deviation from the truth of the gospel.[50] In sum, vv. 19–20 do not describe the nature of

---

[41] Schlier 98–100; Smiles, *Gospel* (1998) 168–177. When engaged in diatribe, Paul is usually very explicit in what he says. See Rom 3:9; 6:1.

[42] Schlier (100) himself notes this. See also Ebeling, *Truth* (1985) 132.

[43] The Antioch incident itself concerns the table fellowship, not the doctrine of justification. It is Paul who brings in the subject, branding Peter's 'table manner' as a denial of justification by faith.

[44] E.g., Cosgrove, *Cross* (1998) 140; Eckstein, *Verheißung* (1996) 57; Fung 123.

[45] E.g., Styler, 'Obligation' (1973) 181–183; Silva, 'Eschatological Struture' (1994) 149; Martyn 258–259. See the sober observation in Keck, *Letters* (1989) 57.

[46] E.g., Dunn 145; Mußner 182–183; Brinsmead, *Response* (1982) 75.

[47] See also 7.3 below.

[48] Martyn 258–259 rightly sees here a note of 'eschatological reservation'.

[49] Rightly Duncan 72; Ridderbos 106–107; Witherington 190; Davies, *Rabbinic Judaism* (1959) 197. See our discussion of the passage in 7.3 below.

[50] The contrast between the Jewish Christians and Paul parallels 5:2–5, where those attempting to be justified in the law are contrasted to 'us' waiting for the hope of righteousness πνεύματι ἐκ πίστεως.

justification but of *faith* as the proper means to justification, stressing that faith in Christ cannot allow any room for the law.

In v. 21 Paul clinches his argument by referring to the death of Christ: 'I do not nullify the grace of God. For if righteousness (δικαιοσύνη)[51] is through the law, then Christ would have died to no purpose'. With an elliptical construction only with a noun and an adjectival phrase, Paul's concentration on the 'how' becomes even clearer: justification is not 'through the law'. The statement is clearly hypothetical, contradictory to the fact,[52] and thus does not tell us anything positive about justification except that it is not 'through the law'. Paul affirms that the death of Christ is somehow the source of justification, but beyond that he does not explain it any further. This rather ambiguous statement on the role of Christ's death confirms once more that Paul's central concern here is to make the negative claim that justification is never 'by the law'.[53]

3.3.2 Abraham and Justification (3:6-29)

In 3:6 Paul brings in the story of Abraham for the first time by citing Genesis 15:6 (LXX) almost *verbatim*: 'Just as (καθώς) Abraham believed (ἐπίστευσεν) God, and it was reckoned (ἐλογίσθη) to him as righteousness (εἰς δικαιοσύνην)'. The fact that he begins his exposition of Abraham tradition with Abraham's justification indicates that justification is the central issue he has in mind.[54] In his quotation, as in the original LXX, God's reckoning is put in the aorist (ἐλογίσθη), indicating that Abraham was in fact justified. The point is clear: Abraham believed God's promises, and therefore God reckoned this as his righteousness, namely, he was justified.

Some people take this to be an unmistakable reference to the realized nature of justification in Galatians.[55] One has to be cautious, however. This

---

[51] The easy switch from the noun and the verb in 2:16–21, 3:19–24 and 5:4–5 makes any attempt to distinguish between the noun/adjective and the verb artificial (see n. 12). Rightly, Dunn, *Law* (1990) 207; Esler, *Galatians* (1998) 141–142. See now Moor, 'δικαιοσύνη' (1998) 27–43. Our view of a future eschatological justification renders such a distinction irrelevant.

[52] Rightly, Barrett, *Paul* (1994) 78: 'the ultimate *reductio ad absurdum*'.

[53] Ambrosiaster here speaks of 'a future life'. Edwards 33.

[54] *Contra* those who connect v. 6 to 3:2–5, making it a scriptural proof for receiving the Spirit 'by faith'. Stanley, 'Curse' (1990) 494–495 (but see 508); Fung 136; Williams, 'Justification' (1987) 92–93; Fee, *Presence* (1995) 390, n. 84; Kruse, *Law* (1996) 77. Clearly, it is the 'obvious' reality of the Spirit that proves the 'controversial' justification by faith, not *vice versa*.

[55] E.g. Ziesler, *Righteousness* (1972) 180. For Barrett too, *Freedom* (1985) 64, this is the only evidence he can adduce in Galatians for realized justification. Also Eckstein, *Verheißung* (1996) 95–96, who considers 3:6 (Gen 15:6) as the fulfillment for Abraham

verse is part of the quotation brought in for the purpose of analogy (καθώς) and *not* part of Paul's own statement about justification.[56] In using Abraham as a paradigm, his interest is limited to the necessary connection between faith and justification, without any intention of reading its present reality out of the 'already' of Abraham's justification.[57] Paul's own conclusion in v. 7 does not make any such claim. In fact, it does not use a *dik-* word at all. What he picks up from the Abraham analogy is the inseparable tie between faith and justification, no more and no less.

3:8–9 furthers the argument in 3:6–7, now utilizing the biblical term, 'blessing'. As he speaks of the Scripture's foreknowledge of justification by faith, Paul uses a present indicative verb with God as its subject: ἐκ πίστεως δικαιοῖ τὰ ἔθνη ὁ θεός (v. 8a). Here too, the present tense expresses 'God's abiding policy'[58] that he justifies the Gentiles by faith, with no clear indication of its temporal aspect.[59]

To offer further scriptural support for his thesis, Paul now appeals to God's oracle of 'blessing' (Gen 12:3; 18:18), thereby defining the Abrahamic blessing in terms of justification (v. 8b).[60] Taking up the gnomic thrust of v. 8a, the conclusion is also put in a gnomic present: 'so that those of faith are blessed (εὐλογοῦνται) together with believing Abraham' (v. 9). The present passive indicative of εὐλογέω, which is very rare in the NT, is never used to describe the result of blessing, for which the passive participle εὐλογημένος is invariably used. In the NT the only other use of the present passive indicative form is found in Heb 7:7, also in a gnomic sense: χωρὶς δὲ πάσης ἀντιλογίας τὸ ἔλαττον ὑπὸ τοῦ κρείττονος εὐλογεῖται. As in the case of justification, the present tense is explained by Paul's focus on the question of 'means', and not, as Eckstein asserts, by his realized eschatological intention to speak of 'das

---

of the 'promise of blessing' quoted in 3:8 (Gen 12:3; 18:18), which has also been fulfilled for the Gentile believers in the form of the Spirit.

[56] Rightly, Yinger, *Judgment* (1999) 167.

[57] In Romans 4 Abraham's justification *before* his circumcision is crucial for Paul. However, the conclusion that Paul draws from ἐλογίσθη αὐτῷ (4:23) is not that we too have been justified but that it is δι᾽ ἡμᾶς οἷς μέλλει λογίζεσθαι (4:24), showing that he has no intention of capitalizing on the *time* of Abraham's justification.

[58] Bruce 156; Burton 160.

[59] *Contra* Eckstein, *Verheißung* (1996) 110, who takes it as 'realen Gegenwart'. Once again, his resort to Romans is noteworthy. Dunn 164 sees a 'deliberate ambiguity', allowing the possibility of 'final justification'. In this way, he speaks of 'God's acceptance…from start to finish', which suits his claim of 'covenantal nomism'.

[60] Rightly, Chrysostom and Augustine in Edwards 39–40; Williams, 'Justification' (1987) 91–100; Hong, *Law* (1993) 131; Witherington 228; Burton 175. *Contra* Cosgrove, *Cross* (1988) 50–51, 60–63 and 'Arguing' (1988) 547, n. 1 who denies such equation. But see Fee, *Presence* (1995) 393.

gegenwärtige Gesegnetwerden durch Gott'.[61] This verse is just another way of saying that 'those of faith are justified' as Abraham was justified by his faith.

However, things are more complicated in 3:14, the conclusion of the whole argument in 3:6–14. Here the blessing of the Gentiles is affirmed once more, now as the purpose of Christ's redemption: 'so that the blessing of Abraham might reach the Gentiles'. This conclusion is followed by another ἵνα clause presenting the gift of the Spirit as result of the Christ event: 'so that we might receive the promise of the Spirit'. If we take the double ἵνα clause as coordinates expressing the same reality,[62] it then means that the 'blessing' is identified, or at least, coincides, with the Spirit, the gift the Galatians already received at the time of their conversion (3:1–5). If this is the case, it then follows that justification, represented by the 'blessing', already happened for the Gentile believers as they came to faith.[63]

It has to be admitted that, grammatically speaking, this is a very plausible interpretation of 3:14, where double clauses are juxtaposed side by side. There are, however, other things to consider before we rush to such a conclusion. First, the argument in 3:6–14 as a whole concerns the claim that justification comes by faith. The initial statement in 3:6–7, first followed by the scriptural argument in terms of 'blessing' (vv. 8–9), is then developed into an antithetical argument of 'curse and blessing' based on the redemption of Christ (vv. 10–13).

Read in this way, it is not the whole v. 14 but only v. 14a that rounds up the argument begun at v. 6, proving why the blessing of justification comes to Gentiles 'in Christ', namely, 'not by works of the law'. Paul's reference to the Spirit in v. 14b is a new development, intended to connect the whole argument (vv. 6–14a) with the 'fact' of the Spirit the Galatians themselves have received (vv. 1–5).[64] By this deliberate association, Paul brings in the Spirit as the experiential support for his argument of justification by faith. That is, the Spirit-clause is a somewhat loose addition to the argument

---

[61] Eckstein, *Verheißung* (1996) 118. Cf. Duncan 91.

[62] So Schlier 140; Mußner 234–236; Bruce 167; R. Longenecker 123; Dunn 179; Eckstein, *Verheißung* (1996) 163; Martyn 321. A minor group of scholars considers v. 14b as dependent on v. 14a. Duncan 103; Betz 152; Bligh, *Greek* (1966) 139.

[63] This is the consensus. See, among others, Williams, 'Justification' (1987) 91–100. Dahl, *Studies* (1977) 133; J. Vos, *Pneumatologie* (1973) 108; Hansen, *Abraham* (1988) 116; Cousar, *Cross* (1990) 117.

[64] Cf. Luz, *Geschichtsverständnis* (1968) 148; Eckstein, *Verheißung* (1996) 163. Structurally, 3:14a corresponds to 3:6–14, and 3:14b to 3:1–5 which does *not* belong to the scriptural argument. See also 7.4 below.

proper (vv. 6–14a) to boost the force of his claim of 'by faith'. We should not, therefore, mingle the two clauses into a single statement.[65]

Secondly, the Galatians who wish to be justified in the law (5:4) certainly do not consider their experience of the Spirit as evidence of their justification. Paul's identification of justification and the reception of the Spirit would have been as much a surprise to the Galatians as it was important for his case. If this had indeed been his intention, then he would have been more explicit identifying the two, probably providing a proper explanation. His failure to do so indicates that he has no intention of making such a point.

Thirdly, in Galatians Paul *never* specifies the Spirit as a concomitant of justification.[66] Certainly they are brought together quite closely, but never equated. On the contrary, when he becomes explicit, he presents the Spirit as the *means* with which or *mode* in which believers wait for their future justification (5:5).

Given these considerations, equating justification/blessing with the gift of the Spirit creates more problems than it solves. Close as they certainly are, justification and the gift of the Spirit do not coincide. The Spirit has certainly come; Paul never says, however, that justification has too.

In 3:11 Paul uses δικ- words twice, once in the quotation of Habakkuk 2:4 and the other in his own explanatory comment. The present indicative in v. 11a is gnomic, stating the 'timeless' truth that no one is justified by the law.[67] The gnomic character is easily confirmed by the declarative conjunction ὅτι at the beginning of the clause and the predicate δῆλον, which is most probably connected to the preceding clause. [68] Also noteworthy is the categorical οὐδείς, which nicely corresponds to ἄνθρωπος and πᾶσα σάρξ in 2:16.[69]

Paul's use of Habakkuk is somewhat problematic. His quotation reads: 'The one who is righteous (ὁ δίκαιος) by faith will live'. Scholars debate whether the prepositional phrase ἐκ πίστεως should be connected to the verb ζήσεται or to the subject ὁ δίκαιος. According to the former, the sentence reads: 'The righteous one shall live by faith',[70] while the latter

---

[65] *Contra* Esler, *Galatians* (1998) 175 who takes both as 'alternative ways of saying the same thing'.

[66] Even in Romans, where justification must coincide with receiving the Spirit, Paul does not bring the two together.

[67] Rightly, Bultmann, *Theology* (1951) 274.

[68] So Mußner 228.

[69] So Mußner 228; Eckstein, *Verheißung* (1996) 134–135.

[70] So AV; NASB; Mußner 227. The Messianic readings of Hays, *Faith* (1983) 150–157 and Cosgrove, *Cross* (1988) 57 are misleading since, as Dunn 174 points out, v. 11b answers to the statement in v. 11a ('no one').

gives the meaning provided above.[71] Either way, his reference to 'the righteous one' is often taken as implying the present nature of justification[72] since it is clear that in its original context the passage does speak of the one who is actually righteous.

Once again, however, we should not squeeze the cited OT text as if it were part of Paul's own, carefully nuanced, statement. As in the case of Abraham's justification (3:6; Gen 15:6), his purpose in appealing to this particular text is clearly defined, as is explicitly stated in his own interpretive comment: 'Now it is evident that through the law no one is justified before God' (v. 11a).[73] From the first, his singular concern is to explain the 'how' of justification and nothing more.[74] Thus, to prove that justification is not by the law but only by faith, he appeals to a text where justification language is combined with the idea of faith. He is not stating how justified people should 'live'. As in the case of the story of Abraham, what he looks for in the Scripture is only the exclusive bond between faith and justification.[75]

By and large Paul's discussion of the Abraham tradition from 3:15 onwards is carried out in terms of 'promise' and 'inheritance' rather than 'justification'. Διχ- words do occur, however, at two significant junctures in his argument. The noun is used in 3:21: 'Is the law then against[76] the promises? Certainly not! For if a law had been given that could make alive, righteousness (δικαιοσύνη) would indeed come from the law' (NRSV). Clearly, Paul assumes that the law has no power 'to give life' (ζωοποιῆσαι). And if this protasis is definitely wrong, it then follows that what is stated in the apodosis is also wrong. Since the law is not 'life-giving', righteousness cannot come from the law.

Here the precise meaning of 'to give life' is debated. Some think it refers to eternal life, while a majority of interpreters opt for the present life given in Christ.[77] Whichever it means, however, it does not necessarily determine the 'when' of justification. In the former view ('eternal life'),

---

[71] So RSV; NEB; Hübner, *Law* (1984) 19, 43–44, n. 15; also Fung 143–145 with detailed discussion.

[72] E.g., Eckstein, *Verheißung* (1996) 142; Ziesler, *Righteousness* (1972) 176; Fung 145.

[73] Cf. Burton 166.

[74] Rightly, Reumann, *Righteousness* (1982) 57–58. Cf. Ziesler, *Righteousness* (1972) 177, n. 1.

[75] In this sense, the view of Sanders that Paul's argument here is 'terminological' has a grain of truth. *Law* (1983) 21–27; *Paul* (1991) 56.

[76] Unlike Dunn 192, the point is the impotence of the law, not its consistency with the promise. Rightly, Martyn 358–359 and *Issues* (1998) 167, n. 15.

[77] The former has Betz 174 and the latter Burton 195 (justification–giving life); Bruce 180; Longenecker 144; Dunn 193–194; Fung 162–163; Eckstein, *Verheißung* (1996) 207.

righteousness could easily be construed as future eschatological. But even in the latter case, it does not necessitate the idea of realized justification since there is no ground for thinking that Paul equates life with justification.[78] Then it would simply mean that the law cannot bring in (future) righteousness since it is now failing to give people genuine life which is essential in receiving future justification (2:20–21; 5:5–6, 25!; cf. 6:7–9). Of course, this futuristic meaning is not explicit within this statement itself, but it is equally true that it does not evidence the present reality of righteousness either.

In 3:24, the verb δικαιοῦν is used in the subjunctive: 'Thus the law was our *paidagogos* unto Christ, so that we might be justified (δικαιωθῶμεν) by faith'. Here Paul, by attributing an utterly negative function to the law, further consolidates the exclusive bond between justification and faith. As in 2:16b, the verb, being a subjunctive, does not have any independent tense value, and therefore does not tell us anything about the time of justification. Also noteworthy is Paul's failure in v. 25 to affirm the present reality of justification as the result of Christ's coming, a move expected by v. 24. The coming of Christ definitely marks the end of slavery, but not the beginning of justification.[79]

3.3.3 *The Hope of Righteousness (5:2–5)*

Justification language is missing in chapter 4,[80] but pops up again at the beginning of chapter 5. In vv. 2–4 Paul utters a series of categorical warnings about the consequence of the Galatian deviation depicted as an attempt to 'be justified by the law': 'You who want to be justified (δικαιοῦσθε) by the law have cut yourselves off from Christ' (v. 4). Though the verb is present indicative, it does not imply that righteousness by the law is a reality, or even a possibility, since for Paul there is no such thing as 'justification by the law', a point stated beyond any doubt.[81] Thus it can only denote the misguided *desire* or *attempt* on the part of the

---

[78] Equating 'righteousness' and 'life' makes Paul's statement quite inept: 'if a law had been given which is able to give righteousness, then righteousness would be by the law'. Rightly, Fee, *Presence* (1995) 398. *Contra* Brinsmead, *Response* (1982) 67; Cosgrove, *Cross* (1988) 59; R. Longenecker 144; Guthrie 107; Dunn 193.

[79] Thus, the context does not provide evidence for a 'liberative sense' of justification. *Contra* Campbell, 'Coming' (1999) 12–13.

[80] This point does not undermine the centrality of justification since Paul uses the concept 'inheritance', which dominates chapter 4, as a scriptural equivalent of justification. See 6.6 below.

[81] See *BDF* §167, 319. *Contra* Cosgrove, *Cross* (1988) 150–151 and Fee, *Presence* (1995) 416.

bewitched Galatians.[82] Yet the Galatians imagine that such a thing is possible, and in their mind, it refers to the justification at God's final judgment.[83]

Over against this fatal dead end, Paul now presents the real alternative in v. 5: 'For we, through the Spirit coming from faith,[84] are eagerly waiting for the hope of righteousness' (ἐλπίδα δικαιοσύνης ἀπεκδεχόμεθα). The genitive is most probably appositional, defining righteousness itself as the object of eschatological anticipation.[85] Paul's use of ἀπεκδεχόμεθα, a word exclusively reserved for eschatological anticipation (Rom 8:19, 23, 25; 1 Cor 1:7; Phil 3:20; cf. Heb 9:23; 1 Pet 3:20),[86] further boosts the future eschatological thrust.

In view of the rather tantalizing nature of Paul's statements on justification so far, this last reference seems crucial since here Paul identifies justification explicitly as a matter of future hope. Up to this point his concern has been only with the 'how' of justification, but now, at this strategic point, he puts this question of 'how' within an unmistakably future eschatological framework by defining justification as a blessing still to be awaited.

Understandably, many interpreters object to this futuristic reading, claiming that in other parts of the letter justification is depicted as a present reality. For example, Fung, citing Schrenk, asserts that 'elsewhere in Galatians ... justification is not mentioned with reference to the future, but appears rather as something already accomplished in the present through faith in Christ. .... Indeed, Paul's conviction that righteousness is imparted now is "the new point in comparison with Judaism"'.[87] If this is the case, justification cannot be an object of eschatological hope and therefore 'hope of righteousness' must be a subjective genitive, referring to 'the realization of the hoped for things pertaining to the state of righteousness conferred in justification'.[88] Then the phrase refers to the hope that 'justified believers' cherish: the hope that issues from, and thus is grounded on, the present justification.[89]

---

[82] That this refers to the intention of the Galatians is confirmed by 4:8 and 4:21, where Paul explicitly employs the verb θέλω.

[83] So, Dunn 267–268.

[84] For this rendering see 7.4 below.

[85] Zerwick, *Greek* (1963) 17; Mußner 350 with most commentators.

[86] Glasswell, *EDNT* 1:407; Hoffmann, *NIDNTT* 2:245. Cf. Kertelge, *Rechtfertigung* (1966) 150.

[87] Fung 225. Cf. Schrenk, *TDNT* 2:205.

[88] G. Vos, *Eschatology* (1930) 30.

[89] So Eckstein, *Verheißung* (1996) 142, 247: 'das mit der Rechtfertigung zugesagte Hoffnungsgut der endgültigen Erlösung'; G. Vos, *Eschatology* (1930) 30; Klein, 'Gottes Gerechtigkeit' (1969) 228; Bruce 41; Matera 189; Fung 224–227, 232–235; Fee,

Though grammatically not impossible, this reading is problematic in two respects. First, one cannot *assume* the present reality of justification in Galatians. To be sure, Paul, except for the present verse, never states explicitly that it is a future hope, but it is equally true that he never affirms its present reality either. Apart from 2:17, where future justification is strongly implied, 5:5 is the only reference to the temporal aspect of justification. It begs the question, therefore, to interpret this verse on the *a priori* assumption of realized justification.[90]

Secondly, this interpretation also creates a serious problem in the flow of Paul's argument. If we take the genitive to be subjective, it means that Paul, quite surprisingly, slips in the new element of hope into his discussion. If his main emphasis is on the present reality of justification throughout, why would he, in this strategic juncture of his argument, suddenly speak of a future hope without bothering to give any further discussion? In this view justification itself may well be explained as present, but the abruptly introduced 'hope' still hangs in the air without any link to Paul's argument so far. Martyn expresses the problem aptly:

> In a letter in which Paul has polemically and consistently said that the human scene-indeed the cosmos itself-has already been changed by God's rectifying deed in Christ's advent and death, it is a surprise to hear him speak with emphasis of hope, the only instance of this term in the letter. And it is a double surprise to hear him refer to rectification as a future event'.[91]

This surprise is, however, an unsolicited one since, apart from the assumption of present justification, there is nothing that prevents us from taking the phrase as an objective genitive: righteousness itself is the object of future hope that believers are eagerly waiting for. This then is another way of saying final salvation.[92]

Thus, quite rightly, most interpreters acknowledge that the phrase refers to future justification.[93] The problem is, however, that they combine this with their prior assumption of realized justification. With this uneasy conflation, some speak of double justification, one initial and the other

---

Presence (1995) 418–419. Zerwick, *Greek* (1963) 17 suggests the rendering 'that which δικαιοσυνή hopes for', with the abstract δικαιοσυνή standing for the concrete οἱ δίκαιοι.

[90] In Romans 'realized' justification does not prevent Paul from speaking of end-time justification.

[91] Martyn 472. See also Cousar 115.

[92] Rightly, Mayer, *ENDT* 1:439. One may call it appositional but in this case the distinction is merely terminological.

[93] E.g., Schlier 234; Mußner 350; Ladd, *Theology* (1974) 442; Cosgrove, *Cross* (1988) 150–152.

eschatological, [94] while others of the future 'dimension' of single justification which will come to its 'consummation' at the *eschaton*.[95] Or, according to Barrett, 'justification, then, is a beginning, and a process; and it leads to a consummation at the future judgment, when God's initial gracious verdict on the sinner is – or, it may be, is not – confirmed'.[96] And it is with this *composite* meaning that most scholars interpret Paul's argument at this point.

The problems of such interpretation are not difficult to show. First, it is exegetically ill-advised. Granted, for the sake of argument, the present reality of justification earlier in the letter, it is fallacious to transfer such meaning to this passage to produce the composite notion of justification, and interpret Paul's argument *here* with that 'richer theology of justification'.[97] This constitutes the fallacy of 'import[ing] into a particular passage a meaning discovered elsewhere, without noticing that the word in the latter passage is modified by a particular phrase or by some syntactical feature'.[98] Indeed, as already noted, the fact that Paul defines righteousness as an object of eager anticipation (ἀπεκδέχεσθαι) makes it clear that Paul has no intention at all of allowing its present reality.

Secondly, the idea of justification as a continuous 'movement' or 'process' is not easy to prove exegetically. Despite its popularity in recent scholarly discussion, Paul's own language lacks such convenient motifs as 'fullness' or 'consummation', even in Romans.[99] Justification may be present (Rom 5:1) or future (Rom 2:1–16; Gal 5:5), but in each case Paul's logic requires a homogeneous concept, either present or future; positing 'justification-as-a-process' seem to obscure his meaning at each point.[100]

---

[94] E.g., Duncan 156; Stuhlmacher, *Gerechtigkeit* (1965) 229; Räisänen, 'Break' (1985) 551, n. 31; Cosgrove, *Cross* (1988) 150 and 'Justification' (1987) 653–670; Witherington 183–184, 369. See the criticism of Stuhlmacher by Donfried, 'Justification' (1976) 95.

[95] E.g., Martyn 254; Eckert, *Verkündigung* (1971) 42–43. Cf. Käsemann, *Questions* (1969) 170.

[96] Barrett, *Freedom* (1985) 64–65. For Jeremias, *Message* (1965) 65, justification as 'antedonation of God's final gift' is 'the beginning of a movement towards a goal, namely towards the hour of the definitive justification, of the acquittal on the day of judgment, when the full gift is realized'. See also Stuhlmacher, *Reconciliation* (1986) 72; Reumann, *Righteousness* (1982) 58; Dunn 269–70, 272; Witherington 193; Williams 138.

[97] Dunn, *Law* (1990) 208.

[98] Silva, *Words* (1983) 26, referring to Barr, *Semantics* (1961) 218 who calls this 'illegitimate totality transfer'. See also Carson, *Fallacy* (1984) 62.

[99] Instructively, in Rom 5:9–10 the end result of present justification is not its 'consummation' or 'final justification' but 'salvation'.

[100] This is not to deny eschatological 'tension' of any kind, though the word 'tension' seems somewhat unfortunate. Our point here is that such tension should not be sought within the single concept of justification. In the Galatian context we can speak of the

Thirdly, even such a step does not help, as far as the future phase of justification remains. Granted, once again, the presence of justification, one has to admit that such initial justification remains tentative since it is also true that 'God's gift can be lost' and 'God's initial gracious verdict' may not be 'confirmed'.[101] What matters at this point is the appropriate 'life/obedience in the Spirit' on the basis of which God will bestow his final verdict of justification.[102] Then, one is bound to ask, what is the point of affirming the 'already' of 'initial' justification, if it can be revoked later according to one's own performance? Is Paul wasting so much papyrus just to argue for this tentative justification by faith only to contradict it later by introducing future justification which requires not only 'conviction' but also 'behavior'? Does not this hope of righteousness then demolish the very point he has been making throughout the letter?[103]

As an explanation of Paul's *polemical* argument, the synthetic understanding of the 'hope of righteousness' simply does not work. Since we cannot excise the clear motif of hope in this passage, the only viable option is to take justification to be future eschatological pure and simple: 'for we, through the Spirit coming from faith, *are eagerly waiting* for the hope of righteousness'.[104]

Thus far we have examined Paul's use of justification language and demonstrated that in Galatians justification refers to a future eschatological gift that God will bestow at the judgment. We have argued that the common view of realized justification is an unfounded assumption read into Galatians, most probably under the influence of Romans. We have also seen that in a couple of places (2:17; 5:2), Paul implies the future

---

eschatological 'movement' between present sonship and future justification, but not within justification and sonship themselves.

[101] Barrett, *Freedom* (1985) 64–65; Williams 138; Witherington 369.

[102] Stuhlmacher, *Reconciliation* (1986) 84.

[103] Surprisingly, this logical contradiction largely escapes scholarly attention. J. Vos, *Pneumatologie* (1973) 105 thinks that Paul is here 'correcting the enthusiastic view of chapters 3–4' but does not explain how such self-correction works as a polemical response to the crisis.

[104] Betz 262 is a rare example of those who hold on to future eschatological justification. According to him, ἐλπὶς δικαιοσύνης spells out the eschatological character of the Christian salvation: 'justification by faith' is a matter of 'hope' in God. This being so, it is 'not visible and not obtainable now'. See 1.2.6 above. Lyons, *Autobiography* (1985) 172 also makes a passing remark about 'the futurity of justification' for which he lists 2:16, 17; 3:8, 24 and especially 5:4. Mitternacht, 'Assessment' (2002) 411: 'Redemption from this present evil age was expected soon (1:4), but as of now righteousness is a matter of hope and its fulfillment is in the future'. As he reiterates in the note, 'Nobody has arrived as yet. Thus, the matter of dispute between Paul and the influencers was not whether the age to come had actually dawned...' (n. 20).

eschatological nature of justification very strongly. We have noted in particular the importance of Paul's reference to the 'hope of righteousness' in 5:2–5, which presents 'righteousness' explicitly as an object of future hope. In sum, there is nothing in Galatians that suggests justification clearly to be a present reality, while there is clear evidence for its future eschatological nature.

3.4 Broader Exegetical Considerations

Our case is not, however, dependent on these considerations alone. The manner in which Paul develops his arguments in general also corroborates this conclusion. Since justification is the primary issue in Paul's mind, it is natural that it is closely related to other major themes of his argument: life in faith (2:15–21); the Spirit (3:1–5; cf. 2:15–21; 3:6ff.); sonship/the seed (3:6–7; 3:23–29), blessing (3:11 in 3:8–14), promise/inheritance (3:15–25) and freedom (5:1–5). In fact, it is this intricately interlocking character of Paul's argument that makes it so difficult to follow his logic precisely, which also seems to lead most interpreters to equate justification with these related yet distinct concepts.[105]

In the previous section, while arguing for the future eschatological nature of justification, we made the observation that in Galatians Paul never makes an explicit affirmation of the realized nature of justification. This reservation stands out quite remarkably, especially when we compare it with the unabashed affirmation of the present privileges believers have in Christ. Throughout the letter, Paul's affirmation of the believers' present status leaves no room for ambiguity. He himself now lives in Christ/faith (2:19–20). The Galatians, having already received the Spirit (3:2–5; 4:6; 4:29; 5:5), are now sons and heirs (3:7; 3:29; 4:7). They have been baptized into and thus are now clothed with Christ (3:27). Their freedom from the law is also an undeniable reality for the Galatian believers (3:25; 4:31; 5:1, 13).

Surprisingly, however, Paul, while making such unreserved statements about the present status of the Galatians, never, *not even once*, speaks of justification as part of their present status, even though he keeps connecting it with these present indicatives. Under the assumption of realized justification, this glaring failure in an argument which is particularly designed to prove that very point remains inexplicable. This dual observation about the eloquence of Paul in affirming the present status of the Galatian believers and the lack of comparable statements on

---

[105] This is the consensus view. See especially Williams, 'Justification' (1987).

justification almost compels us to conclude that in Galatians justification does not belong to the present indicative of Christian life.

This conclusion becomes even stronger if we compare Paul's discussion in Galatians with what he does in Romans. There too, his main concern is the 'how' of justification, proving that it is only by faith and not by works of the law. Naturally he makes a number of gnomic statements as he does in Galatians, mostly utilizing the noun δικαιοσύνη but also with verbal forms too (e.g., 3:24, 28; 4:5). Illuminatingly, *it is in Romans, where a polemical exigency is far less visible than in Galatians,*[106] *that the present reality of justification is declared with impressive clarity.*

Most remarkable is his liberal use of time indicators in conjunction with aorist or perfect *indicatives*, both of which are completely lacking in Galatians. In Rom 3:21 Paul declares: 'but now (νυνὶ δὲ) the righteousness of God has been made manifested (πεφανέρωται) apart from the law'. Coupled with the perfect πεφανέρωται, the emphatic νυνὶ makes the deliberate stress on the 'now' of justification unmistakable.[107] The same goes for 3:26, where Paul speaks of God's self-demonstration as the One who is just and justifies those who believe Christ ἐν τῷ νῦν καιρῷ. Once again, in 5:9 Paul declares, 'Now (νῦν) that we have been justified by his blood...'

Even without explicit time indicators, this point stands out quite clearly. In 9:30 Paul affirms that 'Gentiles who did not pursue righteousness have attained righteousness (κατέλαβεν δικαιοσύνην), that is, righteousness through faith'. Statements to the same effect are made over and over again throughout the letter (cf. 5:1–2, 9–10; 8:30, 31–34; 14:17). The Paul of Romans leaves us no shred of doubt about the present reality of justification.[108] In Galatians, however, we fail to see any move comparable to that. One is bound to ask why.

Since in Romans justification concurs with 'getting in', it naturally forms the ground for what subsequently comes both in the present and in the future. For example, the present justification provides the ground for peace with God (present) and hope for the glory of God (future):

---

[106] Romans is often thought to present the most 'systematic' exposition of justification. Whether this is true or not, it certainly seems that Paul's discussion there, not provoked by an urgent crisis, is more balanced and less polemical than in Galatians. This consideration provides an important backdrop against which to assess Paul's argument in Galatians. Cf. Donfried, *Romans Debate* (1991).

[107] Rightly, Stählin, *TDNT* 4:1117; Nygren, *Romans* (1949) 144; Bornkamm, *Experience* (1969) 63–64. Käsemann, *Romans* (1980) 92: 'the eschatological turn'.

[108] Cf. Tachau, *Einst* (1972) 81–82. Cranfield, *Romans I* (1975) 266. Its combination with 'reconciliation' and separation from final judgment in an *a minori ad maius* argument makes the present reality of justification more emphatic. Cf. Käsemann, *Romans* (1980) 138.

'Therefore, since we have been justified (δικαιωθέντες) by faith, we have
peace with God through our Lord Jesus Christ. Through him we have
obtained (ἐσχήκαμεν) access to this grace in which we stand, and we
rejoice in the hope of the glory of God' (5:1–2). [109] Thus, it is not
surprising at all that justification joins peace and joy as denominators of
the kingdom of God: 'for the kingdom of God is not food and drink but
righteousness and peace and joy in the Holy Spirit' (14:17). The idea of
present justification as the ground for future hope receives further stress in
5:9, where it serves as evidence for the surety of future 'salvation': 'Since,
therefore, we have now been justified (δικαιωθέντες νῦν) by his blood,
much more shall we be saved (σωθησόμεθα) by him from the wrath of
God'.[110] In Romans 8 too, God's present act of justification is presented as
irrefutable evidence for the reality of God's love, and for that matter, for
the surety of future salvation (8:30, 31–34). Paul says the same thing when
he states that the promise that Abraham would be the heir of the world
comes 'through the righteousness of faith' (4:13). Indeed, present
justification constitutes the ground for future promise.

This is, however, as we have noted, a phenomenon we *fail* to find in
Galatians. While justification is closely related to other present indicatives,
it is *never* posited as their ground as in Romans. All present gifts are
unmistakably affirmed as already present, but without being predicated on
justification (3:25, 26–29; 4:5–7, 28, 31; 5:1, 13). Neither is justification
the ground for the hope of eschatological salvation. In Galatians
justification is never the precondition of the 'kingdom of God' or 'eternal
life', that is, future salvation (cf. Rom 5:9–10; 8:30, 31–34). On the
contrary, it is justification itself that takes the place of honor as the object
of eschatological hope, and the goal of Paul's argument (5:5).

The comparison becomes most fruitful in Paul's discussion of the
Christian life. The necessity of proper ethical behavior receives equal
emphasis in both letters, yet in different ways. In Romans justification
constitutes the *ground* for obedience.[111] Freedom means being 'justified'
from sin (δεδικαίωται, 6:7),[112] while the pre-conversion life of slavery to
sin is ironically described as 'freedom in relation to righteousness' (6:20).
Having been liberated (ἐλευθερωθέντες) from the tyranny of sin, however,

---

[109] This captures both the present and the future of the justified believer. Nygren,
Romans (1949) 195.

[110] Instructively, this is the meaning many scholars read in Paul's reference to the
'hope of righteousness' in Galatians 5:5.

[111] Stuhlmacher, *Romans* (1994) 88 titles 6:1–8:31 'The Righteousness of God as the
Ground and Power of New Life'. The claim of Bottorff, 'Justification' (1973) 424–430
applies to Romans, but not Galatians.

[112] For this translation see Cranfield, *Romans I* (1975) 310–311 and n. 1 there.

believers now 'have become slaves to righteousness' (ἐδουλώθητε τῇ δικαιοσύνῃ) (6:18); their members are now not the weapons of wickedness but of righteousness (6:14). Thus, they are now exhorted to attain holiness by presenting their bodies 'to righteousness' as its slave (6:19). Since justification refers to the radical change of believers' status in the present, they are now 'under the reign of righteousness',[113] and it is only natural that Paul utilizes this language of justification to explicate the nature of Christian life.

Paul does something different in Galatians, however. Nowhere in the letter does he explicitly define the present life of believers in terms of justification.[114] Instead of the 'justified life' (Romans), in Galatians he speaks of 'freedom' to characterize the immediate effect of the Christ event, and therefore, the present state of believers' existence (2:4; 3:13, 25; 4:4; 4:21–31; 5:1, 13).[115] And in contrast to Romans this freedom is never related to justification. (cf. Rom 6:7, 18). Naturally, it is now on this *freedom* of sonship, *freedom* in the Spirit, that Paul bases his moral exhortation: 'It is for freedom (τῇ ἐλευθερίᾳ) that Christ liberated us. Stand firm, therefore, and do not take up the yoke of slavery again' (5:1). 'For you were called for freedom, brothers; only do not use your freedom as an opportunity for the flesh' (5:13).[116] The nature of Christian life as a struggle between the Spirit and flesh is the same in both letters, but in Galatians Paul does not relate it to the idea of justification as he does in Romans (8:1, 4, 10).

For the Paul of Galatians, justification is always the goal toward which he drives his arguments, and never a stepping stone for other more advanced points.[117] There is nothing unusual about this once we acknowledge that in Galatians justification remains a future hope which will only come at the end of the story.[118]

---

[113] Stuhlmacher, *Romans* (1994) 89.

[114] The notion of 'justified life' is in vogue, but without Paul himself making the connection, it certainly begs the question.

[115] As Hübner, *Law* (1984) 135–136 notes, in Romans 'freedom' is a neutral concept, while in Galatians it 'provides the key for interpreting what it is to be Christian'.

[116] Hübner, *Law* (1984) 136, who also notes that the concept of 'righteousness of God' used in Romans as 'the powerful epiphany of the just and justifying God' is missing in Galatians. This coheres with our view that in Galatians justification does not function as the ground for life. Cf. Lategan, 'Developing' (1990) 322. Thus, Paul's ethic in Galatians is rightly called 'ethic of freedom' as does Hansen, 'Conversion' (1997) 213–237.

[117] *Contra* Gundry-Volf, *Perseverance* (1990) 206, who reverses Paul's logic by asserting that Paul uses justification 'to answer the question how a Christian ought to live'.

[118] It is to be noted that this conclusion only concerns the theme of justification. Within the context of Romans, however, it is not difficult to see that a strong future eschatological concern runs through Paul's argument. It is also to be noted that at points

3.5 Contextual Considerations

As most scholars would agree, Galatians is the first extant discussion of justification by Paul. It is crucial for interpreters to remember this context, especially since the letter is all too often read within the framework of later Romans. And here, as all acknowledge, Paul is engaged in a bitter polemic, a fact that leads many scholars to call it a *Kampfeslehre*.[119] This does not mean, however, that here he himself invents the doctrine to defend his own position. Reading through his argument, one certainly gets the impression that justification is a concept familiar to all those concerned, including the Galatians and the agitators behind them. For the Galatians this justification is available 'in the law' (5:4; cf. 4:21), and this strongly suggests that they have a future eschatological justification in mind. His appeal to the Old Testament as the ground of his claim (3:6–14) also points in the same direction.[120]

It is at this point that Paul's alleged 'realized eschatological' *re*definition of justification becomes problematic. The reason is his conspicuous silence on its present reality. It is unmistakable that he is redefining its means[121]; it is not clear at all, however, that he does the same about its time. In this letter the question of 'when' is never a proper topic of its own; we have nothing in the text that might signify such a revisionistic intention. Many would argue that his christological redefinition necessarily *implies* such a realized eschatological twist too. This claim, however, begs too large a question since that is by no means a necessary corollary of being 'in Christ' and 'by faith'.

At this point one has to take particular care not to misconstrue the context of Paul's argument. The present situation is one in which all those concerned are familiar with the notion of justification, and they know it as an eschatological gift: God's vindication of the faithful at the final judgment. Up to this point, so it seems, the 'paradoxical' notion of justification already or even proleptically available in the present remains something unheard of yet. In a situation like this, listening to Paul's sharply focused argument concerning 'justification by faith' *without the benefit of Romans*, would anyone in Galatia, who is immersed in the

---

justification itself seems to appear as a future hope (2:13; 3:20, 30; 5:16, 19). See, for example, Dunn, *Paul* (1998) 467.

[119] Wrede, *Paul* (1907) 123. Cf. Strecker, 'Befreiung' (1975) 479–508.

[120] Cf. Goulder, 'Pauline Epistles' (1987) 490: 'The countermissionaries taught that if you kept God's Law you would be held innocent ("justified") before his judgment seat, and Paul is disputing this'. As Becker, *Paulus* (1998) 297 suggests, Paul the Pharisee probably held this view.

[121] So Räisänen, 'Break' (1985) 146.

traditional water of future justification at the last judgment and thus has never heard of such a thing as justification in the present, have come to conclude that he is radically redefining the tradition so as to paradoxically claim the present realization of justification, namely, even despite his own endorsement of future eschatological justification (5:5)? Given the concept of justification as God's *end-time* vindication which forms the 'common ground', are there any statements in the letter that really compel us to conclude that in Galatians Paul polemically redefines it as a present reality, even proleptically? If, as most interpreters maintain, his burden in this letter involves affirming the present reality of justification, should we not expect him to be outright emphatic, making his point crystal clear, as he is in his later Romans? Given the dire situation in which he finds himself in Galatia, would not his case have been much more compelling, if he had affirmed its present reality explicitly?

The real problem for interpreters to deal with is not the 'small' number of references to the future eschatological justification, but the complete failure on Paul's side to assert its present reality. Read in the context of the Galatian crisis, therefore, the only possible conclusion is that 'Paul does not dispute the common goal shared by his readers, himself and the other missionaries in Galatia, as by the people of Israel generally – "the hope of righteousness"'.[122] If so, the idea of realized justification is misleading from the first.

Paul's alleged view of realized justification misses the point in another important sense. The Galatians have already begun in the Spirit but they clearly want *more*. Paul labels this as their desire to be 'justified in the law'. Then, as far as the Galatians are concerned, the issue is not with what lies behind or what they already enjoy but something that still lies ahead of them. Under the circumstances, his talk of 'present justification' would then be seen as a mere definitional game which fails to address their real concern, i.e., the 'more' that they seek after. They would have responded: 'Oh, you call *that* justification, but that is not what we are up to. What we mean is justification in the future and that is why we are adopting the law'. One may argue that he is trying to convince the Galatians who are still wishing to be justified that they have already been justified, albeit unwittingly, and therefore do not need to seek any further. As we have already seen, however, this is precisely the point we fail to hear in Paul's discussion of the subject.

Kim's recent study on the doctrine of justification in 1 Thessalonians[123] seems to lend an indirect support for our interpretation: his basic claim is

---

[122] Dunn 269. Yet he still thinks that Paul does dispute this by claiming its present reality.

[123] 'Justification' and 'Call' in his *Paul* (2002) 85–100, 101–127.

that despite the lack of the actual term, the doctrine of justification is present in the letter *in nuce*. Since Paul's perspective in the letter is so clearly future eschatological, the doctrine Kim finds in the letter also bears the same mark, revealing the idea of justification as 'God's act of acquittal at the last judgment' or as 'deliverance from God's wrath'.[124]

This means that at the time of writing 1 Thessalonians Paul still held to the traditional concept of justification as acquittal at the last judgment. If so, it significantly heightens the possibility that he had the same, future eschatological view of justification in Galatians too, since both letters are commonly considered as belonging to a relatively early stage in Paul's career. At the least, it clearly shows that Paul did not begin from the start with such a view of justification as is found in later Romans, namely, justification as a present reality.[125]

All our considerations thus far therefore point to the same conclusion: Paul does not say that the Galatians are already justified since he cannot. *For the Paul of Galatians justification is not a present reality yet; it still remains a hope for which the Galatians are to wait.*[126] As Boyarin says, justification 'refers to the situation of the believer at her last judgment... when the question is: Will I be acquitted by the divine court?'[127] In Galatians then justification converges with the idea of future 'kingdom of God' (5:21) and 'eternal life' (6:7–9), namely, future eschatological salvation (See 6.5-6 below). Paul's revision of the Jewish doctrine of justification in Galatians is certainly christological but not eschatological.

---

[124] This position echoes the view proposed by Hengel and Schwemer, *Damascus* (1997) 306–307. For Kim, however, the time aspect of the doctrine is not an important issue, and thus, he has no problem in speaking of 'the Thessalonian Christians who *have been saved or justified*' in the same breath (p. 98, emphasis added). We observe the same move in 'Call', another article on Paul's calling and Isaiah 42. Having identified Paul's mission as proclaiming the gospel as God's justifying righteousness at the last judgment, he continues to speak of 'mak[ing] justification proleptically effective ... already in the present', referring, instructively, to passages in Romans and 1 Corinthians (p. 107). Is there any evidence, however, for such proleptically effective justification in 1 Thessalonians and Galatians?

[125] Ironically, the fact that Paul began with the traditional, future eschatological concept of the doctrine seems to work against Kim's own thesis which explains the doctrine in reference to Paul's own Damascus experience.

[126] The claim of Sanders, *Palestinian Judaism* (1977) 495 that Paul 'does not use the righteousness terminology with *any one* meaning' is not completely wrong.

[127] Boyarin, *Jew* (1994) 117. Nevertheless, Boyarin thinks that in Galatians the doctrine of justification by faith is shared by Paul and his opponents, and not in dispute.

Conclusion

A crucial conclusion has been drawn. What then is the significance of this finding for interpreting Paul's arguments in the letter as a whole? As Ziesler asserts, since Paul's main emphasis in his discussion of justification lies in the 'how' and not the 'when', is the temporal aspect simply 'irrelevant' in understanding his arguments?[128] Ziesler is certainly right to say that Paul's immediate purpose is not the time of justification, but he is wide of the mark when he asserts that it is irrelevant, which is in fact another way of endorsing his prior assumption of realized justification. Inasmuch as justification constitutes the center of Paul's argument, our conclusion means that Paul's sustained polemic of 'not by law but by faith' is his answer to the overriding question, 'how to attain to future justification', which is another way of saying, 'how to attain final salvation'. That is, Paul responds to the problem in the Galatian churches from the perspective of final salvation; he evaluates and deals with the present crisis *as it pertains to their quest for the 'hope of righteousness'*.

This conclusion requires us to reread Paul's argument in a radically different way. To substantiate this conclusion, however, there are further questions to be answered: how can we make sense of this in the context of Paul's argument as a whole?[129] Does this conclusion cohere with the rest of his argument? More specifically, does not this conclusion fly in the face of Paul's unmistakable emphasis on 'sonship', an obviously realized gift? Further, how does it related to such motifs as 'promise' and 'inheritance' which take up the central place in his scriptural argument? In the following three chapters we shall take up each of these key themes to argue that they all play their roles to corroborate Paul's central contention of *future* justification by faith and not by the law.

---

[128] Ziesler, *Righteousness* (1972) 180.

[129] As we noted in the Introduction, this is what Betz fails to do, thereby rendering his view of future eschatological justification unconvincing.

Chapter 4

Son, Seed and Heir: Paul's Sonship Language

For the majority of interpreters the conclusion of the previous chapter will raise an immediate question: if justification, the central theme of Paul's argument, is indeed future eschatological, how are we to explain his equally emphatic affirmation of the Galatians' sonship as a *present* reality? Thus, before we move further, it seems necessary to clarify the function of Paul's 'sonship' language with a view to consolidating our overall thesis that Paul argues from a fundamentally futuristic point of view.

4.1 The Problem of Sonship in Galatia?

4.1.1 Paul's Affirmation of Sonship

The prominence of 'sonship' language in Galatians is unmistakable. At various points in his argument Paul introduces several concepts which can be subsumed under the broad category of sonship. In 3:6–7 he infers the sonship of 'those of faith' from the fact of Abraham's justification. His introduction of the theme is abrupt and carries a note of confidence: 'Thus, take it (γινώσκετε ἄρα) that those of faith, these are (εἰσιν) sons of Abraham' (3:6–7). Taken on its own, it delivers a clear impression that sonship is indeed a very important issue for his case, an impression which seems to be confirmed by the 'leap' from (Abraham's) justification to (believers') sonship.

No less explicit is the discussion of the Galatian believers' sonship in 3:26–29. As he brings his scriptural argument to its conclusion, Paul solemnly affirms: 'for all of you are (ἐστε) sons of God through faith in Christ' (3:26). The vivid sense of reality issuing from this 'enthusiastic' affirmation receives further accent from the motif of baptism into Christ, which, in turn, develops into the ideas of being clothed with Christ and absolute oneness in Christ Jesus (3:28). Then follows the final conclusion: 'If you belong to Christ, you are (ἐστε) then Abraham's offspring, heirs according to promise' (3:29).

The motif of sonship keeps occurring in chapter 4 too. 4:1–7 is, as a whole, based on the motif of son-heir; its conclusion naturally highlights the idea: 'so that he might redeem those who were under the law, and so that we might receive adoption as sons (υἱοθεσία)' (4:5). After a reference to the sonship-testifying Spirit (4:6) Paul concludes: 'so that you are no longer (οὐκέτι) a slave but a son; if a son, then an heir through God' (4:7). Combined with the statement in 3:29, Paul's intention to establish the Gentile believers' sonship is undeniable. In 4:21–31 too, the subject is Abraham's two sons: the son of flesh on the one hand, and the son of promise/Spirit on the other. Here too, his affirmation is clear-cut and confident: 'Now, brothers, you are children of promise, as Isaac was' (4:28). The conclusion of the argument reiterates the same point: 'Therefore, brothers, we are not children of the slave woman but of the free woman' (4:31). As is clear from this brief survey, Paul's is clearly emphatic in affirming the sonship of the Galatians: 'You are *no longer* a slave but a son!'[1]

4.1.2 Is Sonship a Central Theme?

Not surprisingly, most scholars detect in Paul's emphatic sonship language a strong note of polemic aimed at the agitators' low view of the Gentile believers' present status. They are stirring up the Galatians with alarming success claiming that the privilege of sonship, i.e., membership in God's covenant, depends on their receiving circumcision. That is, unless they get themselves circumcised, they will be excluded from this blessed company of children of Abraham (4:17). Having been persuaded by this claim 'solidly' based on the Scriptures, the Galatians are now on the verge of taking up this demand, desiring to secure the hoped-for identity as members of God's covenant people.

If this is in fact what is transpiring in Galatia, it is not difficult to understand the emphatic tone in which Paul affirms the sonship of the Galatians. Appalled by the disastrous move in the Galatian churches, he has no alternative but to take up the issue.[2] So he devotes central sections of the letter to demonstrating that sonship depends only on faith and in no way on circumcision (3:6–7; 3:26–29; 4:1–7; 4:21–31). In sum, it is argued, sonship is the primary issue at stake in Galatia, and this explains the prevalence of the theme in Paul's argument.[3]

---

[1] In the previous chapter we contrasted this to Paul's reservation about justification.

[2] So Barrett, 'Allegory' (1975) 1–16 (here 15).

[3] This is the consensus. According to Hübner, *Law* (1984) 15–16, Paul's argument on sonship is a 'higher order argument' in whose framework the theme of justification is placed. For the Galatians, the main concern was sonship since, persuaded by the agitators, 'they were concerned to ensure that their status was indeed that of sons of Abraham'. For

Taken in this way, Paul's affirmation of the Galatian believers' sonship necessarily carries a strong polemic in it. For the Galatians who are so distressed as even to consider circumcision to rectify their sorry situation, his unequivocal affirmation of their *present* sonship must have elicited a deep sigh of relief: 'We *have* already crossed the boundary; we *are* now sons of Abraham/God!' If so, Paul's affirmation of the Galatian believers' sonship, flying in the face of the agitators who deny such privilege to the uncircumcised Gentiles, necessarily conveys a strong note of realized eschatology. In view of the fact that the Galatians are already 'those of faith', Paul's affirmation of faith as the only condition of sonship simply confirms that they have already become sons of Abraham/God, that is, apart from circumcision. He has turned the agitators' conditional 'not-yet' into an unequivocal 'already'.

Self-evident as this reconstruction may appear to many, however, there are reasons to be cautious. For one thing, 'sonship' is an ambiguous concept, an umbrella term which embraces several distinct motifs in Galatians: 'sons of Abraham' (3:6–7), 'seed of Abraham' (3:29), 'sons of God' (3:26; 4:5–7) and 'children of promise/Spirit' (3:21–31). The idea of sonship can certainly serve as a common denominator of these related concepts; it should not, however, be assumed *a priori* that Paul always wants to score the same point with these variegated terms. Frequently, in an argument a different phrase signals a different purpose. Hence being sons of God is not necessarily the same thing as being sons of Abraham or seed of Abraham; we have to allow the possibility that each has its own distinctive function in its own context. A close investigation of the data is therefore in order before we make any general claims about the theme.

4.2 Justification and Sons of Abraham (3:6–9)

4.2.1 A Logical Leap?

The first discussion of sonship occurs in 3:6–9, initiating Paul's scriptural argument which continues until the end of chapter 4. After a programmatic statement on justification (2:15–21) and a castigating reminder of the reality of the crucifixion (3:1) and the powerful working of the Spirit (3:2–

Paul, too, 'everything depends on what it is that *constitutes* being a son of Abraham' (emphasis original). See, e.g., Burton 155; Wilckens, *Rechtfertigung* (1974) 132; Foerster, 'Abfassungszeit' (1964) 139; Eckert, *Verkündigung* (1971) 75–76; Drane, *Paul* (1975) 24; Beker, *Paul* (1980) 48; Lincoln, *Paradise* (1981) 9–11; Silva, 'Eschatological Structure' (1994) 151; Hansen, *Abraham* (1989) 113; Hong, *Law* (1993) 110, 116; Dunn, *Theology* (1994) 39; B. Longenecker, *Triumph* (1998) 129.

5), Paul resumes his talk of justification, now appealing to the Scripture. He begins with Abraham, which is a very perceptive, possibly inevitable, choice under the present circumstances.[4] The passage he seizes upon is Genesis 15:6, a text deployed once again later in Romans: 'Just as[5] Abraham believed God and it was reckoned to him as righteousness' (3:6). Then follows his own inference: 'Therefore, take it[6] that those of faith, these are the sons of Abraham' (3:7). At first sight, this move sounds like an utter *non sequitur*, since we are not told how the sonship of the Gentile believers can be deduced from Abraham's justification. A more natural inference would be: 'Therefore, take it that for those of faith, their faith is reckoned as righteousness.' Yet, significantly, he avoids this expected conclusion, and instead, claims the sonship of the believing Gentiles. How can we explain this obvious 'leap'?[7]

Many interpreters 'explain' this seemingly awkward move by pointing to the situation in Galatia. Martyn's formulation of this position is representative:

> Taken somewhat "in its own right," the text of Gen 15:6 says nothing about Abraham's descendants. It is because of the work of the Teachers that Paul (a) places his exegetical emphasis on an expression not found in the text, "the descendants of Abraham," and (b) answers a question not posed in that text: "Who is it who can truly be said to be the children of Abraham?"[8]

However, a mere reference to the situation does not in itself provide an explanation of Paul's logic, since one is bound to ask: if sonship is the main issue from the first, why does he appeal to Genesis 15:6 in the first

---

[4] It is possible that Paul is responding to the agitators' use of the Old Testament, as Barrett, 'Allegory' (1975) and R. Longenecker 114 think. As Schlier 86 and Eckstein, *Verheißung* (1996) 94–95 remind us, however, this does not necessarily mean that each of his scriptural arguments should be considered as 'dialogical', a sort of point-by-point refutation. There is no methodological justification for positing a coherent theology of the opponents and then explaining Paul's argument as a case-by-case refutation of the 'building blocks' of their teaching. See our discussion in 1.4 above.

[5] Καθώς is probably not a quotation formula. So R. Longenecker 112; Eckstein, *Verheißung* (1996) 97, 101–102 ('exemplum im Sinn von Urbild und Typos'). *Contra* Betz 140; Hays, *Faith* (1983) 199; Hansen, *Abraham* (1989) 112.

[6] The verb is imperative rather than indicative, which seems to fit better with the argumentative mode. So Bruce 155; Fung 138. Eckstein, *Verheißung* (1996) 103; R. Longenecker 114; Martyn 299 take it as 'an epistolary disclosure formula'.

[7] This 'leap' is frequently noted. E.g., Schlier 129: 'etwas kühne Behauptung'; K. Berger, 'Abraham' (1966) 50: 'unbewiesene Behauptung'; Martyn, *Issues* (1998) 162: 'a strange exegesis'.

[8] Martyn 299–300. See also Beker, *Paul* (1980) 48; Hansen, *Abraham* (1989) 112–113; Foerster, 'Thema' (1937) 292; Hübner, *Law* (1984) 15–16; Witherington 227; B. Longenecker, *Triumph* (1998) 129.

place, a passage which says nothing about Abraham's descendants? He could have appealed to other passages, for example, those in Hosea (1:10; 2:23). Or he could have done something similar to what he does in Romans 9:7–13. A glance at the 'hard-pressed Paul' may make one sympathetic, but it will not make his 'spurious' logic any more convincing for that reason. On the contrary, it only shows what shaky ground he stands on when it comes to his scriptural basis.

Noting this problem, others suggest that we should take v. 7 as an anticipatory conclusion to be consolidated in the following argument.[9] This suggestion is hardly satisfactory, either. If that is in fact the case, then we would expect Paul to restate this intended conclusion at least once more at the end of the argument. As a matter of fact, however, he does not speak of sonship any more until 3:26. It is very doubtful that the Galatians, after hearing what he says in vv. 6–14, should have thought this to be the consolidation of his pre-stated thesis on 'sonship' in v. 7. The καθὼς–ἄρα construction seems to demand an immediate connection with the quoted *exemplum* itself.

4.2.2 Sonship as a Median Motif

If we take sonship as the major point of Paul's argument in vv. 6–9, the flow of his thought becomes very difficult, if not impossible, to follow. Not only is his move from Abraham's justification to Gentile believers' sonship problematic,[10] but his abrupt and isolated reference to sonship (v. 7) in the middle of the sustained talk of justification (vv. 6, 8, 11) also remains puzzling.[11] Inevitably, the question raises itself: is sonship really the main point of Paul's argument?

The overall flow of vv. 6–14 shows that its context is justification (vv. 6, 8, 11), and therefore we have to interpret it accordingly. Undue preoccupation with sonship motif may actually hamper the flow of Paul's thought, since, on a careful reading, his interest in it seems secondary. His argument in vv. 6–7 runs as follows:

καθὼς Ἀβραὰμ ἐπίστευσεν τῷ θεῷ, καὶ ἐλογίσθη αὐτῷ εἰς δικαιοσύνην:
Γινώσκετε ἄρα ὅτι οἱ ἐκ πίστεως, οὗτοι υἱοί εἰσιν Ἀβραάμ.

---

[9] E.g., Hartman, 'Gal 3.15–4.11' (1993) 135: '...the thesis of v. 7 does not form a link' in the chain of logic in 3:6–9; 'it takes 3:8–29 to argue it'. See also Betz 141; Eckstein, *Verheißung* (1996) 102; Dunn 162–163, 183, 208.

[10] Equating justification with sonship, of course, begs the question.

[11] Stanley, 'Curse' (1990) 493 rightly notes the absence of sonship motif in vv. 8–9. Yet, his neglect of justification motif is surprising.

As can be seen from the above, the main point of comparison between 'just as' and 'therefore' is faith: just as Abraham 'believed God' and was considered righteous, 'those of faith' [12] are sons of Abraham. As the insertion of the emphatic οὗτοι indicates, here Paul singles out 'those of faith' and relates them to Abraham. Since the Gentile believers too exercise the same faith, they are sons of *this* Abraham, i.e., *the Abraham who believed and was thereby justified*. The implication of this affirmation is: their faith, just as the faith of Abraham, forms the singular ground for their justification. That is, in v. 7 Paul is not making a typical definition of sonship. What he does here is to modify its boundary in terms of faith: 'those of faith, *only these*[13] are sons of Abraham'. That is, only 'those of faith' will participate in the blessing of justification just as Abraham did.[14]

In this context, then, the sonship motif denotes the effective bond[15] between Abraham and Gentile believers on the basis of common faith, and thereby grounds Paul's logic from .καθώς to ἄρα. It serves as a way of affirming the principle of justification by faith for the Gentile believers. After the scriptural norm of justification by faith established in Abraham (v. 6), Paul's reference to 'sons of Abraham' most naturally conveys the idea that the same principle also applies for Gentile believers. Καθώς describes Abraham's justification by faith; so does ἄρα. In other words, the point of v. 7 is not so much sonship as justification by faith warranted by the experience of Abraham. By establishing a filial relationship between the justified Abraham and the Gentile believers on the sole ground of faith, Paul in fact (re)establishes the scriptural truth of justification by faith for the present Gentile believers. He is not making 'an unproved claim'[16] for the sonship of the Gentile believers; there is no rupture in his

---

[12] The context makes it clear that 'those of faith' means 'those who believe'. Rightly, Betz 142; Dunn 162. *Contra*, Hays, *Faith* (1983) 200–202; *idem*, *Echoes* (1989) 108 who take v. 7 as the 'Vorklang' of Hab 2:4 which he interprets christologically. Martyn 299 claims both meanings.

[13] Being emphatic, it carries the meaning: 'gerade diese–und keine anderen'. Eckstein, *Verheißung* (1996) 105. See also Schlier, 128; Byrne, *Sons* (1979) 148. The attempt of Dunn 166 to allow the Israel before Christ into 'those of faith' is tendentious. In Galatians, faith only comes with Christ (3:23, 25). When he speaks of 'those of faith', Paul has the Galatians in mind.

[14] Marius Victorinus in Edwards 39; Bligh, *Greek* (1966) 131; Lambrecht, 'Abraham' (1999) 526; Hansen, *Abraham* (1988) 115; Choi, 'Spirit' (1998) 184–185.

[15] *BAGD*, υἱός, 1.c.γ. Mußner 219; Byrne, *Sons* (1979) 148: 'spiritual kinship or association'. The reference to the Semitic use of בן in the sense of 'sharing in a particular quality or characteristic' is somewhat different since such usage is usually followed by an abstract noun (e.g. might, beauty, etc.) rather than a personal name. *Contra* Dunn 162–163; Bruce 155.

[16] This phrase is from K. Berger. See n. 7 above.

argument. With the help of the 'sonship' motif,[17] he simply affirms the truth of justification by faith.[18]

This reading is confirmed by the following argument in vv. 8–9, which clarifies the ground on which faith establishes such a filial relationship between Abraham and the *Gentile* believers.[19] Paul first picks up the obvious conclusion of vv. 6–7: 'And the Scripture, foreseeing that God would justify the Gentiles by faith...' (v. 8a).[20] To back up this conclusion, he appeals to another passage in the Scripture: 'All the Gentiles will be blessed in you (ἐν σοί)' (v. 8b).[21] By quoting this oracle, Paul presses two points: 1) the Gentiles are part of God's original plan revealed to Abraham[22] and 2) they will be blessed in Abraham. Hence the Scripture itself decrees that the Gentiles will share Abraham's blessing 'in you', namely, as Abraham's sons. His claim in vv. 6–7 is perfectly legitimate. The question, however, is, why 'by faith'?

It is at this point that Paul's polemic kicks in: the Abraham in whom the Gentiles are to be blessed is, as he has already made clear, the Abraham who 'believed God' (3:6, 9). Since God pronounced blessing for the Gentiles 'in this *believing* (πιστῷ) Abraham' (3:9), it follows that the Gentiles will be υἱοί ᾿Αβραάμ (3:6) by sharing the same faith which brought him the gift of justification.[23] By defining Abraham in terms of faith, Paul makes sonship exclusively a matter of faith, producing a happy

---

[17] This 'sonship' motif anticipates his appeal to Gen 12:3, where the Gentiles are said to be blessed 'in you'.

[18] Commentators dispute whether Paul's sonship statement is polemical or not. Compare Mußner 217; Eckstein, *Verheißung* (1996) 105; R. Longenecker 114 who take it as polemical, and Byrne, *Sons* (1979) 148–149 who points out that Paul's reasoning in vv. 6–7 is inadequate for a polemical response. The polemic is certainly there, but not on 'sonship'. The real clincher is 'justification by faith' secured by the filial bond with Abraham. Cosgrove, *Cross* (1988) 73, 85 perceptively captures the subordinate nature of 'sonship', though still failing to acknowledge the context of justification.

[19] Rightly Eckstein, *Verheißung* (1996) 118–119.

[20] Otherwise, Paul's jumping from 'justification' to 'sonship', and then back to 'justification' again becomes a bewildering anomaly.

[21] Paul seems to be thinking mainly of Gen 12:3, while replacing πᾶσαι αἱ φυλαί with πάντα τὰ ἔθνη of 18:18 or 22:18. In this way, Paul makes this pronouncement address the Gentiles, τὰ ἔθνη. Dunn 164 is incorrect to say that the variation in detail is 'inconsequential'.

[22] Emphasized by Sanders, *Law* (1996) 21; Hansen, *Abraham* (1989) 115; Hays, *Echoes* (1989) 106; Witherington 228. Bruce 156.

[23] *Contra* Byrne, *Sons* (1979) 148, 156, who considers that blessing was received on the basis of prior justification both for Abraham and the believers. This view was suggested as early as in 1912 by G. Vos, 'Spirit' (1912) 101, n. 15, who considers 'justification' as 'the indispensable prerequisite of receiving the εὐλογία' which converges with 'inheritance'. Then, 'justification is a means to an end' namely, to the blessing and inheritance.

liaison between two 'believers': ὥστε οἱ ἐκ πίστεως εὐλογοῦνται σὺν τῷ πιστῷ 'Αβραάμ (3:9).²⁴

For Paul, then, the primary significance of Abrahamic sonship lies in the fact that the Galatian believers are, as Abraham's sons, placed 'in you', and thereby become part of πάντα τὰ ἔθνη, the God-designated beneficiaries of the gospel of justification by faith. That he brings in Abraham with the conjunction καθώς, and also that he paraphrases ἐν with σύν advise us not to press the motif of sonship too hard.²⁵ He is not presenting this argument to resolve the question of sonship. Rather, Paul's purpose is to authenticate his gospel that God justifies the Gentiles by faith. He accomplishes this by bringing in the figure of Abraham who was himself justified by faith, and on that score, has become the recipient of God's gospel message that the Gentiles will also be blessed in him, that is, by sharing his faith. Sonship is a supporting motif serving the argument for justification by faith; its primary function is to express the solidarity between Abraham and the Gentile believers.²⁶

Primarily, then, *Paul is not making an affirmation concerning the Galatian believers' status as Abraham's sons.* His affirmation of the Gentile believers' sonship turns out to be an exegetical device to establish

---

²⁴ In the OT context, the condition of 'in you' is determined by the nations' disposition toward Abraham himself: by blessing Abraham, they will be blessed 'in Abraham' who is the 'source of blessing' (Gen 12:2–3). Paul turns this relationship into that of faith: those who share the same faith are blessed 'in Abraham'.

²⁵ This speaks against Hays' attempt to conflate 'in you' with 'in your seed' in other Genesis texts (Gen 22:8 or 26:4) and interpret it christologically as Paul does in 3:16 and 29. *Faith* (1983) 203–206 and *Echoes* (1989) 106; Eckstein, *Verheißung* (1996) 150. Also Theodoret in Edwards 44; Dahl, *Studies* (1977) 131, 171, 172, n. 20; Meeks, *Urban* (1983) 176–177; Martyn 301–302. According to what Paul says in 3:9, a text Hays misses out at this point, the Gentiles are not blessed 'in' but '*together with*' the faithful Abraham. Rightly, Hübner, *Theologie* (1993) 73. Cf. Hansen, *Abraham* (1989) 126. Cf. *Jewish New Testament*: 'In connection with you'. On the other hand, what Paul concerns himself with in 3:16–29 is not Abraham but only 'his seed', another original recipient of the same promise: καὶ τῷ σπέρματι αὐτοῦ. The Gentiles have the promise in Abraham's seed. But they do so not because 'in you' (3:9) means 'in your seed', but because this promise was originally made to Abraham καὶ τῷ σπέρματι αὐτου (3:16).

Paul utilizes Gen 15:6 once again in Romans 4 (4:3, 9), where Abraham's justification before circumcision is unpacked to prove the truth of justification by faith. Here the connection between Abraham and believers is supported by an opposite move: not the 'sonship' of believers but by the universal 'fatherhood' of Abraham (4:11, 12, 16–18). Just as Abraham's 'fatherhood' is a median point supporting the claim of justification by faith, so is 'sonship' in Galatians. In this respect, Paul's view remains consistent.

²⁶ We see that from 2:15 onward the theme is justification throughout. In 3:1–5 he narrows down to the issue of the Spirit, but he does so because the Spirit is essential in proving his case of 'justification by faith', in a similar way as in 3:14 where his discussion of justification by faith also leads to the talk of the Spirit.

the truth of justification by faith.[27] He is not asking his readers to join him in celebrating the 'already' of sonship. In a context where he perceives a dangerous deviation from faith (1:6ff.; 4:8–12; 5:6–7), his unequivocal affirmation of faith as the only way to justification serves as a stern warning that only those who hold on to faith will be able to participate in the future blessing of justification.

In this connection, we also observe that the idea of 'Abrahamic sonship' does not figure prominently in Paul's subsequent argument. In two places he speaks of 'sons of God' (3:26; 4:5, 7), but this motif belongs to a different realm altogether, and thus, should not be conflated with 'sons of Abraham'. At the end of chapter 3, he sums up his argument with the idea of 'seed of Abraham' (3:29). Here too, the use of σπέρμα instead of υἱός suggests that he is using this notion in a context-specific way in relation to such issues as 'promise', 'inheritance' and 'seed' (3:15 ff.). Though there is an obvious overlap between the two ideas, a simple identification will do violence to the thrust of the text.[28] Even in 4:21–31 where he speaks of Abraham's sons, the issue is not sonship *per se*, but their heirship: 'among two sons of Abraham, which is the rightful heir?' Then, 3:7 is in fact the only place where Paul highlights the 'sons of Abraham' motif, and that in the middle of his argument for justification by faith. This observation further confirms our conclusion that Abrahamic sonship is not in fact the main question Paul is grappling with.

4.3 Sons of God and Seed of Abraham (3:26–29)

4.3.1 The Flow of the Argument

The next passage in which 'sonship' figures prominently is 3:26–29, the concluding section of Paul's argument based on the Abrahamic promise (3:15–29). In this section 'the inheritance' replaces justification as the dominant subject of discussion (v. 19) with 'the promise' taking up the role of faith in the programmatic antithesis to the law. The basic question posed in vv. 15–18 is 'How can one get the promised inheritance, by promise or law?',[29] which Paul answers with a definite 'by promise'. Vv. 19–25 follow this on, taking up the almost inevitable question about the function of the law: Τί οὖν ὁ νόμος; (v. 19). His basic position is clear: inasmuch as the law is unable to give life, it does not compete with

---

[27] Cf. Ropes, *Singular Problem* (1929) 7.

[28] Dunn 163 seems to perceive the difference between the two, but only temporarily. See pp. 183, 208.

[29] Rightly, Bruce 169–170; Braumann, *NIDNTT* 1:285–290.

the promise (v. 20); on the contrary, by shutting up everything under sin, it serves the way of promise (v. 22).

Then Paul declares that with the coming of faith the law exhausted its designated temporary function, with the result that 'we are no longer under the παιδαγωγός' (vv. 23–25). V. 25 then is the conclusion of his discussion, describing the Gentile believers' present relation *vis-à-vis* the law. This negative conclusion stands parallel to the positive statement in v. 29, forming an effective οὐκέτι ... δέ contrast: 'You are *no longer* ... *but* if you belong to Christ, then you are Abraham's offspring...'. Between these two negative and positive statements, vv. 26–28, led by γάρ, function as a *supporting* argument providing the ground for both v. 25 and v. 29: 'since[30] in Christ Jesus you are all sons of God through faith'.[31] Paul seems to be suggesting that in view of the Gentile believers' undeniable status as God's sons, it naturally follows that they are no longer in slavery under the law (v. 25).[32] On the contrary, since[33] they now belong to Christ, they are the offspring of Abraham (v. 29).

This observation is crucial in assessing the function of Paul's sonship language. Structurally, his main emphasis falls on the dual conclusions in v. 25 and v. 29, while the intervening statements in vv. 26–28, in which the motif of divine sonship occurs, support and strengthen these major affirmations. Taken in its specific context, then, the sonship of the Gentile believers in v. 26 is not the main conclusion he intends to draw. Within the argument for the Gentile believers' freedom from the law (v. 25) and their existence as the offspring of Abraham (v. 29), sonship stands as a *subsidiary* motif helping these main points to stand out more effectively. The Πάντες with a capital Π, with which both N/A (27) and UBS begins a new paragraph in v. 26, is therefore fatal to following through Paul's logic.

4.3.2 'Sons of God' as a Subsidiary Motif

Even within the context of vv. 26–28,[34] we perceive that sonship is not Paul's primary concern. As he goes on to explain, the sonship of the Gentile believers is grounded on their being 'in Christ Jesus'. Their

---

[30] With Campbell, 'Eschatological Logic' (1999) 73 one may take γάρ as general and explanatory. Even so, it differs from ἄρα or ὥστε. In other words, Paul is not making a conclusion here.

[31] *Contra* Betz 181; Harnisch, 'Einübung' (1987) 283.

[32] With Eckstein, *Verheißung* (1996) 222.

[33] Taking up the force of vv. 27–28, εἰ in v. 29 becomes 'since'. So Eckstein, *Verheißung* (1996) 224.

[34] Many detect a confessional (baptismal) formula in vv. 27–28. Schlier 174–175; Betz 181–185; R. Longenecker 154–156. Bruce 187 disagrees. See now Campbell, 'Eschatological Logic' (1999) 7–20 for a compelling criticism of the de-contextualizing tendency common to the form-critical approaches.

existence in Christ, brought about by their baptism into Christ, means that they are now clothed with Christ himself: their whole existence is now determined by Christ (v. 27).[35] From this originally neutral statement, Paul then draws a very specific inference that serves his polemical purpose: the absolute equality of all those in Christ.

Several features are worth noting. First, the effective antitheses in v. 28a followed by an explicit statement in v. 28b makes Paul's immediate intention beyond doubt: πάντες γὰρ ὑμεῖς εἷς ἐστε ἐν Χριστῷ Ἰησοῦ. Secondly, his repeated use of such inclusive pronouns as πάντες (v. 26), ὅσοι (v. 27) and πάντες (v. 28b) also adds weight to his emphasis on the singular principle of faith in Christ. Thirdly, we note the unmistakable parallelism between v. 26 and v. 28b, yet with a very interesting variation, namely, the replacement of the previous υἱοὶ θεοῦ by εἷς. If Paul is arguing for sonship, this replacement of 'sons of God' by 'one' would be most tactless. This move shows quite clearly that his thought is very much taken up by the idea of the exclusive effectiveness of being 'in Christ' rather than the motif of sonship.[36]

Fourthly, the transition from vv. 26–28 to the final conclusion in v. 29 also reveals the same tendency. Following up what he has just said, Paul concludes: 'Now if you belong to Christ (Χριστοῦ),[37] you are then the offspring of Abraham'. What Paul takes from his previous statements in vv. 26–28 is not the concept of sonship but the bond with Christ which has been variously expressed either 'in Christ' (vv. 26, 28), or 'baptism into Christ', or 'being clothed with Christ' (v. 27). And from this 'in Christ', and not from 'sons of God',[38] he draws his main conclusion about the Gentile believers' existence as the 'seed of Abraham'.

From these observations we can draw an important conclusion: in this argument *the 'sons of God' motif is not Paul's major concern.*[39] He does

---

[35] As Bruce 184 points out, the idea is not adequately captured by either 'mysticism' of Schweitzer, *Mysticism* (1930) 116; 270 or 'diagram' of Deissman, *Paul* (1957) 239–299 or even the Hebrew notion of 'corporate personality'. Eckstein, *Verheißung* (1996) 221, n. 214. Cf. Beasley-Murray, *Baptism* (1997=1972) 146-151.

[36] Campbell, 'Eschatological Logic' (1999), rightly and rarely, takes this change from 'sons of God' to 'one' seriously. Eckstein, *Verheißung* (1996) 224 makes a perceptive comment that Paul uses εἷς out of his concern to emphasize 'sameness' and 'equality', while he speaks of ἓν σῶμα in 1 Cor 12:12–27 and Rom 12:5 where the motif of 'unity' is on the surface. See also Cosgrove, *Cross* (1988) 73. Cf. Theissen, *Reality* (1992) 181.

[37] This is a genitive of possession. So Zerwick, *Greek* (1963) 15–16; Moule, *Idiom* (1959) 38; Bligh, *Greek* (1966) 156. Schlier 175 goes too far when he speaks of 'Christus selbst'.

[38] Byrne, *Sons* (1979) 173.

[39] Rightly, Boers, *Justification* (1994) 68; Cosgrove, *Cross* (1988) 73, 85; Byrne, *Sons* (1979) 173; (cautiously) Hartman, 'Gal 3.15–4.11' (1993) 143.

affirm the sonship of the Gentile believers. However, this affirmation occurs in a subsidiary argument which serves his main contention about the exclusive validity of faith in Christ: 'So long as you are in Christ, you are all sons of God, in other words, you are all one and the same without any distinction!' And this in turn supports the dual statements concerning the Gentile believers' liberation from the law (v. 25) and their status as Abraham's seed (v. 29). At least in this context, then, the centrality of sonship in Paul's argument cannot be maintained. Scholarly preoccupation with this impressive declaration is understandable,[40] but Paul's logic has to be sustained. All along, his concern is to put the Gentile believers within the boundary of the Seed of Abraham, namely, as the recipients of God's promise (vv. 16, 19), and thereby ascertain their prospect as the appointed heirs of God's inheritance (v. 29). In this passage Paul is indeed most eloquent on the 'sonship' of the Gentile believers, but this eloquence serves something else and is not in itself the final point he wants to hammer home in the present context.

If this reading is correct, the claim that the note of realized eschatology is the main thrust of Paul's argument has to be given up. To be sure, he does make many strong indicative statements on sonship in vv. 26–29. It is also out of question that it constitutes an important part of his Christian convictions. It does not follow from this, however, that it is the main point of *this particular argument*. Since they are not the final points he argues for in the context, they should not be allowed to determine the thrust of his argument as a whole.

4.4 Seed of Abraham as Heirs

4.4.1 'Seed' Means 'Heir'

In v. 29, as indicated by the οὐκέτι–δέ contrast, Paul presents the positive counterpart to the negative statement in v. 25, bringing his argument to its intended conclusion: εἰ δὲ ὑμεῖς Χριστοῦ, ἄρα τοῦ ᾿Αβραὰμ σπέρμα ἐστέ … (v. 29). Since faith has come, we are no longer under the law (v. 25), because through this faith in Christ we have now all become equal sons of God (vv. 26–28). At the same time, by faith we are in the 'Seed of Abraham', who is Christ (v. 29). And since we belong to Christ, we are now the seed of Abraham. And it means that we too, as the seed of Abraham, are given the same promise that Abraham *and* his Seed have received. And at this point we see why Paul focuses on the notion of

---

[40] Betz assigns twelve pages to v. 28 but only one to v. 29.

'Abraham's seed' and 'being in Christ'. By identifying the singular seed exclusively as Christ, and then making this seed inclusive of those who 'believe', he effectively relates God's 'promise' to the Seed (v. 16) to the Gentile believers.

Yet, even this emphasis on the 'seed of Abraham' is not the ultimate point Paul wants to convey. He has not finished yet; it is crucial 'to pay attention to his *conclusions*'. [41] Being Abraham's seed, the Gentile believers are therefore κατ' ἐπαγγελίαν [42] κληρονόμοι. The phrase is appositional, [43] clarifying what he has in mind with 'seed of Abraham' just affirmed: 'Abraham's seed, *therefore,* heirs according to the promise'. From v. 15 onward, Paul's discussion is sustained by the antithesis of promise (ἐπαγγελία) and law. Throughout the argument his concern has been the question of inheritance (κληρονομία) (v. 18). Alongside this, we also hear that this 'promise' is given only to Abraham's single 'Seed' (σπέρμα), who is Christ. And it is clear how v. 29 sums up Paul's train of thought in a fitting conclusion: by faith (διὰ τῆς πίστεως) the believers belong to Christ (ἐν Χριστῷ), and by belonging to Christ who is the only legitimate Seed (εἰ δὲ ὑμεῖς Χριστοῦ), they too take on the identity of Abraham's seed (τοῦ Ἀβραάμ σπέρμα). Since God's promise was addressed only to Abraham and his Seed (v. 16), it follows that the Gentile believers too, as the plural seed within this singular Seed, have now become the recipients of the same promise of inheritance: they are κατ' ἐπαγγελίαν κληρονόμοι.

4.4.2 'Seed' in Context

It is clear by now that even when Paul speaks of Christ as the singular seed of Abraham (v. 16), he already has in mind the Gentile believers who have become the 'seed of Abraham' by believing in Christ. [44] It is also clear that for him the significance of being Abraham's seed lies precisely in the fact that God promised the inheritance to Abraham 'and to his seed' and thus the seed is the only legitimate heir to God's promised inheritance (vv. 16, 19, 22).

For this reason, the term σπέρμα bears a strategic importance in Paul's scriptural argument, since it is by utilizing this motif that he answers the fundamental question 'How does one get the promised inheritance?' with a confident 'by faith'. By faith one is placed in Christ. In Christ, the singular

---

[41] Cosgrove, *Cross* (1988) 51.

[42] In context κατά followed by the accusative 'promise' seems to mean 'with respect to' rather than 'according to'. Cf. *BAGD*, 407. The believers become heirs not as the fulfillment of promise; they are heirs to what is promised. *Contra* Betz 201.

[43] Bligh, *Greek* (1966) 156.

[44] Dunn 185.

'Seed', one also becomes Abraham's seed. Now, as the promise-receiving seed, one is also the heir to God's inheritance. It is, then, by faith that one attains the promised inheritance. In this chain of reasoning, the motif of 'seed' constitutes a crucial and yet subsidiary link sustaining the chief point of 'heirship' of those who belong to Christ.[45]

Thus, we observe that the idea of the 'seed of Abraham' in v. 29 is given a very different role from that of 'sons of Abraham' in 3:7.[46] While the latter is used to denote the Gentile believers' solidarity with *Abraham* and his justification by faith, the former carries a primarily christological function to secure the bond between the believers and *Christ*. Introduced to settle the question about inheritance, the 'seed of Abraham' points to Christ; Abraham is outside Paul's purview at this point since the Seed himself (Christ) is a recipient of God's promise in his own right (*'and* to his seed'). Of course, Abraham is crucial in testifying to the priority of God's promise (3:15, 18), but his role stops there. Unlike in 3:6–7, the filial bond with his person remains irrelevant in this context. In Paul's own argument, 'sons of Abraham' and 'seed of Abraham' play distinct roles, and therefore, should not be conflated with each other.[47]

The same caveat applies to 'sons of God' in v. 26. Throughout the argument the crucial question is who the seed of Abraham is. What is at stake here is God's promise of inheritance given to the seed of *Abraham*. To this question, Paul's answer is that those who believe in Christ are considered the seed by virtue of being in the Seed to whom the promise has been made. Thus, if this particular notion of 'Abraham's seed' is replaced by the motif of 'son of God', Paul's argument would not make any sense at all. Similar though they may look, their distinct functions in context demand that each should be taken on its own terms.

4.5 Sons as Heirs (4:1–7)

Our next passage (4:1–7) confirms that Paul's emphasis on heirship is in fact not accidental. The overall flow of logic is basically the same as that in 3:25–29: the Christ event (3:25a/ 4:4–5), liberation (οὐκέτι, 3:25b/4:7a), status as 'seed of Abraham'/'sons' (3:29a/4:7a), heirship (3:29b/4:7b). However, this sub-section divulges some further interesting points. First, the issue is still heirship, but instructively, the figure of Abraham does not

---

[45] Moore-Crispin, 'Galatians 4:1–9' (1989) 217; Cosgrove, *Cross* (1988) 52, 69, 85.

[46] *Contra* the generalizing interpretation of Burton 210 and most others.

[47] This mistake forces Beker to speak of 'the peculiar shift' and 'inconsistency' in Paul's argument. This decision is partly caused by his failure to note the distinctness of these motifs. *Paul* (1980) 23–58. Hong, *Law* (1993) 45–49 shares the same problem.

appear in the picture at all. Whether Paul's illustration is Jewish or Greco-Roman,[48] the Abrahamic tradition is not in his purview here. That he can speak of sonship and heirship without invoking the figure of Abraham seems not insignificant.[49] Secondly, unlike in 3:26–29, now he does speak of 'son of God' as part of his main point, replacing the motif of 'seed of Abraham' in 3:29. This is due to the change of background in the discussion.[50] His appeal here is not to the scriptural logic of the Abrahamic 'seed-heir' but to the legal one of a 'son-heir' drawn from the everyday life of the Galatian believers.

In any case, Paul's emphasis on sonship is quite explicit: 'in order that we might receive adoption as sons (υἱοθεσία)' (4:5). On adoption, the Spirit is bestowed as the confirmation of this newly established sonship (v. 6). Then the final conclusion follows: 'Therefore (ὥστε), you are no longer a slave but a son!' In this passage too, however, 'sonship' is not the ultimate point Paul intends to make. If it were, Paul, having reached his goal, could well have stopped at this point. After affirming the sonship of the Gentile believers, he goes on to add: εἰ δὲ υἱός, καὶ κληρονόμος διὰ θεοῦ (4:7b). Here we observe exactly the same emphasis on heirship: if you are a son, then, you are also an heir![51]

Now the move from sonship to heirship has become much more explicit. While in 3:29 the motif of heirship is expressed by an apposition added to the statement on sonship, here in 4:7 the thought is expressed in a separate sentence specifically designed to bring out this very point. This makes it quite indisputable that Paul's move from sonship to heirship carries a definite argumentative purpose. This is also confirmed by the fact that the argument itself is introduced as one concerning the state of ὁ κληρονόμος (4:1). Even when he unequivocally affirms the sonship of the Gentile believers, he does so not because the Galatian believers' sonship is contextually crucial on its own terms, but because he needs to establish their *heirship* to God's inheritance. He is at pains to affirm that the Gentile believers are 'seed of Abraham' (3:29) and 'sons of God' (4:7) with the more pressing exigency of demonstrating that they, as the Spirit-possessing sons, are the true heirs to God's promised inheritance.

Again we also note Paul's sensitivity to the context in which he develops his arguments. In the concluding statement, he adds 'heirs according to God'. A first sight, the phrase διὰ θεοῦ, which replaces

---

[48] See 6.2 below.

[49] Paul dispenses with Abraham in a passage in which he makes his emphasis on sonship most explicit. Is Paul really tackling the problem of *Abrahamic* sonship?

[50] That is, it is not because σπέρμα is the agitators' term, as Martyn 374–75, 377 speculates.

[51] See Byrne, *Sons* (1979) 176.

κατ' ἐπαγγελίαν in 3:29, seems rather perplexing. To be sure, since promise also accentuates God's initiative, there is no substantial divergence in thought between the two.[52] Yet there seems to be a good reason for this variation. Despite the fact that Paul argues for the same point of the heirship of the Gentile believers, unlike in 3:15–29, the person Abraham and his promise are not in view; here the idea of σπέρμα and heir κατ' ἐπαγγελίαν would be out of place. Now the talk is directly between God and the Gentile believers as God-adopted sons. Since it is God himself who has adopted them, they, instead of being 'seed of Abraham', are now 'sons of God' and therefore their heirship is said to be διὰ θεοῦ.[53]

4.6 Two Sons, One Heir (4:21–31)

That Paul's real concern does not lie in sonship *per se* but in heirship is confirmed yet once more in the 'allegory of Sarah and Hagar' in 4:21–31.[54] In this paragraph Paul establishes a mutually exclusive antithesis between Sarah-Isaac and Hagar-Ishmael, utilizing antitheses such as freedom vs. slavery, promise vs. flesh and Spirit vs. flesh that have already been established (vv. 21–28) and indeed will dominate his argument until the end (5:1, 13, 16–26; 6:6–9). Then, through an apt application of Scripture to the present situation through the common denominator of persecution (v. 29), Paul claims that it is not those born of flesh, namely, those who are under the law, but those born of promise and the Spirit, who are the true heirs of the promised inheritance. Transforming Sarah's word into a divine

---

[52] In both cases, the point is God's powerful initiative. With most interpreters, e.g., Williams 113 and R. Longenecker 175, though the latter's talk of 'certainty of possession' is misleading.

[53] See Moore-Crispin, 'Galatians 4:1–9' (1989) 218. Romans 8:17 confirms this reading, where believers, as fellow-heirs of Christ, are called 'heirs *of God*', recalling 'heir διὰ θεοῦ' in Galatians.

[54] Since Barrett's influential essay, 'Allegory' (1975), this passage is mostly considered as Paul's 'less than successful' revision of his opponents' more natural exegesis (Gen 17). However, Genesis 17 is not a felicitous text for the agitators either since there circumcision, embarrassingly to the agitators, fails to incorporate Ishmael in the family of Abraham. Rightly, Cosgrove, 'Sarah' (1987) 223. As Martyn 305 thinks, the agitators might have deliberately ignored this, but there could have been no chance with Paul (4:30!). Genesis 17 certainly suits the *exclusivistic* agenda as in *Jubilee* but not the missionary purpose of the agitators. After 2:19–4:7, there is nothing surprising in Paul's claim in the allegory. He has not earned most rather nasty abuses he receives from modern exegetes, e.g., Hays, *Echoes* (1989) 111–112; Calvert, 'Abraham' (1993) 5.

oracle,[55] Paul declares 'for the son of the slave woman *shall not inherit* (οὐ μὴ κληρονομήσει) with the free woman's son' (v. 30).

For our purpose, it is important to note that the contested issue in this passage is not sonship at all. Both Isaac *and* Ishmael are unreservedly called *sons* (δύο υἱούς) of Abraham (v. 22). This would be the last thing Paul wants to say if he is arguing for the sonship of the Gentile believers. It is not even that this comment is part of the Scripture he merely quotes; this is his own depiction of the Genesis story. The very fact that he can casually speak of Ishmael as a *son* of Abraham tells us that sonship is not the real issue Paul is currently concerned with.[56]

Paul's argument itself confirms this point. Abraham has two sons, but both cannot share the same inheritance; one of them should be expelled. That Paul affirms the sonship of Ishmael but excludes him from the prospect of inheritance indicates the precise point he is getting at with his appeal to the tradition. The question he is addressing here then is not 'Who is Abraham's true son?' but 'Which son is the rightful heir?' The criterion is no doubt the respective manner of their births: the birth of freedom/promise/Spirit qualifies the son Isaac as the rightful heir; the birth of slavery/law/flesh deprives the child of Hagar of the prospect of future inheritance.[57] Thus Paul's conclusion at the end that we are not 'children of the slave woman but of the free woman' (v. 31) is not just a repetition of what he has already said about the status of the Gentile believers. After the scriptural verdict that only the 'children of the free woman' are to inherit God's inheritance (v. 30), the statement in v. 31 functions as an affirmation that only those allied with the Spirit, as the children of Sarah, will ultimately receive the promised inheritance.[58]

---

[55] In LXX Gen 21:10, these words are Sarah's ... οὐ γὰρ κληρονομήσει ὁ υἱὸς τῆς παιδίσκης ταύτης μετὰ τοῦ υἱοῦ μου Ἰσαακ. By changing 'my' into 'of the free woman' and dropping the name 'Issac', Paul turns her complaint into a scriptural oracle. Bruce 224–225; R. Longenecker 217. This is probably not a command to exercise church discipline as Hansen, *Abraham* (1989) 146 and Witherington 338 think. Paul quotes this passage to answer the question, 'Who gets the inheritance?'

[56] In Genesis the narrative revolves around the question, 'Who is the true heir of God's promise?' The very late *Tg. Ps -J.* Gen 22:1 has an interesting tradition in which Ishmael and Isaac dispute over the inheritance from Abraham.

[57] The point is the law's inability to bring about inheritance. So, Perriman, 'Rhetorical Strategy' (1993) 41.

[58] If we, as many do, take v. 31 as a mere 'status' statement, it becomes a clumsy repetition, almost ruining the flow of Paul's argument. The point has already been made abundantly clear by v. 27, with v. 28 confirming the necessary result of Paul's allegorical association up to the point. Then vv. 29 relates the Genesis story to the situation in Galatia, and v. 30 sets up the scriptural pronouncement that only the children of free woman will receive the inheritance. Then, the conclusion is inevitable: only we, children of the free woman, will inherit God's inheritance! (v. 31)

That sonship is not Paul's final point but only a stepping stone toward the heirship of the Gentile believers must be beyond doubt. For Paul the significance of their sonship lies in their privilege as heirs, namely, in their status as bearers of God's promise to inherit the inheritance: 'If you are a son, then, also by God's own act, heirs' (4:7).[59]

4.7 Affirmation as Warning

In view of the popularity of the realized eschatological reading of Paul's 'sonship' language, it also seems important to remember that in the Judaism of Paul's day the privilege of sonship was an essentially *relational* concept, which carried a corresponding sense of responsibility within it. Referring to the God-human relationship, the privilege of sonship was not an absolutely fixed status that could be taken for granted as if it were a kind of possession. It certainly referred to the identity of believers but this identity, bound to God the Father, entailed corresponding responsibility which was never to be compromised. In practical terms, the identity of sonship/heirship was clearly *conditional* on the proper discharge of one's obligations as sons.[60] Of course, there was always the danger of forgetting this covenantal dynamic of sonship and becoming presumptuous, but warnings of the fatal consequences of such behavior were not lacking either in the OT (Deut 32:5–6), NT (Mt 3:7–10; Lk 3:7–9; Rom 8:17) or the Rabbinic literature (*m. Sanh.* 10.1–4; *m. Abot.* 5.19).[61]

Paul's use of the concept clearly shows that he is not far from this conditional or dynamic idea of sonship. An instructive case in point is Romans 8:28–30.

---

[59] Though neglected by most, there are a few exegetes who notice the importance of this move. Burton 209 perceptively comments that this added phrase 'recalls the previous mention of the promise and the inheritance ..., and emphasizes the aspect of Abrahamic sonship that is *important to the apostle's present purpose*' (emphasis added). Barrett, *Freedom* (1985) 36 (cf. 28–29) also explains the significance of sonship not only in terms of 'its implication of intimate personal relationship' but also of the fact that Paul 'is using the concept of inheritance'. Cosgrove, *Cross* (1988) 52, 69, 85 too takes a clear note of this point, only to muddle it by assuming that Paul speaks of a 'realized inheritance'. Our finding basically agrees with the assessment of Byrne, *Sons* (1979) 158, 189, who takes 'inheritance' rather than 'adoption' as the overarching theme of Paul's discussion from 3:15–5:1. He is followed by Smiles, *Gospel* (1998) 65–66. See also Shaw, *Authority* (1983) 47–48.

[60] This is emphasized by Hester, *Inheritance* (1968) 39, 92–96; Witherington 290–291. See also Smail, *Father* (1980/1996) 44–46, 151–152. That of course is the essence of the covenant relationship between God and Israel.

[61] See Hester, *Inheritance* (1968) 83–85; Eckstein, *Verheißung* (1996) 106. Cf. Strack/Billerbeck 1:116–121 (2:523).

We know that all things work together for good for those who love God, who are
called according to his purpose. For those whom he foreknew he also predestined *to
be conformed to the image of his Son, in order that he might be the firstborn within
a large family*. And those whom he predestined he also called; and those whom he
called he also justified; and those whom he justified he also glorified (NRSV).

In this remarkable verse, Paul sums up the whole aspect of God's
redemptive work, that is, his foreknowledge, predestination, calling,
justification and glorification, within the frame of God's singular purpose
that those called should be conformed to the image of Christ (συμμόρφους
τῆς εἰκόνος τοῦ υἱοῦ αὐτοῦ), who is the original Son or the Son by birth,
so to speak. The purpose of this conforming process is that they should
also become God's sons and Christ's brothers and sisters, with Christ
himself as the firstborn among many brothers and sisters (εἰς τὸ εἶναι
αὐτὸν πρωτότοκον ἐν πολλοῖς ἀδελφοῖς). The idea is clearly that
becoming God's children involves the process of conformation to the
image of the Son of God, and it would be meaningless to speak of being a
son of God without at the same time speaking of actual acquisition of the
character one is supposed to have as God's son. This explains the meaning
of Paul's affirmation earlier in v. 14: 'for all who are led by the Spirit of
God are sons of God' (ὅσοι γὰρ πνεύματι θεοῦ ἄγονται, οὗτοι υἱοὶ θεοῦ
εἰσιν).
    We find the same thought in Paul's exhortation in Philippians 2:14–15 that
the believes should do everything without grumbling and complaining, so that
(ἵνα) they may become blameless and sincere 'children of God' (ἄμεμπτοι
καὶ ἀκέραιοι, τέκνα θεοῦ). It is well-known that at this point Paul is alluding
to Deut 32:5–6 where Moses denounces the people of Israel for their
ungrateful disobedience. In stark contrast to God's righteousness and sincerity
(v. 4), the people of Israel sinned against God and such defective (μωματά)
behavior resulted in the tragic decision that they are now 'no longer children
to him' (οὐκ αὐτῷ τέκνα) but only 'a perverse and crooked generation'
(γενεὰ σκολιὰ καὶ διεστραμμένη, v. 5). No doubt, this statement is rhetorical
to a certain extent, but it nevertheless accentuates the dynamic and relational
nature of sonship. So in v. 6 Moses castigates the people:

Do you repay the Lord in this way? Are you a people so foolish and unwise? Did
not he himself your father purchase you, and make you, and form you?

Now, reminding his converts in Philippi of this tragic consequences of
persistent disobedience as is exemplified by the people of Israel in the
wilderness, Paul exhorts them not to follow their bad example but become
instead God's blameless children 'among the perverse and crooked
generation' (μέσον γενεᾶς σκολιᾶς καὶ διεστραμμένης) by showing a

disposition befitting God's children.[62] From the way Paul speaks, the privilege of being God's children is never taken for granted but clearly incumbent upon the people's responsible discharge of their filial duty.

We can also consider Eph 1:4–5, a passage well known for its references to predestination. In these verses the idea that one should become 'holy and blameless' (ἁγίους καὶ ἀμώμους) to God is closely knitted together with idea of 'adoption through Christ' (υἱοθεσίαν διὰ ᾿Ιησοῦ Χριστοῦ) to be God's son as the purpose[63] of God's decision made 'before the foundation of the world'. Becoming God's son (εἰς αὐτόν)[64] is inseparable from one's being holy and blameless 'before Him' (κατενώπιον αὐτοῦ). The purposefulness of this connection becomes even more explicit when one considers such phrases as οἱ υἱοὶ τῆς ἀπειθείας and τέκνα ὀργῆς (2:2–3, 5:6) or, positively, τέκνα φωτός (5:8), phrases which accentuate the moral texture of sonship. Indeed, it is almost a truism that God's beloved children should become imitators of God their Father and Christ their brother (5:1).

It is this relational and dynamic nature of sonship that makes one uncomfortable with the consensus view which sees this motif as the object of Paul's unequivocal affirmation. As we saw in chapter 2, for Paul the present disposition of the Galatians virtually amounts to a case of apostasy, which reduces Paul to making a series of scathing accusations concerning their behavior (1:6; 3:3; 4:8–11, 15–16, 21). Of course, he has not given up on the Galatians yet, but in the midst of their gross failure to fulfill their responsibility as God's sons his talk of sonship can hardly be entirely conciliatory. His 'affirmation' of their sonship must have a quite different function in Paul's argument.[65]

In this context we also remember Paul's heartbroken utterance that he is now undergoing the arduous process of childbirth all over again until Christ is formed (μέχρις οὗ μορφωθῇ Χριστός) among the Galatian communities. In view of the way he speaks of sonship, speaking in unequivocal affirmation of the Galatians' sonship would sound simply

---

[62] What Paul does here with the OT story is basically the same as what he does in 1 Cor 10:1–11.

[63] The idea is expressed by an infinitive (v. 4) and a prepositional phrase (v. 5). The material connection between the two verses is missed out by most commentators such as Lincoln, *Ephesians* (1990) and Schnackenburg, *Epheser* (1982).

[64] The precise reference of this phrase is debated. Abbott 9 sees a reference to Christ, on the ground of the prominence of ἐν αὐτῷ in vv. 3–14, but we, without substantiation, take it to refer to God. See Schnackenburg, *Epheser* (1982) 53.

[65] This conclusion concerns specifically Paul's argument in Galatians, not his theology in general. So our statement is not about Pauline theology *per se*, but the polemical note Paul strikes in this particular context.

hollow, since he currently finds the image of Christ, the very essence of their sonship, missing in the Galatian churches.

Indeed the way Paul clinches his argument about sonship suggests that the enthusiastic affirmation of the 'already' is not his intention at all. Thus we observe that his affirmation of the Galatians' sonship in 4:7 is immediately followed by a frontal attack on the incredible nature of their present behavior which, according to him, effectively strips them of their present sonship (4:8–11). This is hardly a realized eschatological affirmation but a stern warning designed to prevent them from losing their status which holds promise for the future.[66] By the same token, Paul's argument in 4:21–31 too is drawn up as an explicit warning to 'those who desire to be under the law' (4:21), that is, those who want to return from their present status as 'children of the Spirit' to their former status as 'children of flesh'.[67] In the same way, the quotation in v. 30 also serves as a warning for those who desire to be under the law, reminding them of the inevitable consequence of this fatal move.[68] This is confirmed by the fact that the allegory is immediately followed by his most stern warning in the whole letter (5:1–4). As part of Paul's response to the problem of apostasy, his repeated affirmation of son-heirship 'in Christ' (3:26–29) and 'through the Spirit' (4:6–7) does not function as a celebration of the 'already' but as an urgent appeal to remain 'in Christ' and 'in the Spirit', the only foundation of their heirship.

4.8 Conclusion

Thus far we have examined various motifs in Paul's argument which can be grouped under the concept of 'sonship': 'son of Abraham' (3:6–7); 'sons of God' (3:26); 'seed of Abraham' (3:29); 'sons (of God)' (4:5–7); 'children of promise/Spirit' (4:21–31). Now we are in a position to draw some important conclusions.

First, in each case in which the 'sonship' language occurs, it does not stand as the main subject of argument, but always functions as a

---

[66] Cf. Hansen, *Abraham* (1988) 139.

[67] This intention seems to explain Paul's preoccupation with the 'slavery' side of his allegory which leaves the positive counterpart incomplete, a phenomenon noted by Cosgrove, 'Sarah' (1987) 224–226; Jobes, 'Jerusalem' (1993) 301.

[68] Romans chapter 8 is instructive at this point. There too, Paul is concerned with believers' son-heirship, with sonship receiving more attention than in Galatians. There, interestingly, Paul's affirmation of believers' sonship is placed in a clearly future eschatological context (vv. 6, 11, 13, 17, 23–25) and combined with a strong imperative of having the indwelling Spirit (v. 9, εἴπερ), namely, of being led by the Spirit by putting the practices of body to death with the Sprit (v. 13, εἰ).

supporting motif for another theme. The context in which these motifs are put to use is either justification by faith (3:6–7), or equality in Christ (3:26–28), or, most notably, the heirship of the Gentile believers (3:29; 4:7, 30–31). It is these, and not 'sonship', that constitute the central point. Hence, as far as Paul's argument goes, we cannot consider 'sonship' as a major issue in Galatians. However weighty a theological concept it may be, it should not allow us to ignore the contextual accent of Paul's argument itself which in fact falls on a different place. Therefore, the impression of 'realized eschatology' inherent in the notion of present sonship should be given up. As far as Paul does emphasize the present status of the Gentile believers as sons and seed, the sense of 'already' is not completely missing, but it is radically qualified by the overall thrust of the argument for which the motif works. The supposition that with his focus on 'sonship' Paul emphasizes what has *already* been accomplished in Christ should also be given up. Sonship is never the central point of his argument, and the danger he perceives in the present crisis forbids any unreserved affirmation of the 'already'. The illusion of 'realized eschatology' associated with the motif of sonship should not be allowed to dominate the overall outlook of his argument.

Secondly, taken in context, the unequivocal affirmations about the 'seed of Abraham' (3:29) and 'sons (of God)' (4:5–7) are not made in order to emphasize the believers' *present* status. When Paul speaks of the Gentile believers as 'seed' and 'sons', he means to show that they are 'heirs', namely, those who carry God's promise for the future inheritance. His affirmations are, therefore, deliberately open-ended and conspicuously futuristic.[69] He is not looking backward; on the contrary, he is pointing to what still lies in the future. Here we should not falsify Paul's perspective on the Galatian situation: whatever the Galatians may say, as far as Paul is concerned, they are simply on the verge of abandoning their faith in Christ. In this context, then, his seeming 'affirmation' functions not so much as a positive celebration of their *present* privilege as a grave warning against their present deviation from the truth of the gospel. In effect, he is saying, 'Do not be mistaken. Only those who persist in faith will be able to enjoy the promised inheritance; those who fall back onto the way of the law are sure to forfeit any prospect of such blessing!' (Cf. 6:7; 5:21).

In view of the current consensus on the idea of 'realized inheritance' as the thrust of Paul's thought, however, our final judgment on the future eschatological outlook of his argument must wait until we have examined the ideas of 'promise' and 'inheritance'. Having clarified the limited

---

[69] To be sure, most interpreters speak of 'realized inheritance', which, however, is begging the question. The future eschatological nature of 'inheritance' will be discussed in the following two chapters.

function of Paul's sonship language, however, we are in a much better
position to assess the character of his discussion on these themes. This is
the task we will take up in the next two chapters.

Chapter 5

Paul's View of Promise

In the previous chapter we examined Paul's use of 'sonship' language and suggested that his major concern does not lie in sonship itself but in the heirship it grounds: sonship matters because being sons also means being the *heirs* of God's promised inheritance. This means that a proper understanding of his argument much depends on a correct interpretation of 'promise' and 'inheritance,' two closely related concepts originating from the Abrahamic tradition. In this chapter we will first take up the motif of 'promise' and examine its function in Paul's reading of the Abrahamic tradition. This will then be followed by a study of 'inheritance' in the next chapter.

5.1 A Fulfilled Promise in Galatians?

In recent scholarly discussion it is a commonplace to understand the concept of promise within the framework of 'promise and fulfillment': the promise(s) given to Abraham and his seed have now been effectively realized through Christ and the coming of the Spirit.[1] Abraham received the promise from God; Christ has fulfilled it. While it is not explicitly denied that Christ too is the recipient of the promise, most scholarly construal of Paul's argument depicts Christ mainly as its fulfiller. Thus Gentile believers too are primarily described as the beneficiaries of that 'fulfilled promise', not the recipients of the promise itself. According to this view, the focus then falls necessarily on Christ, who marks the 'Glaubenszeit mit ihrer Erfüllung der Verheißung'.[2] Ridderbos speaks for many: 'it was He to whom the promise pointed and in whom it was materialized.'[3] If this is the case, it follows that the more Paul speaks of

---

[1] Hansen, *Abraham* (1988) begins his study with these words: 'Since the gospel according to Paul is the fulfillment of the Abrahamic promise, ...' (15). See also e.g., Hooker, 'Covenantal nomism' (1982) 51–52; Watson, *Text* (1994) 190–191, 195.

[2] Mußner 254.

[3] Ridderbos 138.

'promise', in reality, the more he says about its 'fulfillment'; his talk of promise becomes an exposition of his realized eschatology.

With the lack of any explicit statement expressing the idea of fulfillment, this view finds its exegetical ground in two crucial decisions: 1) the identification of the Abrahamic 'blessing' in 3:8–14 with the 'promise' in 3:15–29, and 2) the interpretation of 'the promise of the Spirit' in 3:14 as the fulfillment of the Abrahamic promise discussed in 3:15–29. The purpose of this chapter is to demonstrate that these widely held views are exegetically flawed. We shall first deal with these two consensus views, before tracing Paul's argument to see if he actually speaks of the fulfillment of the Abrahamic promise.

5.2 'Blessing' and 'Promise'

5.2.1 'Promise of Blessing'?

In scholarly interpretation of Galatians, it is customary to connect the 'blessing' in 3:6–14 with the 'promise' in 3:15–29 and 4:21–31: God's pronouncement of the future 'blessing of the Gentiles in Abraham' (3:8; cf. Gen 12:3; 18:18) represents the content of God's 'promise' given to 'Abraham and to his seed' (3:16). The result is the popular notion of *Segensverheißung*.[4] Then, on the basis of Paul's reference to 'the promise of the Spirit' (3:14), this promise of blessing in turn is explicitly identified as the gift of the Holy Spirit (3:14).[5] The promise God gave to Abraham and to his seed was the promise that God would bless the Gentiles through Abraham, which was effectively fulfilled when God bestowed the gift of the Holy Spirit upon the Gentiles who were ἐκ πίστεως.

The fusion of these two arguments enables scholars to make a very significant claim for the notion of the fulfilled promise. We will later have to discuss the important phrase 'the promise of the Spirit' (3:14), but even apart from that, another crucial claim is made. As Beker observes,[6] in 3:10–14 Christ comes in as the one who 'enables' the Abrahamic blessing by removing the curse of the law, while in 3:15–29, he is 'the sole recipient of the promise'. By equating blessing with promise, Christ the 'enabler of the blessing' can now be described as the 'fulfiller of the promise', an idea which is *missing* in Paul's discussion of the 'promise' itself in 3:15–29. Since he is the one who establishes the 'promised'

---

[4] This is the consensus. E.g., Martyn 355; Hübner, *Theologie* (1990) 74; Eckstein, *Verheißung* (1996) 95, 97; Smiles, *Gospel* (1998) 133 ('inheritance').

[5] E.g., Hansen, *Abraham* (1989) 126, 128; Fee, *Presence* (1995) 394–395.

[6] Beker's phrase is 'enabler of the promise'. *Paul* (1980) 47–52.

blessing, he is the fulfillment of the promise.[7] By his talk of promise and inheritance, then, Paul means the 'fulfilled' promise, namely, the 'realized' inheritance.[8]

5.2.2 'Promise' and 'Blessing' Are Distinct

In our view, however, this (con)fusion of 'blessing' and 'promise' with the resultant notion of *Segensverheißung* is an exegetical slip fatal to a proper understanding of Paul's point. To be sure, since both 3:8–14 and 3:15–29 appeal to the same Abraham, one can argue that these two passages are to be taken together. However, we cannot begin by assuming that Paul uses this tradition always for the same purpose and with the same logic. Before we conflate the two, we first have to examine each argument in its own context and find out what Paul is up to in each case. Our claim is that he pursues a different track in each argument, and thus they should not be conflated. In support of our claim, we submit the following four points.

First, in 3:8–14 'promise' does not play any role in Paul's argument apart from 'the promise of the Spirit' which comes, as we shall soon show, from the prophetic tradition. Here God's pronouncement of Gentile blessing serves as the divine warrant for Paul's claim that justification is by faith. For this reason, it is an act of 'proclaiming the gospel' in advance (προευηγγελίσατο) instead of 'uttering promises' (ἐρρέθησαν αἱ ἐπαγγελίαι) (v. 8; cf. v. 16). God's 'gospel message' that the Gentiles will be blessed in Abraham occurs in Genesis 12:3 and 18:18, both of which declare the purpose of Abraham's election: God chose Abraham so that all the Gentiles might be blessed through him.[9]

For this reason, in Paul's thought this is not a *'promise' to Abraham* and his seed, but the *'gospel' for the Gentiles* preached in advance in anticipation of the fact that God will justify them by faith (v. 8). His use of two different grammatical subjects seems indicative of his intention here. 'Foreknowledge' and 'preaching the gospel' obviously belong to God, but Paul posits 'the Scripture' as the subject of this foreknowledge, while God comes in as the subject of gospel itself, i.e., the justifier of the Gentiles: προϊδοῦσα ἡ γραφὴ ὅτι ἐκ πίστεως δικαιοῖ τὰ ἔθνη ὁ θεός (v. 8a). That is, for Paul the statement in v. 8b does not function primarily as

---

[7] See, among others, Eckstein, *Verheißung* (1996) 179–184 who speaks of 'die Verwirklichung der Segensverheißung durch das σπέρμα 'Αβραάμ' and therefore 'die Erfüllung der Verheißung in Christus' (115, 117). Even Beker, *Paul* (1080) 50, who detects 'inconsistency' between 3:10–14 and 3:15–29, still considers Christ as 'the blessing and fulfillment of the promise'.

[8] This is the *opinio communis*. Foerster, *TDNT* 3:785; Hester, 'The "Heir"' (1967) 118–125. See also 6.2 below.

[9] In Genesis the pronouncement is certainly God's promise of blessing intended for Abraham, with the emphasis on בְּךָ (ἐν σοί) as the key to the blessing for the nations.

God's promise to Abraham but as a scriptural testimony to the 'gospel' that God justifies the Gentiles by faith. If by this oracle Paul meant 'the covenant ratified by God' (v. 17), the avoidance of 'God' in favor of 'the Scripture' would become quite puzzling.[10]

Secondly, accordingly, the change of emphasis is also unmistakable. In 3:8–14 Paul speaks for the Gentiles and not primarily for Abraham.[11] In the original Genesis context, it is Abraham himself that God is concerned about. Announcing that 'all the nations will be blessed in you' (12:3a), his main emphasis clearly falls on 'in you' (בְּךָ; ἐν σοί), singling out Abraham as the key to the blessing of all nations and thereby making his oracle a word of blessing for Abraham. In Galatians, however, the thrust changes. Paul's main concern is not Abraham himself but the Gentile believers. His burden at this point is to demonstrate the truth that God justifies *the Gentiles* only by faith and not by the law, and that is the reason why he appeals to this particular passage, namely, a passage which explicitly embraces the Gentiles as an original part of God's plan.

The upshot of Paul's exegesis is, no doubt, his characterization of Abraham, the key to blessing, as ὁ πιστὸς 'Αβραάμ (3:6, 9): the Gentiles will be blessed 'in the believing Abraham'. As Paul himself explains later, that the Gentiles are blessed 'in Abraham' really means that the 'believing' Gentiles are blessed 'together with' (σύν) the 'believing' Abraham;[12] just as Abraham was blessed by his faith, the Gentiles will also be blessed by the same faith. Hence God's word of blessing for Abraham has become for Paul scriptural evidence for the truth of the gospel that οἱ ἐκ πίστεως will be blessed σὺν τῷ πιστῷ 'Αβραάμ (3:9).

This explains the unmistakable emphasis laid on εἰς τὰ ἔθνη in his conclusion of the section: 'so that *to the Gentiles* the blessing of Abraham might come in Christ Jesus' (3:14a).[13] From 3:15 onwards, however, Paul's interest centers on the person of Abraham, for the simple reason that now it is the experience of Abraham himself that provides the proof for Paul's case. God gave the promise 'to Abraham and to his seed' (v.16), and showed his grace to him 'through promise' (v.18). Therefore, despite

---

[10] *Contra* Eckstein, *Verheißung* (1996) 108–109. Since he considers the quoted oracle to be the essence of God's 'promise' given to Abraham (3:15–29), he has to ignore the functional difference between 'the Scripture' and 'God'. To be sure, the Scripture ultimately traces back to God Himself; what is important is, however, to discern the intention behind this varying choice of terms.

[11] Hays, *Echoes* (1989) 105–111 observes that Paul's hermeneutic here is 'ecclesiocentric'.

[12] The comparison is between Abraham and believers. Rightly, Betz 143, n. 41 and 47; Dunn 165–166; Hong, 'Jewish Law' (1994) 169.

[13] With Bruce 156–157; Fung 140; R. Longenecker 115; Dunn 164; *idem*, 'Theology' 132; Hansen, *Abraham* (1989) 84.

the fact that both 3:6–14 and 3:15–29 are based on the Abrahamic tradition, the two arguments are not designed to score the same point. God's 'promise' that God would give *Abraham* the land is certainly different from his 'gospel' that *the Gentiles* will be blessed through him.[14]

Thirdly, we should not attribute undue weight to the temporary motif of 'blessing'. As we have just seen, Paul cites Genesis 12:3 (18:18) because the passage proves that the Gentiles are part of God's original plan. Strictly speaking, then, the idea of blessing is somewhat inadvertently carried in from the passage he needed for that reason. Since the 'Gentile' passage happens to speak of their 'blessing', he does incorporate it into his discussion, defining it in terms of 'justification', which, however, does not mean that the idea itself is a major theme in his argument.[15] Unlike such motifs as sonship, promise, inheritance, all of which take indispensable places in Paul's later argumentation, 'blessing' does nothing more than prove the fact that the Gentiles are indeed part of God's original plan of justification (vv. 9, 14). This limited function for the theme explains why it does not appear again in his subsequent argument, most notably in vv. 15–29.[16] Picking up such a minor theme and connecting it to 'promise' to produce the idea of *Segensverheißung* would be highlighting a point Paul himself has little or no intention to advertise.

Fourthly, in 3:15–29 the promise Paul refers to is the specific promise of the land, which makes it very difficult to include the oracle of blessing within this 'promise' explicitly given to Abraham. In v. 15 onward his bold christological exegesis depends critically on the fact that God's promises were addressed to Abraham καὶ τῷ σπέρματι αὐτοῦ (v. 16), and not καὶ τοῖς σπέρμασιν in the plural. This grammatical argument makes it clear that at this point Paul grounds his thesis not on the tradition in general but on a specific text or texts which contain this very phrase.

The possible candidates are either Genesis 13:15 or 17:8, where God promises to give 'the land of Canaan' σοι [Abraham] καὶ τῷ σπέρματί σου.[17] This phrase also occurs in 24:7, where Abraham reminds God of his earlier promises.[18]

---

[14] S. K. Williams 87 and 'Promise' (1988) 710, rarely, takes a special note of this fact. 'The gospel that Abraham heard' is surely different from 'the promise he and his seed received'.

[15] Cf. Sanders, *Law* (1983) 21.

[16] Rightly, Burton 162; Martyn 321–323; Fee, *Presence* (1995) 395. But their speculation that the word belongs to the agitators is unnecessary.

[17] See Lightfoot 142.

[18] MT and Codex Sinaiticus omit καί in 24:7. In Gen. 12:7 and 15:8 too, the phrase, τῷ σπέρματί σου, occurs, but in these cases it is exclusively to Abraham's seed and not to Abraham himself that God promises the land.

Gen 13:15 ὅτι πᾶσαν τὴν γῆν ... σοὶ δώσω αὐτὴν καὶ τῷ σπέρματί σου ....

Gen 17:8 καὶ δώσω σοι καὶ τῷ σπέρματί σου μετὰ σὲ τὴν γῆν ...

Gen 24:7 καὶ ὤμοσέν μοι λέγων σοὶ δώσω τὴν γῆν ταύτην καὶ τῷ σπέρματί σου

In all these passages, God's promise refers to the specific promise that God would give the land of Canaan to Abraham 'and to his seed'. That is, when Paul speaks of God's promise(s) in this context, he must have the 'promise of the land' in mind.[19]

On the other hand, Paul's point about 'and to your seed' cannot apply to God's oracle of 'blessing' which is addressed to Abraham but never 'and to your seed'. In Genesis 12:3 the oracle is given exclusively to Abraham without his seed coming into the picture at all. In Genesis 18:18 even Abraham himself is referred to as a third person. That is, Paul cannot have drawn such a grammatical argument from these oracles of 'blessing'.[20] Hence God's promise given to Abraham 'and to his seed' must refer to the promise of the land and not to 'blessing'.[21] Naturally, in 3:15 onwards it is the idea of 'inheritance' (κληρονομία), the real content of the promise, that takes up the central place (3:29; 4:7; 4:21–31). Yet, as we have noted, the motif of blessing does not occur beyond 3:14, while the talk of promise and inheritance abounds. This is a phenomenon which is difficult, if not impossible, to explain if Paul is thinking of the blessing of Abraham as the specific content of the inheritance. It seems that the role of 'blessing' is limited within 3:6–14, and in 3:15 onwards Paul, having made his point

---

[19] Daube, *Judaism* (1956) 438 lists two further points: 1) 'it was in connection with a promise of the land that the Rabbis resorted to an interpretation of 'seed' with which Paul's has much in common'; 2) The promise of the land was the general basis for chronological speculations. Also see Burton 185; Schlier 144; Mußner 238; Bruce 171–172; Dunn 185; Betz 157, n. 34; Hester, *Inheritance* (1968) 77; Byrne, *Sons* (1979) 160. Even these, however, still relate the 'promise' to the oracle of 'blessing' in vv. 8–9.

[20] *Contra* Fitzmyer 787; Hong, 'Jewish Law' (1994) 172–173. Recently, Wisdom, *Blessings* (2001) 143, claimed that the promise in 3:16 refers to that in Gen 28:4, another passage that contains the phrase καὶ τῷ σπέρματί σου, on the grounds that it contains 'the blessing of Abraham', a phrase we also find in Galatians 3:14. At this point, however, his focus on 'blessing', the subject matter of his investigation, seems to make him blind to the obvious fact that the passage is not God's promise uttered to Abraham but Isaac's word of blessing for his son Jacob. There 'to you' means 'to Jacob', and 'to your seed', 'to Jacob's descendants'.

[21] Martyn 339–340 states that 'Paul focuses his exegetical attention on the text of Gen 17:8', a text which speaks of the land, not 'blessing'. Yet, he goes on to assert that the 'promise' here refers to the 'blessing' and thus Paul ignores the motif of the land. Similarly, Davies, *Land* (1974) 179; Bruce 171–172; Wright, *Climax* (1991) 174; Eckstein, *Verheißung* (1996) 180.

and thus leaving it behind, takes a different route of promise and inheritance to continue his argument.[22]

Based on these considerations we submit that the 'blessing' is not to be conflated with the 'promise' to produce the composite notion of 'the promise of the blessing', since 3:8–14 and 3:15–29 are two distinct arguments designed to score different points. That is, it is exegetically ill-advised to translate Christ 'the enabler of the blessing' (3:14) into Christ 'the fulfillment of the Abrahamic promise'. Whether Paul considers Christ as the one who fulfils the promise is a matter we shall discuss later. At this point, it is important to realize that 3:8–14, where Christ brings about the blessing of Abraham, does not support the assumption of the 'fulfilled promise'.

In 'the old days' God preached the gospel about the blessing of the Gentiles, and Paul, observing the gift of the Spirit (3:14b), understands that this gospel of blessing is now at work (3:14a). And he, in turn, presents this as a sure proof for the truth of justification by faith. Here nothing is said about the Abrahamic 'promise', for which we have to go to 3:15–29. For now, it suffices to affirm that the gospel of blessing (justification) is *not* to be taken as the content of the Abrahamic promise.[23]

5.3 The Promise of the Spirit (3:14b)

A more important *crux interpretum* is the interesting phrase 'the promise of the Spirit' in 3:14b. The verse consists of double ἵνα clauses, both explicating the purpose of Christ's death on the cross: 'so that the blessing of Abraham might come upon the Gentiles (v. 14a); so that we might receive the promise of the Spirit (τὴν ἐπαγγελίαν τοῦ πνεύματος) through faith' (v. 14b). The genitive here is most probably appositional, specifying the Spirit as the content of the promise, meaning 'the promised Spirit'.[24] Of course, it goes without saying that with this expression Paul intends the reality of the Spirit actually conferred on the Galatian congregation (3:1–5; 4:6). What concerns us at this point is his combination of the two highly significant ideas to produce a single concept: the 'Spirit' and the 'promise'.

---

[22] There is a clear break between 3:14 and 3:15.

[23] In Romans 4 too, justification and promise are distinct from each other: Abraham was 'justified' because of his faith in God's 'promise'.

[24] So, Burton 176 ('metonymic'); Bligh, *Greek* (1966) 140 and most others.

5.3.1 Is the Spirit the Fulfillment of the Promise?

In view of the heavy use of the word 'promise' in subsequent argument
(3:15–29; 4:21–31), most scholars infer that with his reference to 'the
promise of the Spirit' in 3:14 Paul is redefining the content of the
Abrahamic promise in terms of the Spirit. The obvious consequence of this
decision is that the Abrahamic promise (3:8; 15ff.) has now been 'fulfilled'
in the form of God's bestowal of the Spirit upon believers. In Burton's
words, 'The apostle refers to the promise to Abraham and has learned to
interpret this as having reference to the gift of the Spirit'. And this
'blessing of the Spirit, as the initial gift of the new life, is the earnest, and
so the fulfillment of the promise'.[25] A survey of commentaries easily
shows that *it is in fact on this single phrase that scholars ground their idea
of 'fulfilled promise'.*[26]

The effect of this reading is that, by connecting the 'promise' in the
Abrahamic tradition with its present 'fulfillment', it highlights the
eschatological decisiveness of the Spirit for the early Christians. It also has
the advantage of a strong connection with Paul's following discussions. As
R. Longenecker notes, the 'promise' in 3:14 'sets up the presentations of
3:15–4:31, for thereafter it is the word "promise" that dominates the
discussions'.[27]

If this is in fact what Paul means by the 'promise of the Spirit', it
unmistakably delivers a note of realized eschatology, since it means that
the ancient promise of inheritance uttered to Abraham *has already been
fulfilled* by God's bestowal of the Spirit upon the Gentile believers. From
this it also follows that his subsequent discussion of 'promise' and
'inheritance' should refer entirely to the 'fulfilled promise' and 'realized
inheritance' with the Spirit as its main reference. Martyn speaks for many
when he says:

> ... equating the promise with the Spirit, Paul assures the Galatians that they have
> been recipients of that promise for some time, having received the Spirit when they

[25] K. Berger, 'Abraham' (1966) 47 speaks for many: 'In Gal 3 wird das Heilsgut der
Christen, das Pneuma, das sie empfingen (3, 2–5), dargestellt als Inhalt der Verheißung
an Abraham'.

[26] This is the consensus. E.g., G. Vos, 'Spirit' (1912) 101; Schniewind/Friedrich
TDNT 2:584; Dunn, *Theology* (1993) 93; Eckert, *Verkündigung* (1971) 79; Lull, *Spirit*
(1980) 153–154; Silva, 'Eschatological Structure' (1994) 152; Kertelge, 'Gesetz' (1984)
387; Hartman, '3.15–4.11' (1993) 133, 136.

[27] R. Longenecker 125. Similarly, Dahl, *Studies* (1977) 132: 'affirmations about the
Spirit...constitute the framework of Paul's discussion of the promise to Abraham'. See
also Byrne, *Sons* (1979) 156; Hansen, *Abraham* (1989) 127.

were grasped by the gospel of the crucified Christ (3:2). Coming as the Spirit, God's promise institutes and constitutes a new state of affairs.[28]

Focusing on the motif of the Spirit as the fulfillment of the promise and the content of the inheritance, then, Paul's argument in Galatians is a pointed case for a 'realized eschatology'.

5.3.2 The Spirit Is Not Related to the Abrahamic 'Promise'

We have to register a strong objection to this widely held interpretation of the phrase, however. Despite the use of the same word 'promise', there are several problems in associating 'the promise of the Spirit' with 'the *Abrahamic* promise'.

First of all, we begin with the observation that this interpretation is not explicit in Paul's argument itself. Nowhere in the letter does he actually claim that the Spirit should be seen as the fulfillment of the Abrahamic promise. This is the idea scholars infer from the way he speaks of the subject, and the only ground for such inference is the proximity of 'the promise of the Spirit' in 3:14b and the discussion of the Abrahamic 'promise' in 3:16 onwards. Does Paul then brings these two promise phrases close to each other (v. 14b and v. 16) in order to make a subtle yet radical and innovative claim that *the Spirit* means the fulfillment of the Abrahamic promise of *the land*?

Secondly, it is not easy, however, to see the grounds on which Paul has come to associate the Abrahamic promise of the land with the Spirit. The reference to the 'promise' is abrupt and its identification with the Spirit is very casual, lacking any explanation.[29] We get the impression that the idea is familiar to the Galatian ears. This familiarity cannot be assumed, however, for the association of the Spirit and the Abrahamic promise is a phenomenon *unattested* in any other contemporary literature.[30] One may argue that Paul somehow 'has learned to interpret this as having reference to the gift of the Spirit'.[31] Yet, in a polemical situation in which he has to fight with his opponents over the right interpretation of the Abrahamic tradition, this precarious reinterpretation of the 'promise' as the Spirit must have struck them as an expression of sheer desperation. If Paul had really meant that the Abrahamic promise was that of the Spirit, he should have

---

[28] Martyn 323, 353.

[29] This is rightly emphasized by Cosgrove, *Cross* (1988) 85. He then begs the question by using this as the evidence for the prevalence of such identification.

[30] The claim of Dunn 186 that Paul draws the idea from the already established early Christian understanding of 'the Spirit as the beginning of inheritance' is simply unfounded. Where do we have evidence for such notion?

[31] Burton 177.

given a justification for this, which he fails to do anywhere in his letters. In the context there is nothing to compel the readers to make this connection.

For the Jews of Paul's time the Abrahamic promise of the land was a well-established tradition. To be sure, this promise had already come to be understood as eschatological and universal, but the core of the 'land' remained solid.[32] Thus, *the historical constraint must have been too great to allow such a 'precarious' equation allegedly present in 3:14b*. A mere reference to 'the promise of the Spirit', a firmly established motif in its own right, would hardly have been enough to make the Galatians and the agitators notice such a claim. That Paul at this point has not even mentioned 'promise' also renders such an intention improbable.

Thirdly, in the subsequent use of the word 'promise', Paul freely alternates from plural to singular. The plural αἱ ἐπαγγελίαι in v. 16 switches into the singular τὴν ἐπαγγελίαν in v. 17. V. 18 maintains the singular, ἐξ ἐπαγγελίας, but once again the plural comes back, τῶν ἐπαγγελιῶν, in v. 21, only to be followed by yet another singular, ἡ ἐπαγγελία, in v. 22. If Paul had the specific Spirit in mind, this variation between 'promises' and 'promise', especially the repeated use of the plural, would be inexplicable. With the Spirit now present in the Galatian congregation, he would have certainly used the singular invariably. As is often noted,[33] his references to the 'promises' in plural is based on the fact that God's promise to Abraham was made not just once but on many different occasions. If so, this makes it more probable that in speaking of 'promise' or 'promises' he is still thinking of the concrete promises uttered by God in the Scripture rather than the Spirit as the singular and realized content of the promise.

Fourthly, v. 18 clearly identifies the 'inheritance' with the content of God's promise to Abraham. In this verse, it is Paul's controversial claim that this inheritance cannot be 'from the law' but only 'from promise'. On the other hand, the fact that the Spirit came 'by faith' and not 'from works of the law' is the Galatians' actual experience which, clearly, is assumed to be self-evident (3:2–5).[34] It may be that Paul means to claim that the Spirit is in fact the inheritance promised by God, but his discussion of the latter too is focused on its coming from faith rather than its identity with the Spirit.

Fifthly, after 3:14, the Spirit does not appear, at least explicitly, until 4:6, while the talk of promise abounds. In 3:15–29, where talk of the

---

[32] See Brueggeman, *Land* (1977) 179: 'No matter how spiritualized, transcendentalized, or existentialized, it has its primary focus undeniably on land'. Also Byrne, *Sons* (1979) 160.

[33] E.g., Burton 181; Bligh, *Greek* (1966) 143; Williams, 'Promise' (1988) 712–713.

[34] This is widely noted. E.g., R. Longenecker 102; Dunn 153.

Abrahamic promise leads to the affirmation of sonship, the Spirit does not come into the picture at all. On the other hand, in his next argument (4:1–7), where he relates sonship to the gift of the Spirit, the notion of the Abrahamic promise is not in view.[35] Under the assumed relation between the two, this phenomenon is not easy to explain. Having already identified the promise as the Spirit, why would he still speak ambiguously of 'promise' and even confusingly of 'promises' without referring to the Spirit, not even once? This at least tells us that such identification is not important for his subsequent argument. If so, why would he unnecessarily take such a provocative step?

S. K. Williams, in his study of the 'promise' in Galatians, makes a very illuminating observation concerning this point. Having surveyed much scholarly interpretation of the theme, he discovers that most scholars, as they move on to the promise in 3:15–4:31, tend to 'forget' the identification of the promise with the Spirit in 3:14. He laments this inconsistency and proceeds to present his own reading of the Genesis story, trying to show how the Abrahamic promise can be understood in terms of the promise of the Spirit.[36] If the promise of the Spirit does refer to the Abrahamic promise, Williams's complaint is quite telling and should be answered.

A different question can be posed, however. If Paul considers the Spirit as the real content of the promise, why is it that his discussion of the promise stands on its own independently of the motif of the Spirit, thereby inducing scholars to forget the latter? The very fact that Paul's discussion of the promise (3:15–29) makes scholars forget about the Spirit renders the forced identification of 'the promise of the Spirit' with the Abrahamic promise questionable. As Fee realizes, in 3:15–29 'the "promise" does not much refer directly to the Spirit, despite v. 14, but to the "inheritance"'.[37] That is, Paul obviously does not feel the need to invoke the Spirit as he discusses the promise, which makes the latter's alleged identity with the Spirit both improbable and irrelevant.

5.3.3 Functional Identity of the 'Promise' and the Spirit

In 4:21–31 Paul does associate the Abrahamic 'promise' with the Spirit. His initial antithesis of κατὰ σάρκα and δι᾽ ἐπαγγελίας describing two

---

[35] See the discussion below.

[36] Williams, 'Promise' (1988) 709–720. See also Hartman, 'Gal 3.15–4.11' (1993) 133, 136–137; Lull, *Spirit* (1980) 153–154. William's attempt to connect the Spirit with various Abrahamic promises is fanciful, to say the least, which eloquently illustrates the problem of the consensus view.

[37] Fee, *Presence* (1995) 396. Yet, misled by his reading of 3:14 and 4:4–7, he too ends up equating the Spirit with inheritance.

different ways of begetting children (v. 23) is later developed into the more
familiar antithesis of κατὰ σάρκα and κατὰ πνεῦμα (v. 29). Thus it
becomes clear that here δι' ἐπαγγελίας and κατὰ πνεῦμα are functionally
identical. On a superficial reading, this interchange between the two
phrases does seem to suggest that Paul equates the promise with the
Spirit.[38] This is not so, however.

In this passage, Paul bases his allegorical interpretation on the fact that
Isaac was born of God's promise in contrast to Ishmael who was born
'according to flesh'. Thus, the 'promise' in this context most probably
refers to the promise of an 'offspring-heir' to Abraham and Sarah (Gen. 15,
17). Here the dominant idea is God's powerful intervention demonstrated
in Isaac's birth in contradistinction to the normal 'fleshly' way of
procuring an heir as is the case with Ishmael. It has to be δι' ἐπαγγελίας,
namely, by God Himself, since, given the situation, it is simply impossible
to have an heir κατὰ σάρκα. In that the birth is made possible by God's
own initiative intervention, saying it is 'by promise' is *in effect* to same as
saying it is 'by the Spirit of God', and it is this insight that explains Paul's
bold hermeneutical association of the promise with the Spirit. Of course
God's powerful working through His Spirit is something all too familiar to
Paul the apostle throughout his ministry (1 Thess 1:5–6; 1 Cor 2:1–5; Rom
15:14–18; Phil 3:3; cf. Gal 2:7–8), including, to be sure, the Galatian
churches (3:1–5, 14; 4:6). From this intervention of God through the Spirit
in the Galatian churches he discerns the outworking of precisely the same
power of God (the Spirit) paradigmatically revealed in the birth of Isaac
'according to promise'.[39] In other words, the identity he detects between
the promise and the Spirit lies in their *function* of denoting God's powerful
initiative and not in their actual content.[40] Nothing either in this passage or

---

[38] Silva, 'Eschatological Structure' (1994) 156 speak of a correspondence between the
Spirit and the promise, by which he actually means the identity of the two (cf. 152).
Similarly, J. Vos, *Pneumatologie* (1973) 92–93; Lull, *Spirit* (1980) 157; Barclay, *Truth*
(1988) 89; Fee, *Presence* (1995) 414.

[39] This is noted by Schweizer, *TDNT* 6:429; Fee, *Presence* (1995) 415–416; Fung 214,
though they take this as the ground for identifying the promise with the Spirit. Cf. Hays,
Echoes (1989) 115; Martyn, 'Events' (1991) 175–176. Also note the perceptive comment
of Standhartinger, 'Hagar' (2002) 295: 'Dass „durch Verheißung" und „nach dem
Fleisch" einen Gegensatz bilden, ist deutlich. Hinter dieser Behauptung steht die Idee,
dass nicht Abraham, sondern Gott selbst der Vater Isaaks ist'.

[40] In 4:21–31, since Isaac is born 'according to promise', this promise necessarily
refers to that of progeny. This promise of a 'seed' cannot be the same as the promise of
'inheritance' indicated in 4:30 and discussed in 3:15–29, the promise uttered to Abraham
'and to his seed'. In the former, the seed is the content of God's promise; in the latter its
recipient. In Roman 4 too, both the promise of a son given to Abraham alone (4:18–21)
and the promise of the land given 'to Abraham *and to his seed*' (4:13) come into play
without being conflated with each other.

in Genesis or in later interpretations of the Genesis tradition suggests that the Spirit is the actual yet undisclosed *content* of God's promise made to Abraham. Borrowing the phrases of modern translation theories, the principle behind Paul's interpretive move here can be described as 'dynamic equivalence' rather than merely 'literal'. Paul translates the promise into the Spirit, not because they literally refer to the same thing but because the reality depicted by the biblical 'promise' corresponds closely to the reality Paul tries to give expression to with the concept of the Spirit.

Another aspect of God's promise also comes into play. In the Genesis narrative, a question which runs through the whole narrative is 'Who is the real heir?' Since here the promise means that of the land, the real question becomes, 'Who will inherit this promise of the land as Abraham's legitimate heir?' To this question, God's consistent answer is that it is only Isaac, the son born of God's promise, who is the genuine 'heir'. The same logic is present in Paul's argument. Just as the son of promise was considered the genuine heir, now it is only those who are born κατὰ πνεῦμα that are considered as God's true heirs (4:30). And here it is also to be noted that the promise of the land itself, which the Gentile believers 'shall inherit', is not spiritualized in terms of the Spirit. As we shall see once again later (6.3.2 below), his point is that the Spirit *produces* heirs and certainly not that it *is* the promised inheritance.[41]

5.3.4 The Promise in Romans

Paul's interpretation of the same tradition in Romans also speaks against the common equation of the Spirit with the Abrahamic promise. Romans chapter 4, where the figure of Abraham is the subject matter, is a close parallel to Galatians 3:15–18 in that in both places the idea of promise is associated with the notion of inheritance. There too ἡ ἐπαγγελία τῷ Ἀβραάμ stands prominently, occurring four times (4:13, 14, 16). Though some try to find a significant difference between the two arguments,[42] their basic thrusts remain the same in both places. The central thesis of his argument ('by faith, not by law') is the same; even the rhetoric of *reductio ad absurdum* used to affirm the validity of the promise (Gal 3:18; Rom 4:14) is the same. In this *later* discussion of the tradition, the Abrahamic

---

[41] It is therefore mistaken to speak of the 'inheritance of sonship' as some do. E.g., Hester, *Inheritance* (1968) 90–91, 97–97; Dunn 188.

[42] Beker, *Paul* (1980) 37–93 discerns an array of contextual differences, which, according to his view, illustrates the contingent character of Galatians. Though his reading is often very perceptive, he tends to exaggerate the differences between Galatians and Romans, somewhat due to his selective reading. No wonder he often has to state his case with 'except' or 'apart from' attached.

promise (ἡ ἐπαγγελία τῷ ᾽Αβραάμ) is now unambiguously identified as the promise that Abraham and his seed should be the inheritor of the world, that is, the eschatological land (τὸ κληρονόμον αὐτὸν εἶναι κόσμου, 4:13).[43] Does this mean that Paul, having identified the promise as the Spirit in Galatians, is now reverting to the traditional and more literal understanding of it?

The motif of Abrahamic promise occurs once more in Romans chapter 9 and this time the motif is introduced in connection with sonship. This motif finds its parallel in Galatians 4:21–31. After an initial absolute use of the word 'the promises' (αἱ ἐπαγγελίαι) as part of Israelite privileges, Paul introduces in 9:8 the familiar antithesis between τὰ τέκνα τῆς σαρκὸς and τὰ τέκνα τῆς ἐπαγγελίας, the one we also find in Galatians 4:21–31. Then in v. 9 Paul specifies the content of this promise as the promise of a son recorded in Genesis 18:10, and not of future inheritance of the world as it was in Romans 4:13.

In fact, we already have this in Romans 4 too as the promise Abraham is invited to believe in order to be reckoned as righteous (4:17–18). Certainly, this promise, though related to the subsequent promise of the land grounded on the 'righteousness of faith', is not identical with it. Paul describes this promise as one about the 'resurrection' of Abraham's 'dead' body (4:17, 19–21), and in this way connects it with our believing the One who raised Christ from the dead (4:24). In Romans 4 Paul exploits the 'resurrection' motif to make clear the powerful and transforming nature of God's work as he 'justifies the ungodly' (4:25), as is explicated more extensively later in Romans 6. At the same time, one can hardly miss the fact that that he spells out this life-giving grace of God in terms of the work of the Holy Spirit (6:6; 8:2 ff.). This is the functional identity between the promise and the Spirit which we discussed above (see 5.3.3). This shows that Paul is not using 'promise' indiscriminately as a shorthand for something in his own mind but with a clear sensitivity to the diverse contexts in which God's promises were actually made. Again, the Spirit is nowhere in view. Even the parallelism of δι᾽ ἐπαγγελίας and κατὰ πνεῦμα is missing.

Based on these considerations we submit that, except for the mere coincidence of the word 'promise', there is no exegetical evidence anywhere in Galatians to suggest that 'the promise of the Spirit' in 3:14

---

[43] See Dahl, *Studies* (1977) 129–130; Sanders, *Law* (1983) 46; Käsemann, *Romans* (1980) 118–120; Dunn, *Romans* (1988) 212–213. Dunn's assumption of 'fulfillment' is puzzling in view of Rom 8:17. In another place Dahl also thinks that the τὰ πάντα in 8:32 'probably refers nothing short of the eschatological inheritance promised to Abraham and his offspring', thus connecting it with the 'world' in 4:13. 'Atonement' (1969) 139 and 148, n. 19.

refers to the fulfillment of the Abrahamic 'promise(s)'. The concept of 'the promise of the Spirit' therefore should be *irrelevant* to our discussion of the Abrahamic promise in the rest of the letter.[44]

5.4 The Spirit as the Fulfillment of the Prophetic Promise

Although scholars are mostly unwilling to consider the possibility, the notion of 'the promise of the Spirit' may well be a firmly established tradition reflecting the shared belief of early Christians that the gift of the Holy Spirit signifies the eschatological fulfillment of God's promises given through prophets such as Isaiah, Jeremiah, Ezekiel, and Joel.[45] There are some interesting data that point in this direction. First, in Acts 2:33 an almost identical and a bit fuller phrase, τὴν ἐπαγγελίαν τοῦ πνεύματος τοῦ ἁγίου, occurs as part of Peter's Pentecostal sermon. In 2:39 the same idea is expressed absolutely as 'the promise'. The phrase, τὴν ἐπαγγελίαν τοῦ πατρός, now specifying the author of this promise, also expresses the same conviction (Lk 24:49; Acts 1:4).

In all these cases, the promise refer to the belief that the coming of the Spirit marks the fulfillment of God's 'promise' given through the prophet Joel (Joel 2:28–32). In this case the promise is explicitly that of the Spirit; it is not a spiritualized interpretation of a promise for something else. In Lukan tradition then the association of the Spirit with the motif of promise is grounded on the *prophetic* traditions where the Spirit constitutes the specific content of God's promise for the future. Here the Abrahamic tradition does not come into view at all.[46]

Secondly, it is noteworthy that in Ephesians 1:13 too the Spirit is connected with promise: 'the Holy Spirit of the promise' (τῷ πνεύματι τῆς ἐπαγγελίας τῷ ἁγίῳ) with which the believers are sealed in Christ. Interestingly, the word order is reversed, but the idea of 'the Spirit as the content of the promise' is not changed.[47] Here too, as in Galatians 3:14, the author provides no further explanation; familiarity with the idea is assumed

---

[44] The question of Hays, *Faith* (1983) 210–212, 'But how can Paul pose this equation?', to which he attempts to answer in terms of his notion of 'narrative-logic', is an unsolicited one. Isaiah 44:3, the text he adduces as part of his answer has nothing to do with the *Abrahamic* promise. On the contrary, this certainly belongs to the prophetic promise of the Spirit, and thus supports our interpretation rather than his.

[45] Isa 32:15; 44:3; 59:21; Ezek 11:9; 36:26; 37:14; 39:29; Joel 2:28–32. Of course, speaking of the arrival of the age to come is going beyond what is warranted by the evidence we possess, as we shall argue later in more detail. See 6.3 below.

[46] In Acts 7:17 Stephen identifies the Abrahamic promise as that of the land of Canaan.

[47] With NRSV; NIV; Moule, *Idiom* (1959) 175; Lincoln, *Ephesians* (1990) 40.

on the readers' side. As such, the prophetic passages seem a better choice than the Abrahamic tradition in which no reference is made to the future bestowal of the Spirit.

Thirdly, there are indications that Paul's understanding of the Spirit is influenced by the prophetic writings. For example, Paul, in the context of defending his ministry, speaks of the Corinthian believers as Christ's letter, written 'through the Spirit of living God' not on stone tablets but tablets of human hearts (ἐν πλαξὶν καρδίαις σαρκίναις). This seems to be a clear allusion to the prophetic tradition reflected in such passages as Jer 31:33, Ezek 11:19 and 36:26 (cf. Prov 3:3; 7:3).[48] The connection between Paul's view of the Spirit as God's life-giving power (1 Cor 15:45; 2 Cor 3:6; cf. Rom 7:6; 8:2, 10–11, 13) and the prophetic traditions is not hard to draw (Ezek 37:1–14). This then heightens the probability that when Paul speaks of 'promise' in relation to the Spirit, his thought is shaped by the prophetic tradition rather than the Abrahamic one which has nothing to say about the Spirit. Thus Fee concludes: 'it is difficult to escape the conclusion that in Pauline theology when "promise" refers to the Spirit, it also inherently includes the theme of the promised new covenant of Jeremiah by way of Ezekiel, whose purposes are fulfilled by the coming of the Spirit'.[49] Given the evidence we have, it seems that the concept of 'the promise of the Spirit' was so well established among early Christians, including the Pauline churches, that Paul could use it without any fear of misunderstanding even in Galatians where the Abrahamic promise takes up a central place in his argument.[50]

Another option is to take the construction as a genitive of origin or author, which gives the meaning 'the promise originated from, or mediated by, the Spirit'. Then, the phrase expresses the view that the Spirit is what gives the believers a promise, that is, a hope for the future.[51] As we have seen, Paul, while not making the Spirit as the content of the Abrahamic promise, nevertheless posits a functional parallelism between the two focused on the idea of God's initiative. In this respect, this interpretation makes good sense in the Galatian context. It also avoids the problematic equation of the Spirit as the content of the promise itself. Nevertheless, the

---

[48] See Fee, *Presence* (1995) 302–307.

[49] Fee, *Presence* (1995) 395. With this recognition on the one hand, and with his conclusion that in 3:15–18 the promise does not primarily refer to the Spirit on the other he should have come to the same conclusion as ours. See the previous note. Cosgrove, *Cross* (1988) 101 is oblivious to the distinction between these two, and mistakenly adduces Acts 2:34 as evidence for his view.

[50] So Piage, 'Holy Spirit' (1993) 405; Schlier 141; Mußner 235; Thielman, *Law* (1994) 135; Fitzmyer 786: 'Promise not to Abraham, but to the people of Israel through the prophets'.

[51] This is suggested to me by Dr. D. Campbell in a private conversation.

abrupt introduction of the phrase makes it uncertain that by this phrase he is actually intending such an association.

The implication of this conclusion for a proper understanding of Paul's eschatological outlook is considerable. Most scholars take the prevalence of the motif of promise as an indication of the 'promise-fulfillment' perspective with which Paul handles the Galatian crisis.[52] It means that the real emphasis of Paul's repeated talk of 'promise' lies on its present *fulfillment* through the Christ event and, more immediately, through the impartation of the Spirit. For this realized eschatological interpretation Paul's reference to 'the promise of the Spirit' (3:14) provides a seeming exegetical justification.

However, we have demonstrated that this is in fact mistaken. If our interpretation of 'the promise of the Spirit' holds, Paul's talk of the Abrahamic 'promise' should not be related to the Spirit already present in the life of the Gentile believers.[53] It means then that we should not assume that the Abrahamic promise discussed in 3:15–29 and 4:21–31 refers to something that has already been realized. Paul's discussion of the 'promise', based on the Abrahamic tradition, should be interpreted on its own, that is, without being mistakenly related to the Spirit. Without making any hasty connection with '(the promise of) the Spirit', we first have to probe carefully the way the motif of promise functions within Paul's argument. Here, in line with our overall subject, our primary concern will be to see whether Paul really presents the Abrahamic promise as fulfilled or not.

5.5 The History of the Promise

With the question of the relationship of the promise and the Spirit clarified, we are now ready to examine the function of the 'promise' in Paul's scriptural argument which covers most of chapters 3 and 4. We will examine the concept in three stages as it encounters three key figures in its history: Abraham, Christ and the Galatians.

5.5.1 Abraham and the Promise (3:15–18)

The train of thought in this argument is not easy to follow, because Paul here seems to fuse two distinct lines of reasoning into a single argument: 1)

---

[52] This is rightly questioned by Dahl, *Studies* (1977) 121–136.

[53] This is an example of what Silva, *Words* (1983) 26 calls 'confusing the word for reality'. Both the Abrahamic promise of the land and the prophetic promise of the Spirit happen to use the same *word* to refer to different *realities*.

the precedence of the promise, the backbone of the present argument, and 2) Christ as the exclusive seed of Abraham, a point which will serve a crucial role in Paul's later argument (v. 16b). One gets the impression that talk of the singular 'seed' has been inserted into the middle of an argument for the chronological priority of the promise (vv. 15–16a, vv. 17–18). And once v. 16b is bracketed as a parenthesis,[54] the flow of the argument becomes smooth.

In 3:15–18 Paul compares God's promise to the human testamentary principle. The purpose of this analogy is clear: the irrevocability of God's way of dealing with people. A human testament (διαθήκη),[55] once ratified (κεκυρωμένην), cannot be changed or added to by a later hand. Having introduced this principle drawn from a familiar analogy,[56] Paul states the undeniable fact that God did in fact utter his promise to Abraham and his seed: τῷ δὲ Ἀβραὰμ ἐρρέθησαν αἱ ἐπαγγελίαι καὶ τῷ σπέρματι αὐτοῦ (v. 16).[57] Then, with v. 15 and v. 16a put together, the case is settled. The inevitable conclusion follows with a special emphasis (τοῦτο δὲ λέγω): 'the law, which came four hundred thirty years later, does not annul a covenant previously ratified by God (προκεκυρωμένην ὑπὸ τοῦ θεοῦ!) so as to nullify the promise' (v. 17).

From the way Paul formulates the statement his emphasis is this: the promise-covenant was ratified 430 years before the law came (μετὰ τετρακόσια καὶ τριάκοντα ἔτη). Neither is the law the proper way to the inheritance, nor does it make this promise-covenant void (note the repetition of ἀκυροῖ and καταργῆσαι). V. 18 recapitulates precisely the same point: 'If the inheritance was from the law, it would never be from promise' (v. 18a).[58] Yet, it cannot be, because the Scripture makes it clear

---

[54] That is, only temporarily, since v. 16b becomes an indispensable presupposition of Paul's thesis that the coming of Christ marks the end of slavery under the law in 3:19–29. Cf. Fitzmyer 786. *Contra* Burton 509, who considers v. 16b as a post-Pauline gloss.

[55] For this see Hansen, *Abraham* (1989) 127; Hester, *Inheritance* (1968) 74. Cf. Morris, *Preaching* (1965) 91. *Contra* Betz 157 and Schlier 146. Anyway, as Fung 155 notes, the point is not the precise background but the 'inviolability' of the covenant.

[56] This is an *a minori ad maius*. So Mußner 240; Hartman, 'Gal 3.15–4.11' (1993) 138.

[57] Though Paul's primary text seems to be Genesis 13:15 (cf. 17:8; 24:7), his appeal to the testamentary custom may well have been motivated by the fact that later in chapter 15 these promises of God, through a solemn ceremony, are 'ratified' as the very first covenant (διαθήκη, Gen. 15:18). The word 'promise' is missing in the OT but nobody would dispute its appropriateness, as Dunn 187 points out.

[58] Dunn 185–187 turns Paul's antithesis of promise and law as a positive remark on the faith-character of the latter: 'what comes after faith (=law) must be consistent with faith'. This certainly enables him to provide a place for the law and 'the election of Israel', but at the cost of Paul's plain logic.

that it is δι' ἐπαγγελίας that God showed his grace to Abraham (κεχάρισται, v. 18b).

Our exposition thus far is intended to clarify the thrust of v. 18, which is crucial for understanding the function of the promise language within Paul's argument in vv. 15–18. All too often this verse is interpreted as if it was about how Abraham *received* the promised inheritance, to which v. 18b provides an unequivocal answer of 'through promise'. Then the whole discussion in vv. 15–18 about promise and inheritance operates within the personal history of Abraham: God not only promised inheritance to Abraham (v. 16) but he actually *gave* it to him (v. 18b). Already for Abraham the promise has become a *fulfilled* promise.[59] In this way Paul's argument, which is designed to press the chronological priority of the promise (vv. 15–16a), has become an argument based on the dynamic of promise and fulfillment exemplified by the life of Abraham (v. 18).

Against this interpretation, however, we have to present the following four points. First, if this is the case, Paul is in fact presenting two separate lines of reasoning: 1) the chronological priority of the promise (vv. 16–17), and 2) Abraham's experience of actually receiving the inheritance through promise (v. 18b). Paul begins with the one and finishes with the other. Though not impossible, this seems a bit inept since if Abraham had already received his promised inheritance, it alone would have been enough to settle the matter, and Paul would not have had to devise such a 'dubious'[60] chronological argument in the first place.

Secondly, the majority interpretation ignores the thrust of the story in Genesis text itself to which Paul is appealing here. In the Abrahamic cycle, it emerges quite clearly that from the first the promise is not intended for Abraham himself but only for his seed. The very first utterance of God's promise, given at the time when Abraham has set his foot on the 'promised land' for the first time, is that God would give τὴν γῆν ταύτην, the land of Canaan τῷ σπέρματί σου, without mentioning Abraham himself (12:7). In chapter 15, the final bestowal of the land is more explicitly set to a time four generations later (v. 16), and explicitly confirmed as a covenant, repeating God's earlier statement in 12:7 *verbatim*: τῷ σπέρματί σου

---

[59] This is the consensus. E.g., Calvert, 'Abraham' (1993) 4 and more recently, Eckstein, *Verheißung* (1996) 113, 188–189. Cf. Betz 159–160.

[60] Dunn 183, 186; *Theology* (1993) 88, 96–97 brands Paul's chronological logic 'unsatisfactory' and 'dubious', which he thinks is why Paul brings in another ground in 3:18 and drops it in Romans. Blaming Paul, however, does more damage to Dunn himself than to Paul. In a way Paul argument in Romans 4 is chronological too. Cf. Räisänen, *Law* (1983) 43–44.

δώσω τὴν γῆν ταύτην (v. 18).[61] This understanding is also reflected in
Psalm 104 (LXX), where the Psalmist, having referred to God's promise of
the land, tells us that the patriarchs, being small in number, stayed in that
very land as 'strangers' (παροίκους ἐν αὐτῇ) and had to wander from one
nation to another (vv. 11–13; cf. v. 44).[62] Paul seems to be well aware of
this 'fact' in history of his fathers, when he says that the 'promises', not
the land itself, were given to Abraham and to his seed. And his strategic
identification of this 'seed' with Christ as the co-bearer of this promise
(vv. 16, 19) renders it very unlikely that he   thinks of the promise as
already fulfilled within Abraham's lifetime.

Thirdly, and most crucially, we should take careful note of the wording
in v. 18b. Most translations and commentaries, assuming Abraham's actual
reception of the inheritance, take κεχάρισται to be transitive with
ἡ κληρονομία in v. 18a as the omitted but assumed object. Then, with the
supply of the supposedly missing αὐτήν, the clause translates: 'But God
gave *it* (i.e., the inheritance) to Abraham through promise'.[63] This is not,
however, necessarily the best reading of the sentence. Paul's choice of
χαρίζομαι instead of more straightforward words such as δίδωμι[64] and the
lack of an object should be given their full weight. The verb χαρίζομαι can
certainly mean 'to give' but it does so only when accompanied by a direct
object (e.g., Rom 8:32). Without one it takes on the meaning of 'to show
oneself to be gracious to someone', typically with an indirect object of
person. While δίδωμι can retain the meaning 'to give' even when the
expected object is omitted (1 Cor 3:5; 2 Cor 9:9), χαρίζομαι always means
'be gracious' which in certain contexts takes on the sense of 'forgive' or
'be gracious' (Lk 7:21; 2 Cor 2:7; Eph 4:32; Col 3:13). Even with a direct

---

[61] Cf. Foerster, *TDNT* 3:775.

[62] Stephen's opinion in Acts 7:5 that what God 'gave' Abraham 'and to his seed' is
not the 'inheritance' itself but 'the promise to give it to him and his seed' coheres nicely
with Paul's thought here: καὶ οὐκ ἔδωκεν αὐτῷ κληρονομίαν ἐν αὐτῇ οὐδὲ βῆμα ποδός
καὶ ἐπηγγείλατο δοῦναι αὐτῷ εἰς κατάσχεσιν αὐτὴν καὶ τῷ σπέρματι αὐτοῦ. There is
no reason to doubt that Stephen here states something taken for granted as a fact, at least
for his hearers.

[63] So most translations such as NASB, NRSV, RSV, NEB, KJV, JB, NIV. Also Luther
and most commentators. Martyn 337 even clarifies this supplied 'it' as 'inheritance'. On
this ground Foerster, *TDNT* 3:781, n. 26 says 'possession' instead of 'inheritance'. Even
Silva, who is usually very keen on syntactical variation, fails to notice this and sides with
others, providing 'the inheritance' in brackets: 'but it was by promise that God gave [the
inheritance] to Abraham as a gift'. *Galatians* (2001) 192.

[64] In 3:22 Paul uses δίδωμι but then it is the promise and not the inheritance that is
given.

object it can retain such meaning (Lk 7:42; 2 Cor 2:10).[65] Thus the sentence should be rendered, 'God showed Abraham favor through promise', in the sense that giving the promise was an act of showing his grace, and thereby establishing 'promise' as the only abiding covenant.[66] Taken in this way, the point is not Abraham's reception of the inheritance but God's act of giving Abraham the promise as a demonstration of His grace, which is what Paul means by God 'ratifying' his covenant of promise (vv. 16–17).[67] Though it would be fallacious to present it as evidence, the fact that Paul substitutes χαρίζομαι for the much more explicit δίδωμι, the word actually used in Septuagint, also seems to support our interpretation of the verse.

Fourthly, it should be noted that the issue of inheritance, explicitly stated only in v.18a but implicitly present from the first, is not posited *vis-à-vis* Abraham. As the antithesis of law and promise makes clear, it is a Galatian question. For Abraham, who lived 430 years earlier than the law, the antithesis between law and promise would have been a simple irrelevance.[68] Taking up the question how the Galatians are to attain the inheritance, Paul posits two mutually exclusive alternatives before them: promise or law. Then, based on the promise-covenant ratified with Abraham, he demonstrates that it comes only through promise. In v. 18 too, as we have shown, he does not appeal to Abraham to determine how the inheritance was *given* to him. The purpose of v. 18b is to bring home to the Galatians' minds the absurdity of v. 18a by *recapitulating* the fact already stated in v.16, that God's dealing with Abraham was 'through promise'. It does not claim that Abraham actually received the inheritance through promise; it only affirms that God has treated him on the basis of promise-grace. Then in v. 18b Paul is not speaking of Abraham's reception of the inheritance as yet 'another' ground for his argument. Rather, from v. 15 to

---

[65] See *LSJ ad loc. BAGD* 877 allows both possibilities. Eckstein, *Verheißung* (1996) 98, n. 27 and 188, failing to note this syntactical difference, mistakenly insists on 'to give'.

[66] Eckert, *Verkündigung* (1971) 81: 'Dem Abraham aber hat sich durch Verheißung gnädig erwiesen Gott'. He also comments: 'Gott- nachdrücklich an den Schluß gestellt- hat sich ein für einmal für die Verheißung entschieden und Abraham nicht den Gesetzesweg, sondern die Gnade als das Heil geoffenbart'. See also Moltmann, *Hope* (1991) 146; K. Berger, *EDNT* 3:456; Lietzmann 21; Schlier 149; Mußner 242; Hartman, 'Gal 3.15–4.11' (1993) 139; Becker 52; Hays, *Echoes* (1980) 114 ('graced'). Among translations, the German *Einheitsübersetzung* (1979) is a rare exception: 'Gott hat aber durch die Verheißung Abraham Gnade erwiesen.'

[67] Surprisingly, the connection between vv. 16–17 and v. 18 is all too easily ignored.

[68] This point is also clearly reflected on the perfect tense of κεχάρισται in v. 18b, which shows the abiding validity of God's act of grace for the Galatian believers. Moule, *Idiom* (1959) 14–15 calls it the 'perfect of allegory'; Bligh, *Greek* (1966) 145–146; Betz 160, n. 62; Mußner 242; Fung 158.

v. 18 his logic is chronological throughout, for which the early establishment of the promise-covenant with Abraham (v.16), that is, God's dealing with Abraham through promise (v. 18b), is presented as the decisive evidence for the precedence of promise to the later law.

To sum up, Paul makes it crucial for his argument that God gave Abraham his promise(s) nearly 430 years before the law was decreed. On our reading, this is the single point that he makes about the promise *vis-à-vis* Abraham. Once v. 18b is properly understood, we realize that the idea of its 'fulfillment' is not in his mind at all, since his purpose in bringing in Abraham is only to establish the temporal precedence of the promise to the hopelessly 'late' law. Paul points to Abraham as the beginning point of the promise-covenant, and that is all that matters for his argumentative purposes. The dynamic of promise and fulfillment is missing in his interpretation of Abraham story here.[69]

5.5.2 Christ and the Promise (3:16, 19)

We have just shown that in Paul's thought what Abraham received was the promise of inheritance, not the inheritance itself. Does he then, as interpreters unanimously uphold, think that this promise was finally fulfilled by Christ?[70] Concerning the promise itself, how does Christ figure in his argument? Paul does not spend much space discussing this matter, but in a couple of places he explicitly reveals his view of Christ in relation to the promise.

The first statement to look at is, no doubt, 3:16, where Paul identifies the seed of Abraham exclusively as Christ. The problem of Paul's singular interpretation of the collective 'seed' does not concern us here.[71] Whether

---

[69] Many commentators perceive the eschatological character of Paul's idea of the Abrahamic inheritance. See nn. 4–5 in Chapter 6.

[70] Theodore of Mopsuestia and Ambrosiaster in Edwards 44. Burton 155 appeals to vv. 16 and 29, which do not speak of Christ's 'fulfilling' the promise. Hester, *Inheritance* (1968) 65, 67–68, 77–79, 87, 91–92 acknowledges that Christ is described by Paul as the Heir (62–63), but still keeps speaking of him as 'the fulfillment of the Abrahamic promise'. See also Lambrecht, 'Abraham' (1999) 534.

[71] Cf. the charge of Schoeps, *Paul* (1961) 181, n. 3. See Daube, *Rabbinic Judaism* (1956) 440–444. A. Scott, *Christianity* (1961) 154–158 suggests the notion of 'corporate solidarity', taken up by R. Longenecker, *Exegesis* (1975) 123–124. In view of Paul's emphasis on 'singularity', it is unlikely. Cf. Bruce 172.

Some try to explain this move by assuming that 2 Samuel 7:12–14, in which a singular seed of David is promised, functions as a linkage between Genesis and Paul's christological interpretation. Wilcox, 'Promise' (1979) 2–20; Bruce 173; Dahl, *Studies* (1975) 130–131; Meeks, 'Apocalyptic' (1982) 696; Hays, *Echoes* (1989) 85; J. Scott, 'Curse' (1993) 219. There is no indication, however, that Paul assumes on the side of his readers the knowledge of this text. The dynamic of the Genesis story itself is sustained by the effort to affirm Isaac being the exclusive and singular seed over against other

persuasive or not, his intention is clear anyway: the promise was given to Abraham and his 'singular' seed. This seed is, surprisingly, not Isaac but Christ. Then, it follows, it is not only to Abraham but also to Christ that God gave his promise since he gave it to Abraham 'and to his seed' (3:16; Gen 12:3; 18:18; 24:7). In this verse, then, Christ is depicted not as one who *fulfilled* the Abrahamic promise, but as one who *received* it together with Abraham.[72] Despite the illuminating silence of the commentators on this very point,[73] Paul's meaning cannot be otherwise.

The idea of the Christ as the bearer of the Abrahamic promise implied here is in fact explicitly stated in v. 19, in the context of explaining the *raison d'être* of the law. Since the primary issue here is not Christ but the law, once again, commentators mostly miss the significance of Paul's characterization of Christ as the recipient of promise.[74] Having stripped the law of its ability to mediate the inheritance (vv. 15–18), Paul then consolidates his argument by putting the law in its own place: 'Why then the law? It was added because of transgression, till the offspring should come *to whom the promise had been made* (ἄχρις οὗ ἔλθῃ τὸ σπέρμα ᾧ ἐπήγγελται)....' Here Paul's answer is twofold: 1) the law was intended for sin and not for inheritance; 2) it was intended only for a limited time. The *terminus ad quem* of this interim measure is the coming of the seed. The σπέρμα in this verse obviously picks up the talk of the singular σπέρμα in 3:16 identified as Christ: καὶ τῷ σπέρματι αὐτοῦ.

What is more interesting for our purpose is the seeming aside added to the predicate Christ-seed, ᾧ ἐπήγγελται, here rendered '*to whom* the promise has been made'. This is the most probable meaning of the dative in the context in which God utters the promise both to Abraham and his seed Christ: 'Now the promises were made to Abraham and καὶ τῷ

---

competitors such as Eleazer and Ishmael. In view of this, Paul's taking the 'seed' in Genesis text to be a singular is not as strange as is often claimed. What is more striking is his identification of this 'seed' with Christ instead of Isaac.

[72] Hoffmann, *NIDNTT* 3:73. The distorting effect of a prior assumption is most clear in Eckstein, *Verheißung* (1996) 183 who contradicts the plain meaning of the verse by appealing to 3:6–14: 'Er hat nicht wie Abraham selbst den Segen *zugesprochen bekommen* (3.6,9,16,18), sondern ihn durch sein stellvertretendes Sterben am Kreuz *verwirklicht* (3,13f.)' (Emphasis his). Patte, *Paul's Faith* (1983) 211–214 speaks of a sort of 'typological' fulfillment.

[73] Most commentaries, preoccupied with Paul's exegetical *method*, neglect the *meaning* generated by it. But see Schniewind/Friedrich, *TDNT* 2:583; Fung 156. As Sand, *EDNT* 2:14–15 exemplifies, however, acknowledging this does not prevent them from speaking of Christ as the fulfiller of the promise.

[74] Part of the reason is, no doubt, the context in which the law, not the promise, is Paul's primary concern. However, it also seems to have to do with the assumption that Christ *must* be the fulfiller of the promise, as Williams, 'Promise' (1988) 710–711 notes.

σπέρματι αὐτοῦ'.[75] Here then Paul refers back to the very 'seed' who was 'there' with Abraham, or, using the phrase of Hebrews, the seed who was 'in the loins of Abraham' (Heb 7:9–10), as the co-recipient of God's promise in v. 16a, to mark out the end of the law and the resumption or reestablishment of the original promise. Once again, nothing is said about Christ 'fulfilling' the promise. Just like Abraham, he comes in as its recipient. As far as we can tell from the text of Galatians, Paul's view of Christ as the recipient of the promise is beyond doubt.[76]

Even in the later epistle Romans we see that Paul still maintains basically the same view of Christ in relation to God's promise. In the fashion observed in Galatians, his discussion of sonship (8:14–15) leads to the Spirit (8:16), and then to the heirship of believers (8:17): 'and if children, then heirs, heirs of God and joint heirs with Christ (συγκληρονόμοι Χριστοῦ) – if, in fact, we suffer with him so that we may also be glorified with him'. As the prefixed σύν makes clear,[77] Christ is not the one who fulfils God's promise, but one who, as the heir *par excellence*, shares the same promise of God, i.e., the promise of future glorification.[78] Even at the time of Romans, Paul still holds the same view of Christ as the fellow heir of the Gentile believers, which further supports our reading: *in Galatians, Christ is not the fulfiller of the Abrahamic promise but its original co-recipient.*[79]

---

[75] Apart from the prior assumption of 'fulfillment', there is nothing in the context to justify the renderings of JNT: 'about whom'; and NIV: 'until the Seed to whom the promise referred had come'. Also Eckstein, *Verheißung* (1996) 198, 225: 'von dem die Verheißung sagt'; Campbell, 'Coming' (1999) 8: 'in relation to whom the promise was made'; Duncan 112; Donaldson, 'Curse' (1986) 100; Barclay, *Truth* (1988) 90: 'until "the seed" came to inherit the blessing'.

[76] Eckert, *Verkündigung* (1971) 80 speaks of both Abraham and Christ as 'Verheißungsträger'.

[77] Instructively, in Ephesians 3:6 the same idea of συγκληρονόμοι is used to express the equal status of the Gentile believers with the Jewish Christians.

[78] Conzelmann, *Outline* (1969) 206 notes the 'eschatological reservation' in the passage. The attempt of Hammer, 'Comparison' (1960) 271 to interpret the αὐτόν in Rom 4:13 christologically to make him '*the* heir' is falsified by 4:14, where the point is 'heirs' in plural. Even granted his rendering, it does not follow that Christ somehow becomes the 'means to the inheritance'.

[79] Williams, 'Promise' (1988) 710, n. 4 and 718, n. 17. Many acknowledge this point. The puzzle is, however, that this observation of Christ the Heir is often, without justification, overridden by Christ the fulfiller of the promise. For example, Schniewind/Friedrich rightly observe, 'He is the true Heir of the promise, of the universal inheritance, and He determines the fellow-heirs. He who has put on Christ (Gal. 3:27), who is in Christ Jesus (3:28), who belongs to Christ, is the seed of Abraham, κατ' ἐπαγγελίαν κληρονόμοι (3:29)'. Then, somewhat later, citing Rom 15:8, 2 Cor 1:20, and Gal 3:14, they declare that 'the promises have been fulfilled in Christ'. *TDNT* 3:583–584. Hester, *Inheritance* (1968) describes Christ as the fulfillment of the promise by

Paul's depiction of Christ as the Verheißungsträger demands that we should not construe Paul's argument of 'promise' from a 'realized eschatological' point of view. 'Promise' serves a very important purpose in his argument, but it does so not as the 'fulfilled' promise but as the promise in the original sense of the word. Of course, claiming that Christ is not the fulfillment of the Abrahamic promise, we are not relativizing the eschatological decisiveness of the Christ event. Our point is simply that Paul does not explain this significance in terms of the fulfillment of the *Abrahamic* promise.

5.5.3 The Galatians and the Promise (3:19–22)

In what relation do the Galatian believers then stand to this Abrahamic promise? It clearly remained a promise for Abraham; nowhere in Galatians does Paul say that Christ has fulfilled it. Do we then have any indication in his argument that it is somehow realized in the life of the Gentile believers, as most interpreters mistakenly infer from 'the promise of the Spirit' in 3:14?[80] As is clear from vv. 15–18, 21 and 4:21–31, for Paul 'promise' is a conceptual tool employed to highlight the *promissory character* of God's relationship with Abraham in the matters of 'seed' and 'inheritance', namely, his gracious initiative in carrying out his plan with Abraham. Despite the common assumption otherwise, when Paul directly addresses the Galatian situation, the idea of promise does not come up as prominently as other motifs. This observation, in an indirect way, weakens the assumption of a fulfilled promise.

In vv. 19–25 Paul discusses the two competing principles of law and promise, this time focusing on the nature of the former. Paul states: ἀλλὰ συνέκλεισεν ἡ γραφὴ τὰ πάντα ὑπὸ ἁμαρτίαν, ἵνα ἡ ἐπαγγελία ἐκ πίστεως Ἰησοῦ Χριστοῦ[81] δοθῇ τοῖς πιστεύουσιν. Here the function of the

---

incorporating the Gentile believers' justification by faith into the idea of the promise (3:6–9) and extending the promise to include the promise of progeny which, according to him, has been fulfilled in the Gentile believers' becoming the seed of Abraham in Christ (90–91). But the core of the promise is that of the land, that is, of the kingdom. He cannot say that this promise, too, has already been fulfilled, and he does list it as part of 'not yet' (97–98). He then takes the passage where the notion of 'not yet' is most prominent as the ground for 'already'. Similarly J. Scott, 'Curse' (1993) 219; Goppelt, *Typos* (1982) 136–140; Hong, 'Jewish Law' (1994) 172–173.

[80] Lambrecht speaks for many: 'For Abraham that [God's] initiative was still a promise; for the Galatians it has become a reality'. 'Abraham' (1999) 527. Also Dunn 195, 197, 199.

[81] We take it in the sense of 'faith in Christ'. Christ's identity as the genuine 'seed' hangs solely on *his being the carrier of God's promise* as Abraham and not his faithfulness. The question then is how this promise in Christ becomes available for the Gentiles. To this, Paul answers, 'by faith'. Christ was surely faithful, but it is not the point in Paul's argument here. *Contra*, Hays, *Faith* (1983) 110–115; Cousar, *Cross* (1990)

law, now surprisingly called 'the Scripture', is described as that of 'shutting up everything under sin' instead of 'giving life' (cf. 3:21). The purpose[82] of this arrangement is 'so that the promise which comes from faith in Christ might be given to those who believe'. The purpose of the law was not to compete with the promise as a way to inheritance/righteousness. On the contrary, it was there in order to enable the promise to stand firm as the only way to this inheritance of righteousness.

This verse is commonly interpreted in the sense that by believing in Christ the believers receive the 'promise', namely, 'what has been promised'.[83] For some who connect the passage to 3:14, this statement refers primarily to the reception of the Spirit by the believers at the time of their conversion. Or for others, it means the receiving of the benefits promised to Abraham and now realized in Christ such as justification, sonship, inheritance, etc.[84] In either case, the emphasis falls on the realized, and therefore now available, character of the promise, and for that matter, on the crucial significance of the Christ event as the (beginning) point of the fulfillment of God's promise.[85]

On its own, this is a legitimate way of reading the passage.[86] This runs, however, against the clear thrust of the context in which, as observed above, the motif of fulfillment is conspicuous by its absence. If Christ is clearly described as the recipient of the promise, not its fulfiller, it follows that the believers 'in Christ' also share the same identity as its recipient. It is far better then to take 'giving of the promise' in its normal sense, namely, in the sense of giving the promise itself, not its fulfillment. The believers, ἐκ πίστεως, have become the recipients of the same promise of God.[87]

Once we read the passage in this way, we can see how well it fits into the wider context. In vv. 16 and 19 we have seen that Christ is singled out as the sole recipient of the Abrahamic promise. Now here in v. 22 the

---

119; most recently, D. Campbell, 'Coming' (1999). Faith is christological not because it *excludes* any anthropological reference but because this human faith points to Christ. See n. 23 in chapter 3.

[82] Here the conjunction ἵνα can denote either purpose or result, without affecting the flow of Paul's argument. Cf. Moule, *Idiom* (1959) 142–143.

[83] This is the consensus view.

[84] So Hester, *Inheritance* (1968) 55 (Abraham = beginning; believers = fulfillment).

[85] So Hester, *Inheritance* (1968) 48–50, 67, 78, 119, 123. For Beker, *Paul* (1980) 97–98, since the Abrahamic promise 'has been confirmed and fulfilled in Christ', it is 'no longer the object of hope'. Recently, Eckstein, *Verheißung*, (1996) 210, 212: 'Verheißungs*gut*' or 'Verheißungs*gabe*'. Hansen, *Abraham* (1989) 131; Ridderbos 142; Schlier 165; Mußner 254; Martyn 361.

[86] Cf. Heb 11:13, 33, 39 (Cf. 11:9).

[87] *Contra* most interpreters. Eckert, *Verkündigung* (1971) 84 seems the least problematic: '... damit die Verheißung aus Glauben, dem einzigen Heilsprinzip, den an Christus Glaubenden zuteil würde'.

Gentile believers, by way of believing him, join the same rank of promise-bearers together with Christ. In fact, this is also the idea expressed in the following context (vv. 23–29). By faith (cf. v. 26), believers are baptized into Christ and thereby clothed with Christ himself (v. 27). In this way, they now belong to Christ (ὑμεῖς Χριστοῦ), the only legitimate seed of Abraham to whom the promise has been made (vv. 16, 19), and therefore they too are also registered as the same seed of Abraham (v. 29).[88] It means that, on the ground of their faith (διὰ πίστεως) and subsequent inclusion into the σπέρμα proper, the Gentile believers too take on the identity of τοῦ ᾽Αβραὰμ σπέρμα, and therefore carry the same promise together with Abraham and Christ. With God's promise given to them, they now look forward to receiving the promised inheritance: they are κατ᾽ἐπαγγελίαν κληρονόμοι (v. 29).

Hence the history of promise from Abraham to Christ, and ultimately to the Galatian believers, is not a story of its eschatological fulfillment but of its succession, the story of *how God's promise continues to find its proper audience*, or *how God continues to create the heirs to his unchanging promise*.[89] The first successor of this Abrahamic promise is Christ, the only seed to whom God's promises were originally addressed. Then follows those who participate in this rightful seed 'by faith', and are taken up into this history of God's promise. The history of 'promise' still continues, no doubt, until the promise/inheritance is finally given to the promise bearers. Only through this promise, however, in which the Gentile believers participate by their faith in Christ, will they be able to attain to the promised inheritance.

5.6 Promise and 'the Fullness of Time' (4:4)

Along with Paul's reference to the promise of the Spirit in 3:14b, scholars often find the idea of fulfillment[90] and even the 'new age'[91] in the interesting phrase, τὸ πλήρωμα τοῦ χρόνου in 4:4.[92] There the phrase,

---

[88] So Fung 117.

[89] So in Romans 4:16 Paul says: διὰ τοῦτο ἐκ πίστεως, ἵνα κατὰ χάριν, εἰς τὸ εἶναι βεβαίαν τὴν ἐπαγγελίαν παντὶ τῷ σπέρματι, οὐ τῷ ἐκ τοῦ νόμου μόνον ἀλλὰ καὶ τῷ ἐκ πίστεως ᾽Αβραάμ, ὅς ἐστιν πατὴρ πάντων ἡμῶν. Once again, as Paul' use of βεβαίαν makes clear, the point is confirmation, not fulfillment.

[90] G. Vos, *Eschatology* (1930) 26; Ridderbos, *Paul* (1975) 44–49; Hammer, 'Comparison' (1960) 269; Mußner 269; Bruce 194; Kümmel, *Theology* (1973) 144; Cook, 'Prescript' (1992) 517.

[91] G. Vos, 'Spirit' (1912); Schlier 165; Fung 184; Dunn, *Paul* (1998) 420.

[92] This motif finds parallels in other contemporary writings: Eph 1:10; Mk 1:15; Lk 24:24; Jn 7:8, 30; Tobit 14:5; *2 Bar* 40:4; 70:2–71:1; *4 Ezra* 11:44. Also *M-M ad loc* and

corresponding to ἡ προθεσμία τοῦ πατρός in the illustration (v. 3), signifies the time of Christ's coming: 'Then, when the fullness of time came, God sent his son ....' (v. 4). Here the idea of 'the fullness of time' clearly refers to the arrival of the time God had set to send Christ, and in this sense it certainly delivers the sense of eschatological decisiveness. Within the Galatian context, the coming of 'the fullness of time' certainly marks the end of the era of παιδαγωγός and the effective beginning of the time of 'faith' and 'promise' for the Gentile believers.

We should be careful, however, not to overload Paul's language. More specifically, it is certainly squeezing the text too much to combine 'the fullness of time' with the motif of the Abrahamic 'promise' so as to produce the idea of 'fulfilled promise' as a concomitant of the advent of Christ. Three observations can be made. First, since the word can mean many different things depending on context, the precise nuance of the phrase should first be determined within the context of 4:1–7. In this particular argument, the phrase corresponds to ἡ προθεσμία τοῦ πατρός in v. 3. Since the latter clearly refers to the arrival of the time set beforehand by the father, it is also very probable that this should be the dominant sense of 'the fullness of time'.[93]

Secondly, we should note that Paul refers to God sending his son in 'the fullness of time' in order to speak of him 'being under the law'. As is clear from his discussion of the law in 3:19–25, the most crucial point that Paul makes about the law is the 'no longer' of slavery: since Christ came, we are no longer under the law; the designated time of the law has now expired. Here too the same concern is present since Paul concludes his argument in this way: 'therefore, you are no longer slaves but sons!' (4:7a). At least in the Galatian context, Paul's interest in time is dominated by his concern to affirm the *termination* of slavery under the law *after* Christ.

Thirdly, and more decisively, this argument is *not* based on the Abrahamic tradition. The analogy is most probably to Greco-Roman testamentary custom.[94] Even if it has a Jewish provenance,[95] it must be from the Exodus tradition. In other words, here the motif of the (Abrahamic) promise is simply missing. Paul's point here is not incorporation into the community of promise-bearers but the direct adoption by God himself. Instead of the 'seed-heir of Abraham', therefore, the believers are now called 'son-heirs of God'. Of course, Paul's final point is the same (heir), but each time he scores this point by taking a

---

Strack/Billerbeck 3:570. For further references, see also Delling, *TDNT* 6: 283–311; Schlier 195; Mußner 269, n. 114 (Qumran).

[93] NEB; JNT: 'the appointed time'; Lührmann 80.

[94] This is the majority view.

[95] See n. 2 in chapter 6.

different route. It only disrupts his contextual argument to try to read the notion of 'fulfilled promise' into his talk of 'the fullness of time'.[96]

5. 7 Conclusion

Thus far we have traced Paul's use of the concept of promise in Galatians and demonstrated that, contrary to the widespread assumption, he does not use the concept in the sense of a 'fulfilled' promise. Taking his language seriously, we observed that at least in the Galatian context Christ, and therefore believers too, are depicted as the recipients of the Abrahamic promise without any idea of its fulfillment either in Christ or in the believers' lives. This idea of Christ and believers as the promise-bearers fits well with Paul's emphasis on the believers' status as 'heirs according to promise' (3:29; 4:7), a theme we studied in a previous chapter. Motifs such as promise and inheritance have an inherently futuristic logic built into them. Dahl's judgment on the subject seems apropos:

> According to Paul, God has shown, by sending Jesus Christ and by his death and resurrection, that he remains faithful to his promises even though men have broken his Law. God has not yet fulfilled his promises, but he has confirmed that he will fulfill them. The believers have received a guarantee that they are God's children and coheirs with Christ, but they have not yet taken possession of their inheritance.[97].

---

[96] The lack of the 'fulfillment' motif is perceptively observed by Lührmann 80. But his talk of 'change from the one world to the other' and 'the end of the age of the law and the beginning of the age of faith in the Christ event' too is unfounded. Paul's concern here is not the change of 'the world'; neither does he speak of the change in terms of the change of the 'age'.

[97] Dahl, *Studies* (1977) 136. Despite this sober conclusion, however, he too endorses the consensus that the Spirit represents the fulfillment of the Abrahamic promise. Barrett, 'Allegory' (1975) 12 rightly takes 'promise' and 'inheritance' as referring to the future. See also Horbury, 'Land' (1996) 221.

Chapter 6

Inheritance as a Future Blessing

In chapter 4 we examined Paul's use of the sonship motif and observed that his affirmation of the Galatians' status as 'seed of Abraham' (3:29) and 'sons of God (4:7) was designed to bring out their status as God-appointed 'heirs'. We also examined in the last chapter his use of 'promise' and demonstrated the lack of any evidence for the idea of 'fulfilled promise'. Thus there is nothing to prevent us from construing these ideas as pointers to the eschatological future.

What then does Paul mean by the 'inheritance' and the affirmation that the Galatian believers are now 'heirs' (3:29; 4:7)? Speaking of heirship to God's promised inheritance, is he thinking of something the Galatians already possess either partially or in full? Or is this inheritance still a promise to be realized in the future? These are the questions that we are concerned with in this chapter.[1] Since much of Paul's argument concerns the crucial motif of inheritance, to which both 'heirship' and 'promise' point,[2] clarifying its future eschatological character will give us a further confirmation of the future eschatological structure of Paul's argument as a whole.

6.1 The Idea of 'Realized Inheritance'

In the scholarly discussion of the 'inheritance' in Galatians two major approaches can be discerned. First, there are scholars who limit the scope of the 'inheritance' strictly to what has *already* been realized. For them the 'inheritance' means 'the *fully* realized inheritance'. According to this view the edge of Paul's polemic falls on the very point of 'already' and, consequently, the 'superfluous' nature of the Galatians' enthusiasm for

---

[1] This is not the question Paul himself is asking in the letter. We raise this issue to question the widespread but problematic assumption of 'realized inheritance'.

[2] 'It is this concept of the "inheritance" (the content of the promise to Abraham and "to his seed": eternal life), rather than sonship of God, which overarches the whole discussion from 3:15 (implicitly from 3:1) to 5:1 (cf. 5:21)'. Byrne, *Sons* (1979) 189. Similarly, Lührmann 66; Witherington 231.

another inheritance. By bringing out the fully realized nature of the 'inheritance', they argue, Paul intends to demonstrate the sufficiency of faith and the Spirit over against the propaganda of the agitators. Needless to say, the specified 'inheritance' refers to the gift of the Spirit, i.e., 'the promise of the Spirit' (3:14), which, in turn, converges with other 'realized' blessings such as justification, sonship, participation in Christ and freedom from the law. The connotation of the inheritance is rich, but its boundary is strictly confined to what has *already* been realized.[3]

There are, however, a group of scholars who do recognize the future eschatological nature of inheritance. For them too, without doubt, the inheritance has already been realized and thus is now present, at least in part. In this respect, they too share the consensus that Paul's emphasis falls most heavily on the point of 'already'. However, these scholars also acknowledge that 'inheritance' intrinsically belongs to the future. In this way, the term inheritance becomes a comprehensive epithet for 'the sum total of the eschatological blessings' and 'the whole complex of salvation',[4] *partially* realized but still to be consummated in its *fullness*. Here the Spirit marks the decisive beginning point in the realization of the inheritance. Thus, for this group of scholars, it is customary to speak of the Spirit as a 'first fruit' and 'down payment' as in Romans 8:14–17, 2 Corinthians 5:5 and Ephesians 1:13–14 (cf. Tit 3:6–7). The result is the well-known eschatological dialectic of 'already and not yet', with inheritance being 'a uniquely appropriate vehicle for conveying the characteristically Pauline dialectic of present and future'.[5]

---

[3] For Burton 225–226 the inheritance means 'justification, acceptance with God, possession of the Spirit'. The Galatians are heirs 'as present possessors of the inheritance', and Paul's emphasis lies on 'that which is already possessed'. Betz: 'all the benefits of God's work of salvation' (159), but with the Spirit as 'the fulfillment of the promise' (152–153) in mind, what he in fact means is 'God's *present* work of salvation' (160, emphasis added). Eckstein, *Verheißung* (1996) 180, 183, 189, 225 stresses that the dominant idea in the inheritance is the 'present bestowal of salvation' (liberation from the curse, justification, the gift of the Spirit and sonship) and not 'the future consummation of salvation'. Similarly, Smiles, *Gospel* (1998) also places a very strong emphasis on the present reality of salvation (144). For him, the inheritance in Galatians is one of many terms in which Paul conceives of the present 'life of faith' (138, 168), and never 'first fruits' or 'down payment' (74). Cole 103, 111: 'the actual "enjoyment" of the benefits already promised under the will'. He identifies it with the gift of the Spirit. Martyn 323, 342–343, 392: 'the church-creating Spirit' of which the Galatians 'have been recipients for some time'; Fung 152, 177–178: 'the reception of the Spirit, justification and sonship' which are all synonymous; Witherington, 292.

[4] Byrne, *Sons* (1979) 156–157, 160–161, 174–175, 189.

[5] Furnish, *Ethics* (1968) 126–135 (here 128). For him, the inheritance, means 'salvation' and 'life' in the fullest sense of the word, is in the future and thus still to be awaited. 'An "heir" is, by definition, one who …waits for the receipt of something which

Whether acknowledging the eschatological aspect or not, they all agree
on one point: there is an unmistakable element of 'already' in Paul's idea
of 'inheritance', and it is 'the gift of the Spirit' that constitutes the heart of
such 'realized inheritance'. Is this, however, a proper reading of his
argument? The scholarly vote is virtually unanimous at this point. Without
doubt the most crucial evidence for this view of the Spirit as the
fulfillment of the promise is 'the promise of the Spirit' in 3:14b.[6] In the
previous chapter, however, we demonstrated that this particular concept
does not belong to the Abrahamic tradition that Paul discusses in 3:15
onwards. Without this particular phrase, do we then have any other
evidence for the notion of 'realized inheritance'?

At this point, a general observation seems in order. The word
'inheritance' is by definition future-oriented. [7] Hence the notion of
'realized inheritance'[8] is, to say the least, a very difficult, if not self-
contradictory, concept. Not only in early Judaism but also in early
Christianity as a whole the concept was used only for future eschatological
references.[9] Paul himself also belongs to the same tradition (Rom 4:13–14;
8:17). Even in Ephesians and Colossians, where the thrust of 'realized

---

is not yet given'. However, insofar as the heir has 'a new status already', it can be said
that the future 'has decisively entered the present'. Thus Paul can identify the 'promise'
as 'the promise of the Spirit' (3:14), since the Spirit signifies 'the presence in this age of
the power of the age to come'. In this sense, 'the dialectic of present and future finds its
focal point in Paul's concept of the Spirit'. For Furnish, this overlapping of the ages
constitutes the key to the character of Paul's gospel, providing the eschatological
framework of the dialectic 'indicative and imperative', which he considers the essence of
Paul's ethics. See also Foerester, *TDNT* 3:782–785; Schlier 150; Hester, *Inheritance*
(1968) 41; *idem*, 'Heilsgeschichte' (1967) 118–125; Mußner 276–277; Bruce 191, 251;
Hendriksen 140: 'future glory'; Dunn 186, 306–307: 'the inheritance of the Kingdom';
idem, Paul (1999) 466. (In its outlook the whole section of 'Eschatological tension'
resembles Furnish). At one point, Burton 185 does speak of the Spirit as 'earnest', but his
actual definition of the inheritance is that of the former group.

[6] A survey of scholarly interpretation easily shows how much they depend on this
single phrase for their view of a realized inheritance. See below.

[7] A point frequently acknowledged but all too easily compromised, as in Furnish,
Ethics (1968) 126–135 and Dunn 186.

[8] We use this phrase, 'realized inheritance', which is not used by other scholars, to
refer to the consensus way of interpreting the concept.

[9] The word 'to inherit' is 'an eschatological technical term in late Jewish literature,
implying a share in the coming Kingdom'. Jeremias, *Promise* (1968) 68. In Synoptics, we
have such idiomatic expressions as 'inheriting the land'; 'inheriting eternal life';
'inheriting the kingdom'. In Hebrews the motif takes on a special importance. The note
of realized inheritance is there but strictly for Christ (1:2, 4) and people in the past such
as Noah and Esau (11:7; 12:17). For the letter's recipients, the inheritance always refers
to something in the future (1:14; 6:12, 17–20; 9:15; 11:8). The references in other NT
writings also accord with this perspective (1 Pet 1:4; 3:9; Jas 2:5; Rev 21:7).

eschatology' becomes much more prominent, the word 'inheritance' is still reserved for what is yet to come in the future (Eph 1:14, 18; 3:6; 5:5; Col 3:24).[10] The same applies to the Pastorals.[11] *By positing the 'realized inheritance', we are then making the Paul of Galatians a glaring exception within the tradition of early Judaism and early Christianity, including Paul himself.* This is by no means impossible, but it certainly is unusual, to say the least. Of course, one can posit the idea, but not without unequivocal evidence.

6.2 A Realized Inheritance in 4:1–7?

Apart from 3:15–29 and 4:21–31, Paul also discusses the theme of 'heir' in 4:1–7, a passage we did not take up in the last chapter since it does not concern the Abrahamic promise. Do we have here evidence for a realized inheritance? The passage divides into three sections: illustration (λέγω δε, vv. 1–2), application (οὕτως καὶ ἡμεῖς, vv. 3–4), and further explication (vv. 5–7). Much ink has been spilled to determine the provenance of the illustration (vv.1–2) and the metaphor of 'adoption' (v. 5).[12] As Burton states, however, this problem does not really affect the flow of Paul's argument.[13] The real interpretive problem lies in what is already clear. Regardless of its possible provenance, the illustration clearly describes ὁ κληρονόμος, who is presently a νήπιος, and still ὑπὸ ἐπιτρόπους καὶ οἰκονόμους. Nevertheless, being an heir, he is also said to be the κύριος πάντων.

At first glance it seems that Paul compares those before Christ to an 'heir' and 'master' before his coming-of-age. After προθεσμία, he then

---

[10] On this basis, Hammer, 'Comparison' (1960) 267–272 asserts that Paul's concept of '(realized) inheritance' is different from that in Ephesians.

[11] In the Pastorals, the motif occurs only once in Titus 3:7. There the eschatological character stands out clearly both by its contrast to the 'already' of justification (δικαιωθέντες) and by its combination with the hope of eternal life (κληρονόμοι γενηθῶμεν κατ' ἐλπίδα ζωῆς αἰωνίου).

[12] There are four major views about the provenance of the imagery. (i) For the Roman law, see Hester, *Inheritance* (1968) 18–19, 59 and *passim*; Lyall, *Slaves* (1984) 67–99; Byrne, *Sons* (1979) 174; Dunn 210; Williams 107. (ii) For a Hellenistic legal background, see Schlier 189; Mußner 266; Moore-Crispin, 'Use' (1989), 203–223; Witherington 281–283. (iii) For a Jewish provenance, see Rossel, 'Adoption' (1952), 233–234; Theron, 'Adoption in the Pauline Corpus' (1956) 6–14; most eloquently J. Scott, *Adoption* (1992) 121–186, who argues extensively for an 'Exodus typology' in Paul's illustration. (iv) Ridderbos 152 thinks that Paul appeals to the 'a generally current usage' and not any specific legal system. Some remain open on this issue, e.g., R. Longenecker 164; Fung 180, n. 59.

[13] Burton 215.

becomes a full-grown adult who, as κύριος πάντων, finally enters into full possession of his designated inheritance. Then, it seems, the redemption of Christ is likened to a kind of 'spiritual maturity'[14] or 'coming-of-age' after which the child 'heir-master' gains full authority over his inheritance. 4:1–7 then is clearly a case for the 'realized inheritance'. The 'heir' at the conclusion must be an heir in actual possession of the promised inheritance (4:7).[15]

Plausible as it may sound, however, this reading overlooks the problem posed by Paul's illustration. The talk of a 'child-heir' and 'master' is fine in itself, but surprise sets in when he says that this heir is no better than a slave: οὐδὲν διαφέρει δούλου. That Paul at this point 'overdraws the picture' is frequently observed,[16] but the problem runs deeper: the picture of an heir-in-slavery is not a mere exaggeration but an outright contradiction in Paul's own terms. For him κληρονόμος is an epithet strictly reserved for 'those who are in Christ' (3:26–29), while 'slavery' characterizes anyone before or outside Christ (5:1, 13), who can never join the rank of the heir (4:21–31). His clear-cut antithetical thinking in the letter simply does not allow any room for such a hybrid as 'heir-in-slavery' (4:7!). He seems to be mixing up the oil of heirship and the vinegar of slavery, thereby creating a sheer impossibility. How can anyone be a 'son' and 'heir' even before τὸ πλήρωμα τοῦ χρόνου? How can such a radical change as υἱοθεσία be likened to mere coming-of-age? By likening the Christian before Christ to an heir, is not Paul contradicting himself?[17]

Since Paul's illustration contains two mutually contradictory notions (heirship vs. slavery), it is very risky to take an interpretive key from the illustration itself.[18] The important thing is to observe how Paul himself develops his argument. Illustration is, after all, only an aid and not the main point in an argument. It is the actual point he draws from it that should be the key to the meaning of the argument.[19]

---

[14] Fung 179. The quoted phrase is the title he gives to this passage.

[15] So most interpreters, recently, Dunn, *Paul* (1998) 466.

[16] As Martyn 387 puts it, 'Focusing his attention on the motif of slavery, Paul overdraws the picture because he anticipates the way in which he will use it'. See also Anderson, *Theory* (1996) 149 (ὑπερβολή); Burton 215; Schlier 188; Eckert, *Verkündigung* (1971) 89; Betz 203, n. 12; Mußner 267. This partly explains the difficulty of the provenance problem.

[17] Cf. Hester, 'Heir' (1967) 121 identifies this as 'one of the, if not the, most difficult part of the illustration'. This problem has not been sufficiently appreciated. See n. 28 below.

[18] Cousar 93 also notes this but insufficiently. Cf. Byron, *Slavery* (2003) 183.

[19] *Contra* J. Scott, *Adoption* (1992) 126: 'And, in so far as vv. 1–2 compose the "illustration," they hold the hermeneutical key to the whole passage'. Rightly, R. Longenecker 164: 'Paul, *being more interested in application than precise legal details,*

One possible, and widely held, solution to this problem is to take the illustration as a description of the Jewish Christians before Christ.[20] Such a solution, however, falls to the ground by the very fact that 4:1–7 closely follows 3:29 where 'heirs' already includes both Jews and Gentiles. That the heirship becomes real only in Christ, the singular Seed of Abraham (3:17, 29), simply denies the possibility that Paul should designate the Jews before Christ as 'heirs'. From the first he is speaking of both Jews and Gentiles.[21]

How then are we to interpret Paul's argument here? Several interesting features in his argument come to our attention. First, his preoccupation with the slavery motif stands out immediately: the heir is ὑπό[22] ἐπιτρόπους καὶ οἰκονόμους and οὐδὲν διαφέρει δούλου. As already noted, this is an intentional exaggeration, an anomaly serving to divulge what Paul is really up to with his talk of 'child-heir'.

Paul's conscious focus on 'slavery' continues as he moves on to the application (οὕτως καὶ ἡμεῖς). The term νήπιος remains, but now it is only about slavery: ὑπὸ τὰ στοιχεῖα τοῦ κόσμου[23] ἤμεθα δεδουλωμένοι (v. 3).[24] The subsequent explication further confirms this intention of

---

made the specifics of his illustration conform to his purpose. No illustration is required to represent exactly every aspect of a situation in order to be telling or meaningful.' (Emphasis added). See also Martyn 386.

[20] According to Dunn 210–223, even though they had been God's elected 'sons' all along, they were in virtual slavery under the control of the guardians and trustees (= the law). Then, on their coming-of-age (προθεσμία, τὸ πλήρωμα τοῦ χρόνου), God sent his Son (v. 4) and redeemed them from this slavery under the law (v. 5a). So far so good, but then the problem sets in. If the Jewish Christians were ὑπὸ τὰ στοιχεῖα τοῦ κόσμου before Christ, were their condition not the same to that of the Gentiles enslaved by τὰ ἀσθενῆ καὶ πτωχὰ στοιχεῖα (v. 8)? And what does υἱοθεσία mean (v. 5b)? How can they receive another 'adoption' while already being 'sons'? One may argue that at this point Paul widens the audience, and his subsequent talk of 'adoption', 'receiving the Spirit', 'sonship' and 'heirship' all concern the Gentile Christians too. But Paul keeps speaking of 'we' (v. 5b) without any indication of such change. This way of reading is certainly very handy in maintaining the *Heilsgeschichtliche* continuity, but Paul's logic seems too antithetical for that. Also, with minor variations, Belleville, 'Under Law' (1986) 68; Bruce 193–196; R. Longenecker 165. Witherington 288–290, to make the picture neater, reads ὑμῖν in v. 5 instead of the more strongly attested and generally accepted ἡμῖν. J. Scott, *Adoption* (1992) 121–186 differ from these in that he limits the reference to the Jews to vv. 1–2 (Exodus-type) and takes the whole of vv. 3–7 as referring to believers' redemption (New Exodus-antitype).

[21] Rightly, Burton 215; Schlier 193; Mußner 268; Betz 204; Byrne, *Sons* (1979) 182.

[22] As Dunn 211 points out, Paul's use of this preposition is deliberate.

[23] See n. 31 in chapter 2.

[24] So Mußner 268, rightly considers that the emphasis lies on 'das an den Schluß gestellte, rhythmisch retardierende δεδουλωμένοι' (268); 'Der Apostel sagt nicht νήπιος,

Paul's. The redemption of Christ means the liberation from slavery under the law: τοὺς ὑπὸ νόμον ἐξαγοράσῃ (v. 5a); υἱοθεσία and the resultant sonship is the simple antonym of slavery: ὥστε οὐκέτι εἶ δοῦλος ἀλλὰ υἱός (v. 7a).

On the other hand, Paul's 'neglect' of other motifs is also unmistakable. Just like the child-heir (vv. 1–2), 'we' (v. 3) too were νήπιοι, but this time we are not depicted as 'heirs'. The motif κύριος πάντων also lacks its counterpart in the otherwise neat parallelism between the illustration and the application.[25] It is only natural since in reality the Christians before Christ had never been such a privileged people. Before 'the fullness of time', we are neither 'heir' nor 'master of all'.[26] Illustration fails at this point, and therefore Paul simply drops these motifs as he proceeds to the application. [27] Furthermore, while the application describes both before and

---

sondern δοῦλος, wahrscheinlich im Rückblick auf das ἤμεθα δεδουλωμένοι in v. 3' (276). Also Eckert, *Verkündigung* (1971) 87–90; Schlier 190. Cf. Dunn 210.

[25] Much confusion is caused by κύριος πάντων in v. 2. The phrase is usually rendered 'owner of all', namely, 'possessor of all the promised possessions' (Burton 211; Betz 202; Mußner 267: 'Besitzer'). There are, however, reasons to question this interpretation. First, it is very unlikely that Paul should intend to say that the Galatian believers are already 'possessors of *all* possessions'. However we translate the phrase, the issue is not the prospective inheritance becoming realized. The young heir, though not free enough to dispose it, already possesses and enjoys his inheritance. The only restriction is that he cannot dispose it at will. Thus, most scholars end up saying *Verfügungsrecht* as the point of difference between the baby-heir and the mature one. Then, the issue at stake is not so much the 'already' and 'not yet' of the inheritance as freedom or sovereignty over it. Even in the illustration itself, then, Paul's main concern is not the actualization of the promised inheritance but the change from slavery to freedom.

More importantly, however, Scott has convincingly demonstrated that the whole phrase should be taken as a *Hoheitstitel*. It refers to 'lord of all' and not, as most scholars assume, 'owner of all'. The idea of 'patrimony is simply not mentioned'. Again, the point is not the 'possession' of things, but the condition of 'sovereignty' and 'freedom', intended to produce a strong contrast to the status of 'slavery'. J. Scott, *Adoption* (1992) 130–135. Paul's sole interest in this passage lies in the notion of freedom-slavery and not of 'possession'. It runs against the intention of Paul himself to take this phrase as the evidence for the idea of 'realized inheritance'.

[26] So Mußner 268 (also 271): 'wir waren in der Zeit der Sklavenschaft eben noch keine "Söhne", sondern wurden es nach 3, 26 erst in Jesus Christus durch den Glauben'. Martyn 386, puts it more strongly: 'Paul has no intention of implying that human beings have been God's sons all along, only waiting for the day of their majority. On the contrary, they have been actual slaves, and have therefore to be made into sons'.

[27] By and large, scholarly exposition of this passage is quite ambiguous and confusing due to undue emphasis on the illustration and failure to capture Paul's main point. A good illustration is found in Hester, 'Heilsgeschichte' (1967) 118–125. On the one hand, he says that 'Paul does not say that the heir ceases to be son and heir and becomes lord and owner' (124). In fact, 'he does not cease to be a νήπιος' (122). On the other hand, however, he also states that this heir, once νήπιος, is now given 'a position of mature

after 'the fullness of time', the illustration stops short before telling the story after προθεσμία. Having made his point about the slavery of the child-heir, Paul immediately moves on to his main story without bothering to return to the unfinished illustration.[28] Undue preoccupation with such 'false' motifs will thus ruin the flow of his argument.

The way Paul develops his arguments makes it clear that his concern is not to discuss the *future* of the child-heir, neither his coming-of-age nor his taking possession of a future inheritance.[29] Starting from the illustration about a child 'heir-master', we might expect such a development. Yet, the story he actually tells is not προθεσμία but υἱοθεσία (v. 5a);[30] instead of coming of age and taking possession of the inheritance, he has only now become a son and heir: 'If you are a son, you are also an heir' (v. 7).[31] Heirship was the beginning of Paul's argument; it is also its conclusion.[32]

Paul's initial reference to 'the heir' is best taken in a proleptic sense, spoken from the vantage point of the *present* sonship and heirship: 'when the (now adopted) heir was still in slavery'.[33] It is probably the force of what he said at the end of chapter 3 about 'heirs' that prompted him to begin this argument with the same word. However, since human custom at this point does not really cohere with the redemption in Christ that Paul intends to describe, he has to caricature it to a drastic degree.[34] Even then,

---

responsibility, who is heir and lord of all' (125). His concern for 'Heilsgeschichte' ('already-not yet') is clear enough, but we cannot help wondering how these contradictory statements 'explain' Paul's logic. This sort of ambiguity is present in most interpreters.

[28] So Martyn 389.

[29] As pointed out, the heir's being 'master of all' is not part of Paul's actual conclusion. Likewise the motif of 'immaturity' is also left out. Cf. Schlier 190: '[a]uf νήπιος selbst liegt kein Ton'. See also Martyn 389.

[30] NIV wrongly translates 'adoption' virtually in the sense of coming-of-age: 'we might receive the *full* rights of sons'. (Emphasis added).

[31] Here υἱοθεσία means adoption, not the state of sonship. Rightly, J. Scott, *Adoption* (1992) 175–177; Moore-Crispin, 'Use' (1989) 214.

[32] Dunn 210, and more recently, Brawley, "Contextuality" (2002) 111. *Contra* Burton 226–227. See the perceptive discussion in Anderson, *Theory* (1996) 148.

[33] The proleptic nature of Paul's reference to 'heir' and 'master of all' is perceived by Burton 211–212, but he still mistakenly construes the picture as that from (initial) sonship to actual possession of inheritance.

Martyn 386 speaks of Paul's 'freedom' to 'reaches beyond the legal picture of vv. 1–2, making adoption a chief motif of vv. 5–7'. It may be true, but then the illustration itself becomes rather meaningless. Paul, who first met the risen Christ as late as on his way to Damascus, could say that God had set him apart for the gospel even before he was born. A similar retrospective perspective seems to be at work here.

[34] Martyn 387: 'a useful metaphor is not an image projected from the (human) known into the (divine) unknown. Things are the other way around. A metaphor true to the gospel is produced by the incursion of the unknown into the orb of what is presumed to

his use of the illustration is highly selective, dropping those motifs unsuitable for his purpose.

4:1–7 is not a follow-up of the point presented in 3:15–29 (heirship, 3:29). It is a new argument pressing precisely the same point (heirship, 4:7) from a different angle.[35] As we observed in chapter 4, in 3:15–29 Paul argues for heirship using the motif of σπέρμα. Now in 4:1–7 he makes the same point with the motif of υἱοθεσία. In 3:15–29 they are heirs because they are 'seed' of Abraham participating in *the* Seed; now they are heirs because they have become 'sons' by the work of *the* Son (4:4) and His Spirit (4:6). The mediation is always through Christ, but he is now the 'Son of God' rather than the 'Seed of Abraham'.[36] Thus each time Paul approaches the subject from a different angle but what he tires to affirm remains the same: that the Gentile believers are now heirs, either as the seed of Abraham (3:15–29) or as the sons of God (4:1–7). Naturally, we do not hear anything about the actual possession of the inheritance by this heir. Just as we failed to find any indication of 'realized inheritance' in 3:15–29, here too we do not see any evidence that this is part of Paul's intention.

6.3 Inheritance and the Spirit

In view of the fact that the Spirit is usually hailed by interpreters as the content of 'realized inheritance', it is necessary to clarify the relation between the inheritance and the Spirit at this point. Since in scholarly discussion this decision mostly depends on the 'eschatological' view of the Spirit as the mark of the new age, we shall deal with this point first, before we move on to examination of the data in Galatians.

6.3.1 The Spirit, the New Age?

Speaking of Paul's view of the Spirit, scholars frequently claim that for him the Spirit signifies the time of fulfillment, the arrival of the longed-for new age.[37] Of course, this is not a claim Paul himself makes but an inference scholars make on the basis of the alleged 'intertextuality'.

---

be the known'. The situation is comparable to Jesus' parables, in which vivid realism and striking 'distortion' mix together to make the intended effect upon the audience.

[35] R. Longenecker 161; Dunn 210.

[36] This difference is observed by Martyn 306, 392 and *Issues* (1997) 7–24. However, his claim that the 'descent from Abraham' is introduced by 'the Teachers' which Paul replaces with his own 'descent from God' ruins his insight.

[37] Schweizer, *TDNT* 6:422; Hamilton, *Holy Spirit* (1957) 31, 39; Hill, *Greek Words* (1967) 269; Ridderbos, *Paul* (1975) 64–68, 87; Silva, 'Eschatological Structure' (1994) 150; J. Vos, *Pneumatologie* (1973) 87; Lull, *Spirit* (1980) 170; Fee, *Presence* (1995) 383, 385; Marshall, 'Eschatology' (1997) 57.

Widely held as it may be, there are good reasons to question the propriety of this logic.

First, it is widely acknowledged that the Spirit does not feature prominently in the Jewish eschatological speculation of Paul's day.[38] This does not render an 'eschatological' view of the Spirit impossible but certainly much less likely. Barclay[39] detects the note of eschatological fulfillment in *Jubilees* 1:23–25, but it is an overinterpretation. While it is true that the passage, building on diverse OT passages (cf. Deut 10:16; 14:1; 31:27; Lev 26:40; Neh 9:2; 2 Chr 6:38; 30:6; Jer 31:9; Hos 1:10), speaks of the revitalization of Israel, the motif of 'new age' is simply missing. God's creation of 'a holy spirit' certainly means the creation of 'sons of the living God' (v. 25), which is, however, predicated on their 'cleaving to me and to all my commandments' (v. 24) as the result of God 'cutting off the foreskin of the heart' (v. 23). The point of the passage is, just as in Old Testament passages on which it is based, not the prediction of the new age in the form of the Spirit but the hope of God's decisive intervention perceived as the only solution to the inveterate problem of disobedience (cf. *Ode Sol.* 11:2).

In *1 Enoch* 61:11 too, the motif of the spirit occurs in connection with various ethical qualities. Not surprisingly, we notice that the scene here is that of judgment where the Elect One, now seated on the throne, 'shall judge all the works of the holy ones in heaven above, weighing in the balance their deeds' (61:8) and 'judge the secret ways of theirs' and 'their conduct' (61:9). The point is that one is hard pressed to demonstrate the notion of the spirit or the Spirit carrying in itself some kind of 'eschatological' significance. Of course, it is possible that Paul may have used these texts to formulate his own, 'eschatological' view of the Spirit, but we do not see any clear sign that he is doing that. These texts, standing on their own, do not allow us to speak of the Spirit as a mark of a new age. It is modern scholars who read that note into the texts and then adduce them as evidence for their understanding of the Spirit.

Secondly, to justify this inference therefore scholars typically refer to OT prophecies in which the Spirit is spoken of as a gift of the future (Isa 32:15; 44:3; 59:21; Ezek 11:19; 36:26; 37:14; 39:29; Joel 2:28–32).[40] For

---

[38] Sjöberg, *TDNT* 6:384; J. Vos, *Pneumatologie* (1973) 51, 63; Isaacs, *Spirit* (1976) 82–84. *Contra* Davies, *Rabbinic Judaism* (1970) 208–226; Hill, *Greek Words* (1967) 232 speak of 'a strong hope for the outpouring of the Spirit in the future' but *without* adequate evidence. Note the warning in Levison, 'Spirit' (1997) 57 against the danger of manipulating the 'background' data.

[39] Barclay, *Truth* (1988) 83–85.

[40] Barclay, *Truth* (1988) 83–85; Schweitzer, *Mysticism* (1930) 160; Davies, *Rabbinic Judaism* (1970) 216–217; Furnish, *Ethics* (1968) 130; Bruce, *Paul* (1977) 207; Dunn, *Theology* (1993) 107.

example, Fee claims that '[i]n the light of this kind of intertextuality, one can hardly miss the eschatological implications of Paul's understanding of the Spirit – as fulfillment of God's promised gift of Spirit at the end of the ages'.[41] Fee is overly confident here. While a futuristic thrust is clearly there, the idea of a 'new age' seems to be the product of proof-texting. As is clear especially in Ezekiel, the main concern of the prophets falls on moral renewal, symbolized by the revivication of dry bones. Quite naturally, here 'a new spirit' stands functionally synonymous with 'a new heart' (Ezek 36:26; 37:14; 39:29). In other texts mentioned above too, one does not have to look long to find where the real concern lies. For the prophets the Spirit was not so much the sign of the new age as the source of authentic obedience. Assuming Paul's dependence on the OT tradition for his view of the Spirit, it is perhaps more likely that he seizes on the main motif of moral transformation without necessarily claiming the presence of the new age.[42] That the Spirit *ipso facto* signifies the new age is by no means an obvious inference from these passages.

Thirdly, we have to pay serious attention to the fact that in Galatians Paul *never* makes a statement to such an effect. To be sure, it is not impossible that this idea is so manifest as to obviate any reference to it, but it is extremely unlikely. If this realized eschatological concern is, as scholars usually assume, central to Paul's thought, his silence on the point is striking, especially in view of his extensive discussion of the Spirit. Moreover, granted such an implication as *one* aspect of the Spirit, it still remains that the Spirit also means many other things. Mere references to the experience of the Spirit, therefore, would not have helped the Galatians to detect which possible aspect Paul actually means; if he had really intended the 'new age', he would have said so explicitly, which he fails to do in any of his letters. It is too risky a procedure to construe Paul's argument based on an inference which may or may not be the case.

In this respect, it is also worth noting that we do not find any clear evidence in other early Christian writings for the claim that the Spirit marks the arrival of the new age. In order for the logic of intertextuality to work, this association of the Spirit and the new age should be strong and obvious to anyone familiar with the prophetic promise of the Spirit in the Old Testament. Even in Acts 2 where we come closest to the 'eschatological' view of the Spirit, however, Peter's immediate purpose seems to be convincing those at the scene of the authenticity of the

---

[41] Fee, *Presence* (1995) 304. He comments on 2 Cor 3:6, which he also applies to Galatians.

[42] In early Christian thinking Paul is prominent by his emphasis on the ethical role of the Spirit. Bultmann, *Theology* (1951) 336; Davies, *Rabbinic Judaism* (1970) 177, 220–221; Hill, *Greek Words* (1967) 275; Isaacs, *Spirit* (1976) 87.

phenomena as the signs of the promised Spirit rather than claiming the arrival of the awaited new age on the basis of what is happening before his eyes. If this intertextual logic is not something obvious to everybody, the scholarly claim that Paul views the Spirit as the sure sign of the new age cannot hold the water, for the simple reason that people would not have possibly guessed what he intended to say, unless he makes himself loud and clear on this point. And as is indicated by scholars' heavy dependence on intertextuality, this is precisely what he fails to do in his extant writings.[43]

For Paul the Spirit is most of all a living reality, the presence of the risen Christ himself, through whom his work in the past becomes an ever-relevant reality for believers in the present (3:1; cf. 2:19; 6:14). It is not mere theological shorthand for the 'new age'. His emphasis on the Spirit is therefore not so much a gesture of alleged intertextuality as an act of reminding his converts of the very foundation of their Christian existence[44] with a view to showing what ultimately matters and what is at stake in their pursuit of the hope of righteousness. More will be said on this in the final chapter.

Instead of resorting to the inherently uncertain and often subjective logic of intertextuality to create the notion of a new age about which Paul himself does not seem to care much and reading his argument in that creative line, we first need to hear what he does say *explicitly* about the Spirit and begin to follow his argument on that basis.

6.3.2 The Spirit in Galatians

So the final judge of the matter is, of course, the data in Galatians itself. Within Galatians the only possible evidence for this view is the phrase 'the promise of the Spirit' (3:14b), but we have already seen that it cannot be interpreted in this way. The real question is whether the way in which Paul speaks of the Spirit throughout the letter compels us to accept the 'novel' idea that it means the realization of God's promised inheritance.[45] The answer is definitely in the negative.

First, as is clear from the way Paul argues, it is by no means self-evident to the Galatians that the inheritance comes through promise and not by the law. Paul has to *argue* for the point, just as he has to prove that justification is by faith (2:15–21). Things are different, however, when it

---

[43] See our discussion in 7.1.

[44] This is noted by Betz, 'Spirit' (1974) 146; Lull, *Spirit* (1980) 42; Fee, 'Conversion' (1997) 175.

[45] Dahl, *Studies* (1977) 133 ('evidentiary proof'); Betz 25, 28–29; Lull, *Spirit* (1980) 39, 42–43; Barclay, *Truth* (1988) 84–85; Dunn, *Theology* (1993) 60; Williams 84–85; *idem*, 'Justification' (1987) 91–100.

comes to the Spirit. For him, the Galatian believers' reception of the Spirit belongs to a historical fact. Precisely because this fact is so obvious, he can build his case on it by throwing a rhetorical demand at the 'foolish' Galatians: 'Have you received the Spirit by hearing of faith or by works of the Law?' (3:2, 5). If the 'inheritance' refers to the Spirit, however, it then means that he now argues (3:15–18) for what he had previously assumed to be obvious (3:2–5)! Hence inheritance, which he argues to be by promise, must be something other than the Spirit, which even the 'foolish' Galatians know to have come by faith.[46]

Secondly, as we pointed out in the last chapter, in 3:15–29, where Paul deals with the dual themes of promise and inheritance extensively, the Spirit does not come into his argument, at least not explicitly. If the inheritance actually refers to the Spirit, this failure to make an explicit connection between the two also becomes very difficult to explain. If he had had the Spirit in mind throughout the argument, would he not have made this clearer?

Thirdly, the role of the Spirit in relation to the inheritance also points in a rather different direction. In 4:6, after speaking of God 'sending the Spirit of his Son' to the newly adopted sons, he affirms their heirship on the basis of this sonship (4:7). Here the Spirit either identifies or institutes[47] the Gentile believers as God's sons. In the context the primary function of the Spirit, specified as the Spirit 'of His Son',[48] is to ensure an effective bond between the 'Son' and the 'sons', and *not* to identify the content of the inheritance.[49] If Paul meant the Spirit by the 'inheritance', his argument, especially his conclusion in v. 7, becomes very awkward. He would then be saying in effect: 'If you are a son, then you are also the one who possesses the inheritance of the Spirit,' as if their reception of the Spirit needs an argument! It would be a most inept truism that practically ruins the force of his argument.[50]

---

[46] Scholars who associate the Spirit with the inheritance fail to notice this problem.

[47] The precise meaning of ὅτι in v. 6 is debated. It may either by causal ('since') or explicative ('that'). For recent discussion see Fee, *Presence* (1995) 406–408. Paul himself does not seem interested in making such distinction. Rightly, Dunn 219.

[48] That the addition of 'of His Son' is intentional is frequently noted. E.g., Burton 222–223; Schlier 198; Mußner 275; R. Longenecker 173–174; Dunn 220; Fee, *Presence* (1995) 404–406. Since the Spirit concerns sonship, they should have reconsidered their identification of the Spirit with the inheritance.

[49] *Contra* Moore-Crispin, 'Galatians 4:1–9' (1989) 219 and many others.

[50] Fee, *Presence* (1995) 396, while sensing this awkwardness, still asserts that the inheritance means 'becoming God's children in the new aeon' and 'the inclusion of Gentiles among God's children'. Then he complains that 'Paul's fluid use of metaphor causes the argument to become a bit fuzzy at the end'. This alleged ambiguity is in fact caused by the discrepancy between Paul's 'future' inheritance and Fee's own 'realized' one.

This becomes even clearer in 4:21–31. Here the backbone of the argument is the clear-cut antithesis between ὁ κατὰ πνεῦμα and ὁ κατὰ σάρκα. Paul cannot be clearer: the latter is absolutely denied any possibility of inheritance (4:30); it is only ὁ κατὰ πνεῦμα that is guaranteed the promised inheritance. Here the Spirit 'qualifies' the child as the rightful heir and thus 'guarantees' him the prospect of the promised inheritance, and therefore, in its function, corresponds to the 'promise' in the case of Isaac's birth. Just as God's promise established Isaac as a God-designated heir, it is now the work of the Spirit that puts the Gentile believers on the same rank of heir.[51] The Spirit *enables* believers to receive the inheritance; it never is its content.

Fourthly, perhaps one may argue that Paul intends to correct the Galatians' futuristic concept of 'inheritance' by defining as the Spirit they have *already* received as though he was saying, 'Look, the Spirit that you have received by faith, that is the very inheritance that you are looking for!'[52] Yet, nowhere in the letter do we find indications that he is at pains to make this point. The only possible instance of such a move is, once again, 'the promise of the Spirit' in 3:14b, but even there the connection between the 'promise' and 'the Spirit' is more assumed than argued for. His arguments seem to have been designed for a different purpose.

Lastly, in a later part of the letter too, Paul's view of the Spirit remains the same. It is 'through the Spirit', Paul affirms, that the Galatians are to wait for the hope of righteousness (5:5). The fruit of the Spirit is an absolute 'prerequisite' for entering the future kingdom of God (5:19–24). It is only by sowing for the Spirit that one can reap the harvest of eternal life 'from the Spirit' (6:7–9). If the Spirit is equated with the inheritance, all these statements fail to make any sense.

In sum, in Galatians the Spirit is never the content of the 'realized inheritance'. In all the passages discussed above the Spirit is mentioned in the light of the future: the hope of righteousness, the kingdom of God or eternal life.[53] In this letter, the Spirit is never identified as (part of) the inheritance; it is always the *means* to or *condition* of the God-promised inheritance.[54] It is simply wrong to draw the notion of 'realized inheritance' from Paul's description of the Spirit.

---

[51] See 5.3 above.

[52] Witherington 292. This point is necessarily implied by the identification of the inheritance with the Spirit.

[53] Observe the unequivocally future eschatological thrust of 5:16–26 and 6:7–9. As already seen, even the reminder in 3:1–5 is couched in a future eschatological perspective ('beginning and ending'). The assertion of Smiles, *Gospel* (1998) 144 that 'the Spirit does not point to the future fulfillment' is simply not true.

[54] Typically, the simple dative πνεύματι (3:3; 5:5; 5:16, 18, 25) or κατὰ πνεῦμα (4:29) is used.

6.4 Inheritance in Context

Since the motif of 'promise/inheritance' originates from the Abrahamic
story in Genesis, it is clear that Paul cannot discuss the subject apart from
that tradition. God promised to Abraham that he would give him and his
descendants 'the Land' as their inheritance. Therefore, 'promise-
inheritance' is originally an Abrahamic question.

On the other hand, however, Paul also considers the issue to be crucial
for the Galatian believers, as is clear from his affirmation that the
'inheritance' does not come 'by the law' but 'through promise'. So he
endeavors to affirm that not only Abraham but also the Galatian believers
are 'heirs according to promise' (3:29). That his interest in the
'inheritance' goes beyond the Abrahamic tradition is most clear in 4:1–7
where he discusses the 'inheritance' without referring to the Abrahamic
tradition. Not only are the Galatians heirs 'according to promise'; they are
also heirs 'through God' (4:7).

The dual orientation of the 'promise/inheritance' (Abraham and the
Galatians) provides an interesting feature in Paul's discussion of the
subject. Anchored in God's promise to Abraham, the association of the
'promise/inheritance' with 'the land' never disappears from its purview,[55]
and the 'promissory' character of God's way of dealing with Abraham
continues to remain normative for its proper understanding (3:18).[56] Yet,
since the Galatian believers live in a different time and space, the promised
'inheritance' necessarily takes on a very different meaning. The promise
remains effective, but 'the land' is now transformed into a Christian hope.

There is, then, both continuity and discontinuity in Paul's conception of
the Abrahamic 'promise-inheritance'. This point will become very
important as we try to determine the precise meaning of the promised
'inheritance'. In what sense is the Abrahamic 'promise-inheritance' still
relevant to the Gentile believers? Within the Galatian context, what does
the 'inheritance' ultimately refer to? How would Paul, a first-century Jew
now committed to the risen Christ, have understood the meaning of the
Abrahamic promise of the Land?

Whether introduced by Paul himself or by the agitators, it seems almost
certain that the inheritance the Galatians know of is a future eschatological
one, a point suggested by the futuristic understanding of 'inheritance' in
early Judaism and early Christianity in general. Especially in early Judaism,
the expectation of a future inheritance is closely related to the strong
emphasis on the necessity of keeping the law as the means of receiving this

---

[55] See n. 32 in chapter 5.
[56] The perfect force of κεχάρισται in 3:18 is frequently noted.

future inheritance. If the concept is from the agitators,[57] they have probably taught the Galatians that they will participate in the promised inheritance only by performing works of the law.[58]

Under such circumstances Paul's silence on the 'what' or 'when' of the inheritance serves as an eloquent testimony to the fact that he was not at odds with them at least on these points. His discussion of the subject is extensive, but the only 'correction' he makes to the traditional teaching is that the inheritance is not 'by law' but 'by promise' and 'through the Spirit'. His concern is sharply focused on a single point: the inheritance comes 'through promise' (3:18, 23, 29); the Gentile believers are now its heirs 'through promise' (3:29; 4:7, 21–31). He simply assumes that everybody knows what the inheritance refers to and the most natural inference from this is that all the parties involved in the Galatian crisis are in full agreement with its future eschatological character.[59] This contextual consideration also makes the assumption of 'realized inheritance' quite difficult to maintain.[60]

6.5 Inheritance and the Kingdom of God

This leads us to the crucial passage in 5:21 where Paul associates the 'inheritance' with the 'kingdom of God': ἃ προλέγω ὑμῖν, καθὼς προεῖπον ὅτι οἱ τὰ τοιαῦτα πράσσοντες βασιλείαν θεοῦ οὐ κληρονομήσουσιν (5:21b). This stern *Drohwort* (Haufe), an integral part of Paul's apostolic message,[61] follows a long vice-list describing various

---

[57] For the possibility that the concept is introduced by Paul himself, see our discussion of 5:21 below.

[58] A survey of early Christian writings tells us that one's commitment to Jesus did not necessarily involve a radical change in their eschatological outlook.

[59] We also presented a similar argument for 'justification'. See chapter 3. Scholarly failure to notice this fairly obvious point well illustrates the danger of 'historical reconstruction' approach which makes Paul argue for something about which he is actually silent.

[60] Marius Victorinus in Edwards 50: inheritance = 'receiving eternal life'. On this Byrne, *Sons* (1979) 160 comments: 'But the sudden introduction of κληρονομία in v. 18 shows that Paul, in line with the inter-testamental Jewish tradition understands the 'land' promise in an eschatological sense: the "inheritance" awaiting Israel in the last age'. This is closer to the direction in which we are heading. Nevertheless, he takes this inheritance also as a realized one, mainly in the form of the Spirit (156, 163).

[61] 'As I have warned you before' refers to his previous teaching activity among the Galatians. As most scholars agree, this was a staple component in his apostolic preaching among the Gentiles. Betz 284–285; Lull, *Spirit* (1980) 35–36; Williams 22–23; Mußner 383; Bruce 251; R. Longenecker 258; Dunn 306; Martyn 497–498. Lightfoot 25 and 212 speculates that Paul uttered this warning on his second visit to Galatia.

symptoms of 'works of flesh' (5:10–20a). Paul's point is clear enough: if one is led by the flesh and thereby produces evil behavior, one will be excluded from the eschatological inheritance of the kingdom of God.

Assuming that Paul's argument in chapters 3 and 4 concerns 'realized inheritance', scholars frequently read this explicitly futuristic passage in the light of the eschatological 'tension' of the 'already and not yet', with the Spirit understood as the 'first fruits' and 'down payment' of the final kingdom yet to be consummated.[62] That the idea of 'already' is the result of a mistaken exegesis has already been made clear. Even granted the assumption, however, this involves a dubious procedure. As we noted in our discussion of 5:5 in chapter 3, to conflate the assumed notion of 'already' with the clearly futuristic thrust of Paul's statements here constitutes the well-known fallacy of 'illegitimate totality transfer'. The 'already and not yet' may be a legitimate scheme for a systematic synthesis of the diverse aspects of Paul's eschatological thinking, but it in no way means that we can impose this synthetic notion on each statement smoothing out its specific contextual edges. In this particular context, Paul's manifest intention is to warn the Galatians that improper conduct in the community will certainly disqualify one for the future kingdom. Importing the notion of 'already' at this point ruins the effect he wants to produce with this stern *Drohwort*.

Interpreters also frequently obscure the explicit eschatological thrust by rendering βασιλεία θεοῦ as 'realm of God' or 'dominion of God'.[63] That this will not do has been clearly demonstrated by Kvalbein.[64] The motif of 'inheriting' or 'entering' with which the 'kingdom of God' is typically combined in Synoptics and Paul, renders the idea of 'dominion' quite unlikely. Both for Jesus and Paul the kingdom of God refers to the 'eschatological inheritance, the content of all the awaited gifts of salvation'.[65]

---

[62] Dunn 307; Fee, *Presence* (1995) 443. Cf. Bruce 251.

[63] Duncan 173; Lull, *Spirit* (1980) 175–176; Fung 261–262; Witherington 406–407. As Martyn 497 points out, Paul's use of προλέγω ('warn ahead of time') anticipates the day of Judgment.

[64] 'Kingdom of God' (1997) 60–84 (esp. 64–71). Kvalbein refers to G. Dalman, *The Words of Jesus* (1902) who observed the syntactical difference between *malkuth* or *malkutha* and βασιλεία τοῦ θεοῦ which corresponds not to the former but to such motifs as 'coming aeon', 'the coming world' or 'life in the world to come'. See *m. Sanh.* 10.1–4; *m. Abot.* 3.16. Luz, *EDNT* 1:204: 'As the use of εἰσέρχεσθαι indicates, the idea of an "area" is present in the word βασιλεία, not the functional notion of sovereignty'. Also Goulder, 'Already?' (1994) 30, n. 32; Hester, *Inheritance* (1968) viii. Cf. Moore, *Judaism* (1927) 94–95.

[65] Merk, *Handeln* (1968) 73–74. See also Martyn 497. The similar warning in 1QS 4:12–14 is often cited (Martyn; Mußner).

The importance of Paul's 'kingdom of God' statement for a proper understanding of his concept of 'inheritance' is great. By connecting the motif of the Abrahamic inheritance with the future kingdom of God, Paul makes a clearly future eschatological definition of the former. The conclusion is, then, quite simple: with his talk of the 'inheritance' in Galatians he most probably means the eschatological salvation, namely, the kingdom of God (5:21) and eternal life (6:7–9) as he specifies later in the letter. On the one hand, the figure of Abraham remains determinative since the hope of eschatological salvation is so closely associated with God's promise to Abraham. On the other hand, it is now a Galatian question, since this ancient promise of the land is now understood to be the promise of the eschatological land for them, i.e., the future kingdom of God and eternal life.

Explicitly or implicitly, [66] however, it has been asserted that this particular statement should be separated from Paul's earlier discussion of 'inheritance'. Two grounds are normally given.

First, it has been asserted that the future eschatological use of κληρονομεῖν stands at variance with Paul's earlier use of the term for a realized inheritance.[67] This is clearly begging the question, however, since, as we have shown, his discussion in 3:15–4:21 by no means requires the meaning of 'realized inheritance'. The evidence available rather points in the opposite direction.

Secondly, many have argued that the statement, originating from the early Christian (baptismal) catechism, contains ideas which are 'not quite Pauline', and therefore, 'in some tension with Paul's theology'.[68] But a charge of this kind is usually precarious, and this one seems to be no exception. That βασιλεία θεοῦ is 'somewhat rare' in Paul is a matter of personal opinion; one can equally say that fifteen occurrences in the whole Pauline corpus is by no means meager, especially compared with other letters in the New Testament.[69] More importantly, the idea of '(not)

---

[66] That is, by ignoring the 'inheritance' motif in this passage. This seems to be a majority way of resolving the alleged 'tension'. Some focus on the kingdom motif, while others ignore the passage completely (e.g., Williams).

[67] Betz 285; Donfried, 'Kingdom' (1987) 185; R. Longenecker 258. Eckstein, *Verheißung* (1996) 189 similarly asserts that the statement in 5:21, which is more in line with Rom 4:13, is different from the inheritance in Galatians 3–4 which stresses the present bestowal of salvation. Without explanation Schnackenburg, *Kingdom* (1963) 285 also asserts that in chapters 3 and 4 Paul does not associate the inheritance with the kingdom of God.

[68] Gager, 'End-time' (1970) 325–337 (333); Betz 285; Donfried, 'Kingdom' (1987) 185; R. Longenecker 258.

[69] 1 Thess 2:10–12; 2 Thess 1:5; Gal 5:21; 1 Cor 4:20; 6:9, 10; 15:24, 50; Rom 14:17; Eph 5:5; Col 1:13; 4:11; 2 Tim 4:1, 18. Cf. Heb 1:8; 2 Pet 1:11.

inheriting the kingdom of God' is an integral part of Paul's apostolic preaching, and this flies in the face of such an argument.[70] The assertion that οἱ πράσσοντες is at variance with his normal usage also does not carry any weight.[71] One also needs to remember that this particular phrase occurs only rarely in the Synoptic gospels (Mt 25:34). Nothing in this statement prevents us from making a fruitful connection between Paul's discussion of the Abrahamic inheritance in chapters 3 and 4 and the motif of 'inheriting the kingdom of God' and 'eternal life'.

There are, in fact, many positive grounds for reading the two concepts in close connection. First, there is a potential problem in Paul's logic that can be avoided. Galatians, by common agreement, is the most polemical and emotionally charged among his writings. Considering the high stakes (apostasy), this is hardly surprising. So he is at great pains to refute the destructive claim of the law-upholding agitators and to reaffirm the truth of 'by faith', 'through promise', and 'through the Spirit'. According to the majority view, it is the notion of a 'realized inheritance' as defined in terms of the Spirit that plays a critical role in sustaining his case. If that is the case, however, his explicitly future eschatological use of 'inheritance' in such a stern 'eschatological warning' (5:21b; 6:7–9) deals a fatal blow to the very point he has been trying to establish.[72] Paul has run the whole gamut of argument to prove the 'already' of the inheritance; now the Galatians hear that this is not the case at all. Given such high stakes in Galatia, this is the last thing he would dare to do. The critical nature of the crisis demands a single, consistent perspective throughout the letter.[73] Since Paul is explicitly eschatological in the later part of the letter, it is more probable to suppose that his earlier argument about 'inheritance' should also be structured in the same future eschatological perspective.

Secondly, Paul has already taught (προεῖπον) the Galatians about 'inheriting the kingdom' and therefore presupposes familiarity with the

---

[70] See n. 61 above. In two places the statement is introduced by a reminding formula or another: 'I warn you in advance, as I did so before' (Gal 5:21); 'Do you not know' (1 Cor 6:9). We should not think that it was only part of Paul's 'missionary' (initial) preaching, distinguishing it from Paul's preaching in general. See Furnish, *Ethics* (1968) 98–111. Paul presupposes familiarity with the thought on the side of his Gentile readers. Would anyone have preached an idea so actively which is not quite harmonious with one's own thought?

[71] As Fee, *Presence* (1995) 443 points out, the word ποιέω is more traditional since it is brought in as the result of Paul's citation of Lev 18:5 in 3:12.

[72] On a realized eschatological reading, even speaking of 'tension' is an unjustified understatement.

[73] Or, is Lightfoot's (63) confident judgment that 'The Epistle to the Galatians is especially distinguished among St Paul's letters by its unity of purpose' still wishful thinking?

concept on their part;[74] the only 'inheritance' they presently know of is that of the eschatological kingdom of God (5:21). If so, it is very probable that the Galatians, without an explicit indication otherwise, associate Paul's talk of the Abrahamic 'inheritance' with the inheritance they are waiting for, namely, the 'kingdom of God' and 'eternal life'. To these people, then, his belated reference to '(not) inheriting the kingdom of God' probably serves as a natural confirmation of their understanding of his argument.

Thirdly, the close linguistic link between οὐ κληρονομήσουσιν in this verse and the similar phrase in 4:30 has to be considered: οὐ γὰρ μὴ κληρονομήσει ὁ υἱὸς τῆς παιδίσκης μετὰ τοῦ υἱοῦ τῆς ἐλευθέρας. Already in this text inheritance is in the future, promised to those who are born of the free woman, namely, of the Spirit (4:23, 28–29, 31). Here the negative pronouncement of 'will never inherit' applies to 'the son of the slave woman', namely, the son born κατὰ σάρκα (4:23, 29). Similarly in 5:21 the warning is addressed to those who walk 'by the flesh' (σαρκί) and practice τὰ ἔργα τῆς σαρκός (5:16–21a), involving the promise that those who walk according to the Spirit bearing its fruit will surely inherit the kingdom of God. The similarity both in the Spirit-flesh antithesis and their actual wording suggests the close association of the two statements.[75]

Fourthly, from the tradition-historical perspective, the idea of 'inheriting the kingdom of God' or 'inheriting eternal life' (cf. 6:7–9), corresponding to the Jewish idea of 'the age to come' and 'life in the new aeon', has its origin in the same Abrahamic promise of the land. Space precludes detailed exposition, but a survey of inter-testamental literature easily shows that the idea of 'inheriting the new aeon' and similar motifs are firmly rooted in the promise of the land given to Abraham and to his children.[76]

To be sure, Furnish, like many others, contends that Paul derives the idea of 'inheritance' in 3:15 onward directly from the Abrahamic tradition, while the idea of 'inheriting the kingdom of God' is taken from the early

---

[74] So Bruce 251.

[75] This is especially so if we remember the aural nature of ancient 'reading'. Cf. Stanton, 'Law' (1996) 100–101; Harvey, *Listening* (1998), especially chapter 8 on Galatians.

[76] See, e.g., *Ps. Sol.* 14:10; *1 Enoch* 40:9; *4 Macc* 18:3; *Test. Job* 18:6–7; 47:1; *2 Bar.* 44:13; *4 Ezra* 7:96; *2 Enoch* 9:1; 10:4–6; 66:6. Also see Friedrich, *EDNT* 2:298; Schweitzer, *Mysticism* (1930) 210; Kvalbein, 'Kingdom of God' (1997) 68; Hester, *Inheritance* (1968) 29–36, 79; Byrne, *Sons* (1979) 68–70. Gager, 'End-time' (1970) suggests its origin in 'a common rabbinic *topos*' present 'in discussions about heretics' (333) which is, of course, rooted in the Abrahamic promise of the land. Closer to Paul is the data in Matthew 5, where 'inheriting the land' stands parallel to possessing 'the kingdom of heaven' (vv. 3, 5, 10).

Christian tradition. [77] But even if we grant this probably unlikely assumption,[78] it does not amount to much, unless one also claims that Paul is unaware of the motif's tradition-historical origin in the Abrahamic tradition. But this is falsified by his own, future eschatological understanding of the Abrahamic promise in Romans where he interprets the promise as about 'to be the heir of the world' (4:13).

That is, it is very unlikely that when Paul speaks of 'inheriting the kingdom of God', an idea ultimately founded on God's 'promise of the land', he intends something quite different from the Abrahamic 'inheritance' (of the land) to which he has already referred (3:15–29; 4:21–31). [79] Apart from the question-begging assumption of a 'realized inheritance', there is nothing that prevents us from relating the idea of 'inheriting the kingdom of God' to Paul's discussion of the Abrahamic 'inheritance'. His discussion of the Abrahamic inheritance in Galatians chapters 3 and.4 and his talk of the 'inheriting the kingdom of God' belong together. In both places, the 'inheritance' refers to the future inheritance of eschatological salvation.

By the same token, it also seems certain that the reference to 'reaping eternal life' in 6:7–9 should be included within the notion of the inheritance. Both are set within the same framework of the Spirit-flesh antithesis with the same purpose of eschatological warning. Moreover, a comparison of this passage with other passages such as Romans 2:7 and 1 Corinthians 15:50 makes it clear that in Paul's thought the eschatological kingdom practically converges with such ideas as 'eternal life', 'the imperishable' and 'glory'. All are various expressions of the same reality of future eschatological salvation.[80]

An important conclusion has been drawn: the kingdom of God-eternal life is the 'inheritance' that Paul has been discussing throughout the letter. This means that from the first Paul's discussion of the 'promise/inheritance' is structured from a consistently future eschatological perspective. His strong emphasis on the 'heirship' of the Gentile believers and his repeated claim that the 'inheritance' is only 'through promise' and 'by the Spirit' are therefore *not* retrospective

---

[77] Furnish, *Ethics* (1968) 127; J. Vos, *Pneumatologie* (1973) 30 (26, n. 1); Haufe, 'Gottes Reich' (1985) 467–472; Betz 285; Brinsmead, *Response* (1982) 164–170; Donfried, 'Kingdom' (1987) 185; R. Longenecker 258; Martyn 498; Duling, 'Kingdom' *ABD* 4:65–66.

[78] As already noted above, outside Paul, the precise phrase, 'inheriting the Kingdom of God' occurs only very rarely (Mt 25:34). *Did* 7.1 and *Herm*. Sim 9.16.2–4, passages that Betz adduces as evidence, are hardly close enough to prove the claim.

[79] In Justin we have the connection between 'Abraham's seed according to flesh' and 'eternal kingdom'. *Dial* 140.

[80] Rightly, Friedrich, *EDNT* 2:279.

thoughts looking back on what has already transpired and is now present. On the contrary, by his sustained talk of 'heir' and 'inheritance', he repeatedly draws the Galatians' attention to what still lies in the future. Pointing to the eschatological future, Paul's consistent claim in the letter is that the Galatians will be able to attain the 'inheritance' (eschatological salvation) only by holding on to faith and by being led by the Spirit.[81]

6.6 Inheritance and Justification

Having identified the 'inheritance' as final salvation (the kingdom of God and eternal life), we are now faced with an important question: how does this inheritance relate to the hope of righteousness, the central concern of the letter? The answer is not far away. Earlier in our study we argued that justification/righteousness in Galatians is depicted as an exclusively future eschatological gift.[82] Then, in the preceding and the present chapters, we demonstrated that the 'promise-inheritance', identified as the 'Kingdom of God' (5:21) and 'eternal life' (6:7-9), also point to the same future of eschatological salvation. The implication is clear: justification and inheritance, both being future eschatological, are just another way of referring to the same reality of final salvation. The hope of righteousness is not different from the hope of the future Kingdom of God and of eternal life.[83]

Paul's actual treatment of these two themes as functional synonyms confirms our conclusion. The first case in point is 3:18 and 3:21.

> for if the inheritance is by the law,
> it is no longer by promise (v. 18).

> for if a law that has the power to give life had been given,
> righteousness would have been by the law (v. 21).

The parallelism between the two verses is fairly strong. Both employ a rhetorical *argumentatio ad absurdum*, positing a hypothetical situation (εἰ γάρ) in which ἐκ νόμου instead of ἐξ ἐπαγγελίας[84] comes in as the answer.

---

[81] In *2 Clement* 5:5, without referring to the Abrahamic tradition, 'the rest of the coming kingdom and eternal life' (ἀνάπαυσις τῆς μελλούσης βασιλείας καὶ ζωῆς αἰωνίου) is called 'the promise of Christ' (ἡ ἐπαγγελία τοῦ Χριστοῦ).

[82] See chapter 3.

[83] Since Paul envisages future salvation as a single reality, this conclusion presents itself very naturally.

[84] In v. 21 the actual phrase is missing, but the following statement in v. 22 shows that the thought is clearly there.

What is noteworthy here is the switch from 'the inheritance (v. 18) to 'the righteousness' (v. 21). The major contested issue throughout is, of course, the inheritance (3:15–29), but the fact that Paul can casually speak of 'the righteousness' while discussing the inheritance suggests that for him the two are functional synonyms.

A similar correspondence is also observable in 3:22–24.

> But the scripture has imprisoned all things under sin,
> so that the promise from faith in Jesus Christ might be given to those who believe (v. 22).

> Now before faith came,
> we were imprisoned and guarded under the law until faith would be revealed.
> Therefore the law was our disciplinarian until Christ came,
> so that we might be justified by faith (vv. 23–24).

The two statements are similar both in idea and structure: the negative function of the law leading to the positive consequence of faith. The only noticeable difference is that the latter looks at the situation with its effect on human beings in mind, while the former focuses on the law itself.[85] As he describes the consequence or purpose of the enslaving function of the law, Paul speaks at once of 'receiving the promise' (v. 22) and 'being justified' (v. 24), thereby giving the impression that they are basically analogous. Since the 'promise' is that of 'inheritance' (vv. 15–18),[86] here too, we can see the correspondence between the promised inheritance and justification.[87]

A similar correspondence between inheritance and justification is also visible in Paul's move from 4:21–31 to 5:1–5.[88] In both passages the argument is sustained by the stark antithesis of ἐλευθερία/πνεῦμα versus δουλεία/νόμος. In the allegory of Sarah and Hagar the child who belongs

---

[85] So Martyn 362, noting the appearance of 'we' in v. 23. The suggestion that the 'we' in v. 23, in contra-distinction to τὰ πάντα in the previous verse, refers to 'Jews' should be rejected. *Contra* R. Longenecker 145; Dunn 197–198. Dunn's conscious emphasis on the 'positive' nature of Paul's view of the law, without doubt, born out of his concern for the *heilsgeschichtliche* continuity seems off the mark, at least in Galatians.

[86] So Schlier 145; Fung 165; Dunn 195.

[87] This clear convergence of inheritance and justification is mostly missed out. Fung 165–166, 176–177, is a rare exception. In his words, 'justification by faith is seen to be the fulfillment of the promise made to Abraham' (177). His view is, of course, that of 'realized inheritance/justification'. Cf. Mußner 254. The inheritance and righteousness certainly converge, but they do so as future eschatological blessings.

[88] Scholarly uncertainty over the role of 5:1 illustrates the unity of Paul's running argument between 4:21–21 and 5:1–6. Williams 132. Cf. Merk, 'Beginn' (1969) 83–104 (with a survey); Matera, 'Culmination' (1988); Harnisch, 'Einübung' (1987).

to the realm of freedom/promise/Spirit will receive the promised inheritance, while the one belonging to the realm of slavery/law is expelled from the household of the promise. Similarly, in 5:1–5 Paul affirms that it is only by persevering in the freedom of the Spirit that one will get to the 'hope of righteousness', while resorting to 'yoke of slavery' (the law) simply means excision from Christ Himself. Remaining in the Christ-given freedom of the Spirit will bring the inheritance, i.e., the hope of righteousness; turning back to the law will only cause an expulsion from the promise, since it only means a fall from Christ and his grace. His talk of 'promise/inheritance' drawn from the Abrahamic tradition is in fact just another way of expounding the same truth of justification by faith.[89]

According to our exposition, then, Paul is no anomaly in the futuristic understanding of the Abrahamic tradition in early Judaism and Christianity. There is, of course, no denying that he is an innovative interpreter of his tradition. Yet his innovation is mainly christological, which does not involve a realized eschatological redefinition of the promised inheritance in terms of the Spirit. Christ came; the Galatians received the Spirit. This does not, however, affect the validity of God's ancient promise of 'the land'. On the contrary, now both Christ and the Spirit are seen as God's final confirmation, rather than fulfillment, of this promise (cf. 2 Cor 1:20!), and as the only way through which to attain to this promised inheritance of God's eschatological land which Paul and other early Christians called 'the Kingdom of God' (5:21b) in which they are to receive the gift of God's justification (5:5) and eternal life (6:7–9).[90]

6.7 Conclusion

The conspicuously future eschatological thrust of Paul's argument, much of which is taken up with the discussion of promise and inheritance, has become clear. In the Galatian context this 'inheritance' is clearly used as an epithet for eschatological salvation drawn from the Scriptures, namely, the kingdom of God and eternal life. It has also become clear that this future inheritance is not different from the hope of righteousness (5:5), the central subject of Paul's argument. From first to last, then, Paul's argument is sustained by one single aim: to demonstrate that future salvation comes

---

[89] Cosgrove's claim that inheritance is never designated as justification is a superficial one. *Cross* (1988) 60, 64, n. 44; 'Arguing' (1988) 547.

[90] Isaiah 60:21(LXX) expresses the eschatological hope that in the future the people of Jerusalem will be 'righteous' and 'inherit the land forever'. As is easily confirmed by Matthew 5, both 'inheriting the land' and 'inheriting the kingdom of God' belong to the same tradition of the Abrahamic promise of the land.

only 'by faith', 'through promise', and therefore, 'by the Spirit'. It can be variously phrased as 'justification', 'inheritance', 'Kingdom of God' or 'eternal life', but the point remains the same: one will be able to attain it only πνεύματι ἐκ πίστεως.

The purpose of this consistently eschatological argument seems fairly obvious. By writing the letter, Paul warns of the dreadful eschatological consequences of the Galatians' present deviation from the gospel and encourages them to persevere in faith and the Spirit so that they may be able to attain to the hoped-for salvation. It is from this future eschatological perspective that he perceives the development in Galatia as a crisis. From the same perspective he also develops his theological argument in which he presents faith and the Spirit as the exclusive means of attaining future salvation. [91] As far as this eschatological 'not yet' remains, it is crucial to hold on to faith and the Spirit since only in that way is one able to attain to the promised inheritance, the hope of righteousness. And this is why the present crisis in Galatia, namely, the Galatians' departure from the Spirit, constitutes such a critical matter.

---

[91] This is what we already anticipated in chapter 2.

Chapter 7

Paul's Christological Argument

Paul's future eschatological perspective in Galatians has become clear. Our examination of Paul's argument thus far, however, leaves a crucial dimension of it untouched: his interpretation of the Christ event. Following Paul's argument, it is not difficult to see how crucial his view of the Christ event is in sustaining his argument.[1] Not surprisingly, therefore, in scholarly interpretation of the letter it is this christological focus that is thought to form the foundation of Paul's realized eschatological perspective. By associating the contested privileges such as righteousness and inheritance exclusively with the Christ event in the past which supposedly marked the inauguration of the new aeon, Paul tells the Galatians that those blessings have *already* been bestowed on those who exercise their faith and thereby have participated in Christ, for which the gift of the Spirit serves as the evidence *par excellence*. With these privileges already available without the law, Paul's polemic against the law is then particularly focused on its *eschatological superfluity*. It is by pointing at the 'already' established by the cross of Christ that Paul effectively demolishes the anachronistic 'not yet' of the agitators.[2]

In this chapter, we make two major claims. First, this 'realized eschatological' interpretation is the outcome of reading a theology into Paul's contextual argument (sections 1–3). In a sense, this is a difficult

---

[1] This is widely noted. Gaventa, 'Singularity' (1991) 149; Weima, 'Gal. 6:11–18' (1993) 90–107; Cook, 'Prescript' (1992) 511–519; Fee, *Presence* (1995) 380. It is misleading, however, to posit Christ as 'one of the main matters in dispute' as Grayston, *Dying* (1990) 69 does. Cf. Kertelge, 'Gesetz' (1984) 385. Paul is not debating about Christ but responding to the crisis caused by circumcision with his own interpretation of the Christ event.

[2] This is the consensus. See 1.2 above. As Hübner, *Law* (1984) 18 puts it, 'why do you therefore seek to take the circuitous route by way of circumcision and thus by way of the law when it is not in the least necessary, nay more, when it is not in the least possible?' Also Lincoln, *Paradise* (1981) 11; Johnson, *Writings* (1986) 308, 311; Keck, *Letters* (1988) 72–73; Barclay, *Truth* (1988) 102–103; Hong, *Law* (1993) 27, 76–78, 88–89, *passim*; *idem*, 'Perspective' (1991) 1–16; Wright, 'Gospel' (1994); Eckstein, *Verheißung* (1996) 225; Smiles, *Gospel* (1998) 73–74, 142–146, 182, 217; Dunn, *Theology* (1993) 99–100. Cf. Stuhlmacher, *Reconciliation* (1986) 81.

task, because the Christ event *is* a past event. This being so, it is all too easy to read 'realized eschatology' into Paul's language which may have no such implication at all. Paul speaks of the event in the past tense because he cannot do otherwise, but it does not necessarily mean that he is pressing a realized eschatological logic for the Galatians. Our thesis is that once we read Paul's christological argument as his response to the problem of *the Galatian apostasy* we will see clearly that it does not show any such intent. This will be followed by a second, more positive claim that Paul's focus on the Christ event is his way of highlighting the critical role of the Spirit in the Galatians' quest for justification and inheritance (section 4).

7.1 Does Christ Mark the New Age?

Scholarly interpretation of Pauline eschatology typically turns on the notion of a 'new age' or 'the age to come'. We cannot treat this highly significant issue extensively at this point; nevertheless, a brief discussion seems necessary in view of the popularity of the motif in the interpretation of Paul's argument in Galatians.

7.1.1 Rescue from the Present Evil Age (1:4)

In Paul's interpretation of Christ's death as the rescue 'from the present evil age' (ἐκ τοῦ αἰῶνος τοῦ ἐνεστῶτος πονηροῦ), scholars commonly see an explicit expression of realized eschatology, supposing that Paul interprets the Christ event as the 'dawn of the new age' or 'the turn of the ages'.[3] However, several considerations make us wary of such conclusion.

First, as Betz points out,[4] the issue here is 'the liberation "out of" the evil aeon and not of the change of the aeons themselves'. What Paul means is, 'while the present evil aeon continues, Christ's coming and the gift of the Spirit have granted freedom to the believers in Christ'.[5] In Galatians Christ's work of redemption (3:13; 4:5; 5:1, 13) marks the beginning of the battle between the Spirit and the evil flesh, which is to be fought with a

---

[3] This is the majority view. E.g., G. Vos, *Eschatology* (1930) 12, 24; Davies, *Rabbinic Judaism* (1970) 36; Wengst, *Formeln* (1972) 61; Ladd, *Theology* (1974) 38, 68–69; Brinsmead, *Response* (1982) 61–67, 189; Meeks, *Urban* (1983) 176; Silva, 'Eschatological Structure' (1994) 146; Hong, *Law* (1993) 77–78; Adams, *World* (2000) 224, 227; Martyn 90, 101.

[4] Betz 42; R. Longenecker 8. Witherington 77 notes this, still opting for the 'new age'.

[5] Silva, 'Eschatological Structure' (1994) 146 retorts that Betz's 'objection would be valid if Paul could not think in terms of an overlapping of the ages' (146). This begs the question. Where do we find evidence for the idea? See the next section.

vivid awareness of the 'not yet' (5:1–6; 5:21b; 6:7–9).[6] The Christ event surely marks the crucial turning point, but in Paul's language this 'turning' is never that of the *ages*.

Second, the wording 'the *present* evil age' renders the intention of 'realized eschatology' unlikely. The predicate ἐνεστώς, replacing the usual οὗτος or νῦν, is clearly emphatic, accentuating 'the threatening presence'[7] of this evil age. This is certainly an unlikely step to take if Paul means to suggest the present reality of the new age.[8] That at the outset of the letter he labels the time *after* Christ as 'the *present* evil aeon' must be taken seriously.

Thirdly, the unusual form of 'the present evil age' is also noteworthy. That this 'age' or 'world' is evil is a Pauline commonplace (Rom 12:2; 1 Cor 1:20; 2:6, 8; 2 Cor 4:4; Eph 5:16), but the actual phrase '*evil* age' occurs only here, with an emphasis on its morally evil character.[9] This emphasis fits nicely with the preceding reference to Christ's death 'for our sins'. It seems that Paul, by stressing the evil nature of this age, intentionally highlights the moral consequence of Christ's redemption. It is not difficult to see the relevance of this emphasis to what he is to say later in the letter, especially in chapters 5 and 6 (3:22!; 5:24!). In sum, Paul's references to the Christ's 'rescue from the present evil age' (1:4) do not suggest the inauguration of the new age by Christ's redemption.

7.1.2 New Age in Paul?

More generally, scholars commonly suppose that for Paul the new age is somehow already inaugurated in the present, thereby producing characteristic 'overlapping of the ages' which forms the fundamental framework of his theology as a whole. A two-age scheme in Paul is a reasonable supposition, but the way he speaks of the matter hardly enables us to affirm the present realization of the new age. A few considerations can be made.

First, Paul *never* speaks of 'the coming age' in his undisputed writings.[10] Given the fundamental importance that scholars confer on this

---

[6] Rightly, Grayston, *Dying* (1990) 70: the redemption is that from our 'hopeless situation' but not into the 'new age'.

[7] Smiles, *Gospel* (1998) 72. Also Mußner 51; Schlier 33: 'etwas drohendes Hereinstehendes'.

[8] Rightly, Furnish, 'Christological' (1993) 113: 'Neither "new creation"...nor "new age" is specifically in view here'. As Sänger, 'Argumentationsstrategie' (2002) 391 notes, in Romans 8:38 ἐνεστῶτα stands parallel to μέλλοντα.

[9] So Lightfoot 71; Burton 13; Longenecker 9; Smiles, *Gospel* (1998) 73.

[10] This is noted by Conzelmann, *Outline* (1969) 207. At this point, most scholars seem to have a predetermined penchant for the two-age scheme. Keck is typical: '*Although*

scheme, his silence on this key motif is striking. Despite the scholarly tendency to relativize the significance of this silence, it is indeed a phenomenon very hard, if not impossible, to explain on the assumption of the 'realized' new age, especially in contrast with his heavy reference to 'this age'. His failure to mention the motif can mean either that the age to come is still yet to come or that he does not feel it necessary to stress it, even if it is already here. If, as many scholars believe, he really takes the inauguration of the age to come as the starting point of his theology, one cannot help asking whether it is realistic to say that he is busy exploiting the rich implications of this inauguration without feeling it necessary to affirm it, *not even once*, throughout his extant letters.

Secondly, the phrase, 'the coming age' occurs in Ephesians 1:21 but somewhat later we also come across the plural 'the coming *ages*' (2:7), implying many more ages still to come. This is a very unusual expression to use to say the least, if Paul was thinking in terms of the two-age scheme. More significantly, this 'coming age', despite the strong realized eschatological emphasis that runs through the letter, definitely lies in the future. If we follow Paul's language faithfully, we have to conclude that at least in Ephesians the Christ event did not inaugurate the new age.

Thirdly, the closest Paul moves to such an idea is his reference to 'the ends of the *ages*', both in the plural (1 Cor 10:11). Now believers stand at the end of many ages, not just of the present one.[11] Even if the plurals are merely rhetorical, though unlikely, standing at the end of the ages is certainly a far cry from the actual arrival of a new age.

Fourthly, the way Paul alternates between 'this age' and 'this world' (κόσμος) in 1 Corinthians as the opposite *not* of 'the coming aeon' *but* of 'God' also suggests that the intended contrast is more ontological or moral than eschatological (1:20–21, 27–28; 2:6, 8, 12; cf. Rom 12:2).[12] Paul's arguments in these passages do not require the idea of a new age, whether

---

Paul never uses the entire phrase, his references to "this aeon" show that he *assumes* the duality'. *Letters* (1988) 74.

[11] Hays' clever rendering, 'on whom the ends of the ages have met' is mistaken. Granted the dual meaning of the plurals, what he needs is the 'end' (τέλος) of one and the 'beginning' (ἀρχή) of the other, not two 'ends' (τελή) of them. Unlike the English 'end', the Greek τέλος never refers to the 'beginning' end. This reading comes from his otherwise excellent study, *Moral Vision* (1996) 20, 56, n. 14. Perhaps, we can present this as an illustration about how scholarly preconception can make the text say what they want to hear.

[12] Cf. Adams, *World* (2000) 227. Certainly, Paul does not mean that God belongs to the age to come.

realized or not. Judging from Paul's own writings, the notion of 'the overlapping of the ages' seems out of the question.[13]

7.1.3 Intertextuality?

Since Paul never speaks explicitly of a 'realized' new age, scholars mostly resort to the logic of intertextuality supposedly generated by his use of Jewish apocalyptic motifs: 'revelation', [14] 'the Spirit', [15] 'Jerusalem above'[16] and most crucially, 'new creation'.[17] The logic is simple. In the Jewish apocalyptic tradition these motifs are associated with the new age. Paul uses them to describe the effect of the Christ event in the present. By so doing, he *in effect* claims that the waited-for eschaton/new age has been inaugurated through the work of Jesus Christ.

Despite its being a virtual consensus, this view builds upon several questionable assumptions. First, the Gentile Galatians, if they are to detect such a subtle move at all, must have substantial familiarity with the Jewish apocalyptic thought-world. But it is not easy to imagine that the Gentile Galatians, living at the heart of the Greco-Roman world, knew the Jewish apocalyptic well enough to catch the radical claim of 'new age' supposedly communicated by such a subtle means. [18] Paul the Jew might have entertained such a possibility, but it would have most probably been lost on the ears of the Gentile Galatians.

Secondly, the logic of intertextuality requires that these motifs are 'technical terms', i.e., virtual synonyms of the 'new age', which automatically conjure up the idea of 'new age' *regardless of context*. If they also contain other connotations, more than one intertextual inference is possible, and readers would be left wondering which aspect of these

---

[13] Baumgarten's sober assessment of relevant data in *Apokalyptik* (1975) 180–184 seems to have been lost in the enthusiastic hail of Paul the apocalyptic.

[14] Bornkamm, 'Revelation' (1974) 95–96: since the word originally refers to 'a freshly commencing, aeon-changing, eschatological act of God', Paul, by speaking of 'the "coming" of faith', 'gives the apocalyptic idea a radical new twist, by relating it no longer to a saving event which is yet to come but to that which has already been realized'. Also Kim, *Origin* (1984) 72, 274; Martyn (see Introduction).

[15] See 6.3 above.

[16] Most strongly, Lincoln, *Paradise* (1981) 18–22 followed by Hansen, *Abraham* (1989) 149–150. Also see Mußner 326; Cosgrove, 'Sarah' (1987) 231; Lambrecht, 'Abraham' (1999) 528. Despite his otherwise strong realized eschatological interpretation, Martyn 440 is much soberer: 'the community that is *both above and future*, being ready to descend to earth *at the parousia*' (emphasis added). For a sober assessment of the data against the background of the Jewish thought, see Horbury, 'Land' (1996) 219–222.

[17] See 7.3 below.

[18] In reality, for this sort of subtle method to work, the tradition has to be an integral part of one's world-view so as to generate an immediate response to any change to it.

potential meanings Paul intends. This sort of exclusivity is indeed too big
an assumption to make. For example, Mell makes a strong case for the
technical meaning of the 'new creation',[19] but is its bond with the 'new
age' strong enough to exclude other connotations and disallow any further
change of meaning? When Paul invokes such motifs as 'revelation' or 'the
Spirit' in relation to the Christ event, is the idea of 'new age' as obvious as
is usually assumed?

Thirdly, even granting that these motifs are technical terms for 'new
age', Paul's application of them to the present condition does not
necessarily mean the arrival of the new age. An easier inference would be
that *he uses these words in different senses*. He takes them up out of their
original contexts and puts them to a very different use, that is, to speak of
the immediate consequence of the Christ event without necessarily
implying the presence of the new age.[20] The rabbinic use of the 'new
creation' motif shows how easily this can be done (*Gen. Rab.* 39:14).
Changing the meaning of words would have been much easier than turning
the ages themselves. Especially when Paul himself never makes any
explicit claim to such effect, why should *we* draw such a difficult inference?

Fourthly, despite scholarly willingness to endorse the idea, one has to
remember that for Paul's contemporaries for whom the new age is so
obviously 'not yet', the claim of a 'new age' must have been a very
difficult idea to convey unless one makes it absolutely clear. Yet in his
extant writings Paul never speaks of a 'new age'; on the contrary he
himself explicitly states that the new age is still in the future (Eph 1:21;
2:7).[21] Under the circumstances, no sensible person would think that his
use of such motifs is a roundabout way of claiming the arrival of the
awaited new age. Just a few allusions are not enough for such an
'incredible' claim. Even if he kept saying 'new age' repeatedly, people
could not have helped asking back, 'What on earth do you mean by that?',
probably thinking that he is using the term 'new age' very strangely.

Fifthly, instructively, Paul's use of another 'apocalyptic' motif belies
the alleged intertextual logic of the new age: the apocalyptic birth pangs
(4:19; cf. 4:27; 1 Thess 5:3). To be sure, this motif too is associated with
the eschaton but its reference is not to the new age itself but to the
tribulation which *precedes* it, namely, the *antecedent* events to the

---

[19] Mell, *Neue Schöpfung* (1986) 47–257.

[20] Concerning the 'new creation', Adams, *World* (2000) 226 recognizes this
possibility without pursuing it further. Baumgarten, *Apokalyptik* (1975) 169–170, while
still subscribing to a realized eschatological view, thinks that Paul 'radically
decosmologized' the meaning of this phrase.

[21] Even if not Pauline, the letter certainly belongs to Pauline tradition. And the
author's overall realized eschatological tendency suggests that this idea comes from Paul.

birth/coming of the Messiah (1QH 11:9–11; cf. Mk 13:8; Mt 24:8; Rev 12). As the imagery goes, the mood is a desperate 'not yet' rather than that of a confident 'already'. Paul's application of this imagery to his present ministry is therefore suggestive. By depicting his ministry as 'apocalyptic' birth pains, Paul in effect labels the present crisis 'an instance of the last-ditch effort by which God's enemies hope to thwart the eschatological redemption of the elect'.[22]

The thrust of the imagery is clear: the present situation 'preclude[s] a simple reference to the Galatians' birth as a punctiliar event accomplished in the past'.[23] That is, the intertextual meaning generated by this motif is precisely the opposite: with Christ yet to be born, the Galatians are now in the pre-messianic period. Hence, an appeal to the logic of apocalyptic intertextuality is inherently self-defeating, for the simple reason that Paul's use of the apocalyptic motifs is confusing in its possible eschatological implications. This means that the alleged eschatological intertextuality is not part of Paul's intention behind his use of 'apocalyptic' motifs. Speaking of the presence of the new age in Paul, widespread as it may be, is certainly going beyond the evidence in Paul himself.

7.2 Christ and the Law

Now we move on to Paul's interpretation of the Christ event in terms of liberation or redemption from the law. All too often, due to the theological weight of the subject (Christology), interpreters fail to perceive the immediate purpose of Paul's discussion. Our aim in this section is to bring out its *contextual* meaning, no doubt, with a view to showing the problem of a realized eschatological reading. We discuss Paul's christological argument in three parts: 3:10–14; 3:15–29 and 4:1–7.

7.2.1 Christ and the Curse of the Law (3:10–14)

Apart from the adumbration in 2:19–21, 3:10–14 is Paul's first extant interpretation of the Christ event in relation to the law, which follows up his argument concerning the blessing of Abraham in 3:8–9.[24] Here Paul takes several radical steps. First, he draws a dark picture of the law. That one is not justified 'in the law' (v. 11) is familiar (2:16), but Paul presses this shared conviction one step further. Instead of providing the blessing of justification, the law only incurs curse: 'all who belong to works of the law

---

[22] Martyn 430.
[23] Martyn 429.
[24] Sanders, *Law* (1983) 22; Dunn 169.

are under a curse' (v. 10)[25]. Together with this, he also drives a clear wedge between law and faith: 'the law is not of faith' (v. 12). Depicting the law as demanding exclusive allegiance to its own 'way of life' (3:12),[26] he simplifies the matter as a clear-cut 'either/or'. Thirdly, Paul reinterprets the shared conviction of Christ's death 'for us' (ὑπὲρ ἡμῶν)[27] by relating it to the curse of the law: 'Christ redeemed us from the curse of the law' (v. 13).[28] By relating the law with curse and defining Christ as the redemption from this curse of the law, the point of the whole argument is clear: the blessing of justification, and the Spirit for that matter, are only 'in Christ Jesus' and 'by faith' (v. 14). The conclusion in v. 14 then is no mere reiteration of justification by faith in 3:6–9.[29] After 3:10–13, the claim is more specific: the blessing comes to the Gentiles 'in Christ Jesus' and *not ἐξ ἔργων νόμου as the foolish Galatians (and the agitators behind them) would have it*. Since justification requires liberation from the curse of the law, the Galatians, if they are to be justified, should stay clear of the law.[30] Christ and the law are mutually incompatible.

Arguing for this incompatibility, Paul's immediate point is that Christ's soteriological significance ('for us'), which is assumed to be obvious, involves our liberation from the curse of the law. He grounds this controversial interpretation on a further claim that Christ himself became

---

[25] The curse is not just possibility but reality. *Contra* Stanley, 'Curse' (1990) 500; Witherington 233; Williams 90; Spanje, *Inconsistency* (1999) 202–203. The only reason Paul *actually* gives for this is people's failure to keep the law *in toto* (v. 10b). Cf. Luz, *Geschichtsverständnis* (1968) 149. Paul's conviction is surely christological, which, however, inevitably involves an anthropological judgment. *Contra* Sanders, *Palestinian Judaism* (1977) 482–484; Donaldson, 'Curse' (1986) 101; Cousar, *Cross* (1990) 114.

[26] Rightly, Choi, 'Spirit' (1998) 189. The contrast is not between 'performance' and 'faith'. *Contra* Mußner 230–231; Westerholm, *Law* (1988) 113–114; Kruse, *Law* (1996) 84. Dunn's assertion (117) that Paul's quote of Lev 28:5 is 'essentially a positive view' is prejudiced. After v. 10 and before v. 13, this is an ironical way of announcing death (curse) rather than life. The covenant was not 'effective ... for Israel' during the time before Christ (175–176); they were 'under the curse' and in effect outside the covenant (3:11, 13, 22), as Dunn himself, self-contradictorily, acknowledges (178).

[27] Whether this is pre-Pauline (Betz 150; R. Longenecker 121–122) or not (Dunn 177) is a question we cannot answer with certainty.

[28] Eckstein, *Verheißung* (1996) 153–154; Räisänen, *Law* (1983) 59. Whether Paul develops such a view for the first time here or has already done so, probably in the light of his Damascus experience, is an issue attracting lively scholarly discussion. Strecker, 'Befreiung' (1975) 479–508; Stendahl, *Paul* (1976) 23–40; Räisänen, *Law* (1983) 229 (256–263); Dunn, *Law* (1990) 89–107; Suhlmacher, *Reconciliation* (1986) 68–93, 110–168; Kim, *Origin* (1984) 269–311.

[29] Many interpreters fail to appreciate the polemical note directed at the 'judaizing Galatians'. E.g., Dunn 168–180; Wright, *Climax* (1991) 153–156; Donaldson, 'Curse' (1990) 94–112.

[30] *Contra* Sanders, *Law* (1983) 25–26, v. 13 is therefore crucial for Paul's argument.

the curse on behalf of us: γενόμενος ὑπὲρ ἡμῶν κατάρα (cf. 2 Cor 5:21; 1 Cor 1:30). It is to justify this second claim that he appeals to the Christ event. To be precise, his concern is not Christ's death itself but the specific information that he died 'on a tree' since it is this particular fact that provides the necessary justification of his association of Christ's death with curse: 'Cursed is everyone who hangs on a tree' (Deut 21:23).[31]

In this antithetical logic of law/curse and Christ/redemption we do not see any particular intention of capitalizing on the 'already' of the latter. Christ surely liberated us but turning this into 'an act in which the law was robbed of its universal power to curse'[32] is squeezing Paul's language too much since it ignores the Galatian context in which the curse of the law *is* posing a serious threat. Speaking of curse and redemption, therefore, Paul's primary concern is the Galatians in the present, not the Jewish Christians[33] or humanity in general[34] in the past: 'All who *are* (εἰσίν) of works of the law *are* (εἰσίν) under a curse' (v. 10); 'Christ redeemed *us*' (v. 13).[35] That is why Paul, addressing the Gentile Galatians, presents Christ as *our* liberation from the curse of *the law*.

In the context of the Galatian crisis, this statement clearly functions as a way of warning the Galatians that their attraction to the law, instead of bring about the hoped-for justification, in fact means losing the freedom they have attained in Christ and returning to the curse of the law.[36] Could anyone in the Galatian churches have missed the sharp lash of criticism when Paul announces, '*All* who (ὅσοι) belong to works of the law are under curse' (v. 10)?[37]

---

[31] Rightly, Eckert, *Verkündigung* (1971) 78. For this verse see Wilcox, 'Upon the Tree' (1977) 85–99. For the data in Qumran (4QpNah; 11QTemple 64:6–13), see Fitzmyer, *Advance* (1981) 125–146.

[32] Martyn 321; *idem*, 'Crucial Event' (1996); Luz, *Geschichtsverständnis* (1968) 153. Scholarly failure to relate v. 10 to v. 13 is surprising. If the law had lost its cursing power, taking it up would not do any harm to the Galatians.

[33] *Contra* Lightfoot 140; Betz 148; Donaldson, 'Curse' (1986) 95; Hong, *Law* (1993) 141; Wright, *Climax* (1991) 154. The problem of this view is 'we' in v. 14, which refers to the Galatians. Cf. Räisänen, *Law* (1983) 19: 'Now, it would be strange, if the pronoun tacitly changed its reference in v. 14'.

[34] *Contra* Byrne, *Sons* (1979) 153, 182; Bruce 167; Dunn 176–177; Cousar, *Cross* (1990) 116.

[35] Addressing the Galatians, 'us' includes the Galatians. See Hübner, *Law* (1984) 150.

[36] Rightly, Spanje, *Inconsistency* (1999) 202–206. Cf. Stanley, 'Curse' (1990) 501 and Patte, *Paul's Faith* (1983) 48–57. The view of Donaldson, 'Curse' (1989) 102 that Paul interprets the Christ event as liberation from the curse of the law because it 'is not possible to make an end run around the law and those in its domain' misses the point.

[37] Esler, *Galatians* (1998) 254, n. 9; Sanders, *Paul* (1991) 57–58. Martyn 317, n. 105 notes that Paul turns to such words as κατάρα and ἐξαγοράζω 'for the Galatian situation', but still fails to bring it to bear on his interpretation of v. 13.

7.2.2 Abraham, Christ and the Law (3:15–29)

In 3:15–25 Paul's polemic continues but now with a chronological logic. His argument is twofold (vv. 15–18, vv. 19–29). First, the law came much later (μετά) than the promise covenant which had already (πρό) been ratified by God (vv. 16a, 18). On the basis of the testamentary principle of finality adduced in v. 15, it then follows that the law is not the proper channel of inheritance (v. 17). Second, Christ marks the termination of the law as our παιδαγωγός.[38] Since Christ too is a recipient of God's promise as Abraham's Seed (vv. 16, 19), his coming marked the effective reinstitution of the promise covenant, and therefore the end of our imprisonment under the control of the law (vv. 19–25). Again, the result is that the inheritance is only available 'through promise', that is, 'in Christ' (vv. 26–29). Paul's logic is clear. In relation to the promise, the law came too late; in relation to Christ/faith, it had run its course when he finally came. Between Abraham on one side and Christ on the other, the law is, so to speak, edged out.[39] Therefore, the law has no place in the Galatian believers' quest for justification/inheritance which is only 'by promise'.

Here Paul's logic is consistently chronological, as is confirmed by his liberal use of temporal references.[40] The law came 430 years after (μετά) the promise which had been ratified earlier (προκεκυρωμένην, v. 17). The law had been here only 'until' (ἄχρις οὗ) the Seed came (v. 19). We were under the law 'before' (πρό) the coming of faith, namely, only 'until' (εἰς)[41] the revelation of faith (v. 23).[42] The law had been our disciplinarian 'until' (εἰς) the time of Christ (v. 24). Thus, 'Now that faith has come, we[43] are no longer (οὐκέτι) under the παιδαγωγόν' (v. 25).

---

[38] This has been the subject of intense scholarly discussion. For attempts to highlight its positive role, see Young, 'Paidagogos' (1987) 150–176 (with extensive background discussion); Belleville, 'Under Law' (1986) 53–78 (59–63); Lull, 'Pedagogue' (1986) 481–498 which also contains a bibliography for the negative view.

[39] Cf. Conzelmann, *Outline* (1969) 223; Watson, *Text* 190–191; Barrett, *Paul* (1994) 73.

[40] Cf. B. Longenecker, *Triumph* (1998) 118; Witherington 262; Donaldson, *Gentiles* (1997) 65.

[41] In both v. 23 and v. 24, the sense is clearly chronological. So most commentators, e.g., Duncan 121–122, 128; Betz 178; Mußner 257; R. Longenecker 148–149; Bruce 183. *Contra* Burton 200 ('pregnant use'); Fung 169–170. Paul's emphatic point in this verse is that the law was our custodian *only* until Christ so that our justification may be *exclusively* by faith in Christ.

[42] That is, revelation of 'faith', not 'Christ'. Paul speaks of the revelation of many 'things' (e.g., Rom 1:17, 18; 2:5; 8:18; 1 Cor 2:10; Phil 3:15) or of the *risen* Christ (1 Cor 1:7; 2 Cor 12:1; Gal 1:12, 16; Eph 3:3; 2 Thess 1:7) but never of 'Christ' to denote his first coming.

[43] See nn. 33–35 above.

The way Paul appeals to the Christ event also changes accordingly. Since Christ now functions as a carrier of God's promise, and since Paul's logic is mainly chronological, all Paul needs to claim the priority of the promise and the temporary function of the law is Christ's 'coming' (vv. 19, 23, 25). Thus, how he died ('hanging on a tree', 3:13) or how he was born ('being born of a woman'/'under the law', 4:4) is not relevant for this particular argument.

Is Paul's point here, as most scholars believe, the eschatological superfluity of the law? The chronological thrust of the argument and especially the statement in v. 19 seem to imply this idea. We have to be careful, however, since the law *is* still alive and active, which is eloquently illustrated by 'the present Jerusalem' (4:25) and now, to Paul's dismay, by the crisis in Galatia. The Galatian crisis itself presupposes the ongoing relevance of the law and its curse (3:10; 4:8–11; 5:1).[44] The change happens to us, not to the 'law'. The demise Christ's coming occasioned is not that of the law itself but that of *believers' slavery*. 'But now that faith has come, *we* are no longer subject to a disciplinarian' (3:25). This forms an interesting contrast to the idea of Christ as 'the end of the law' in Romans (10:4). It is simply not true to say that the coming of Christ rendered the law eschatologically 'obsolete' or 'inoperative',[45] not even the *nuda lex* ('naked law').[46] It is precisely because the law is so lethal, cursing and enslaving those who are under it, that the Galatians' foolish wish to be under the law constitutes such a serious crisis.

In the context in which the Galatians want to take up the law, Paul's chronological argument can hardly be a realized eschatological affirmation of the 'already' of freedom from the law and the superfluity of the latter. This sort of announcement is meaningless anyway since the Galatians can join the law and thereby scrap this 'no longer' and 'already' anytime they want, as indeed they wish to do now. With the law posing a serious threat to the Galatians' quest for God's inheritance (3:18), Paul's chronological argument, accentuating the *incompatibility* of the law with promise and faith,[47] functions as a strong *warning* to the Galatians of the consequence of their foolish behavior. One is either ἐν Χριστῷ or ὑπὸ παιδαγωγόν; one cannot belong to two different 'periods' at the same time. Of course, they can choose to belong to the 'time' of the law, but then it means they *lose* the freedom Christ has brought for them (3:25–26), and *return* to their

---

[44] Paul's use of 'the Scripture' for 'the law' (v. 22) may be an indication of this. Belleville, 'Under Law' (1986) 56, 58 disputes the equation of the two, but the parallelism is too strong to be explained away. Compare v. 22 and vv. 23–24.

[45] *Contra* Hübner, *Theologie* (1993) 83 and most others.

[46] *Contra* Cranfield, 'Law' (1964) 62–63; Hong, *Law* (1993) 125–169.

[47] So Cosgrove, *Cross* (1988) 71.

former life in slavery, with the result that they will also lose the promised inheritance which only comes by faith. Paul's logic here is not that of realized eschatology.

7.2.3 Christ and Slavery under the Law (4:1–7)

Paul's discussion of Christ in 4:1–7 combines the motif of 'liberation from the law' in 3:10–14 and the chronological thrust and emphasis on 'heirship' in 3:15–29. Here too, Paul's skilful use of time references, contrasting the times 'before' and 'after' Christ, effectively highlights the law's incompatibility with Christ. In the illustration (vv. 1–2) we hear that the heir does not differ from a slave 'during the time when' (ἐφ' ὅσον χρόνον) he is a minor, and he is under guardians and trustees 'until' (ἄχρι) the time set by the father. The contrast between slavery and liberation becomes more explicit in the explication (vv. 3–5): 'when' (ὅτε) we are minors, we were under the elements of the world (v. 3), but 'when' (ὅτε) the fullness of time came, God sent his Son. The result is our redemption from the law and adoption as sons (v. 5), leading to the exclamation: 'οὐκέτι you are a slave ἀλλά a son!' (v. 7a).

As we have seen,[48] Paul's description of the time before Christ is singularly colored by the motif of 'slavery' under the law (vv. 1–2, 3). Then 'the fullness of time'[49] came, and God sent His Son accordingly (cf. 3:25). This may have been enough in another context, but Paul continues: Christ was 'born of a woman' and 'came under the law'. The purpose is obvious: 'so that he might redeem those who were under the law' (v. 5a), and 'so that we[50] might receive adoption as sons' (v. 5b). Paul's point is simple: since the very purpose of Christ's coming is our redemption from the law, commitment to him necessarily entails the dissolution of any relation to the law. The result is, of course, exactly the same: the law and Christ do not mix.

Once again, Paul's depiction of the Christ event is determined by the specific point he wants to get across in this particular argument. As in 3:10–13 the salvific significance of Christ's death is presupposed. His immediate claim here is that it involves liberation from the law.[51] That Christ redeemed us from the law is backed by the fact that he too came to be 'under the law', which is further justified by the fact that Christ was

---

[48] See 6.2 above.

[49] See n. 96 in chapter 5.

[50] See nn. 33–35 above.

[51] 3:10–14 is designed to prove that the Abrahamic 'blessing' does not come from the law. Accordingly, its 'curse' receives accent, with Christ becoming the redeemer from this 'curse'. In 4:1–7 the law itself is at issue, and therefore Paul drops 'curse' and simply speaks of 'the law'.

'born of a woman'. This time it is Christ's incarnation, not his 'hanging on a tree' (3:13) nor his 'coming' (3:15–25), that Paul needs to maintain his claim of 'freedom from the law'.[52]

Here too, we should be careful not to squeeze Paul's declaration, 'You are no longer slaves but sons!' (4:7a).[53] To be precise, his point is the termination of our slavery,[54] and not the eschatological obsoleteness of the law which remains as relevant as ever. In fact, for the Galatians in whose life the 'Abba' cry plays an essential role, Paul's declaration of sonship as evidenced by the Spirit is nothing more than a reminder of what they already know.

What is really surprising is Paul's claim that this Spirit-sonship, which involved freedom from pagan idolatry, also involves freedom from *the law*. Addressed to the Galatians who are on the verge of joining it, this then is in no way an unconditional endorsement of their unchangeable sonship. On the contrary, this emphatic 'no longer' functions as a sharp warning, revealing the true nature of their behavior and its consequence, as is easily confirmed by his charge of apostasy in the following verses (4:8–11). What Paul is actually saying to the Galatians is that they should not come under the law again if they are to remain as God's sons and heirs.

In sum, throughout the letter the upshot of Paul's christological argument is the *incompatibility* of Christ and the law. Each time, Paul presses this point from a different angle: Christ means liberation from the curse of the law (3:10–14), the end of the law as our *paidagogos* (3:15–25) and liberation from the slavery under the law (4:1–7). In turn, these claims are supported by appealing to different aspects of the Christ event according to the immediate need of Paul's logic: 'hanging on a tree' (3:10–14), 'coming' (3:15–25) and 'being born of a woman' (4:1–7).

Paul's appeal to the Christ event is therefore highly contextual and shows no particular intention of pressing a realized eschatological point. The Galatian crisis itself, in which the law is by no means obsolete or superfluous, falsifies a realized eschatological reading of Paul's christological argument. That Paul's logic is not eschatological is further confirmed by the allegory in 4:21–31 where both the law and promise, corresponding to the flesh and Spirit respectively, form *synchronic* alternatives for the Galatians to choose.[55] Paul's point throughout is not that the law is chronologically outdated, but that it is fatal, placing one

---

[52] Our concern is to discern the contextual nature of Paul's use of the Christ event and not to drive a theological wedge between the incarnation and the crucifixion. See the caution by Hooker, *Adam* (1990) 15.

[53] See Grayston, *Dying* (1990) 81–82.

[54] Cf. NEB; Lührmann 80.

[55] Cf. Boers, *Justification* (1994) 70.

under the sway of the flesh, the consequence of which is exclusion from God's inheritance (3:3, 10, 19–25; 4:3–5, 8–11, 30; 5:1, 18).[56]

7.3 Paul's Polemical Use of the 'Crucifixion' Motif

Interestingly, Paul does not use the term crucifixion in his christological argument itself (3:10–4:7), but he uses it three times as he speaks of himself and of the Galatians (2:19–20; 5:24; 6:14–16). Not surprisingly, these passages too are frequently adduced as evidence for Paul's realized eschatological perspective. But once again, proper attention to the context indicates that this is a misreading of Paul's intentions. The purpose of this section is to substantiate this claim.

7.3.1 The Crucified Paul I (2:17–21)

The first use of the crucifixion image occurs in 2:19–20. The passage is variously construed, but in our view the whole section is Paul's criticism of Peter's behavior as a breach of 'the truth of the gospel' (v.14), namely, the truth of justification by faith. As Paul sees the matter, Peter's withdrawal from the table fellowship with Gentile believers amounted to labeling the Jewish Christians 'sinners'. Inasmuch as their associating with Gentiles was encouraged by their belief that justification is only available in Christ, Peter's behavior in effect rendered Christ himself as 'the agent of sin' (v.17). Moreover, it also meant 'reinstating' the law which had already been demolished as incapable of providing righteousness (v. 16), making Peter himself a 'transgressor' (v.18). Paul's manifesto in vv. 19–21 serves as a polemic against 'hypocritical'[57] dispositions such as Peter's, and against the propaganda of the agitators for that matter. Using Peter's blunder as the launch pad, Paul declares his own stance *vis-à-vis* the law.[58]

Shocking as it must have been in the ears of other Jewish Christians, Paul unequivocally announces that his commitment to the crucified Christ involves his own death too, that is, his death in relation to the law: διὰ νόμου[59] νόμῳ[60] ἀπέθανον (v. 19). The shock doubles as he continues

---

[56] Mitternacht, noting on 5:5, rightly asserts that 'the dispute between Paul and influencers was not whether the age to come had actually dawned' but about 'the living conditions of the new creation within the prevailing evil age'. 'Assessment' (2002) 411, n. 20.

[57] Cousar 48 notes the observation of Wilckens, *TDNT* 8:565 that in Hellenistic Judaism the word also carried the meaning of 'apostasy', which coheres well with the Galatian problem of apostasy (1:6).

[58] Similarly, Anderson, *Theory* (1996) 134.

[59] 3:13 and 4:4–5 seem to provide the most reliable key to this cryptic phrase. So Tannehill, *Dying* (1967) 58–59; Bruce 143; Fung 123. *Contra* Burton 133; Duncan 70.

to say that he died to the law 'with a view to living in relation to God' (v. 19). This is a bold polemic since it suggests that the law is only a *hindrance* to his life in relation to God.[61] Paul had to abandon the law because he simply could not have any life in relation to God while living under the law.[62] Thus, any attempt to deny his 'death in relation to the law' by rebuilding it can only mean a flat denial of his God-oriented life. So Paul cries, 'I do not nullify the grace of God!'[63]

It is to justify this refusal to take up the law again that Paul brings in the cross of Christ. His focus, even fixation, on the motif of death is unmistakable.[64] For him committing himself to Christ means *participating* in his death/crucifixion (v. 19), which also involves his death in relation to the law.[65] And, as the perfect συνεσταύρωμαι indicates, it is the reality of his death, namely, his severance from the law, that characterizes his present life in faith. Of course, Christ's resurrection too is presupposed (1:12, .16), but this should not obscure Paul's immediate purpose of accentuating his separation from the law. Thus, even this 'Christ living in me' is now perceived in the light of his death rather than resurrection: who 'loved me and gave himself for me' (v. 20).[66] Verse 21 further confirms this: 'for if righteousness was from the law, Christ would have died in vain!' (v. 21). The effect of Paul's focus on the death motif is clear: his faith in the crucified Christ does not allow any room for the law.[67]

Is this crucifixion of 'I' intended, as most scholars think, as a description of 'believers' objective position in Christ',[68] including the Galatians, with the 'I' being 'universal' or 'paradigmatic'?[69] That, however, is to blunt Paul's polemic edge.

---

[60] The primary connotation is 'separation'. Burton 132; Fung 122; Martyn 256. Cf. Romans 6:2, 10, 11; 7:6.

[61] So Burton 134; Duncan 70–71. Cf. Ebeling, *Truth* (1985) 147.

[62] One senses a strong polemic against the view of the law as a source of life. Deut 30: 15–20; 32:47; Ps 119; Prov 3:1 f.; Sir 17:11; 45:5; Bar 3:9; 4:1; *m. Abot* 2:7–8; *4 Ezra* 7:17, 21; 14:30. But see Ezek 20:25.

[63] Cf. Lightfoot 119.

[64] Cf. Hays, 'Christology' (1989) 278.

[65] Here Paul assumes that Christ's death is a death *vis-à-vis* the law.

[66] The two aorist verbs clearly point to Christ's death on the cross. See J. Vos, *Pneumatologie* (1973) 86: '[z]u beachten ist aber, daß Christus nicht in seiner Funktion als Auferstandener, sondern in der Funktion des Gekreuzigten erscheint'. See also Furnish, 'Christological Assertion' (1993) 113–115; Cousar 61.

[67] Mußner 179; Brinsmead, *Response* (1982) 75.

[68] Burton 136; Fung 123, following Ladd, *Theology* (1974) 485.

[69] So most scholars, e.g., Betz 121; Kümmel, '"Individualgeschichte"' (1978) 140; Kertelge, 'Rechtfertigungslehre' (1968) 218–219; Martyn 102, 280.

First, in the context of the Antioch incident, the passage is part of Paul's polemical and personal manifesto.[70] As his emphatic *refusal* in v. 21 shows,[71] the main point is his *determination* to make Christ the exclusive center of his life in contradistinction to the disposition of Peter. No doubt, this *presupposes* a christological foundation, but that is not what Paul is getting at. It is Paul himself who tore down his relationship to the law; it is he who, unlike Peter, refuses to rebuild it (v. 18).

Secondly, in the context of the Galatian crisis too, Paul's statement functions as a *rebuke* of the wayward Galatians.[72] As we have seen,[73] Paul's view of the present state of the Galatians is a bleak one, a disposition so *different* from his own: apostasy (1:6; 3:3; 4:8–11; 5:7); 'ending with flesh' (3:3); 'not obeying the truth' (5:7). Addressed to those who, desiring to be under the law (4:21), are turning a blind eye to Christ crucified (3:1), Paul's announcement of his own crucifixion 'with Christ' and 'to the law' can hardly be an affirmation of their faith in Christ.[74] No doubt, the truth of dying with Christ remains universal, equally applicable to the Galatians. The trouble is, however, that they themselves, enticed by the law, are *abandoning* this truth.[75] For this reason, Paul even changes the shared confession about 'Christ's death ὑπέρ ἡμῶν into his own personal experience of Christ 'who loved μέ and gave himself ὑπέρ ἐμοῦ', a move witnessed only here in his entire writings.[76] Thus, his criticism of Peter, like his autobiographical narrative as a whole,[77] is his criticism of the behavior of the deviating Galatians.[78] Precisely because his attitude is

---

[70] Rightly, Witherington 190; Ridderbos 106–107; Duncan 72; Davies, *Rabbinic Judaism* (1970) 197; Burton 132, 134. *Contra* Weder, *Kreuz* (1981) 176–177.

[71] Rightly, Lambrecht, 'Reasoning' (1996) 59; Ebeling, *Truth* (1985) 150; Smiles, *Gospel* (1998) 186–188. *Contra* Burton 140; Schlier 104.

[72] Brinsmead, *Response* (1982) 69, 188 notes this, but still misses his own point.

[73] See 2.2 above. The contrast between Paul's uprightness and the Galatians' deviation forms a major feature in Paul's argument (1:6–9; 4:12, 16; 6:12–15).

[74] Rarely, Suhl, 'Galaterbrief' (1987) 3113.

[75] The criticism of Schlier by Eckstein, *Verheißung* (1996) 44 therefore also applies to Eckstein himself. Faith itself is now at issue not only between Peter and Paul but also between Paul and the Galatians. See Chrysostom.

[76] Here 'we' is traditional and 'I' a contextual adaptation (cf. Rom 8:31–39). Cf. Berényi, 'Gal 2,20' (1984) 529. Tannehill, *Dying* (1967) 57 worries about 'false subjectivising' but the real problem here is ignoring the context and reading too much theology into Paul's words.

[77] The Antioch incident concludes Paul's autobiographical narrative whose parenetic function is well acknowledged. Lyons, *Autobiography* (1985) 124–164; Gaventa, 'Galatians 1 and 2' (1986) 309–326; Williams 76–82; Stowers, *Letter Writing* (1986) 109; Cosgrove, *Cross* (1988) 145–146; B. Dodd, 'Paradigm' (1996) 90–104.

[78] So Ridderbos 98; Schlier 87–88; Betz 113–114 and n. 14; Smiles, *Gospel* (1998) 103–105.

paradigmatic, it is also a stinging criticism of the Galatians who are attracted to the law.[79]

7.3.2 The Crucified Paul II (6:14–15)

Paul uses the crucifixion motif once again at the end of the letter, this time to contrast his apostolic disposition to the flesh-oriented policy of the agitators (vv. 12–13). Paul is adamant: 'May I never boast of anything except the cross of our Lord Jesus Christ' (v. 14a). Here, to boast does not mean 'to brag' but 'to have confidence in'[80] or, in light of v. 16, 'to live according to', used here to describe his and his opponents' dispositions. It is to explain this policy of his that he brings in the crucifixion motif: through the cross[81] the 'world' has been crucified to him. Not only that, but he too has been crucified to the world. V. 15 explains why: 'for neither circumcision nor uncircumcision is anything; but a new creation is everything!'[82]

For many, Paul's talk of double crucifixion, together with the motif of the 'new creation', provides evidence for his realized eschatological outlook.[83] According to Martyn, what we have here is 'the death of one world and the birth of another', i.e., the dawn of the new age, occasioned by the cross of Christ.[84] Again, this claims too much. We make two points.

First, the crucifixion here is a very specific one. The world is not crucified in an absolute sense but only 'in relation to me'. This qualification is crucial since it clearly implies that otherwise the world still exists. Moreover, it is only the world that is crucified; Paul remains alive. The point is the dissolution of relationship. With the world crucified he cannot have any relationship with it. The opposite is equally true. With Paul crucified to the world, the latter cannot have anything to do with him.[85] The crucified subject is different each time; the result is exactly the same: with one party gone, the relation between the two breaks up. That is,

---

[79] Thus the 'I' here is certainly 'paradigmatic but not 'incorporative' as Cummins, *Antioch* (2001) 217 suggests. In the present polemical context, it is 'paradigmatic and exclusive'.

[80] Boyarin, *Jew* (1994) 81.

[81] Alternatively δι' οὗ may refer to Christ but with no meaningful difference. Rightly, Betz 318.

[82] Within Galatians, 'the world' is the sphere of the flesh, 'the order of material creation and everything under its sway, independent of the control of the Holy Spirit'. Guthrie 150–151.

[83] So Tannehill, *Dying* (1967) 64; Fung 307; Witherington 450. Dunn 341 even changes the imagery into the mutual crucifixion of *Christ* and the world.

[84] Martyn 564. See also B. Longenecker, *Triumph* (1998) 36 and many others.

[85] Cousar 151: 'continuing presence of the world'.

Paul here 'uses the image of crucifixion to emphasize his own lethal separation from his previous, cherished and acknowledged identity'.[86]

Secondly, context has to be considered. The immediate contrast is between Paul and the agitators, two competing ministers to the confused Galatians.[87] The statement is Paul's *personal* manifesto, a depiction of his apostolic disposition polemically juxtaposed to the policy of his opponents, as the emphatic and contrastive ἐμοὶ δέ (v.14) makes clear.[88] That is, this is not an objective theological statement about the effect of the cross of Christ[89] but about Paul himself. This being so, it is clear that this statement does not apply to the agitators. For those who boast of flesh the world has not been crucified.[90] Though largely ignored, it is equally clear that the Galatians are not included either.[91] Indeed, there is a sense in which this manifesto is paradigmatic, in that it describes how the Christian existence *should* be.[92] Yet, given the Galatians ending with the flesh despite the vivid display of the Christ crucified (3:1, 3), it is hardly possible that Paul should intend to include the Galatians within this 'I' statement. On the contrary, his resolute manifesto of 'only the cross' serves as a criticism of their attraction to the policy of the agitators.[93]

This manifesto is backed up by the following statement: οὔτε γὰρ περιτομή τί ἐστιν οὔτε ἀκροβυστία ἀλλὰ καινὴ κτίσις (15). Given the lack of the specific term 'new age' in Paul, it is this motif of 'new creation' that scholars adduce as the strongest evidence for Paul's realized eschatology.[94] In this respect, it is quite unfortunate that scholarly

---

[86] Martyn 564. See also Tannehill, *Dying* (1967) 63; Minear, 'Crucified World' (1979) 396.

[87] Cf. Witherington 449.

[88] This is widely noted. E.g., Burton 354; Ridderbos 224; Mußner 414; Fung 306. Cf. R. Longenecker 293.

[89] *Contra* G. Vos, *Eschatology* (1930) 48; Cousar 150–151; Fung 307. This reads too much theology into Paul's crucifixion *metaphor*.

[90] See Weima, 'Gal 6:11–18' (1993) 93, 94–95 among others.

[91] *Contra* Tannerhill, *Dying* (1967) 64; Mußner 414; R. Longenecker 295; Mell, *Neue Schöpfung* (1989) 293.

[92] Lyons, *Autobiography* (1985) 151–152 speaks of 'the "formerly-new" contrast of redemptive history personalized in Paul's self-description and made paradigmatic for the experience of every Christian'. Paul's problem is that this paradigm is now *not* working with the Galatians.

[93] Similarly, Paul also sets himself up against Peter with a view to criticizing the behavior of the Galatians (2:15–21).

[94] Cf. *Jub* 1:29; 4:26; *1 En* 72:1 (cf. Isa 65:17; 66:22; Rev 21:1; 2 Pet 3:13; *1 En* 91:16–17; *4 Ezra* 7:75; *2 Bar* 32:6; 44:11–12). As Keck, 'Apocalyptic' (1984) 236 puts it, 'While Paul never says that "the age to come" has arrived, he does speak of "new creation"'. See also G. Vos, 'Spirit' (1912) 93–94; Stuhlmacher, 'Erwägungen' (1965) 2–

discussion of the passage is mainly focused on the thrust of this ambiguous concept itself (individual, communal or cosmological)[95] without paying sufficient attention to the meaning *Paul* gives it in the context of his argument.

For Paul this 'new creation', whatever its original meaning may have been, functions as a 'rule' (τῷ κανόνι τούτῳ) or 'standard' according to which he has been conducting himself and according to which the Galatians are supposed to conduct themselves (στοιχήσουσιν).[96] As the rule to walk by, the standard of 'new creation' easily merges with the motif of the Spirit, according to which the Galatians are urged to walk: εἰ ζῶμεν πνεύματι, πνεύματι καὶ στοιχῶμεν (5:25).[97] Moreover, its parallelism with 'faith working itself out through love' in 5:6[98] makes Paul's *moral* use of the concept unmistakable.

Paul's concern here then is not the nature of the new creation itself but the disposition of the Galatians *vis-à-vis* this new creation. Whether individual, communal or cosmological, his demand is that the Galatians should *'participate* in the new order of existence',[99] that is, they should conduct themselves according to this rule of 'new creation', and precisely this 'participation' is the problem he is presently concerned with.[100] His demand is simple: 'Do not resort to the flesh (circumcision and uncircumcision) as the agitators do, but to the real means of justification, the 'new creation'! The unusual, conditional benediction[101] that follows makes it unmistakable: 'Peace and mercy to anyone who walk according to this rule' (6:16). His barbed retort in v. 17 confirms that the Galatians are

---

3, 7–8; Mell, *Neue Schöpfung* (1989) 304, 324; Weima, 'Gal 6:11–18' (1993) 93, 100–101; Ortkemper, *Kreuz* (1967) 34; Baumgarten, *Apokalyptik* (1975) 169–170.

[95] A good survey is available in Mell, *Neue Schöpfung* (1989) 9–32. As Reumann, *New Creation* (1973) 89–99 points out, the context lacks any cosmological note. Even granted the cosmological meaning, it cannot refer to the 'new age', since for Paul this cosmological renewal of the creation belongs to the future (1 Cor 7:31; 15:27–28; Rom 8:19–22; Phil 3:20–21). See Adams, *World* (2000) 227 who, despite his own recognition of this, still opts for a quasi-cosmological, realized eschatological, reading.

[96] Guhrt and Link, *NIDNTT* 3:399–400. It is not the 'criterion of *salvation'* as Mell, *Neue Schöpfung* (1989) 317 asserts but the standard for *human conduct*. Cf. *1 Clement*. 1:3; 7:2; 41:1.

[97] Matera, 'Culmination' (1988) 88.

[98] Eckert, *Verkündigung* (1971) 37; Snodgrass, 'Justification' (1986) 86. Another parallel in 1 Cor 7:19 speaks of 'keeping God's commandment'. Despite the caveat by Drane, *Paul* (1975) 65 and Räisänen, *Law* (1983) 67, these parallels are the most immediate data for determining the thrust of the 'new creation' in Paul. Furnish, *Ethics* (1968) 201; Ridderbos, *Paul* (1975) 286.

[99] The phrase comes from Fung 308 with emphasis added.

[100] We demonstrated this in chapter 2.

[101] As Betz 321 rightly notes, the condition 'implies a threat'.

not doing very well in this respect, and this is why he has to utter this warning (cf. 1:6; 3:3–4; 4:12–20; 5:7).

Paul speaks of the mutual crucifixion between the world and himself to accentuate the absolute disjuncture between his own stance and the world-oriented disposition of the agitators, with the radical image of 'crucifixion' encapsulating his resolute refusal to compromise his unwavering orientation to the cross of Christ. Paul also employs the motif of 'new creation' to describe this life-disposition as the rule he has consistently been following, to which he now urges the wayward Galatians to return. Here Paul is not announcing 'the death of one world and the inauguration of another'. Speaking of the 'objective and eschatological' reality occasioned by the cross of Christ is, therefore, missing the point.[102]

7.3.3 Crucifixion of the Flesh (5:24)

Paul also uses the crucifixion motif in 5:24. The context is his exhortation to the Galatians to follow the Spirit instead of the flesh (vv. 16–26): 'Those who belong to Christ crucified (ἐσταύρωσαν) the flesh together with its passions and desires' (v. 24). This negative statement is followed by a positive exhortation: 'if we live by the Spirit, let us also conduct ourselves by the Spirit' (v. 25).

As is widely noted,[103] now believers come in as the crucifying agents with the flesh as the crucified victim. Put in the aorist, the most likely reference of this crucifixion is what happens at conversion or baptism:[104] 'the decisive act taken at the beginning of their Christian experience'.[105] Naturally, the primary focus falls on the action of believers. As Fung says, 'in turning to Christ and becoming members of his body, they radically renounce fellowship with sin, whose seat is the flesh'.[106] Here too the intention is not difficult to see, namely, to highlight 'a decisive separation from the Flesh, a separation so radical as to amount to the death of the Flesh'.[107]

Yet, many interpreters want to go further. Speaking of crucifixion, it is argued, Paul posits a deliberate link between believers' crucifying action and the crucifixion of Christ. For example, Fung remarks, 'It is only on the basis of their spiritual participation in the historical crucifixion of Christ

---

[102] Paul's concern is the behavior of the Galatians, not the death of Christ itself. In this sense, Paul's use of crucifixion language stresses the fact that 'dying with Christ needs to be worked out in the believer's life'. Hooker, *Adam* (1990) 45 (see the whole chapter).

[103] E.g., Martyn 501; Barclay, *Truth* (1988) 117; Tannerhill, *Dying* (1967) 61.

[104] The difference between the two is immaterial.

[105] Dunn 315.

[106] Fung 274.

[107] Martyn 501.

and by the Spirit's power that believers can hope to fulfill the ethical obligation to crucify the flesh with its passions and desires'.[108] Even when he speaks of believers' action, then, he still looks askance at the cross of Christ, thereby creating a 'mysterious blend of divine initiative and enabling, and human response and commitment'.[109] The talk then is as much about the cross of Christ as the action of believers at the conversion.

The effect of this blending is clear: the eschatological decisiveness assigned to the cross of Christ is transferred to the crucifixion of believers. In effect, their crucifixion amounts to 'participation' in the crucifixion of Christ, which marks the eschatological defeat of the flesh.[110] Then, their crucifying of the flesh, referring to 'a completed action in the past' and stressing 'the finality of the act',[111] takes on the sense of a perfect: 'they have crucified' – a past event with present results or implications. This then turns out to be another case of the same crucifixion Paul speaks of in 2:20 and 6:14.[112]

With the flesh clearly still alive (5:16–17), however, the tone has necessarily to be moderated. As Bligh says, 'in fact the perfect would not be appropriate, since the flesh once crucified does not remain crucified. The crucifixion has to be continued'. Thus he proposes to take this aorist as an '"inceptive aorist" which signifies the commencement of an action which still goes on'.[113] 'That victory is decisive, but it is paradoxically incomplete'.[114] With 'the past victory in baptism' now leading to 'the constant reenacting of that victory in the daily life of the community', we enter familiar territory. This turns out to be yet another 'instance of the famous Pauline "already" and "not yet"'.[115]

Questions do arise, however. First, why should the motif of crucifixion always be a reference to the cross of Christ? Of course, the imagery ultimately traces back to Christ's crucifixion, but does it mean that Paul cannot use the image without referring to it (cf. Mt 16:24)? Here scholars seem to be squeezing Paul's metaphor a bit too hard.

---

[108] Fung 275. See also Tannerhill, *Dying* (1967) 62: '... it is only through Christ's crucifixion that men are able to crucify the flesh'. *Practically*, what does this statement mean?

[109] Dunn 315. See also Ortkemper, *Kreuz* (1967) 37.

[110] So Fung 275; Barrett, *Paul* (1994) 72; B. Longenecker, *Triumph* (1998) 65.

[111] Guthrie 41.

[112] So Smiles, *Gospel* (1998) 166. Here Suhl, 'Galaterbrief' (1987) 3127 ruins his own insight gained in 2:20.

[113] Bligh, *Greek* (1966) 205.

[114] Martyn 501.

[115] Martyn 501; See also Ladd, *Theology* (1974) 474; Ridderbos, *Paul* (1975) 62–63; Dunn 315.

Secondly, combining believers' crucifixion of the flesh with Christ's cross to produce the paradoxical 'already and not yet' runs against the thrust of the context. As Lull rightly points out,[116] this statement has to be read in relation to Paul's exhortation in vv. 16–23, where the flesh, far from having being defeated, remains as powerful as ever. If Paul had intended to point out the 'already and not yet' nature of the flesh, he would have done it here, instead of drawing such an almost fatalistic picture. Paul's concern here then is not the eschatological status of the flesh but the Galatians' disposition *vis-à-vis* the flesh or the Spirit.[117] Inevitably, therefore, the talk of 'eschatological victory' over the flesh creates undue tension, which in turn necessitates uncalled-for linguistic juggling.

Thirdly, Paul's choice of word may not be insignificant here. This time he uses an aorist, unlike the perfect verbs he uses for himself (συνεσταύρωμαι, 2:20; ἐσταύρωται, 6:14). In the context of the crisis in which the Galatians are presently *allied with the flesh* (3:3; 4:8–11, 12–20; 5:7), this change is not difficult to understand: he cannot refer to their crucifixion of the flesh as a present reality simply because that is not true. Of course, they, like Paul, crucified the flesh at the time of their conversion. However, while he always keeps the flesh (the law and the world) crucified, the Galatians are now reviving their crucified flesh, so to speak. And this is why he has to remind them of their *past* act of 'crucifying the flesh', to contrast it with their present allegiance with it (3:3).[118]

Thus far we have examined Paul's use of the crucifixion motif. Twice he uses perfect verbs to depict his resolute and consistent disposition in the gospel, and once he uses an aorist to remind the Galatians of their conversion to Christ. In both cases the motif accentuates the note of separation between life in Christ/faith and in the law/flesh. The purpose is, of course, to challenge the backsliding Galatians and encourage them to remain in or return to the truth of the gospel. The note of realized eschatology usually associated with the motif is a figment of scholars' theological imagination.

---

[116] Lull, *Spirit* (1980) 115.

[117] So Stott 150: '[i]t is not now a "dying" which we have experienced through union with Christ; it is rather a deliberate "putting to death".... This is Paul's graphic description of repentance, of turning our back on the old life of selfishness and sin, repudiating it finally and utterly'. See also Brandenburger, *NIDNTT* 1:401; Weder, *Kreuz* (1981) 199–200.

[118] Cf. Mitternacht, 'Assessment' (2002) 413–416. In chapter 2 we noted how Paul reprimands the Galatians by contrasting their 'running well' in the *past* with their *present* deviation from the gospel. Paul does exactly the same thing here.

Before we move on to a new section, let us briefly summarize the result of our discussion thus far. Since Christ already came and died on the cross, and since redemption from the curse of the law is inherently grounded on this past event, Paul's appeal to the Christ event is, to a certain degree, necessarily retrospective. Yet, having examined the way he actually appeals to this pivotal event and his use of the crucifixion motif for that matter, it has become clear that the point he drives at is not its eschatological decisiveness or sufficiency which supposedly renders the law obsolete or superfluous.

Rather, Paul's interpretation of the Christ event is formulated in such a way that highlights the mutual incompatibility of Christ/faith and the law. And, as we saw in the preceding chapters, this thesis of incompatibility is presented in the context of the Galatians' quest for their ultimate salvation which is variously termed righteousness, inheritance, the kingdom of God or eternal life. Paul certainly points to the past, but he does so with the specific purpose of rectifying the fatal mistake of his converts in the present, which is accomplished by pointing to its devastating consequence for their future destiny. It is not true therefore to say that 'the dominant temporal scheme of Galatians is then/now ... not now/yet-to-come'.[119] Looking at the work of Christ, 'he looks at the future in the light of the past so as to see how to live in the present'.[120]

7.4 Christ and the Spirit

Apart from its polemical function discussed thus far, there is another important aspect of Paul's christological argument that needs to be examined, namely, its conspicuous emphasis on the role of the Spirit. Since Paul's main points are summed up as 'in Christ' and 'by faith', to clarify this point will prove crucial for a proper grasp of Paul's thought.

7.4.1 Christ Living in Paul (2:20)

We begin with the statement in 2:20. Here Paul says that his present life in faith, in stark contrast to his former life under the law in which Paul himself (ἐγώ) was the subject of existence, has a completely new ground: 'Christ living in me'. As the foundation of his new existence, 'Christ living in me' here seems to be an allusion to the Spirit, that is, the Spirit of his Son (4:6). As Fee perceptively suggests, the clause 'Christ lives in me' is

---

[119] Williams, 'Promise' (1988) 711–712. The dominant contrast is the 'then' of 'running well' and the 'now' of apostasy. See 2.2 above.

[120] We borrow the words from Goldingay, *Approaches* (1990) 122.

'a kind of shorthand for "Christ by his Spirit lives in me"'.[121] This
supposition is supported by the observation that it is typically the Spirit
rather than Christ that is depicted by Paul as living or dwelling 'in us'.[122] It
is this Christ-in-the-Spirit living in Paul that enables him to live in relation
to God, which he could not do in his life under the law, and that is why he
had to die to the law and take up faith in Christ. The idea of the Spirit is,
however, not explicit at this point, and thus we move on to our next
passage.

7.4.2 The Crucified Christ and the Spirit (3:1–5)

Paul's focus on the death of Christ continues in 3:1 (cf. 2:19–21). What
concerns us at this point is the suggestive move from the crucified Christ
(v. 1) to the Spirit (vv. 2–5).[123] That these two form a single argument is
clear. His charge of foolishness (ἀνόητοι) in v. 1 corresponds to the
equally rhetorical demand in v. 2 and more directly to οὕτως. ἀνόητοί
ἐστε in v. 3. Clearly, he brings in both Christ (v. 1) and the Galatians'
receiving the Spirit by faith (vv. 2–5) as *the* clincher of his claim of
justification by faith.[124]

This connection has not yet been properly explained. Vos begs the
question by asserting that Paul here brings in the *Tauftradition* in which
participation in Christ's death and the gift of the Spirit are combined as
expressions of 'das in der Taufe geschenkte Heil'.[125] Fee's claim that Paul
appeals to the experience of the Spirit since the theological argument in
v. 1 is not sufficient to 'secure their allegiance to his gospel'[126] is hardly
satisfactory either. Considering that Paul begins with the crucified Christ
(v. 1) but moves quickly to the Spirit which takes up his *main* interest here
(vv. 2–5), more probable is the supposition that he appeals to Christ
crucified in order to speak of the Spirit. In other words, Paul here appeals
to the crucified Christ as the exclusive source of the Spirit.[127]

---

[121] Fee, *Presence* (1995) 374. He rightly remarks that it is only a matter of 'emphasis
in a given context' whether Paul speaks of 'indwelling Christ' or 'indwelling Spirit'.
Most relevant is Romans 8:9–10 where 'the Spirit of God' and 'the Spirit of Christ' are
clearly interchangeable with 'Christ'.

[122] So R. Longenecker 93; Duncan 72; Ridderbos 106; *Paul* (1975) 232; Conzelmann,
Outline (1969) 209; Bruce, *Paul* (1977) 209.

[123] See Lull, *Spirit* (1980) 54–55. Most commentators pass over this move.

[124] So R. Longenecker 101; Brinsmead, *Response* (1982) 68; Eckstein, *Verheißung*
(1996) 121. *Contra* Cosgrove, *Cross* (1988) 39–61; Stanley, 'Curse' (1990) 492–495.

[125] J. Vos, *Pneumatologie* (1973) 87.

[126] Fee, *Presence* (1995) 382.

[127] Paul's focus on the Christ crucified was motivated by his desire to ground his
converts' faith on 'God's power' which expresses itself in the activity of the Spirit. See 1
Cor 2:1–5.

Paul's repeated emphasis on receiving the Spirit not ἐξ ἔργων νόμου but ἐξ ἀκοῆς πίστεως confirms this interpretation (2–5). However we translate ἀκοὴ πίστεως,[128] its focus on the Christ crucified remains unchanged (3:1). That is, it is Paul's proclamation of the crucified Christ that constitutes the indispensable *Sitz-im-Leben* of the gift of the Spirit[129]. It was by the 'message' of the crucified Christ,[130] or the Galatians' 'hearing' it,[131] that they received the Spirit. Inasmuch as faith means one's commitment to the crucified Christ (2:20), receiving the Spirit by faith is just another way of saying receiving the Spirit on the ground of the work of Christ. At least in this context then, both Christ and faith in him are seen in the light of their being the source of the Spirit.

7.4.3 Redemption from the Law and the Spirit (3:14; 4:6)

Paul's emphasis on the Spirit in his christological argument is also visible in his deliberate association of Christ's redemptive work with the gift of the Spirit. In 3:10–14 his argument ends with double ἵνα clauses, juxtaposing the blessing of Abraham and the promise of the Spirit as the dual purpose of Christ's redemption from the law's curse. Our concern here is the second clause about the Spirit. The argument in 3:10–14 forms part of the larger argument concerning the 'blessing' which began at 3:8. Thus he may well have stopped after 3:14a, which, as we have seen,[132] forms a perfect conclusion for the whole argument (3:6–14a). Yet, significantly, he adds another clause about the Spirit which seems quite obtrusive in its context,[133] and thereby makes a *deliberate* connection between Christ's work of liberation from the law and the coming of the Spirit. Led by a purpose-denoting conjunction (ἵνα), this remarkable clause claims that the Spirit is in fact the very *purpose* or the direct consequence of Christ's work of liberation.[134]

Paul does the same thing in 4:1–7. Again, his reference to Christ's redemption from the law (v. 5) soon leads to the thought of the Spirit: 'God sent his Spirit into our heart, crying "Abba! Father!"' (v. 6). This time the link between Christ's redemption from the law and the coming of the Spirit is much more explicit than in 3:14. First, he uses the same 'sending formula' (ἐξαπέστειλεν) for both 'his Son' and 'the Spirit',[135]

---

[128] See the surveys in Hays, *Faith* (1983) 143–146 and Fung 131.

[129] Lull, *Spirit* (1980) 53–95; Cousar 66.

[130] So Hays, *Faith* (1983) 146–148; Fung 131–132; Eckstein, *Verheißung* (1996) 86–88; Martyn 284, 286–289.

[131] So Williams, 'Hearing' (1989) 82–93; Dunn 154–155; Witherington 212–113.

[132] See 3.3 above.

[133] The Spirit is missing in 3:6–14, as R. Longenecker 123 observes.

[134] Rightly, Kremer, *EDNT* 3:120.

[135] So Fee, *Presence* (1995) 402, 404–405; Martyn 391; R. Longenecker 173–174.

indicating that the two are part of a single package. Secondly, he identifies the Spirit as 'the Spirit of His Son', with the clear implication that the coming of the Spirit is in fact not different from the coming of the Son himself.

Here too this move is deliberate since Paul's argument does not require a reference to the Spirit.[136] The idea of redemption and adoption (v. 5) leads smoothly to the conclusion in v. 7. Yet the flow is 'diverted' and made to run through the experience of the Spirit. Paul's intention to lead his talk of Christ to the work of the Spirit is unmistakable.[137] As in 3:14, one has to note, he presents believers' sonship based on Christ's work of redemption from the law as effective ground or *reason* for God's sending of the Spirit: '*Because* (ὅτι) you are sons, God sent his Spirit...' (v. 6). Once again, the work of Christ is understood in the light of the gift of the Spirit.

7.5 Faith and the Spirit

Our observation above has another important corollary: Paul also presents faith in the light of the Spirit, that is, primarily as the source of the Spirit. This is hardly surprising since for Paul faith, referring to believers' commitment to the person of Christ, carries an intrinsically christological orientation.[138] We have already looked at 3:1–5, where he presents both the death of Christ and ἀκοὴ πίστεως as the only ground for the coming of the Spirit, and 3:14b in which he reminds the Galatians that they have received the Spirit, the purpose of Christ's death, διὰ τῆς πίστεως. Just as the Galatians received the Spirit 'by faith', the blessing of justification comes to the Gentiles 'in Christ'.

The same thought seems present in 3:21–22, though it is not explicit. Here the contrast is between law and promise. Paul says that the law is not the source of righteousness because it does not have the 'power to give life'. This life-giving power belongs to the promise, which therefore is the exclusive source of righteousness. And in v. 22 he says that this promise comes ἐκ πίστεως. Here, as many interpreters note, the 'power to give

---

[136] Paul refers to the Spirit in 4:6 for the first time since 3:14.

[137] Rightly, G. Vos, 'Spirit' (1912) 110.

[138] So Donaldson, *Gentiles* (1997) 116–117; Räisänen, 'Break' (1985) 546. Faith, love and hope all refer to the single entity of believers' disposition. Paul speaks of faith to denote its christological orientation and love for its horizontal, ethical dimension. Seen in its eschatological dimension, this becomes 'perseverance of hope' (1 Thess 1:3).

life' is almost certainly an allusion to the Spirit,[139] making the promise a functional equivalent of the Spirit. This then is practically the same as saying that the Spirit is 'by faith'.

Another case in point is πνεύματι ἐχ πίστεως in 5:5. Normally both are taken as two independent adverbial phrases, both describing the manner of eschatological waiting: 'through the Spirit' *and* 'by faith'. This is by no means an unnatural meaning, either exegetically or theologically. Yet in view of Paul's manifest concern to stress that the Spirit comes only 'by faith' (3:2–5, 14b, 21–22), it seems better to take ἐχ πίστεως as an adjectival phrase qualifying the immediately preceding πνεύματι, with the result of 'through the Spirit that comes from faith'.[140] As in the case of his appeal to Christ, Paul's emphasis on faith too is intended to bring out the crucial role of the Spirit.

It has become clear that Paul, by focusing on Christ and faith in him, in fact points to the importance of the Spirit that comes from *faith* in *Christ*. This means then that in Paul's talk of 'in Christ' and 'by faith' it is the Spirit that receives his ultimate emphasis. This is further confirmed by the way he develops his argument in 4:1–7 and 4:21–31. In 3:13–14 we have both the Christ event (v. 13) and faith (v. 14b) as the ground of the experience of the Spirit. In 4:1–7 the link between the Christ event and the coming of the Spirit remains the same, but now nothing is said about faith. Then, in his allegorical summary of his theological argument in 4:21–31,[141] we notice that the antithesis is now neither between law and Christ nor between law and faith but between law and Spirit. Both Christ and faith are prominent by their absence, while it is the Spirit alone that effectively sustains Paul's antithetical argument.[142]

Of course, that does not mean that Christ and faith are any less crucial for Paul's argument. It does show, however, where his ultimate emphasis falls: the Spirit. Thus, Fee is right to observe that the ultimate antithesis in Paul's polemic against the law is between Spirit and flesh,[143] since both Christ and faith, which both stand in antithesis to the law, ultimately point to the work of the Spirit. *In short, in Galatians saying 'in Christ' and 'by*

---

[139] Williams, 'Justification' (1987) 96–97; Cosgrove, *Cross* (1988) 65–69; Fee, *Presence* (1995) 398. It seems clear enough in 2 Cor 3:6 which alludes to Ezek 37: 5, 14.

[140] So Chrysostom; Lull, *Spirit* (1980) 126; Cosgrove, *Cross* (1988) 152; Sloan, 'Law' (1991) 53; Haufe, 'Geistmotiv' (1994) 190. Cf. Burton 278.

[141] Major themes in Paul's argument converge here: slavery-freedom; law-promise; flesh-Spirit. Thus, there is a grain of truth in Boyarin's claim that this passage is 'the climax of the entire argument and preaching of the letter, in which all of its themes are brought together and shown to cohere'. *Jew* (1994) 32.

[142] Cf. Boers, *Justification* (1994) 66; Siker, *Disinheriting* (1991) 45.

[143] Rightly, Fee, *Presence* (1995) 383. See also Duncan 80–81.

faith' amounts to saying 'through the Spirit'. Paul's christological emphasis turns out to be an emphasis on the crucial role of the Spirit.[144]

7.6 The Spirit as the Key to Paul's Argument

In the context where Paul deals with the questions of justification and inheritance, the implication of this emphasis on the Spirit is clear: justification and inheritance come only *through the Spirit*. Justification is available only 'in Christ' (2:17; 4:14a; 5:2–4) whose redemption from the law forms the foundation of the work of the Spirit (3:1–5, 14b; 4:6). Inevitably, it is also only 'by faith' (2:16–21; 3:11, 24), since it is faith that incorporates believers into the person of Christ (2:19–20; 3:26–28). In saying this, Paul's meaning then is that justification comes only through the Spirit. The point is succinctly expressed by his own summary of his argument: ἡμεῖς γὰρ πνεύματι ἐκ πίστεως ἐλπίδα δικαιοσύνης ἀπεκδεχόμεθα (5:5). It is 'through the Spirit' that we, who seek to be justified 'in Christ' (2:17; cf. 5:2, 4, 6), are waiting for the hope of future righteousness, and this Spirit comes only 'from faith'. Here Paul's emphasis on the role of the Spirit as the means of proper eschatological anticipation stands out quite impressively.[145]

Needless to say, the same goes for 'inheritance'. Inheritance is only 'through promise' (3:18, 29),[146] and this promise comes only ἐκ πίστεως (3:22). In 4:6–7 heirship to God's promised inheritance is depicted as the function of the Spirit. In the allegory of 4:21–31 it becomes clear that 'promise' is in fact another (biblical) way of saying 'the Spirit' (28–29),[147] which is the indispensable qualification for participating in the inheritance (30). In the final analysis, then, Paul's thesis is simple: the Spirit is what ultimately matters because the Spirit is the only way to justification and inheritance. This is indeed the force of his charged demand at the beginning of his argument proper: τοῦτο μόνον θέλω μαθεῖν ἀφ' ὑμῶν· ἐξ ἔργων νόμου τὸ πνεῦμα ἐλάβετε ἢ ἐξ ἀκοῆς πίστεως; (3:3).

---

[144] Crownfield, 'Problem' (1945) 498; Lull, *Spirit* (1980) 25; Barclay, *Truth* (1988) 83; R. Longenecker 123; Witherington 211: '[t]he Spirit is at the heart of the matter and so plays a vital role in his acts of persuasion'. This is one of the central concerns of Fee's study, *Presence* (1995).

[145] Hamilton, *Spirit* (1957) 34. Unlike Fee, *Presence* (1995) 417 and many others, the eschatological thrust is not a new element here.

[146] The actual phrases varies: ἐξ ἐπαγγελίας, δι' ἐπαγγελίας (3:18a, b) and κατ' ἐπαγγελίαν (3:29) without any significant change of meaning.

[147] See 5.3 above.

In this sense, we can also call his argument in Galatians pneumatological as well as future eschatological. The significance of this emphasis on the Spirit in his argument as a whole will be discussed in the next chapter, where we attempt to make sense of both the future eschatological thrust and the strong pneumatological accent in Paul's argument as his response to the crisis in the Galatian churches.

Chapter 8

Paul's Future Eschatology and the Galatian Crisis

The future eschatological thrust of Paul's argument in Galatians has become clear, and therefore the main task of this study is now accomplished. As we have just indicated, however, our thesis will not be complete unless we are able to show how his future eschatological argument actually works as a response to the present crisis in Galatia. The purpose of this last chapter is, therefore, to make sense of his future eschatological argument in the concrete context of the Galatian crisis.

Three major issues are involved here. First, we shall inquire about the nature of the Galatian crisis. In chapter 2 we already identified the apostasy of the Galatians as the real problem with which Paul grapples. Now we need to ask further: in what sense does their behavior constitute a case of apostasy? Our thesis in this section is that Paul speaks of apostasy primarily because of the moral, or behavioral deviation of the Galatian converts from the truth of the gospel which he defines in terms of 'faith working itself out through love', not because of certain doctrinal implications of circumcision and the law[1].

Secondly, in line with this, we also need to clarify the thrust of Paul's emphasis on faith and the Spirit which we identified in chapter 7 as characterizing his theological response to the crisis. That is, what does he mean when he claims that future justification and inheritance can only come about 'through the Spirit'? We shall argue that in both the theological and the ethical sections the purpose of Paul's emphasis on the Spirit is not doctrinal or apologetic but pastoral, in that he considers the Spirit mainly as it pertains to the proper conduct of the Galatian converts.

This will in turn lead us to the issue of the nature of the opposing mission in the Galatian churches. Paul's consistent concern about

---

[1] Here I use the terms 'moral' and 'morality' without the negative connotation often attached to these words, especially in Western Protestant scholarship. 'Morality' is not something opposite to the 'gospel' but an indispensable dimension of it, as long as we do not mean by the 'gospel' a certain ethereal idea which does not touch our corporeal existence. In Paul, the term 'obedience', which in fact is the ultimate goal of his apostolic ministry, conveys what we mean by 'morality'. See our discussion in the conclusion below. Also see our cautionary remark on pp. 203–204.

'obeying' the truth throughout the letter leads us to suppose that moral rigor is not really part of the agitators' program. This claim runs, of course, against the typical reconstruction of the agitators' mission as 'law-observant. In this section we shall argue that this picture of a 'law-observant mission' cannot be reconstructed from Paul's reports about them in Galatians, however 'rhetorical' they may be. We shall take up these three questions one by one, after discussing the problems of the dominant way of construing Paul's argument in the letter.

8.1 Two Arguments in Galatians?

In our *Forschungsbericht* at the beginning of this study, we have identified the awkward relation between chapters 3 and 4 and chapters 5 and 6 of Galatians as the chief problem of the realized eschatological reading of Paul's argument. Now, as we inquire into the nature of the Galatian apostasy, we can present this very problem as the reason why the traditional, doctrinal construal of the crisis should be reconsidered as the proper interpretation of his argument.

8.1.1 Opinio Communis

In current scholarship it is widely thought that Paul's argument in Galatians consists of two distinct, though related, sets of argument, one 'theological' and the other 'ethical'.[2] In this dual construal of his argument, it is the theological, i.e., the doctrinal discussion in chapters 3 and 4 that forms his main response to the crisis in Galatia with the ethical exhortation in chapters 5 and 6 either further qualifying/clarifying or supplementing this main argument. Scholars differ on how to relate the moral exhortation to the main, theological part of the letter,[3] but this distinction itself seems to be fairly well-established.[4]

On this view, the 'central' section, being 'theological', deals with the immediate crisis in Galatia which is essentially dogmatic in nature. The cause of the crisis is, of course, the Galatians' attempt to get themselves circumcised, and possibly, to take up the law. For Paul, however, for Gentile believers to receive circumcision of necessity means to acknowledge the insufficiency of faith in/of Christ, and therefore, amounts

---

[2] Barclay's scheme of 'identity' and 'pattern of behavior' nicely captures the consensus.

[3] See the survey in Barclay, *Truth* (1988) chapter 1.

[4] This is true even for those who consider chapters 5 and 6 as the main part of Paul's argument. E.g., Choi, 'Spirit' (1998) 47–51.

to a flat denial of faith itself (cf. 2:21; 5:2–4).[5] Not that there is any visible deterioration in the life of the Galatians, except that they are adding 'works of the law' to their existing 'life in faith'.[6] In Paul's *dogmatic* reasoning, however, this very addition somehow[7] means a denial of faith, *despite the fact that their 'life in the Spirit' remains as vivid as ever, at least, in the opinion of the Galatians and the agitators.*

Accordingly, Paul's emphasis on the Spirit too is understood mainly in terms of its doctrinal significance: Paul focuses on the Spirit because it can serve as evidence of the realized nature of justification and inheritance, namely, as evidence of the eschatological superfluity of circumcision and the law (cf. 3:1–5, 14b). In a sense, it is the Galatians' doctrinal 'ignorance' (3:1, 3) of the significance of the Spirit that causes them to turn to the law, and it is also this ignorance that Paul wants to rectify by drawing their attention to the Spirit as the fulfillment of God's promise.

---

[5] According to Hooker, *Pauline Pieces* (1979) 25–27, the law, symbolizing 'the effort to achieve salvation by one's own effort', 'violates the logic of grace manifested in the death of Christ'. Betz 48; Mußner 54–55; Lull, *Spirit* (1980) 38–39; Dunn 40; Kruse, *Paul* (1996) 102–103; Wright, 'Gospel' (1994) 234. Hansen, 'Paradigm' (1994) 198.

[6] Cousar 20. He expresses the idea as 'icing on the cake' (67).

[7] With no explicit answer to this question available in Paul, scholars suggest many different reasons for such decision. 'Legalism' is the traditional answer, but after E. P. Sanders, sociological and eschatological explanations become increasingly popular. See 1.2 above. The solution presented in the present study focuses on the ethical dimension of Paul's argument.

Boyarin, *Jew* (1994) presents an interesting view. Based on his own hermeneutical flesh-spirit dualism, he explicitly affirms that 'for Paul "Christian ethics" is simply the true interpretation of "Jewish Law" and always has been'. Yet, this explicit affirmation of the moral dimension of Paul's perspective receives an idiosyncratic, ideological twist, since he defines 'the moral and religious necessity of humankind' as Paul's desire 'to erase all distinction between ethnos and ethonos, sex and sex and become one in Christ's spiritual body' (85). For him, Christian ethics is the true interpretation of the Law, precisely because it 'replaces the difference of the doing of *many* material practices with the logos of one ideal fulfillment' (140, emphasis his).

Boyarin does define 'the spiritual' in terms of 'the law of faith working through love' (94, 105) but this moral concept is strategically retranslated into 'a new, single human essence' which forms the answer to Paul's 'profound concern for the one-ness of humanity' (52–56, 106). Even the crucifixion is understood as 'the erasure of the difference between "Jew and Greek" and their reconstitution as the new single People of God', which is 'the fundamental message of Galatians and ultimately of all of Paul' (76). Here we see that the ethical dimension is effectively explained away by the ideology of 'the unification of humanity' (36). It is not surprising, since, for him, the ethical dimensions remain only 'a consequence of the hermeneutic' (105). He claims that 'there is no contradiction between an ethical reading' of Paul's argument and 'a hermeneutical one' (95–105; the quote is from 97), but what actually happens is a practical subordination of the ethical to the hermeneutical notion of 'one-ness'.

Here it is also widely assumed that the agitators require of the Galatians not only circumcision but also 'observing the law'. This means that the agitators, keen on doing what the law commands, also show a strong moral sensitivity. Fighting against this morally-sensitive, law-upholding, theology of the agitators, then, Paul's denunciation of 'works of the law' inevitably involves repudiation of moral effort (works) to keep the law seen as the denial of faith, with this faith now radically redefined as either 'faith-as-trust'[8] or 'the faithfulness of Christ'[9] to exclude any human endeavor within its purview.

If this is the case, it necessarily means that Paul's moral demand of 'walking by the Spirit' in chapters 5 and 6 cannot be considered as a direct response to the crisis caused by the agitators' law-upholding mission.[10] For many interpreters it is his anti-law polemic in the theological section that explains the inclusion of moral exhortation in his argument. For the agitators and the Galatians his outright criticism of (observing) the law can certainly be taken as giving a blank check for moral libertinism. Hence, in order to prevent the possible (inevitable?) moral confusion or misunderstanding to which his polemic may give rise, he had to issue a strong warning, making it clear that his criticism of the law by no means compromises the importance of proper conduct. According to this view, then, Paul's exhortation becomes a 'warning' against a potential problem that may arise from his own argument in the earlier part of the letter.[11]

Other scholars perceive a real moral problem in Galatia, but then they attribute this problem not to the 'law-upholding' agitators but to Paul himself who supposedly failed to provide his Gentile converts with adequate practical moral provision comparable to the detailed moral directions in the Mosaic law.[12] For these interpreters, such moral confusion

---

[8] Many interpreters think that Paul is redefining the traditional 'faith-as-obedience' (Sir 44:19–21; 1 Macc 2:52; *Jub* 17:15–18; CD 3:2; *m. Abot* 5:3) in terms of 'faith-as-trust'. Betz 141; Fung 135; Dunn 161–162; Martyn 297–298; Witherington 225–226. If so, however, would he have said what he says in 5:6? His revision is certainly christological but not moral.

[9] In this case, even (human) faith becomes irrelevant. For major proponents of this view, see chapter 3, n. 22.

[10] Notable exceptions are Howard, *Crisis* (1991) 11–14; Lull, *Spirit* (1980) 113–130; Brinsmead, *Response* (1982) 164–192.

[11] Besides commentaries, see Eckert, *Verkündigung* (1971) 134; Schnabel, 'Ethics' (1995) 270; Eckstein, *Verheißung* (1996) 248–249.

[12] Examples of those who posit a sort of 'moral deficit' as inherent in Paul's gospel include Betz 273; Barclay, *Truth* (1988) 60–74; Dunn 285; Gaventa, 'Singularity' (1991) 157; Lategan, 'Developing' (1994) 321; Murphy-O'Connor, *Paul* (1996) 200; Williams 28; Martyn 19.

We should take care not to minimize the serious moral concern that dominates Paul's apostolic ministry from first to last. Despite the persistent misunderstanding partially

among the Galatians, visible even before the intrusion of the agitators provides a partial explanation for the willingness of the Galatians to open themselves up to the law-upholding mission of the agitators. In this case, Paul's moral emphasis on the Spirit in chapters 5 and 6 primarily serves an apologetic function, 'defending' the moral efficacy of his Spirit-oriented gospel.[13]

Whether one understands Paul's moral exhortation as a warning or a defense, however, it remains unchanged that it cannot belong to Paul's main response to the Galatian crisis itself caused by circumcision (and the law), and thus, one ends up having two distinct sets of argument with two very different points of emphasis.

8.1.2 Problems of the Opinio Communis

This dualistic construal of Paul's argument in terms of 'theology and ethics' raises a number of difficult questions in the flow of Paul's argument. First of all, we have to recognize that Paul's response in 2:15–5:12 is hopelessly ineffective for a dogmatic argument. With flat disagreements over such critical issues as faith and law,[14] and with the Galatians inclined to the wrong side, the vital thing for him to do to win them over is to demonstrate *why* his 'narrow' position should be the real gospel. As Sanders remarks, the view of the agitators is 'an entirely reasonable position' solidly based on the Scriptures,[15] while Paul himself

---

based on a misinterpretation of his 'repudiation' of the law, Paul's mission is never morally lax or deficient. Paul himself defines his apostolic mission of 'proclaiming the gospel' in clearly moral terms: 'obedience of faith' (Rom 1:5; 15: 16, 18; 16:26), a concern easily confirmed by such statements as Phil 2:14–18 and 1 Thess 3:9–12. Thus, as is easily ascertained by his reminder in 5:21, Paul's concern for his converts' proper moral conduct is consistent and uncompromising. To be sure, Paul's gospel is not just another ethical system, since it is solidly ground on God's redemptive work through Jesus Christ and the Holy Spirit, thus creating what Jacque Ellul calls 'true moral situation'. However, this conviction should not be used as a means of emptying or relativizing the anthropological-moral dimension of the gospel, thereby reducing Paul's gospel to a mere ideology without anchorage in the concrete context of human life.

[13] Scholars do not agree over the degree of moral uncertainty. Jewett, 'Agitators' (1971) 209: 'libertinism'; Betz 8–9, 273: 'flagrant misconduct'; Barclay, *Truth* (1988) 106, 218: 'moral insecurity/confusion'; Ebeling, *Truth* (1985) 251: 'deep sense of insecurity'. On the other hand, Drane, *Paul* (1975) 8 and B. Longenecker, *Triumph* (1988) 80, n. 13 explain Paul's moral exhortation as 'a consequence of his own theological presentation', without postulating moral laxity on the Galatians' part. Still the apologetic thrust remains the same.

[14] For the agitators and the Galatians presently under their auspices, the law, far from nullifying faith, supplements and completes it. See Martyn, *Issues* (1998) 7–24, 141–156.

[15] Sanders, *Law* (1983) 18. See also Räisänen, *Law* (1983) 183; Goulder, 'Pauline Epistles' (1987) 489: 'The counter commission has the Bible, the Church and reason entirely on its side'.

is something of a lone wolf. Under the circumstances, his repeated charge of apostasy must have struck the others as nonsensical,[16] unless he was able to convince them why it has to be so. Yet this crucial explanation is precisely what he *fail* to provide, as the diversity of scholarly opinion on this ironically confirms.[17] It is not that Paul gives up on the Galatians; he is confident of persuading the Galatians back to his own gospel (5:10). Indeed, his matter-of-fact manner of throwing charges[18] gives us the impression that he assumes that his accusation will make immediate sense to the Galatians. In other words, Paul must have a reasonable ground for such a confident denouncement of the behavior of the Galatians.

Secondly, we should not miss the fact that Paul's language itself does not show any sign of dealing with two distinct issues. His concern with the law/circumcision, the immediate cause of the crisis, does not stop at the end of his theological argument but runs on right to the end of the letter (5:1–4, 14, 18, 23; 6:12–13, 15).[19]

More suggestive is Paul's consistent use of the Spirit-flesh antithesis to depict the crisis both in the theological (3:3; 4:21–31) *and* the ethical sections (5:16–26; 6:7–9). In fact, the heart of the present crisis lies in the fact that the Galatians are abandoning the Spirit and ending with the flesh (3:3), to which his demand that they should follow the Spirit instead of the flesh (5:16–18; 6:7–9) comes as a perfect answer. To be sure, many interpreters speak of two distinct uses of this dualism, 'theological' (non-moral) and 'moral', limiting the flesh in 3:3 and 6:12–13 strictly to circumcised flesh.[20] Why, however, do we need to resort to an artificial dichotomy of moral and non-moral when Paul himself does not show any intention of making such distinction? Granted a reference to circumcision,[21] His use of the evocative 'flesh' instead of the more neutral 'circumcision' would be hard, if not impossible, to understand, if he had meant to avoid the moral connotation the word normally delivers.[22]

---

[16] This is noted by Guthrie 61; Dunn 40; Anderson, *Theory* (1996) 149.

[17] For the agitators Paul's 'argument' is only a series of *non sequiturs* in variation. So Sanders, *Palestinian Judaism* (1977) 552; Howard, *Crisis* (1991) 52–53; Watson, *Paul* (1986) 64 are justified to fail to find any 'theological' ground for his rejection of the law.

[18] For this reason, T. Martin, 'Apostasy' (1995) 437–461 speaks of an apostasy to their former 'paganism'.

[19] Thus, speaking of 'a real return to law-language' is misleading, since it has always been Paul's central concern. *Contra* Brinsmead, *Response* (1981) 164, 200.

[20] E.g., Burton 148; Barclay, *Truth* (1988) 204; Hansen 80. But see R. Longenecker 239.

[21] Eckert, *Verkündigung* (1971) 75 doubts such a reference.

[22] See Keck, *Paul* (1989) 101; Frey, 'Antithese' (1999) 45 (68) –77. The effect of this deliberate association is widely noted. E.g., Cousar 67–68; Cassirer, *Grace* (1988) 39–40, 43.

Thirdly, and more seriously, this dualistic construal of Paul's argument creates an insuperable contradiction within his polemic. The problem is simple: Paul's relentlessly moral claim that future salvation requires proper obedience (5:21; 6:7–9) contradicts his emphatic claim of 'justification by faith' as commonly understood. As we have seen, many scholars think that here Paul's main purpose is just to warn the Galatians of the danger of libertinistic behavior. Even if this is the case, it only means that he carries out this task so effectively that he practically demolishes his own claim in the earlier part of his argument. As long as one subscribes to a doctrinal understanding of his theological argument, this logical contradiction cannot be avoided.[23]

Not surprisingly, there are attempts to ease the tension by turning Paul's explicit moral demand (imperative) into a sort of doctrinal discussion (indicative). Some scholars do so by taking his conditional exhortation as a description of identity. For. example, Fung interprets Paul's warning in 5:19–22 in this way: 'those who consistently behave in ways that are opposed to God's nature (cf. 1 Cor 6:9 f.) show thereby that they have not accepted God's rule through Christ in their lives'.[24] This is not, however, what Paul says there. He never says that improper conduct evidences that one has never been a believer.[25] Even when he charges the Galatians of blatant apostasy (1:6; 3:3; 4:8–11; 5:7), he means a return to their former slavery and not their having never come to God at all. His intention is pastoral exhortation, not theological discussion of who are in and who are out (cf. 1 Jn 2:19).[26]

Another way of alleviating the tension is to consider Paul's ethical section as a defense of the Spirit's moral efficacy.[27] This view is not entirely misleading, since his exhortation does presuppose his conviction about the superiority of the Spirit over the flesh, as is reflected on the strong promissory note of his command in 5:16–18.[28] But this is a

---

[23] This is highlighted by Jewett, 'Agitators' (1971) and Martin, *Foundations* (1986) 152–158.

[24] Fung 261–262. See also Cole 164; Gundry, 'Grace' (1985) 11; Fee, *Presence* (1995) 443.

[25] The passage that suits Fung best would be 2 Cor 13:5. Even there, however, Paul's paraenetic purpose is clear: 'so that you may not do wrong'; 'that you may do what is right' (v. 7). Paul is not testing the authenticity of his converts' faith but motivating their improvement (v. 10).

[26] *Contra* Esler, *Galatians* (1998) 205–239.

[27] E.g., Betz 28–29; *idem*, 'Defense' (1979); Lull, *Spirit* (1980) 113–130; Barclay, *Truth* (1988) 106–145; Gundry-Volf, *Perseverance* (1990) 141–154, 203–216.

[28] The construction οὐ μὴ τελέσητε carries this note. See *BDF* §365; Zerwick, *Greek* (1963) 149–150. Martyn 529; Barclay, *Truth* (1988) 111; Burton 299; Merk, *Handeln* (1968) 71; Parsons 'Being' (1988) 242; Hansen, 'Conversion' (1997) 225.

presupposition, not the main point of his discourse here. The dominant mood of these chapters is exhortative, not apologetic. Moreover, would Paul really think that the Spirit needs his *defense*? A more serious difficulty of this 'solution' is, of course, the actual situation in Galatia. With the Spirit apparently failing to produce its promised fruit for the Galatians, thereby precipitating their embrace of the law, would mere verbal affirmation of the Spirit's efficacy do any meaningful job for its defense?

Since Paul's moral demand as the non-negotiable condition for final salvation is so inexorable, any attempt to harmonize it with his supposed emphasis on the sufficiency of 'faith' does violence to the plain thrust of his exhortation.[29] That is, as long as we posit a sort of doctrinal threat to faith caused by circumcision and the law in chapters 3 and 4, his moral demand in chapters 5 and 6 leaves us with no real possibility of finding coherence between the two sections of his argument. The choice before us is thus simple: either Paul is juxtaposing two mutually contradictory arguments side by side[30] or we have to turn the question the other way round. That is, is it really the case that Paul's 'theological' argument in chapters 3 and 4 deals with a doctrinal issue?

8.2 The Moral Crisis in Galatia

Bearing these problems in mind, we shall argue in this section that the Galatian crisis is primarily a moral one.[31] This conclusion is based on the observation that Paul himself responds to the crisis essentially in moral terms, which is the immediate concern of our inquiry here. Our thesis about the future eschatological nature of his theological argument thus far already anticipates this conclusion; our task here is to bring it out to the surface.

---

[29] Spanje, *Inconsistency* (1999) 180–189 tries to resolve the 'inconsistency' between justification by faith and judgment by deed by saying that the latter is addressed to 'haughty self-assured Christians'. As long as both come from the same Paul, such a differentiation of audience does not really solve the problem of 'inconsistency'.

[30] Cf. Räisänen, *Law* (1983) 62.

[31] By saying this, we do not mean to deny the presence of other issues. The real-life situation is always complex and therefore allows different ways of looking at it. A good example is, as is frequently attempted by modern scholars, to investigate the dimension of identity as it relates to the current crisis. Here our contention is simply that the moral dimension of the crisis is what stands on the foreground in Paul's perception.

8.2.1 Circumcision as a Moral Problem

The obvious starting point is Paul's treatment of circumcision, the issue *par excellence* in the present crisis in Galatia.[32] On a dogmatic view of the issue, as already noted, circumcision poses a threat to the gospel due to its 'doctrinal' implication as a denial of faith. Under the circumstances, resisting the lure of circumcision should not only be the necessary but also the *sufficient* solution to the problem, at least for the present crisis. In the words of Mauer: '[i]n Galatien dreht sich alles um einen einzigen Punkt, um die Frage der Beschneidung. *Ihre Annahme oder Ablehnung* ist das Bekenntnis, durch das man sich für das Gesetz oder für die Gnade...entscheidet'.[33]

Is this, however, the way Paul actually treats the matter? His unequivocal prohibition in 5:4 seems to suggest this very thing. We should read further, however. Having warned the Galatians of the danger of circumcision, he surprises them by stating that 'in Christ Jesus neither circumcision nor uncircumcision has the power[34] but only faith working itself out through love' (5:6). This way of putting the matter is by no means an accidental misrepresentation, since he reiterates precisely the same point at the end of the letter: 'for neither circumcision nor uncircumcision is anything; but a new creation is everything!' (6:15)

The importance of these statements is clear: in a letter designed to impress on the Galatians the absolute necessity of avoiding circumcision, Paul places both circumcision *and uncircumcision* together under the same negative column of 'of no power'.[35] For one thing, this makes it clear that remaining uncircumcised is not the real answer he has in mind; the latter is as unsatisfactory as the former in defining one's faith. This then falsifies the common view that for Paul circumcision constitutes a doctrinal denial of faith, and thus its refusal has to be the affirmation of one's faith. Circumcision is clearly of no use, but then, so is uncircumcision. That is, the real problem Paul detects in Galatia runs much deeper than the question of circumcision *per se*.[36]

---

[32] So Burton 272; Eckert, *Verkündigung* (1971) 31–71; Boers, *Justification* (1994) 62–65; 70–71. Circumcision, as Barclay, *Truth* (1988) 45–46 puts it, is 'one fact which is incontrovertible', and therefore, forms 'a secure base from which to analyze the Galatian crisis'.

[33] Cited from Eckert, *Verkündigung* (1971) 40 (emphasis added). Most recently, Nanos, *Irony* (2002) 58 speaks of the incompatibilities of 'the good message of inclusion by circumcision versus the good message of inclusion apart from circumcision' competing with each other in Galatia.

[34] See our discussion of this passage below.

[35] See Williams 138. Cf. Martyn 472.

[36] Mitternacht, "Assessment" (2002) 410 is certainly right to think that 'more is at stake' behind Paul's words in 5:6, but it does not necessarily prevent one from positing a

According to Paul's own affirmation, the *only* thing that matters is 'faith working itself out through love' (5:5) or a 'new creation' (6:14),[37] which constitutes the heart of the 'truth' (5:7) or 'rule' (6:16) to which the Galatians have to conform. Here both 'faith and love' and the rule of 'new creation' come into the picture as alternatives or solutions to the problem of circumcision. What we need to note here is the fact that these alternatives to circumcision and uncircumcision are *moral* entities. As Johnson remarks in a different context, these are 'not abstract terms but living qualities, which could be described behaviorally in terms of the attitudes and actions'.[38] Faith as the antithesis of circumcision is familiar. What is significant at this point is Paul's definition of faith in terms of love, something becoming active (ἐνεργουμένη)[39] through love. Love is, of course, 'the synopsis of Christian life',[40] which represents the gist of Paul's exhortation to 'walk according to the Spirit' in chapters 5 and 6. We have also observed the close parallelism between the 'new creation' and the Spirit as the standard of Christian conduct (6:14–15; 5:25).[41]

Does this then mean that Paul gives a moral answer (faith-love) to a doctrinal problem (denial of grace/circumcision)? Is this the first crack of an opening through which he is to sneak in 'the whole law'? Indeed, most interpreters read this statement as if it were his attempt to 'clarify' or 'qualify' his own earlier statement on 'faith'.[42] This change of thrust is, however, not visible in the text.[43] Clearly, both 'faith working itself out through love' and the 'new creation' are presented not as a (moral)

'no salvation without circumcision' theology on the part of the agitators. In other words, Paul's answer is not necessarily the opposite of the agitators' position.

[37] See 7.3 above.

[38] Johnson, *Writings* (1986) 94. The comment is made while he gives a general description of the qualities of early Christian experience.

[39] For the thrust of this participle, see Mulka, 'Fides' (1966) 174–188; Furnish, *Love Command* (1972) 97; Bligh, *Greek* (1966) 193; Mußner 353–354. However we construe the participle, the *actual convergence* of faith and love remains the same. Clearly, both refer to different *aspects* of believers' disposition which is *indivisible*. For this reason Paul can freely refer to the disposition of the Thessalonians either as 'work of faith', 'labor of love' or 'perseverance of hope' (1 Thess 1:3; 5:8): faith (3:2, 5, 7, 10); faith and love (3:6); love (3:12). Also see Phil 2:15–17 in which Paul defines 'the sacrifice and service of your faith' in clearly ethical terms.

[40] Williams 143. He says that for Paul faith denotes the 'vertical' and love the 'horizontal' aspect of Christian life.

[41] See 7.3 above.

[42] So most scholars, e.g., Williams 138; Fung 230; Cousar 117. This is analogous to the tendency to consider 2:19–20 as the ethical defense of Paul's argument of justification by faith instead of considering it as part of the argument itself.

[43] Cf. Crownfield, 'Problem' (1945) 492: 'Surely he would have made it clear that he was turning from one misunderstanding to its polar opposite'.

consequence of (justifying) faith[44] but as the very definition of faith, and thus, as the alternative to the problem of circumcision itself (5:2, 4, 6).[45] That is, this is just another case of the *same* antithesis between law and faith which colors the whole of his 'theological' argument. After all, as is widely acknowledged, these statements occur at the clinching points of his argument.[46] That is, it is 'faith and love' as a *single* entity that forms Paul's solution to the crisis of circumcision (5:2, 4, 6). The 'relational turn'[47] at this point is rightly noted, but it is equally clear that this 'relational turn' is made as the answer to the very question of circumcision.

If Paul himself defines faith in terms of love (5:6) and demands it of his Gentile converts (5:13–14), his emphasis on faith necessarily involves a demand of the pattern of behavior through which it expresses itself, namely, the pattern of 'love' (2:19–20; 5:5–6). In other words, his polemic against circumcision is from the first more moral than doctrinal.

Paul's real problem with the Galatians is not that they want to receive circumcision but that they, in so doing, are neglecting their life of 'faith and love' and the pattern of the 'new creation' which Paul takes to be the only thing that counts. Of course, circumcision does pose a serious threat to faith; hence such a stern warning against it (5:2–4). This is not, however, because Paul's thinking is 'controlled by a deeper logic'[48] but simply *because it causes the Galatians to deviate from the pattern of faith and love.*[49] In other words, his words in 5:2–4 are not doctrinal statements exposing the hidden theological meaning of circumcision, but a context-

---

[44] *Contra* R. Longenecker 229 who considers v. 6b as an addition to v. 6a.

[45] Cf. Morris, 'Faith' (1993) 290: 'we must not take Paul's emphasis on faith to mean that he is doing away with the importance of obedience'. The only way to heed to this caveat will be to acknowledge the ethical nature of faith itself. Thus Luther's distinction between 'the faith that justifies' and 'a faith that includes love' does not work at this point.

[46] On 5:6 see Burton 279; R. Longenecker 229; Dunn 260–261; Eckert, *Verkündigung* (1971) 39; Becker, *Paulus* (1998) 290; Johnson, *Writings* (1986) 312. On 6:12–16 see Minear, 'Crucified World' (1979) 398; Weima, 'Gal. 6.11–18' (1993) and references there.

[47] Russell, 'Argumentation' (1995) 338. Betz 22 thinks that v. 5 is a 'summary of doctrine of justification' and v. 6 of 'doctrine of the church'. This 'turn' is, of course, becoming explicit what is implicit, and not the new introduction of a moral logic into a doctrinal argument.

[48] Hooker, *Pauline Pieces* (1979) 25.

[49] Thus in Philippians, where no such threat is clearly in view, circumcision is described as something as useless as dung but not necessarily harmful (3:4–9). In Romans, Paul's depiction becomes much more positive: now circumcision is said to be the 'seal' of justification (4:11), not an antithesis to it as in Galatians. Paul even says that it has its own benefits, though he stops short of explaining what that benefits might actually be (3:1).

specific warning tailored to fit the situational need in Galatia in which misguided enthusiasm for circumcision is currently drawing the Galatians away from what Paul considers to be the truth of the gospel–faith working itself out through love.

Dogmatically, neither circumcision nor uncircumcision has any relevance to the definition of 'faith' and 'new creation'. In the Galatian situation, however, circumcision seems to be propagated in such a way that causes the Galatians to neglect what is really important, namely, faith working itself out through love. In this particular situation, then, circumcision, otherwise an *adiaphoron*, does become a threat to faith, and that is why Paul has to denounce circumcision the way he does in 5:2–4. It is for this reason that uncircumcision, which is as useless as circumcision, can never be an adequate answer to the crisis caused by circumcision. In Paul's eyes, the real crisis in Galatia is a moral one; so is the solution that he suggests to the Galatians.

8.2.2 The Law as a Moral Problem

Interestingly, Paul's argument does not remain with such local issues as circumcision and calendar observances. Rather, he considers circumcision as an inseparable part of 'the whole law' (5:3), and launches a serious polemic against the law *in general* (3:19–25; 4:21–31; 5:4). At first glance this might give the impression that Paul's argument cannot be a moral one, since he is fighting against the very law, 'the epitome of morality'. However, a sober look at his treatment of the subject[50] in fact reveals a consistent moral concern on his part. In a nutshell, his criticism of the law is focused primarily, though not exclusively, on its *moral impotence*, its incapability to enable those who belong to it to actually carry out its own requirements (cf. Romans 8:3). His criticism of the agitators too is not aimed at their rigorous yet misguided effort to observe the (whole) law but their *failure* to do so (6:12–13; 5:3; cf. Romans 2).[51] That is, he is not criticizing the actual *observance* of the law.

An instructive case in point is Paul's promissory statement that the Galatians 'are not under the law' if they are led by the Spirit' (5:18). Strangely, most interpreters fail to capture the real point of this statement as they read the idea of superfluity into Paul's language: the Galatians 'do

---

[50] The literature on Paul's view of the law is enormous. For surveys, Barclay, 'Observations' (1985) 5–15; Westerholm, *Law* (1988) 1–105; Moo, 'Paul and the Law' (1987) 287–307; Thielman, *Plight* (1989) 1–27; *idem*, *Law* (1994) 14–47; Hong, *Law* (1993) 11–15; Schreiner, *Law* (1993) 12–31 with a substantial bibliography (253–272).

[51] B. Longenecker, 'Until Christ' (1999) 93–100 convincingly demonstrates the intentional convergence of Paul's portrait of the agitators and 'works of the flesh' listed in 5:19–21.

not *need* to be under the law', since 'the Spirit provides all the necessary guidance in the fight against the flesh'.[52] This is not, however, the plain sense of Paul's words. What he actually says is that those who are led by the Spirit *are* not under the law. Reversing the statement, the Galatians will end up being under the law, if they, as they are doing now, continue to forsake the Spirit.

At this point, it is important to realize the pregnant meaning of 'being under the law' in Paul's argument. For Paul, it means nothing other than being under its *curse* (3:10), imprisoned under sin (3:22–23) and enslaved under the flesh (4:3, 9, 21–31).[53] Thus his point is that the Galatians are not under the curse of the law, only if they walk according to the Spirit.[54] Here too, as in 5:6, following the Spirit and bearing its fruit stands as the only effective solution to the problem of the flesh and the consequent curse of the law. That is, for Paul the danger of the Galatians' attraction to circumcision/law lies in the fact that they are thereby entangled into the deadly pattern of 'works of the flesh' whose end is nothing but curse and eternal destruction.

Two further points support this conclusion. First, Paul deliberately links the law with the flesh in an inexorable dualism. After what he says in 3:3 and especially 4:21–31, where the law and flesh are virtually synonymous, the implication of the moral explication of the same dualism in 5:16–26 and 6:7–9 is unmistakable.[55] In 5:16–18 too the intentional interchange between 'gratifying the desire of the flesh' and 'being under the law' is beyond doubt.[56] Secondly, the phrase ἔργα σάρκος, in view of the close association between law and flesh (3:3; 5:16–18), is probably a deliberate allusion to ἔργα νόμου.[57] In effect, he seems to be saying that life under the law, necessarily interlocked with the force of the flesh, only produces 'works of the flesh'.

In fact, this moral critique of the law is not limited to the ethical section. As early as in 2:19 Paul claims that 'life under the law' does not allow any life in relation to God. This is why he had to die and adopt a new 'pattern

---

[52] Betz 281 and Barclay, *Truth* (1988) 116 respectively. See also Gundry-Volf, *Perseverance* (1990) 152; Fee, *Presence* (1995) 438.

[53] Rightly, Hong, *Law* (1993) 61, 149–169, 184; Schreiner, *Law* (1993) 77–81; Hansen 172; Fee, *Presence* (1995) 392.

[54] Rightly, Ladd, 'Spirit' (1975) 216; J. Vos, *Pneumatologie* (1973) 30.

[55] So Howard, *Crisis* (1991) 12–14; Lull, *Spirit* (1980) 114–116; Barclay, *Truth* (1988) 210; Thomson, *Chiasmus* (1995) 136–139.

[56] So Mußner 378; Sloan, 'Law' (1991) 49; Hong, *Law* (1993) 165; Martyn 496.

[57] Rightly, Ebeling, *Truth* (1985) 258; Dunn 301; R. Longenecker 252–253; Fee, *Presence* (1995) 441; B. Longenecker, *Triumph* (1998) 74–78.

of life' in faith (v. 20).[58] In other words, Paul does not mean to replace life of doing the law with life of trust; his point is getting out of the blind alley of 'being under the law' for the authentic 'life in relation to God'.

Precisely the same idea is reiterated later in a generalized statement: the law does not have the power to give life (3:21), a claim that contradicts the cherished convictions of Judaism concerning the life-giving role of the law. The statement becomes even more poignant and innovative once we remember the cherished hope of 'life' through the bestowal of the Spirit, in that it effectively shut the law off from this eschatological hope.[59]

That this conclusion involves a moral judgment[60] is clear not only from the tradition Paul alludes to[61] but also from the way he describes the real function of the law in moral terms: it was given only as a jailer dealing with 'sin' (3:19). Whether it refers to its preventive role or aggravating effect,[62] the fact remains unchanged that the only thing it can do is to shut everything 'under sin' (3:22). Since the law pronounces curse upon those who fail to carry out its demand, this is in reality another way of saying 'under curse' (3:10).[63] It is not certain doctrinal implications of the law but its *inability to bring about obedience* that Paul wants to hammer home with his 'polemic' against it.[64] This is the *irony* of 'belonging to the law'.

Thus, Paul's emphatic claim that the Spirit is never from the law (3:2–5),[65] is an essentially moral criticism of the law, since only the life-giving power of the Spirit (Rom 8:11; 1 Cor 15:45; 2 Cor 3:6. Cf. Jn 6:63) can enable the believers to fulfill the law which is summed up in its demand of

---

[58] 2:19–20, the summary of Paul's ethics, forecasts the full-blown discussion in chapters 5 and 6. E.g., Brinsmead, *Response* (1982) 78. Does this not belie the neat theology/ethics division?

[59] One can think of the familiar vision of the revivification of dry bones in Ezekiel 37: 1–14, where God's spirit is said to be the agent of life: καὶ δώσω τὸ πνεῦμα, μου εἰς ὑμᾶς καὶ ζήσεσθε (v. 6, 14; cf. v. 10; 39:29).

[60] Thus, 'making one alive' involves moral renewal. Rightly Ridderbos 141; Drane, *Paul* (1975) 24, 154, n. 52. *Contra* Byrne, *Sons* (1979) 162, n. 103.

[61] In Ezekiel, as in the prophetic tradition in general, giving the Spirit primarily aims at change of heart: from disobedience to obedience (36:26–28).

[62] Paul's moral polemic seems to point to the negative effect of the law.

[63] So Wilckens, *Rechtfertigung* (1974) 92; Sloan, 'Law' (1991) 35–60.

[64] This is noted by Howard, *Crisis* (1991) 11–14; Lull, *Spirit* (1980) 113–130; Brinsmead, *Response* (1982) 164–192; B. Longenecker, *Triumph* (1998) 119–122, 134–142; Schreiner, 'Perfect Obedience' (1985) 254–278; Wilckens, *Rechtfertigung* (1974) 77–109; Hansen, *Abraham* (1988) 150–154; Hooker, *Adam* (1990) 61. It will be interesting to ask whether Paul's view here is influenced in any way by Ezekiel's 'puzzling' statement about the law which is unable to give life (20:25; but also see 20:11, 13, 21).

[65] The law's inability to give the Spirit is emphasized especially by Cosgrove, *Cross* (1988) 39–86.

love (cf. Rom 8:1–4). [66] This seems to be what Paul means by his suggestive expression 'the law of Christ'. [67] B. Longenecker nicely sums up the moral nature of the Galatian crisis:

> The recommendation that Christians should observe the law was not, in Paul's view, simply a *cognitive* error in need of a theological corrective. Instead, it opened the way for Christians to be pawns of superhuman influences other than that of the Spirit of God. At stake, in Paul's mind, is *Christian character enlivened by the Spirit* and evidenced within human relationships. [68]

That Paul responds to the problem of circumcision/the law with an essentially moral argument suggests that as far as Paul himself is concerned, the crisis in Galatia is perceived to concern a behavioral problem: *the Galatians' deviation from the Spirit-inspired pattern of faith and love caused by their hollow enthusiasm for circumcision and the law.* And this is what he means when Paul charges the Galatians of apostasy (1:6), of *abandoning the Spirit* for the flesh (3:3), and of allowing the troublemakers to prevent them from obeying the truth (5:7). It is this deplorable situation in which the Galatians are backsliding from their life in the Spirit that explains why Paul has to make the Spirit as the central point of his argument.

8.3 Paul's Moral Emphasis on the Spirit

In the preceding chapters we argued that Paul perceives the crisis in Galatia primarily in the light of its implication for the Galatians' quest for final salvation, the ultimate goal of their coming to Christ. In the light of the moral nature of the crisis, then, his criticism is clear: by deviating from their life in the Spirit, and thereby exposing themselves to the threat of the flesh which the law has no power to overcome, the Galatians are in effect putting their hope of future salvation at serious risk.

This is immediately clear in the ethical section of the letter in which Paul's exhortation to the Galatians forms a virtual exposition of the

---

[66] Lohse, *Ethics* (1991) 163.

[67] Scholarly discussion mostly concerns its relation to Mosaic law and Jesus tradition. Dodd, 'ENNOMOS CHRISTOU' (1968); Davies, *Torah* (1952) 92–93 and *Rabbinic Judaism* (1970) 111–146; Schürmann, 'Gesetz' (1974); Stuhlmacher, *Reconciliation* (1986) 110–133; Martyn 554–558; *idem, Issues* (1997) 235–249. See the surveys and further literature in Barclay, *Truth* (1988) 125-145; Hong, *Law* (1993) 173–183.

[68] B. Longenecker, 'Until Christ' (1999) 106 (emphasis his). See also his *Triumph* (1998) in which he puts strong emphasis on the moral thrust of Paul's argument. Of course, we disagree with his realized eschatological viewpoint.

function of the Spirit in Christian life. According to what Paul says there, the Spirit is not so much evidence of realized salvation as a mode or power of new life which enables believers to attain to the hoped-for salvation. Here, by the Spirit Paul means 'life in the Spirit', and thus, the *moral* thrust of his argument stands out unmistakably. The burden of this section is to show that this moral logic is equally crucial for Paul's theological argument about justification and inheritance.

8.3.1 Justification and 'Faith Working Itself Out through Love' (5:5–6)

The moral thrust of Paul's argument of 'justification by faith' becomes clearest in 5:2–6 in which he sums up his whole argument on the subject. In antithesis to the dead end of 'justification by the law' (5:2–4), Paul presents before the Galatians the real alternative: ἡμεῖς γὰρ πνεύματι ἐκ πίστεως ἐλπίδα δικαιοσύνης ἀπεκδεχόμεθα (v. 5). The moral thrust of v. 6 has already been explained. Our concern at this point is that he presents this moral notion of 'faith working itself out through love' (v. 6) as the only answer to the question of justification (v. 5): 'we are waiting for the hope of righteousness by the Spirit which comes from faith, *for* in Christ Jesus neither circumcision nor uncircumcision has any power but only faith working through love'.

Scholars usually overlook its connection with the preceding statement on justification.[69] Even when it is acknowledged, the future eschatological thrust is mostly left out.[70] On the assumption of realized justification, however, this severance results in virtual reversal of Paul's perspective, turning the statement of hope into 'an excellent description of [present] righteousness in Christ'.[71] Barclay speaks of 'the stark alternatives of the two ways of life', but for him too its eschatological context remains irrelevant. Surprisingly, even 'the hope of righteousness' to be awaited is taken to be one of the 'benefits' of *present* identity, 'the distinguishing marks of the true Abrahamic covenant as it is *fulfilled* in Christ'.[72] He cannot, of course, ignore the eschatological motif completely, and admits the presence of the motif of the final judgment, which is, however, already 'partially anticipated in the justification'.[73]

---

[69] See, e.g., Witherington 370. B. Longenecker, *Triumph* (1998) never touches v. 5.

[70] So Fung 228; Matera 189; Fee, *Presence* (1995) 419–420.

[71] Ziesler, *Righteousness* (1972) 179. See also Bornkamm, *Paul* (1975) 153. For Ziesler, it provides support for his claim that for Paul righteousness is both 'forensic' and 'ethical', for this verse 'implies a new being as well as a new standing'. His talk of 'first fruit' is rightly criticized by Reumann, *Righteousness* (1982) 58.

[72] Barclay, *Truth* (1988) 93 (emphasis added). See also pp. 94, 216–220, 223.

[73] Barclay, *Truth* (1988) 101. Similarly, Weder, *Kreuz* (1981) 193–195; Glasswell, *EDNT* 1:407. We do *not* deny the identity-making function of hope in the present; what we deny is the assertion that this is the *primary* thrust of the passage. The issue is

To grasp the point Paul drives at, it seems quite crucial to give ἰσχύει in v. 6 its full meaning: 'be capable of', 'have the power to do something' (cf. Phil 4:13; Lk 13:24; Jas 5:16).[74] Typical renderings of the word such as 'to be of avail' or 'to matter'[75] ignore this basic motif of power in it and thereby obscure the meaning of his statement. In the present context in which he speaks of two different, competing, attempts to attain to the 'hope of righteousness' (vv. 4–5), it takes on the meaning of 'to be capable of leading one to eschatological righteousness'.[76] It is not simply that circumcision and uncircumcision 'do not matter' or are 'irrelevant' for those who are already justified.[77] His specific claim is that these things are *impotent*, that is, incapable of leading the Galatians to the hoped-for righteousness (cf. 3:21; cf. Romans 8:3). Receiving circumcision itself, just as remaining uncircumcised, does not help at all in the Galatians' quest for justification. It is only 'faith working itself out through love' that has the power to bring about justification. This is why believers are to await the hope of righteousness 'through the Spirit' since 'faith working itself through love' is the very function of the Spirit.[78]

So here, by defining 'through the Spirit' and 'by faith' in terms of love, Paul in effect claims that the life of love sustained by the Spirit is the only mode of waiting for the hope of righteousness.[79] When he seizes upon the Spirit as the only means of justification (5:5), he is then primarily thinking of his *moral* function (5:6). For him the Spirit constitutes the sure proof of 'justification by faith', not because it signifies the present reality of justification but because it enables believers to maintain the life of love which is the *sine qua non* for reaching future justification.[80] As Cosgrove

---

justification and it remains a hope. See the perceptive comment of Bonnington, 'Review' (1999) 149–150.

[74] So Louw/Nida 677; Paulsen, *EDNT* 2:208. The notion of religious distinction is not in view here. *Contra* Hansen 157 and Martyn 472–473.

[75] So Barclay, *Truth* (1988) 93; Ziesler, *Righteousness* (1972) 179; B. Longenecker, *Triumph* (1998) 63, 82; Eckert, *Verkündigung* (1971) 43; Fung 228.

[76] Betz 263, n. 94; Mußner 351–352: 'das Hoffnungsgut der Gerechtigkeit zu bringen vermag'.

[77] *Contra* Bultmann, 'Ethic' (1924) 214; Kertelge, *Rechtfertigung* (1966) 149. Unlike Gundry-Volf, *Perseverance* (1990) 207, Ridderbos, *Paul* (1975) 179 and Ziesler, *Christianity* (1990) 116, the context, dealing with 'justification', *is* clearly soteriological (5:5).

[78] Merk, *Handeln* (1968) 71: 'Die Liebe ist „tatsächlich nichts anderes als das Leben im Geist."' See also Schnabel, 'Ethics' (1992) 272.

[79] Betz 264: '[n]othing but this love is the basis of the Christian eschatological hope (5:25–6:10)'.

[80] Sanders, *Palestinian Judaism* (1977) 516 is misleading to speak of 'salvation by grace' and 'punishment and reward by deeds'. Interestingly, *1 Clement*, who affirms Paul's doctrine of justification by faith (5:7; 32:3–4), interprets Genesis 15:5–6 as James

puts it, 'Paul understands life in the Spirit as the precondition of authentic ethical engagement, the ultimate justification of which remains future'.[81]

If, as most interpreters acknowledge, this sums up Paul's whole argument in the letter,[82] it follows that *throughout his argument* his emphasis on faith as the only way to justification in fact presupposes its morally active nature. That is, his argument that (future) justification comes only by faith is from the first a *moral* argument, in the sense that the morally active nature of faith should be taken into consideration. And that is indeed a most appropriate point to highlight in the current situation in which his converts are showing signs of deviation from this all-important pattern of faith and love.

8.3.2 Inheritance and Life in the Spirit (5:16–26)

Just as life in the Spirit forms the *sine qua non* for receiving future justification, it is also the only means of receiving God's promised inheritance. In his allegory of Sarah and Hagar couched in the characteristic Spirit-flesh dualism, Paul makes it clear that only those born of the Spirit will participate in God's inheritance, while those born of the flesh will be expelled from this community of children of promise. The theme of inheritance continues in his exhortation in 5:16–26, with the inheritance now specified as the future kingdom of God (v. 21b).[83] Paul's demand in this passage is simple: 'walk according to the Spirit' (vv. 16, 18). Otherwise, one will not be able to inherit the promised kingdom. V. 17, depicting the Spirit and the flesh as two mutually contradictory powers dominating human life, further strengthens the urgency of his demand by accentuating the inexorable conflict between the two forces:[84] one either follows the Spirit or the flesh; there is no third option.[85]

---

does (10:1–7; 30:3!; 31:2). Did this author, far closer to Paul than we, and Luther for that matter, really misunderstand the apostle?

[81] Cosgrove, *Cross* (1988) 150. For him, however, justification is not the issue, and thus this recognition remains inconsequential to Paul's main argument.

[82] See n. 46 above.

[83] For justification of taking the two passages together, see 6.4.

[84] This passage is difficult. See the survey of possible interpretations in Barclay, *Truth* (1988) 112–115. Mußner 377–78 thinks that the Spirit and the flesh neutralize each other so as to create 'freedom of choice' for believers. Paul presupposes human freedom, but the negative thrust of v. 17b renders his view unlikely. Betz 278–281 takes the passage as a case of (unpauline!) fatalism, which flies in the face of Paul's unmistakable confidence in the superiority of the Spirit reflected in vv. 16 and 18. Cf. Jörg Frey, 'Antithese (1999) 45–77.

[85] This is acknowledged by most interpreters, e.g, Burton 302; Barclay, *Truth* (1988) 114–115; R. Longenecker 246; Fee, *Presence* (1994) 434–447; B. Longenecker, *Triumph* (1998) 70.

The dualistic perspective has already been made clear in 3:3 and 4:21–31; now its *moral* texture comes to the fore.[86] The antithesis between Spirit and flesh is not just a matter of passive belonging (identity); it requires active decision on one's behavior. Being born of the Spirit means actually *walking* (περιπατεῖτε, v. 16; στοιχῶμεν, v. 25) by the Spirit and being born of the flesh in fact means *gratifying* (τελέσητε, v. 16) the desires of the flesh.[87]

Paul's point here is that only by 'walking in the Spirit' will the Galatians be able to avoid gratifying the desires of the flesh (v. 16) and doing its works (vv. 19–21)[88] which is a sure way of disqualifying oneself from the inheritance of God's future kingdom. Though not expressed, the other side of the story is equally clear: only by following the Spirit, and thereby producing 'the fruit of the Spirit',[89] will the Galatians be able to participate in this promised inheritance.[90] Here too, Paul presents life in the Spirit as the indispensable condition for receiving future salvation.[91] Paul's claim that inheritance comes from the Spirit (4:7, 21–31) is from the first a moral argument.

Paul's argument in Galatians, both the theological and the ethical, therefore shows a clearly moral logic. His problem with the Galatians is their deviation from their life in the Spirit (3:3). Since for him this pattern of life in the Spirit constitutes the *sine qua non* for participating in future salvation (justification, inheritance, the kingdom of God and eternal life), their deviation from the Spirit can only mean that they are foolishly jeopardizing their hope of this salvation. Hence the desperate call to these wayward Galatians: 'walk according to the Spirit!'

Seen in this way, Paul's moral exhortation in chapters 5 and 6 is not just a confusing or even potentially self-contradictory qualification of his 'main, theological' emphasis on faith-as-trust but *the continuation of his consistent moral polemic against the apostatizing behavior of the Galatians*. His extensive argument in chapters 3 and 4 does provide crucial 'theological' groundwork for his demand, hammering home on the

---

[86] Rightly, B. Longenecker, *Triumph* (1998) 70; Barrett, *Freedom* (1985) 46.

[87] In Romans 8, 'indwelling of the Spirit' (9, 11) is the same as 'walking according to the Spirit' (4) and 'kill the practices of the body' with the Spirit' (13).

[88] Paul presupposes the superior power of the Spirit over the flesh as is implied by the strong promissory note in v. 16b (οὐ μὴ τελέσητε). See *BDF* §365; Zerwick, *Greek* (1963) 149–150. Martyn 529; Barclay, *Truth* (1988) 111; Merk, *Handeln* (1968) 71; Parsons 'Being' (1988) 242.

[89] See W. Barclay, *Flesh* (1962); Barclay, *Truth* (1988) 106–215; Fee, *Presence* (1995) 439–54.

[90] Rightly, Lull, *Spirit* (1980) 175; Fee, *Presence* (1995) 443.

[91] See Hester, *Inheritance* (1968) 86; Yinger, *Judgment* (1999) 247; Watson, *Paul* (1986) 64; Hansen 177; Hamilton, *Eschatology* (1957) 21–23.

Galatians the fact that their *future salvation* is available only in the Spirit. Yet, as we have seen thus far, this theological logic aims at the Galatians' deviation from this Spirit and therefore already carries a strong *moral logic* within it, which only becomes *explicit* in the later part of the letter.

In the final analysis, it is this demand that the Galatians should remain in or return to their life in the Spirit that constitutes the major purpose of Paul's writing this letter. In this sense, we can indeed call the ethical section the 'culmination' and 'climax' of his response to the crisis in Galatia.[92] In conclusion, Galatians as a whole is therefore his coherent response to the singular problem of the apostasy of the Galatians, which comes out quite clearly, once we recognize the essentially future eschatological and moral character of Paul's perspective.

A caveat seems necessary at this point: by speaking of the moral function of the Spirit, we do not mean to say that the moral dimension exhausts the meaning of the Spirit in Paul's gospel. The same goes for his criticism of the law. We do claim that morality is an indispensable dimension of the gospel, not just a consequence or corollary of it, and indeed we are of the opinion that this is something which still awaits proper attention from Pauline scholars. We do not claim, however, that Paul's 'good news' is 'good' simply because it brings about effective ethical performance. Faith in Christ means more than proper moral conduct; the former involves the latter, but can never be replaced by it. And its resultant pattern of life is not just another moral system, since it is grounded on God's creative and life-giving love manifested in the death and resurrection of Christ Jesus and working in the lives of believers. Thus its aim cannot be mere 'goodness' or observing certain rules but a pattern of life obedient to the holy will of God, which Paul calls 'walking according to the Spirit'. What we are trying to bring out is the simple fact that this new existence involves moral dimension not merely as a consequence to the gospel understood as theology but as an indispensable and crucial dimension of the gospel itself.

In addition, it should also be noted that our heavy emphasis on the moral dimension of Paul's gospel is not intended as a balanced exposition of his gospel as a whole but as a clarification of the contextual argument in Galatians which specifically deals with the moral deviation of the

---

[92] In this respect, Cosgrove, *Cross* (1988); Fee, *Presence* (1995) 367–471; Witherington 193, 217 and Choi, 'Spirit' (1998) 16 and *psssim* are closer to our view, though their realized eschatological interpretations of the 'theological' section differ from ours. The claim of Matera, 'Culmination' (1988) that chapter 5 and 6 are the 'culmination' of the letter is somewhat misleading, since for him the real culmination occurs in 5:1–12 and 6:11–18 and *not* the ethical section proper. For him the ethical section still remains secondary.

Galatians from their life in the Spirit. Of course, our reading does draw
attention to the importance of moral dimension (obedience) in Paul's
gospel as a whole, but it is hoped that this position is not taken to be a
blatant moral reductionism.[93]

8.4 Paul's Opponents in Galatia

With our exposition of Paul's argument completed, we are now in a
position to say a few words about the nature of the agitators' mission in
Galatia.[94] Though much about their activity inevitably remains obscure,
our study does make one thing clear: in view of the inherently moral thrust
of Paul's polemic against them, the *moral* observance of the law is not part
of their agenda. They certainly demanded circumcision (5:2–3; 6:12–13)
and probably the Jewish calendar, too (4:10). We do not have any
evidence in Galatians, however, that the agitators' demand involves a
rigorous moral concern, at least not a successful one. Paul's description of
them actually runs in the opposite direction.

8.4.1 Paul's Moral Polemic

That Paul is not fighting against a law-observant, that is, morally rigorous,
mission can be shown by the fact that such a hypothesis creates an
insoluble contradiction in the flow of his argument. The problem is simple.
In chapters 5 and 6 Paul *demands* with utmost seriousness (part of) what he
himself has categorically *rejected* in earlier chapters.[95] The 'tension'
between these two seemingly contradictory thrusts of the letter is well
captured by Barrett:

> Paul's criteria are neither doctrinal nor institutional, but the transformation of life in
> love. Even so, however, his position is a difficult one for there may be *little
> observable difference* between the fruit of the Spirit and works of law. He is obliged
> to walk on a knife edge between the alternatives of flinging away the moral content
> of Christianity and the conversion of it into a new legal system.[96]

In Dunn's words, 'Paul is thus engaged in a delicate art of trying to have
his cake and eat it, that is, trying to retain some emphasis of the law while

---

[93] I thank Professor Jörg Frey for pointing out this potential misunderstanding.

[94] What is the starting point for other scholars is therefore the end result of exegesis
for us.

[95] Cf. Ropes, *Singular Problem* (1929) 22–24; Crownfield, 'Problem' (1945).
However, this does not support the two-front theory either, as far as one section cancels
out the other.

[96] Barrett, *Freedom* (1985) 46 (emphasis added); Barclay, *Truth* (1988) 140–145.

dispensing with others'.[97] Here interpreters face an unavoidable question: in what sense does his 'Pneuma-Ethik' differ from the 'Tora-Ethik' he criticizes?[98] In Paul's own language, what distinguishes his 'law of Christ' from the 'law of Moses'?

Many solutions are proffered. Hübner's attempt to distinguish between 'all the law' (5:3) and 'the whole law' (5:14) is rightly discarded.[99] Also not uncommon is the distinction between 'quantitative' and 'qualitative' obedience or 'inner' and 'external' obedience.[100] Another popular view is to differentiate 'doing' the law from 'fulfilling' it, with the latter taken in the sense of 'eschatological fulfillment'.[101] This linguistically and contextually subtle[102] solution, however, is based on a misreading of Paul's statement which does *not* speak of an 'eschatological fulfillment' of the law in terms of Spirit-inspired love.[103] Paul speaks of 'fulfillment' but it is not the Spirit but the 'one word' (ἐν ἑνὶ λόγῳ) of the love commandment within the Mosaic law itself (Lev 19:18!) that fulfils 'the whole law' (ὁ ... πᾶς νόμος). To be precise, it is not even that the whole law 'is fulfilled', either presently or gnomically; it comes to us already fulfilled

---

[97] Dunn, *Theology* (1993) 116.

[98] These terms come from Mußner 364.

[99] Hübner, *Law* (1984) 36–41. See the critique in Barclay, *Truth* (1988) 136–137. Cf. Hong, *Law* (1993) 172.

[100] E.g., Furnish, *Ethics* (1968) 188-194; Hübner, *Law* (1984) 37; Dunn, *Theology* (1993) 111–114. Similarly, Moule, 'Obligation' (1967) 389–406: 'obedience as self-righteousness' vs. 'obedience as faith'; Kim, Paul (2002) 89: 'doing works of the law' vs. 'new obedience', referring to Käsemann. The talk of 'moralism' is also common as in Houlden, *Ethics* (1973) 34; Schlier, *TDNT* 2:497; Cousar 67; Schweizer, 'Lasterkataloge' (1975) 467. Even Snodgrass, 'Justification' (1986) 72–93 falls into a similar trap: 'obedience based on works righteousness' vs. 'saving obedience in response to God's grace'. The concern behind this solution is well taken, but it is pastorally meaningless and inapplicable. If I, as one justified in Christ, am zealous to obey God's will in view of God's final justification, is it an expression of 'works righteousness' or 'saving response' to God's grace? Paul's problem was simple disobedience, not obedience wrongly motivated.

[101] Examples include Betz 275; R. Longenecker 242–243; Matera 197; Westerholm, *Law* (1988) 201–205; Barclay, *Truth* (1988) 135-145; Hong, *Law* (1993) 177–183; Hansen, 'Conversion' (1997) 230; B. Longenecker, 'Defining' (1996) 91–93; *idem, Triumph* (1998) 83–88.

[102] Thielman, *Law* (1994) 140. It is suggestive that Barclay ends up appealing to the notion of *ambiguity*. *Truth* (1988) 140, 142–145.

[103] Cf. Russell, 'Argumentation' (1995) 341. Even as a moral defense, this would be too dangerous a statement to make, if Paul's intention is to banish the law completely out of sight. As Romans 6 aptly illustrates, Paul has his own way of expounding the moral nature of his gospel without making any reference to the law. Why then, in this critical situation, would he run the risk of making his moral demand in the name of the law? So Bandstra, 'Recent Developments' (1990) 259–260 (against Westerholm).

(πεπλήρωται).[104] Paul is simply urging the Galatians to practice the love command in which the whole law stands fulfilled.

Most of all, however, this sort of linguistic juggling[105] fails to make any *practical* sense. However one interprets Paul's language, it does not change the brutal fact that the love Paul demands as the heart of his ethics is precisely the same love required by the Mosaic law, that is, part of what he has urged the Galatians to reject. It is Paul himself who says that love, the concrete working-out of faith (5:6), is the gist of the very law (5:13–14). That is, he *does* take up 'the moral standards of the law'. Therefore, if we construe his argument as a doctrinal objection to the observance of the law including its 'Tora-Ethik', the conclusion is inevitable: he is contradicting himself.[106]

This conclusion is, however, an unsolicited one. If Paul does have a 'deeply-ingrained impulse to maintain a place for the law within his understanding of the gospel',[107] it is absurd to imagine that he would disparage the *ethic* of Torah in the first place. It is Paul who highlights the absolute importance of obedience in the name of the law (5:13–14), and it necessitates the conclusion that moral observance of the law is not part of his opponents' agenda.[108]

---

[104] In effect, this amounts to 'summed up'. So Furnish, *Ethics* (1968) 200 and *Command* (1972) 97; Schlier, *TDNT* 3:681; Schrage, *Ethics* (1988) 206–207. *Contra* Martyn, 'Crucial Event' (1996) 48–61 who attempts to explain this 'fulfillment' or 'perfection' as an act of Christ.

[105] It is an irony that scholarly discussion of Paul's ethics is often too theoretical and dialectical to follow. Fine theoretical explanations abound; *practical* implications are often difficult to see.

[106] Cf. Ropes, *Singular Problem* (1929) 24.

[107] B. Longenecker, 'Defining' (1996) 91–94 (here 94).

[108] In this respect, without being able to go into detail, we need to point out one questionable assumption often made in scholarly discussion: the unrealistically optimistic estimation of the *practical* value of the Torah as a moral guide for the Gentiles. Of course, there is a sense in which the law could be called the 'epitome of morality'. Nevertheless, its *practical* usefulness for the Gentiles living in Roman Asia Minor should not be exaggerated. To them, much of what the Law says was obsolete or irrelevant for obvious cultural and geographical reasons. And those moral injunctions readily applicable to them were mostly moral commonplaces already available from their own Hellenistic moral traditions, as Collins, *Jerusalem and Athens* (1986) 137–174 persuasively demonstrates. The distinctive points of the Law, such as circumcision, Sabbath, and dietary regulations, were more religious or ritual than moral, and this explains why these elements came to function as effective Jewish identify markers. Of course, this is not to deny the role of the Torah in contemporary moral discourse completely; the moral rigor of the theocratic Torah religion surely left strong impressions upon the contemporary Gentiles. But such a contribution has more to do with moral sensitivity than with its practical value as a moral guide for one's everyday life. This consideration requires a realistic reexamination of the hypothesis that tries to explain the

8.4.2 The Agitators Are Not Observing the Law (6:12–13)

This coheres nicely with what Paul says about the agitators. According to his report in 6:12–13, they want (θέλουσιν), and indeed compel (ἀναγκάζουσιν), the Galatians to be circumcised. Yet Paul also criticizes them that 'they themselves are not keeping the law'. This is a criticism he cannot afford to make if the agitators are actually law-observant. This statement therefore strongly suggests that these people are not really concerned with 'keeping the law', while being very anxious to get the Galatians circumcised.

In scholarly reconstruction of the Galatians situation, however, this verse is frequently played down for various reasons. For some this remark does not necessarily contradict the law-observant character of Paul's opponents since it only reflects Paul's former, (Pharisaic) legal standard,[109] or his conviction that no one can keep the whole law.[110] This is unlikely, however. Paul may well have such belief but it does not obviate the conspicuous gap between 'not keeping the law' and 'not keeping the whole law' (5:3 and 5:14; cf. 3:10). According to Jewett, Paul makes this accusation because 'they annulled grace and rest on their boasting', and thereby 'denied and perverted the truth of the gospel which the law itself affirmed'.[111] However, this reads too much into Paul's language. The way Paul speaks makes it clear that he accuses them on their own ground. Howard asserts that this accusation of Paul rather confirms that the Galatians believed the contrary, and that Paul's charge only refers to their association with the uncircumcised Gentiles, which supposedly constitutes a breach of the law.[112] In view of their strong demand of 'ritualistic' elements of the law such as circumcision and the calendar regulations, however, this is very unlikely. As Esler notes,[113] Paul's talk of 'keeping the law' most probably refers to its ethical dimensions.

More frequently, scholars explain away this statement by appealing to its polemical nature. For example, Barclay, taking these verses as an 'exaggerated polemic point', turns Paul's word completely upside down: 'Paul's snide remark that they do not really keep the law does not disprove but rather, paradoxically, confirms our impression from the rest of the

---

crisis in Galatia in terms of moral attraction to the Law on the part of the Galatians. What kind of concrete moral problems or needs were there, which Paul's gospel could not meet but the Torah could?

[109] So Howard, *Crisis* (1991) 15–16; R. Longenecker 293; Witherington 449.

[110] So Hansen, *Abraham* (1988) 119; Schreiner, *Law* (1993) 64–65.

[111] Jewett, 'Agitators' (1971) 201–202.

[112] So Howard, *Crisis* (1991) 15–16. Cf. Sanders, *Law* (1983) 23.

[113] Esler, *Galatians* (1998) 183–184.

letter that the agitators expected the Galatians to observe the law in conjunction with their circumcision.'[114] For him Paul's statement is a groundless slander aimed to 'show up his opponents in the worst possible light with the hope of weaning the Galatians away from them'.[115] This suggestion is intriguing, especially in view of Barclay's own recognition:

> If he was attempting to persuade the Galatians to abandon the 'other gospel', what he says about it must have been both *recognizable and plausible in their ears*. Thus the letter is likely to reflect fairly accurately what Paul saw to be the main points at issue.[116]

Yet Barclay does not follow his own advice. It is fair to say that Paul's talk of their motivation '*merely* to avoid persecution' needs a grain of salt. But he is not necessarily throwing a slander when he speaks of their 'boasting in the flesh'. If they concentrate their attention on circumcision in particular, Paul's statement can be a fair depiction of their activity.

On Paul's remark about them 'not keeping the law', Barclay misses the point completely. If the agitators are presently launching a law-observant mission, it means that the Galatians are now witnessing to their strenuous zeal to obey the law. Under the circumstances, such a groundless *ad hominem* slander, instead of helping Paul 'weaning the Galatians away from them', would have been a kiss of death in that it would damage his own personal integrity.[117] Are we to believe that Paul is so naive as not to anticipate such a result? That this statement concerns the 'character' and 'motivation' does not exempt it from the need of being 'plausible'.[118] In a highly polemical and critical situation, one is required to pay more meticulous attention not to misrepresent one's opponents, even their character and motivation, because a slight slip on that point could easily destroy one's whole case by damaging one's own *ethos*.[119] A polemic may

---

[114] Barclay, 'Mirror-reading' (1987) 87; *Truth* (1988) 64–65 (here 85).

[115] Barclay, 'Mirror-reading' (1987) 75. Already Räisänen, *Paul* (1983) 96; Watson, *Paul* (1986) 62. Also B. Longenecker, *Triumph* (1998) 32–33; Smiles, *Gospel* (1998) 191.

[116] Barclay, 'Mirror reading' (1987) 76.

[117] Cf. Williams 25.

[118] See the (self-contradicting) admission of Martyn 563. The reservation of R. Longenecker 293 and Eckert, *Verkündigung* (1971) 34–35 is therefore misleading. Cf. Mußner 413–414.

[119] In a personal conversation, Dr. Barclay pointed out that among ancient authors such practice was a commonplace, of which Josephus is an excellent example. But such tactic of personal slander presupposes effective control of information about the victim criticized, a privilege Paul does not have here. Given a strong bond with his converts, such an *ad hominem* tactic will work very powerfully as in Philippians 3:2 ('dogs'; 'evil workers'; 'mutilators') and 3:18–19 ('enemies of the cross'). But having lost their affection and become their 'enemy' (Gal 4:16), and especially with his opponents as the

well be 'evaluative' but it will have its intended effect only in so far as its 'descriptive' makes sense to the hearers.[120]

The easy tone of Paul's remark can best be explained as the reference to the clearly selective disposition of the agitators, highlighting certain elements of the law, while neglecting others.[121] Instructively, Martyn comments on this verse that the 'Teachers' are 'allowing themselves a ... flexibility' of practicing certain parts of the law, 'while leaving aside numerous other parts' and yet 'being nevertheless convinced *in their own minds* that they are fully observant of the Law'.[122] In Paul's mind, however, 'they are not keeping the law'.

8.4.3 Observing the Whole Law (5:3)

This conclusion is supported by Paul's statement in 5:3. In this verse, Paul warns the Galatians: 'Once more, I, Paul, say to each of you who are circumcised that you are obliged to keep the whole law!' The impression is that presently they are not intending to observe the whole law, which in turn implies that they have not been taught to do so.

Naturally, those who posit a 'law-observant mission' in Galatia try to weaken the force of this statement. Howard suggests that Paul's point is this statement is that circumcision makes one a debtor (ὀφειλέτης), namely, a slave to the law, with the 'whole' expressing the severity of such servitude.[123] Yet, 'obligation' is a far cry from 'slavery'; Paul would have said 'slavery' explicitly if he had meant it, instead of making such an ambiguous remark.

A more typical solution is that of Kümmel: 'Paul did not try to inform the Galatians with a fact new to them in 5:3 but to remind them again (πάλιν) of a known fact to which they had not paid sufficient notice'.[124] If so, one must ask, how would his readers have responded? Their immediate answer would be: 'Oh, yes, thank you for reminding us. Well, in fact, that's exactly what we are told to do and are trying to do'. What then would the argumentative force of this remark be? If Paul really wants to

---

Galatians' new frame of reference, such a tactic will do more harm than good, unless it makes good sense in their doubtful ears. Whatever Paul says about the agitators, they would gauge it against the real agitators they are observing with their own eyes. The suggestions of Nanos, *Irony* (202) and Mitternacht, 'Assessment' (2002) also share the same problem.

[120] The 'evaluative-descriptive' antithesis of Hansen, *Abraham* (1988) 191 is a false one.

[121] Crownfield, 'Problem' (1945) 493, 497 without taking his claim of 'syncretists'.

[122] Martyn 563 (italics added).

[123] Howard, *Crisis* (1991) 16.

[124] Kümmel, *Introduction* (1975) 300, followed by Eckert, *Verkündigung* (1971) 41–42; Barclay, *Truth* (1988) 64; Fung 222; B. Longenecker, *Triumph* (1998) 30–33.

'hammer home their full unpalatable implications',[125] he would have made clear *why* they are so 'unpalatable'. Simply rehearsing the agitators' own point without clarifying what he is up to seems to be a very unusual way of 'hammering home' his real point. Or, is the thought expressed, which most interpreters take to be a Jewish commonplace (cf. *m. Abot* 2:1; 4:2; *4 Mac* 5:20–21; Sir 7:8; 1QS), so difficult for the Gentiles to grasp as to require such a solemn declaration by Paul? If the agitators had been concerned to impose 'the total observance of the law' on the Galatians, would such a notion not be the first thing they would have learned from them? Does not their willingness to take up circumcision, the last and hardest step in the proselytization,[126] indicate that they, if taught, would have been fully conscious of the need to keep the whole law? The plausibility of the Galatians' 'naiveté' or 'insufficient realization' is more apparent than real.

In order for this statement to have its intended warning effect, it must be either that the agitators had not made the point clear (the agitators are being selective), or the Galatians are resisting their demands except for circumcision and calendar regulations (the Galatians are being selective). Since the latter clearly runs against the impression we get in the letter (cf. 1:6; 3:1; 4:12–20; 5:7–8),[127] the only viable option seems to be that the agitators themselves are selective in their demands. Thus even Martyn, whose 'Teachers' are thoroughly law-observant, concedes that they are extending 'indulgence' to the Galatians in their demand.[128] This means, then, the construct of 'law-observant' mission is from the first a mistaken one, as is illustrated by the glaring self-contradiction in the readings of those who champion such a view, especially with their interpretation of 3:10![129] Paul's statements in 5:3 and 6:13 necessitate the conclusion that

---

[125] Barclay, 'Mirror-reading' (1987) 75.

[126] According to Philo, circumcision is the most repugnant of all Jewish laws (*Spec.* 1.1–11).

[127] Their willingness even to receive circumcision means that they are prepared to go all the way in the law, if they are required to do so.

[128] Martyn 470. This is widely noted. Brinsmead, *Response* (1982) 64, 87, 160, 193; Jewett, 'Agitators' (1971) 207–208; Sanders, *Law* (1983) 29. See further references in Barclay, *Truth* (1988) 62, n. 75.

[129] R. Longenecker, commenting on 3:10, says that 'Undoubtedly the Judaizers *had quoted* this passage [Deut 27:26] as being decisive'. Then commenting on 5:3, he remarks: 'The fact that Paul here points out that circumcision obliges one to keep all of the prescriptions of the Mosaic law implies that the Judaizers *had not yet mentioned this*'. Similarly, Martyn takes Deut 27:26 quoted in 3:10 as 'the Teachers' own text' and remarks, 'One supposes that it was with such scriptural passages that they *threatened* and *frightened* the Galatians'. Then at 5:3 he retreats, 'Perhaps the Teachers are extending a[n] ... indulgence to the Galatian Gentiles, *failing* to require that they observe every commandment' (470). Barclay, *Truth* (1988) 64 and 67 falls into the same trap. Equally

the agitators are not law-observant in the proper sense; the law as a moral guidance is not part of their agenda.[130] It is Paul, not the agitators, who brings in 'the whole law' into the discussion.[131] In short, the 'law-observant mission' cannot be reconstructed from the text of Galatians.[132]

8.4.4 Paul and the Agitators

Since circumcision signifies the initiation into the Jewish community,[133] the agitators are in effect teaching that salvation is only available for the Jews. What the agitators believe is, then, the salvation-historical privilege of the Jews based on God's special, covenant relationship with them. It is then nothing other than their *Erwählungsbewußtsein* as God's people (cf. 2:15; 5:6; 6:15) or as descendants of Abraham (3–4) that they resorted to as the guarantee of their participation in God's eschatological salvation (cf. *Jubilees* 15:26).[134] Since it is not one's ethical performance but the salvation-historical privilege that becomes crucial for one's salvation, it is not difficult to understand why they, at least in Paul's eyes, exhibit relative indifference to moral questions.

In contrast to these agitators who rely on God's grace of election without paying sufficient attention to God's relentless moral demand as the 'condition' of final salvation, Paul presents in Galatians an inherently moral polemic in which he emphasizes the indispensability of 'ending with the Spirit', namely, the pattern of 'walking by the Spirit' as an appropriate response to God's grace of calling and thus as the disposition 'worthy of God who calls us into his Kingdom and glory' (1 Thess 2:12; Eph 4:1). Paul's criticism is that the Galatians, persuaded by a sort of ill-advised enthusiasm, begin to compromise what is never to be compromised, namely, 'faith working itself out through love' (5:6), which he posits as the only 'truth of the gospel' (5:7). For Paul, this means that they are now 'ending with the flesh' (3:3), and this is nothing but an act of giving up the

---

unintelligible is Mußner's assertion (348) that the agitators taught the soteriological necessity of observing the law without informing the Galatians that circumcision entails the need to keep the whole law. In different context, Brinsmead says that the opponents are only focusing on circumcision and other ritualistic laws, while still considering themselves as 'an ethical movement'. *Response* (1982) 177.

[130] Similarly, Vielhauer, 'Gesetzesdienst' (1975) 545. Now also Mitternacht, 'Assessment' (2002) 408–409.

[131] Rightly, Brinsmead, *Response* (1982) 87; Kertelge, 'Gesetz' (1984) 384.

[132] It is possible that the agitators may have their own system of ethics. What is crucial to note, however, is that *for Paul* it can never be an authentic ethical provision. For him genuine obedience with love at its centre is possible only through the Spirit and he denies this privilege of the Spirit to those under the law.

[133] See chapter 2, n. 99 above.

[134] Cf. Lull, *Spirit* (1980) 172.

only path leading to their salvation. Hence such a desperate call for a return to the life of 'walking according to the Spirit'.[135]

---

[135] Thus Paul's argument in Galatians parallels his similar polemic against 'the Jews' in Romans 2. For this frequently misinterpreted passage, see especially Watson, *Paul* (1986) 109–122 and Snodgrass, 'Justification' (1986) 72–93. Cf. Boyarin, *Jew* (1994) 86–95. A good historical analogy of Paul's moral critique of complacent reliance of God's grace of election is the stinging criticism by John the Baptist of those who rely on their being 'children of Abraham' as giving a sure immunity to the impending wrath, namely, as automatically guaranteeing their future salvation (Lk 3:7–8; Mt 3:7–9). Similar perspective seems to lie behind such passages as Mt 21:33–44 (43!); Jn 8:37–41; *Ps. Sol.* 18:4; *m. Abot* 5:19. See Bruce, *Fulfilled* (1978) 61–64.

Chapter 9

Conclusion

The purpose of this study has been to demonstrate the fundamentally future eschatological perspective of Paul's argument in Galatians. Refuting the widespread reading of the letter in terms of realized eschatology on the one hand, and demonstrating Paul's future eschatological concern on the other, the study has presented a rather unconventional interpretation of Paul's argument in Galatians. Although summaries are provided at the end of each chapter, it seems useful to bring the main points of the study together at this point.

9.1 Summary of the Present Study

9.1.1 The Problem of Apostasy as the Context of Paul's Argument

Focusing on what Paul himself explicitly says about the crisis in Galatia instead of hazarding a hypothetical reconstruction of it, we have made two important points about the context of his argument. First, the problem that Paul deals with in Galatians is the apostatizing behavior of the Galatians (anthropological), not with the erroneous theology of the agitators (doctrinal). That is, the letter is not a record of his theological debate with his rival missionaries but a pastoral letter in which he rebukes the Galatians for their deviation from the truth of the gospel and exhorts them to return to it.

Secondly, the way he deals with the problem indicates that Paul attempts to dissuade the Galatians from the present backsliding by highlighting the fatal consequence which such behavior entails for their future. This makes us expect that his theological argument too, as part of his response to the crisis, is framed in a similar, future-oriented perspective instead of a realized eschatology.

9.1.2 Paul's Future Eschatological Argument

In line with this, our main concern has been to clarify the fundamentally future eschatological thrust of Paul's theological argument. We have done so by demonstrating that the primary framework of Paul's theological argument is future eschatological salvation and not what has already been realized through the Christ event.

(a) Justification, the central issue in Galatians in the light of which Paul perceives the significance of the present crisis, does not refer to a present reality but the final justification at the judgment, a point which receives further confirmation from a comparison with the data in Romans and also from the consideration of the theological context of the letter.

(b) Unlike the widely held view, sonship is not the main issue in Galatia. An analysis of such motifs as 'sons of Abraham', 'seed of Abraham' and 'sons of God' indicates that they are all median motifs, employed to accentuate Paul's main points which are either justification (3:6–9) or the heirship of believers (3:15–29; 4:1–7, 21–31), with each of these motifs performing a distinct role in Paul's argument. We have also stressed the idea of responsibility inherent in the biblical concept of sonship.

(c) We have also argued that the notion of a 'fulfilled Abrahamic promise' is a mistaken one. This thesis is based on a number of exegetical revisions. 1) The argument in 3:6–14 (blessing) is distinct from that in 3:15–29 (the promise). 2) 'The 'the promise of the Spirit' (3:14) does not signify the fulfillment of the Abrahamic promise. 3) The Abrahamic promise of the land is yet to be fulfilled. God gave Abraham the promise, and Christ-Seed, as a co-recipient of the same promise, mediates it to those who become seed by believing and being incorporated in him.

(d) And, naturally, the inheritance, the major subject of Paul's scriptural argument (3:15–29; 4:21–31), also refers to an inheritance in the future. Refuting the notion of 'realized inheritance', we have argued that the motif of 'inheriting the kingdom of God' (and eternal life) is related to the Abrahamic promise of the land, thereby making the 'inheritance' another epithet for final salvation together with the 'kingdom of God' and 'eternal life'. The notion of future inheritance therefore also converges with justification, another name for the same final salvation.

Paul's claim throughout the argument is therefore that one can attain to eschatological salvation (justification, inheritance, kingdom of God, eternal life) only by faith, namely, only by remaining in Christ, since he is the only source of the Spirit, God's life-giving power.

9.1.3 Paul's Christological Argument: Incompatibility, Not Superfluity

Accordingly, contrary to the widespread assumption, Paul's christological argument does not show a structure of realized eschatology. His singular purpose is to dissuade the Galatians from taking up the law by impressing on the Galatians its utter incompatibility with their commitment to Christ. In each subsection of his christological argument (3:10–14; 3:15–29; 4:1–7)

Paul repeats this critical point, but each time with a different argument which he justifies by exploiting a different aspect of the Christ event. His application of the crucifixion motifs to himself (2:19-20; 6:14) and to the Galatians (5:24) is also guided by his desire to drive a wedge between the law and faith in Christ.

Together with this, we have also shown that Paul presents the Christ event, and faith in him for that matter, as the source of the Spirit which forms the ultimate foundation of his argument. This makes his christological argument an essentially a pneumatological one. That is, by claiming that justification/inheritance is only 'in Christ' and 'by faith', he is in fact telling the Galatians that they will attain to it only by remaining 'in the Spirit'.

9.1.4 The Moral Nature of the Galatian Crisis

Paul's emphasis on the Spirit is basically of moral character. That the Galatians will reach future salvation 'through the Spirit' in fact means that they will receive their final salvation only by 'walking according to the Spirit' instead of the flesh. Not surprisingly, therefore, Paul understands the crisis in Galatia primarily in moral terms. The real problem does not lie in the alleged doctrinal implications the act of circumcision may involve but in its making the Galatians deviate from the truth of the gospel, the pattern of 'faith working itself out through love' and the standard of 'new creation', which can be summed up as 'life in the Spirit'.

Naturally, Paul's polemic against circumcision/law is moral too, focusing on its inability to produce a genuine pattern of behavior, which in his opinion is only possible through following or being guided by the Spirit. This also leads us to suspect that the mission of the agitators is not a 'law-observant' one in the sense that they are also stressing the importance of proper obedience to the moral elements of the Torah.

All in all, Paul's demand is that the Galatians should remain in or return to the lifestyle of faith and love sustained by the Spirit. Our main thesis has been that he makes this appeal not by stressing what the Galatians already have in Christ but by warning them of the inescapable eschatological consequence of their present deviation from the life in the Spirit. Abandoning the Spirit for the sake of the flesh, Paul says, will put their future in jeopardy: their justification, the promised inheritance, the kingdom of God and eternal life which all refer to the eschatological salvation itself, the ultimate goal of their coming to Christ.

9.2 Implications for Pauline Study

The present study represents a plea for a reassessment of Paul's eschatological perspective in Galatians. Inevitably it also asks for a re-evaluation of the place of ethics in his gospel. Since much of the result of our study goes against the grain of current Pauline scholarship, it will be useful to discuss the implications of our study on some key issues.

9.2.1 Pauline Eschatology

Though our thesis only concerns eschatology in Galatians, it also carries significant implications for the study of Paul's eschatology as a whole. This is all the more so since Galatians is frequently considered as the clearest example of his realized eschatological outlook. For example, Marshall contends, '[w]e can also see in Paul's writings ... that the parousia or future coming of Jesus occupies a secondary place compared with other aspects of his person and work. For example, it is insignificant in Galatians'. This in turn serves to consolidate the impression that '[t]he centre of gravity in Paul's theology lies in the past and not in the future, although the future hope is one pole of the context for Christian living now'. Even when it is acknowledged that 'Paul works within the horizon of the future coming of Christ and the establishment of the kingdom of God, and for him this is a living hope', the final word tends to run in the opposite direction: 'But the central content of his message is not the future coming of Christ but his incarnation, death, and resurrection.'[1] Our study has shown that the impression that future eschatology is insignificant in Galatians is a gross misreading, which in turn questions Marshall's claim about the 'center' of Paul's gospel.

This is not, of course, a call to discard the cross of Christ and posit instead his *parousia* as the real center of his gospel. Such a step would cause even more disastrous distortion of his gospel which *is* about 'Christ and him crucified' (1 Cor 2:2). The real problem rather seems to be the tendency to treat these themes (Christology, eschatology) as independent theological motifs which occupy certain compartmentalized portions of Paul's thought, often competing against each other for the place of honor in his mental universe. There is also the unfortunate tendency to treat

---

[1] Marshall, 'Eschatology' (1997) 49. Similarly, Baird, 'Eschatology' (1971) 314–327; Boyarin, *Jew* (1994) 35–36: 'It seems to me to be a serious hermeneutical error to make one's interpretation of Paul dependent on the apocalyptic expectation, which is after all not even mentioned once in Galatians, rather than the apocalyptic fulfilment which has already been realized in the vision of the crucified Christ'. Dunn, *Paul* (1998) 465: 'Paul's gospel was eschatological not because of what he still hoped would happen, but because of what he believed had already happened' (italics removed).

Paul's future eschatological language as a mere motivating tactic in his ethical discourse.

However, driving an artificial wedge between the cross and the *parousia* or highlighting one at the cost of the other does more to obscure Paul's thought than to clarify it. For Paul both 'Christ and him crucified' and 'the Day of Christ' are like pillars which sustain the whole structure of his gospel, and without either one of which the other simply loses its meaning. Thus Paul's future eschatological perspective cannot be reduced to an isolated 'motif' which may be relativized or even sacrificed according to situational exigencies. On the contrary, for him the coming of Christ forms an unavoidable goal of the present life, without which the crucifixion, indispensable as it may be, would end up being an aborted attempt on God's side to save his people.

In Galatians, as we have seen in our study, the urgent situation forced Paul to speak more of the present, explicating its meaning in the light of the Christ event in the past and the work of the Spirit in the present. Yet, he does all this with a clear view to bringing out the meaning of the present crisis for the Galatians' quest for final salvation which is, after all, the ultimate purpose of their coming to Christ. In other words, the observation that future eschatology is not a *topic* in a letter should not turn into the claim that it therefore lacks a future eschatological *perspective*. If it is nearsighted to say that in 1 Thessalonians Paul completely neglects the cross and considers Christ solely in terms of his future *parousia*, we should take equal care not to commit the opposite but equally fatal mistake. The interpreter's task is to try to understand how Paul carried out his ministry and worked out his theology between these two horizons, that is, in the light of Christ who was crucified, is present among his people in the Spirit, and is to come to bring everything to its due completion.

In this respect, we also believe that one commonly-accepted construction of Paul's eschatological thinking, namely, the idea of a 'tension' between the already and the not yet, needs serious re-examination.[2] The notion of 'tension' seems to be the product of an artificial juxtaposition of an 'already' against a 'not yet' by scholars, and not a natural result of close exegetical investigation. For Paul, what has already happened does not seem to stand in uneasy tension with what will happen in the future. On the contrary, Paul speaks of what has happened as the indispensable ground for the future hope, all as closely knitted parts in God's ongoing drama of salvation. Namely, the relation between the two is not exactly one of tension but one of more organic interaction, with the former necessarily moving toward the latter within the frame of divine

---

[2] Most responsible for this is, of course, O. Cullmann, *Time* (1950) and *Salvation* (1967).

faithfulness. The investigation of the precise nature of this interaction calls for a study of its own.

9.2.2 The Place of Ethics in Paul's Gospel

Another crucial corollary of Paul's future eschatological perspective is the importance of ethics in his gospel. We have claimed that he perceives deviation from the pattern of faith and love rather than circumcision itself as the essence of the Galatian apostasy. In line with this we have also argued that he develops an extensive theological argument with a view to dealing with this eminently practical problem, which becomes explicit in the later part of the letter. Thus, according to our suggestion, what needs to be explained is not the existence of the ethical sections at the end of the letter but how Paul uses extensive theological argument to back up his call for a return from apostasy to the truth of faith and love. Focusing mainly on eschatology, our treatment of ethics has been inevitably brief (chapter 8), but even our cursory discussion has shown that ethics, far from being a mere implication of Paul's gospel proper, is in fact at the heart of what Paul calls 'the truth of the gospel'.

Thus our reading of Galatians poses a serious question to the normal way of construing the structure of Paul's gospel in terms of 'theology' and 'ethics'. No one would deny the importance of ethics in Paul's gospel but the fact that we often describe him in the dual terms of theology (doctrine) and ethics seems to show a persistent assumption that the former is more crucial than the latter.

One inevitable result of such dichotomy is the confusion of the theological logic of indicative-imperative with the eschatological logic of imperative-future salvation.[3] For example, much scholarly resistance to acknowledging the explicitly conditional nature of Paul's ethical imperative is motivated by the desire to preserve the precedence of indicative over imperative. This is a legitimate concern since there is no denying that God's indicative precedes human obedience. This does not mean, however, that the latter can be subsumed under the shadow of the former, thereby losing its imperatival edge. To be sure, the whole of Paul's ethical talk is based on the conviction about God's effective working through the Spirit. However, this theological conviction does not obviate the necessity of human obedience which is clearly presented as an indispensable process through which God accomplishes his redemptive purpose, the ultimate indicative. Some would call such obedience 'evidence' instead of 'condition' but giving it different names does not make any practical difference since the indicative-imperative dynamics is

---

[3] This is similar to the distinction between 'warrant/telos' and 'sanction' discussed in Keck, 'Rethinking' (1996) 3–16.

by no means an automatic process but something that requires genuine *human effort.*[4] And in most cases Paul's moral exhortation is not motivated by the theological intention of showing the effectiveness of the 'indicative' which is assumed to be obvious, but by the eminently practical and pastoral purposes of keeping his Gentile converts vigilant by pressing on them the absolute necessity of proper conduct for 'inheriting the kingdom of God'.

This explains the rather disturbing phenomenon that while Paul's own moral directives are very simple and straightforward, scholarly exposition of them tends to be too 'theoretical' and 'dialectical' for people with common sense to follow, often rendering them impractical and thus quite useless as a moral guide.[5] Very often, one cannot help feeling that academic discussion of Paul's ethics does more to mystify or muddle up issues than to clarify them. For example, some scholars try to explain the function of Paul's moral directives in Galatians in terms of 'evidence' for the divine indicative which logically precedes human effort. If this process was more or less automatic, we would not have any problem. But such a turn does create a serious theological problem in the context of Paul's pastoral situations, where obedience is *never* a matter of course.[6]

From his extant letters, it is not difficult to see that disobedience presents a major cause of anxiety for Paul the pastor. If successful moral performance provides evidence of God's preceding indicative, how then can one interpret the agonizing reality of disobedience? The only answer seems to be that the disobedient person has never been saved in the first place, for the simple reason that he fails to show proper evidence. Yet, clearly, Paul does not treat the problem of disobedience in this way. Although he by no means underestimates the seriousness of human disobedience, neither does he throw up his hands, crying 'Now I can see that you have never been saved!' He describes cases of disobedience among his converts as an incredible return to their former, unsaved state, and never as proof of their not having come to Christ in the first place. Dealing with the problem of disobedience, his purpose is always to make them come back to obedience, not to prove theologically the hollowness of their faith on the basis of such disobedience. Speaking of evidence may be

---

[4] Paul often conveys this idea through the notion of God's 'calling', an idea which stresses the purposefulness of God's redemption.

[5] Cf. Stendahl, *Paul* (1976) 97: 'Learned persons have even become accustomed of late to speaking about "dialectic" – a method which can be dangerous because it could be one of those subtle ways in which words neutralize one another, although theologians claim rather that they seek a creative tension between the words'.

[6] This is the problem many scholarly works on ethics suffer from. That is, they speak as if this move were smooth and easy, when in reality it is exactly the opposite!

legitimate theologically, but merely invoking it will never do for a concerned pastor like Paul.

It seems that the consistent moral concern that runs through Paul's gospel and his mission of 'proclaiming' it is a subject that still awaits serious scholarly attention.[7] That is, we are yet to grasp the rich implications of the fact that Paul's writings are all results of his *pastoral* engagement with his converts in one way or another. And once we pay more attention to this context, we will be able to appreciate his unwavering concern for his converts' obedience which inevitably sets the direction for his theologizing activity.

Despite the bad press under which the term 'morality' often finds itself, especially among Western Protestant scholars, this call for proper recognition of Paul's moral concern should not surprise us, since it is nothing more than a call to acknowledge the fact that his gospel, as God's power of salvation, addresses *real* human situations. In other words, the gospel is not a theological system which then has anthropological implications, but something that from the first concerns the religious-moral context of human existence. For the same reason, his gospel is not a philosophical system devised on a desktop but the gospel message proclaimed in the actual context of his apostolic ministry. Our emphasis on the ethical dimension of Paul's gospel is nothing more than a request to see the context in which it is actually proclaimed and believed.[8]

9.2.3 The Galatian Eschatology and Pauline Chronology

Another implication of our study concerns the chronology of Paul's writings. Many interpreters think that the allegedly strong emphasis on the present phase of salvation in Galatians forms a stark contrast with the future eschatology of 1 Thessalonians, and take it as evidence for the relatively late date of Galatians. Our thesis that Galatians shows a strong future eschatological perspective brings this sort of argument to the ground. Galatians does not show a realized eschatological perspective, and therefore, one cannot attribute it to a later date for that reason. If we employ the same logic, the future eschatological outlook of Galatians, which is similar to that of 1 Thessalonians, supports the view that these two writings belong to the same (early) period of Paul's writing career.

Ultimately, however, it begs the question to draw a conclusion about Pauline chronology from his theology since it already *assumes* a sort of development in Paul's eschatological thinking, presumably from a future

---

[7] Malherbe has been a prominent exception to this. See for example, *Paul and the Thessalonians: The Philosophic Tradition of Pastoral Care* (1987) and more recently 'The Apostle Paul As a Pastor' (1999).

[8] See below for more on this.

eschatology to a more realized one. Yet this development is precisely the point that is yet to be demonstrated.[9] At this point it suffices just to note that it is therefore begging the question to use the allegedly realized eschatological viewpoint in Galatians as evidence for the late date of its writing.

9.2.4 Justification and the Development of Paul's Thought

Our thesis of future eschatological justification in Galatians also has significant implications for Paul's view of justification in general. For one thing, the usual custom of taking the data in Romans ('righteousness of God' and 'justification of the ungodly') as the starting point of discussion and treating Galatians as a supplement will not do, since Paul clearly uses the concept in different ways in both letters. If our thesis is correct, we have to posit certain changes from a future eschatological doctrine of justification in Galatians to a more complicated one in Romans in which both the present and future justification occur side by side. This recognition requires a more thorough investigation into the precise thrust of Paul's justification language in both letters, especially in Galatians.

Secondly, our thesis also has a crucial bearing on the origin of Paul's doctrine of justification. Many scholars, assuming that Paul from the beginning considers justification as a present gift, suggest that he first gained this insight into 'justification of the ungodly' from his encounter with the risen Christ on the Damascus road which is understood as his own experience of God's justifying grace. That Paul still considers justification as an end-time gift in Galatians indicates that this speculation is an unlikely one. This may explain the lack in Galatians of such themes as the present revelation of 'righteousness of God' and 'justification of the ungodly'. This also seems to explain the surprising failure on Paul's side to connect his conversion/call with justification, despite his emphasis on both themes. With justification still being an end-time gift, it certainly did not occur to Paul to describe the 'revelation of his Son in me' (1:16) as a personal example of present justification.

Thirdly, does this mean that Paul's thought about justification developed? Our thesis makes it clear that Paul uses the *dik-* words in different ways in each letter. The question then is whether this change of definition also involves a change in his theology. The decision is not an easy one, but in our opinion it is not necessarily the case, since change in words does not always involve change in thought structure itself. In Galatians the issue at hand is justification, a term which Paul uses to refer to final salvation (eternal life). That this future justification (final

---

[9] Cf. The attempt of Dodd to trace such a development in 'The Mind of Paul: I' (1933) and 'The Mind of Paul: II' (1934) and the critique by Lowe, 'Examination' (1941).

salvation) happens to be the immediate issue, of course, does not mean that he attributes no significance at all to the 'getting in'. On the contrary, it is not difficult to see that even in Galatians it does remain determinative. It is just that Paul calls it by different names such as redemption, sonship and freedom. On the other hand, in Romans Paul uses the term 'justification' to describe the initial 'getting in', and thereby gives a new twist to the meaning of the word. Again, however, this change in meaning does not indicate that Paul now considers 'getting in' as the major point of salvation, thereby relativizing the importance of final salvation. A comparison of both letters tells us that despite Paul's flexible use of the justification terminology, the overall structure of Paul's thought remains remarkably consistent. The decisiveness of 'getting in' is obvious in both letters but so is the absolute necessity of 'being led by the Spirit' which is the only path toward the goal of final salvation.

Indeed, it is not difficult to show that the same future eschatological thrust characterizes much of Paul's argument in Romans, as is the case in Galatians. As noted above, justification itself is future as well as present (2:13; 3:20, 30; 5:16, 19). The fact of justification in the present leads immediately to the theme of the hope of God's future glory in chapter 5 (5:2, 5). The same future eschatological concern also frames Paul's Christ-Adam typology (5:17–19, 21). Paul's discussion of two contrasting modes of life is also carried out with a clear view to the necessary eschatological consequence (τὸ τέλος) of each disposition (6:21, 22), a perspective effectively summed up by the concluding statement (v. 23). In chapter 7 Paul deals with the specific problem of the law and therefore his immediate focus is the present, but his future eschatological perspective emerges again in chapter 8 with impressive clarity (vv. 6, 11, 13, 16–17, 18–25, 28, 31–39).

This brief consideration suggests that although Paul's use of certain terminology may change case by case, the underlying reality described by his language remains fairly consistent. In turn, it will also be possible to demonstrate that this consistent structure is the very thing we also find in his other letters, for example, 1 Thessalonians. It should be remembered that this and other letters often prove troublesome for those who try to find the core of Paul's gospel mainly on the basis of Galatians and Romans, often positing the Jew-Gentile problem as the controlling factor of his theologizing.

9.2.5 The 'Center' of Paul's Gospel

This is not the place to go into this complex issue in any level of detail, but our discussion above seems to have an important bearing on this question. The phenomenon discussed in the above section can easily be understood, if we consider the fact that Paul is not writing as a systematic theologian striving for conceptual clarity but as a pastor who engages with his converts through the multifarious activity of 'proclaiming' the gospel. This flexibility on the terminological level may explain why scholarly attempts to arrive at the 'core' of Paul's theology in terms of certain theological concepts (justification, reconciliation, participation in Christ, and others) remain relatively unsuccessful, despite the wide agreement on the essential coherence of his theological thinking.

At the same time, it also suggests that we should search for the coherence of Paul's gospel from a somewhat different perspective, namely, not just in the 'narrow' and static realm of Paul's *theology* but in the much broader and dynamic context of his apostolic *ministry*. Given the fact that Paul's life is guided by his sense of calling as the apostle to the Gentiles, it would be a perfectly sensible thing to expect this sense of calling to give consistency to what he does and thinks in the course of his ministry. *That is, we should perhaps begin our search for the center of Paul's gospel at the pastoral context in which it is proclaimed.* Thus, rather than asking about the center of his theology, it will be more to the point to ask 'What is the ultimate aim of Paul, the apostle to the Gentiles?' Perhaps in this way we will be able to get much closer to what undergirds and guides the course of Paul's apostolic ministry.

This brings our study to an end. Our main thesis has been that, contrary to the widely held view, Paul's argument in Galatians shows a clearly future eschatological perspective. How cogent our thesis is, of course, is something for the readers to decide. However the readers may decide about our thesis as a whole, it is our hope that those questions discussed and answers proposed in this study will challenge other students of Paul to read his argument in Galatians in a different light, and thereby contribute to a better understanding of the letter as well as of Paul's gospel as a whole.

Bibliography for Secondary Literature

Achtemeier, Paul J., 'Finding the Way to Paul's Theology: A Response to J. Christiaan Beker and J. Paul Sampley'. In Jouette Bassler ed., *Pauine Theology. Vol 1: Thessalonians, Philippians, Galatians and Philemon*. Minneapolis: Fortress, 1991, 25–36.

Adams, Edward, *Constructing the World*. SNTW. Edinburgh: T&T Clark, 2000.

Anderson, R. Dean, *Ancient Rhetorical Theory and Paul*. Kampen: Kok Pharos, 1996.

Arnold, Clinton E., 'Returning to the Domain of the Powers: *Stoicheia* as Evil Spirits in Galatians 4:3, 9'. *NovT* 38 (1996) 55–76.

Auerbach, Erich, *Mimesis: The Representation of Reality in Western Literature*. Princeton: Princeton University Press, 1953.

Baird, W., 'Pauline Eschatology in Hermeneutical Perspective'. *NTS* 17 (1971) 314–327.

Bandstra, A. J., 'Paul and the Law: Some Recent Developments and An Extraordinary Book'. *CTJ* 25 (1990) 249–261.

_____, *The Law and the Elements of the World. An Exegetical Study in Aspects of Paul's Teaching*. Kampen: Kok, 1964.

Barclay, John M. G., 'Mirror-Reading a Polemical Letter: Galatians as a Test Case'. *JSNT* 31 (1987) 73–93.

_____, *Obeying the Truth*. SNTW. Minneapolis: Fortress Press, [1988] 1991.

_____, 'Paul and the Law: Observations on Some Recent Debates'. *Themelios* 12 (1985) 5–15.

Barclay, William, *Flesh and Spirit: An Examination of Galatians 5.19–23*. London: SCM Press, 1962.

Barr, J., *The Semantics of Biblical Language*. Oxford: Oxford University Press, 1961.

Barrett, C. K., 'The Allegory of Abraham, Sarah, and Hagar in the Argument of Galatians'. In J. Friedrich *et al.* eds., *Rechtfertigung* (Ernst Käsemann FS). Tübingen: Mohr/Siebeck, 1976, 1–16.

_____, *Freedom and Obligation*. London: SPCK, 1985.

_____, *Paul: An Introduction to His Thought*. Louisville, KT: Westminster/John Knox Press, 1994.

Baumgarten, J., *Paulus und die Apokalyptik*. Neukirchen: Neukirchener, 1975.

Baur F. C., *Paul, the Apostle of Jesus Christ. His Life and Work, his Epistles and his Doctrine*. Trans. E. Zeller and A. Menzies. 2 volumes. London: Williams & Norgate, 1875.

Beasley-Murray, G. R., *Baptism in the New Testament*. Biblical and Theological Classics Library. Carlisle: Paternoster Press, [1962] 1997.

Becker, Jürgen, 'Der Brief an die Galater'. In J. Becker and U. Luz, *Die Briefe an die Galater, Epheser und Kolosser*. NTD 8/1. Göttingen: Vandenhoeck & Ruprecht, 1998.

_____, *Paulus: Der Apostel der Völker*[3]. Tübingen: Mohr Siebeck, [1992] 1998.

Beker, J. Christiaan, *Paul the Apostle: The Triumph of God in Life and Thought*. Edinburgh: T. & T. Clark, 1980.

_____, 'Recasting Pauline Theology: Coherence-Contingency Scheme as Interpretive Model'. In Jouette Bassler ed., *Pauine Theology. Vol 1: Thessalonians, Philippians, Galatians and Philemon*. Minneapolis: Fortress, 1991, 15–24.

Belleville, L. L., '"Under Law": Structural Analysis and the Pauline Concept of Law in Galatians 3.21–4.11'. *JSNT* 26 (1986) 53–78.

Berényi, Gabriella, 'Gal 2,20: A Pre-Pauline or A Pauline Text?' *Biblica* 65 (1984) 490–537.

Berger, K., 'Abraham in den paulinischen Hauptbriefen'. *MTZ* 17 (1966) 47–89.

_____, 'χαρίζομαι'. *EDNT* 3:456–457.

Berger, Peter L. & Luckmann, Thomas, *The Social Construction of Reality. A Treatise in the Sociology of Knowledge.* New York: Doubleday/Anchor Books, 1967.

Best, T. F., 'The Apostle Paul and E. P. Sanders: The Significance of Paul and Palestinian Judaism'. *RQ* 25 (1982) 65–74.

Betz, Hans D., 'In Defense of the Spirit: Paul's Letter to the Galatians as a Document of Early Christian Apologetics'. In Schüssler-Fiorenza ed., *Aspects of Religious Propaganda in Judaism and Early Christianity.* Notre Dame: University of Notre Dame Press, 1976, 99–114.

_____, *Galatians: A Commentary on Paul's Letter to the Churches in Galatia.* Hermeneia. Philadelphia: Fortress Press, 1979.

_____, 'The Literary Composition and Function of Paul's Letter to the Galatians'. *NTS* 21 (1975) 353–79.

_____, 'Spirit, Freedom, and Law'. *Svensk Exegetisk Arsbok* 39 (1974) 145–60.

Bjerkelund, C. J., '"Vergeblich" als Missionsergebnis bei Paulus'. In J. Jervell *et al.* eds., *God's Christ and His People* (N. A. Dahl FS). Oslo: Universitätsforlaget, 1977, 175–191.

Blass, F., and Debrunner, A., *A Greek Grammar of the New Testament and Other Early Christian Literature.* Trans. and ed. by R.W. Funk from 19th German edition. Chicago: Chicago University Press, 1961.

Bligh, John, *Galatians in Greek: A Structural Analysis of St. Paul's Epistle to the Galatians with Notes on the Greek.* Detroit: University of Detroit Press, 1966.

Boers, Hendrikus, *The Justification of the Gentiles: Paul's Letter to the Galatians and Romans.* Peabody, MA: Hendrickson, 1994.

Bonnington, M., Review of P. Esler's *Galatians. Tyndale Bulletin* 50 (1999) 141–155.

Bornkamm, Günther, *Early Christian Experience.* Trans. P. L. Hammer. London: SCM Press, 1969.

_____, *Paul.* London: Hodder and Stoughton, [1969] 1975.

_____, 'Revelation of Christ to Paul on the Damascus Road and Paul's Doctrine of Justification and Reconciliation. A Study in Galatians 1'. In R. Banks ed., *Reconciliation and Hope* (Leon Morris FS). Grand Rapids: Eerdmans, 1974, 90–103.

Bottorff, J. F., 'The Relation of Justification and Ethics in the Pauline Epistles'. *SJT* 26 (1973) 421–430.

Bouwman, Gijs, 'Christus Diener der Sünde' *Bijdragen* 40 (1979) 44–54.

_____, 'Die Hagar- und Sara-Perikope (Gal 4,21–31). Exemplarische Interpretation zum Schriftbeweis bei Paulus'. *ANRW* 2.25.4 (1987) 3135–3155.

Boyarin, D., *A Radical Jew: Paul and the Politics of Identity.* Berkeley: University of California Press, 1994.

Brandenburger, E., 'Cross' (σταυρός). *NIDNTT* 1:391–403.

Braumann, G., 'Children etc.' (τέκνον and υἱός). *NIDNTT* 1:285–290.

Brawley, Robert L., 'Contextuality, Intertextuality, and the Hendiadic Relationship of Promise and Law in Galatians'. *ZNW* 93 (2002) 99–119.

Brinsmead, B. H., *Galatians – Dialogical Response to Opponents.* SBLDS 65. Chico: Scholars Press, 1982.

Bruce, F. F., *Commentary on Galatians.* NIGTC. Grand Rapids: Eerdmans, 1982.

_____, *Paul: Apostle of the Heart Set Free.* Grand Rapids: Eerdmans, 1977.

_____, *The Time Is Fulfilled: Five Aspects of the Fulfilment of the Old Testament in the New*. Exeter: Paternoster Press, 1978.

Brueggemann, Walter, *The Land: Place as Gift, Promise, and Challenge in the Biblical Faith*. Philadelphia: Fortress, 1977.

Bultmann, Rudolf, 'Zur Auslegung von Galater 2,15–18'. In Erich Dinkler ed., *Exegetica: Aufsätze zur Erforschung des Neuen Testaments*. Tübingen: J.C.B. Mohr (Paul Siebeck), 1967, 394–399.

_____, 'The Problem of Ethics in Paul'. In Brian Rosner ed., *Understanding Paul's Ethics*. Grand Rapids: Eerdmans, [1924] 1995, 195–216.

_____, *Theology of the New Testament, Vol 1*. Trans. K. Grobel. New York: Charles Scribner's Sons, 1951.

Burton, Ernest de Witt, *A Critical and Exegetical Commentary on the Epistle to the Galatians*. ICC. Edinburgh: T. & T. Clark, 1921.

Byrne, Brendan, *'Son of God' – 'Seed of Abraham'*. Analecta Biblica 83. Rome: Biblical Institute Press, 1979.

Byron, John, *Slavery Metaphors in Early Judaism and Pauline Christianity*. WUNT 2. Reihe 162. Tübingen: Mohr Seibeck: 2003.

Calvert, N. L., 'Abraham'. *DPHL* 1–9.

Campbell, Douglas, 'The Coming of ΠΙΣΤΙΣ in Galatians, Chapter Three (vv. 22–26)' *Paper Delivered at a Day-Conference at King's College London* (1999) 1–49.

_____, 'The Eschatological Logic of Paul's Gospel for Gender as Suggested by Galatians 3.28a in Context'. 1998 1–125. *Unpublished*.

_____, *The Rhetoric of Righteousness in Romans 3.21–26*. JSNTSS 65. Sheffield: Sheffield Academic Press, 1992.

Carson, D. A., *Exegetical Fallacies*. Grand Rapids: Baker, 1984.

Carson, D. A., O'Brien, P. T., and Seifrid, Mark A., *Justification and Variegated Nomism: A Fresh Appraisal of Paul and Second Temple Judaism. Volume I: The Complexities of Second Temple Judaism*. WUNT 2.Reihe 140. Tübingen: Mohr Siebeck: 2001.

Cassirer, Ernst, *Grace and Law: St. Paul, Kant, and the Hebrew Prophets*. Grand Rapids: Eerdmans, 1988.

Choi, G. J., 'Living by the Spirit. A Study of the Role of the Spirit in Paul's Letter to the Galatians'. Ph. D. Dissertation. Iliff School of Theology & University of Denver, 1998.

Cole, Alan, *Galatians*. TNTC. London: The Tyndale Press, 1965.

Collins, John, *Between Athens and Jerusalem: Jewish Identity in the Hellenistic Diaspora*. New York: Crossroad, 1986.

Conzelmann, Hans, *An Outline of the Theology of the New Testament*. Trans. J. Bowden. NTL. London: SCM, 1969.

Cook, David, 'The Prescript as Programme in Galatians'. *JTS* 43 (1992) 511–519.

Cosgrove, Charles H., 'Arguing Like a Human Being'. *NTS* 34 (1988) 536–549.

_____, *The Cross and the Spirit: A Study in the Argument and Theology of Galatians*. Macon, Georgia: Mercer University Press, 1988.

_____, 'Justification in Paul: A Linguistic and Theological Reflection'. *JBL* 106 (1987) 653–670.

_____, 'The Law Has Given Sarah No Children (Gal 4:21–31)'. *NovT* 29 (1987) 219–235.

Cousar, Charles B., *Galatians*. Interpretation. Louisville: John Knox Press, 1982.

_____, *A Theology of the Cross: The Death of Jesus in the Pauline Letters*. Overtures to Biblical Theology. Minneapolis: Fortress Press, 1990.

Cranfield, C. E. B., *The Epistle to the Romans*. 2 vols. ICC. Edinburgh: T&T Clark, 1979.

_____, 'St. Paul and the Law'. *SJT* 17 (1964) 43–68.

Crownfield, Frederic R., 'The Singular Problem of the Dual Galatians'. *JBL* 64 (1945) 491–500.

Cullmann, Oscar, *Christ and Time* : The Primitive Christian Conception of Time and History. Trans. Floyd V. Filson. Philadelphia: Westminster Press, 1950.

_____, *Salvation in History*. Trans. Sidney G. Sowers. London: SCM Press, 1967.

Cummins, S. A., *Paul and the Crucified Christ in Antioch: Maccabean Martyrdom and Galatians 1 and 2*. SNTSMS 114. Cambridge: Cambridge University Press, 2001.

Dahl, N. A., *Studies in Paul*. Minneapolis: Augsburg, 1977.

_____, 'The Atonement: An Adequate Reward for the Akedah?'. In *Neotestamentica et Semitica* FS M. Black, eds., E. E. Ellis and M. Wilcox. Edinburgh: T. & T. Clark, 1969,15–29. Now in *Jesus the Christ: The Historical Origins of Christological Doctrine*. Ed., Donald H. Juel. Minneapolis: Fortress Press, 1991, 137–151.

Daube, David, *The New Testament and Rabbinic Judaism*. London: Athlone, 1956.

Davies, W. D., *The Gospel and the Land: Early Christianity and Jewish Territorial Doctrine*. Los Angeles: University of California Press, 1974.

_____, 'Paul and the Law. Reflections on Pitfalls in Interpretation'. In M.D. Hooker *et al.* eds., *Paul and Paulinism*. (C. K. Barrett FS). London: SPCK, 1982, 4–16.

_____, 'Paul and People of Israel'. *NTS* 24 (1977) 4–39.

_____, *Paul and Rabbinic Judaism: Some Rabbinic Elements in Pauline Theology*. London: SPCK, 1970.

_____, *Torah in the Messianic Age and/or in the Age to Come*. JBLMS. Philadelphia: SBL, 1952.

Davis B. S., 'The Meaning of ΠΡΟΕΓΡΑΦΗ in the Context of Galatians 3.1'. *NTS* 45 (1999) 194–212.

Deissmann, Adolf, *Paul: A Study in Social and Religious History*. Trans, W. E. Wilson. New York: Harper & Brothers, [1927] 1957.

Delling, G., 'πληρόω κτλ.' *TDNT* 6:283–311.

DeVries Carl E., 'Paul's "Cutting" Remarks About a Race: Galatians 5:1–12'. In G. F. Hawthorne ed., *Current Issues in Biblical and Patristic Interpretation* (M. Tenney FS). Grand Rapids: Eerdmans, 1975, 115–120.

Dodd, B. J., 'Christ's Slave, People Pleasers and Galatians 1.10'. *NTS* 42 (1996) 90–104.

Dodd, C. H., 'ENNOMOS CHRISTOU'. In *More New Testament Studies*. Manchester: Manchester Univeristy Press, 1968, 134–148.

_____, 'The Mind of St Paul: A Psychological Approach'. *BJRL* 17 (1933) 91–105.

_____, 'The Mind of Paul: Change and Development'. *BJRL* 18 (1934) 69–110.

Donaldson, T. L., 'The "Curse of the Law" and the Inclusion of the Gentiles: Galatians 3.13–14'. *NTS* 32 (1986) 94–112.

_____, *Paul and the Gentiles*. Minneapolis: Fortress Press, 1997.

Donfried, K. P., 'Justification and Last Judgment in Paul'. *ZNW* 67 (1976) 90–110.

_____, 'The Kingdom of God in Paul'. W. Willis ed., *The Kingdom of God in Twentieth-Century Interpretation*. Peabody, MA: Hendrickson, 1987, 175–190.

_____, ed., *The Romans Debate*. Peabody, MA: Hendrickson, 1991.

Drane, John W., *Paul: Libertine or Legalist?: A Study in the Theology of the Major Pauline Epistles*. London: S.P.C.K., 1975.

Duling, Dennis, 'Kingdom of God'. *ABD* 4:49–69.

Duncan, George S., *The Epistle of Paul to the Galatians*. MNTC. London: Hodder and Stoughton, 1934.

Dunn, James D. G., *Baptism in the Holy Spirit: A Re-Examination of the New Testament Teaching on the Gift of the Spirit in Relation to Pentecostalism Today*. London: SCM Press, 1970.

_____, *The Epistle to the Galatians*. Black's New Testament Commentary. Peabody, MA: Hendrickson, 1993.

_____, *Jesus, Paul and the Law*. Louisville, KT: Westminster/John Knox Press, 1990.

_____, *The Theology of Paul the Apostle*. Grand Rapids: Eerdmans, 1998.

_____, *The Theology of Paul's Letter to the Galatians*. NTT. Cambridge: Cambridge University Press, 1993.

_____, *Romans 1–8*. WBC. Waco, TX: Word, 1988.

Ebel, G., 'Walk' (περιπατέω). *NIDNTT* 3:943–947.

Ebeling, Gerhard, *The Truth of the Gospel: An Exposition of Galatians.* Trans. David Green. Philadelphia: Fortress Press, 1985.

Eckert, Jost, *Die urchristliche Verkündigung im Streit zwischen Paulus und seinen Gegnern nach dem Galaterbrief*. Regensburg: Friedrich Pustet, 1971.

Eckstein, Hans-Joachim, *Verheißung und Gesetz: Eine exegetische Untersuchungen zu Galater 2,15–4,7*. WUNT 86. Tübingen: J.C.B. Mohr (Paul Siebeck), 1996.

Edwards, Mark J., ed., *Galatians, Ephesians, Philippians*. ACCSNT 8. Downers Grove: IVP, 1999.

Engberg-Pedersen, Troel, 'Response to Martyn'. *JSNT* 86 (2002) 103–114.

Esler, P. F., *Galatians*. New Testament Readings. London: Routledge, 1998.

_____, 'Group Boundaries and Intergroup Conflict in Galatians: A New Reading of Gal. 5:13–6:10'. In Mark G. Brett ed., *Ethnicity and the Bible*. Leiden: E. J. Brill, 1996, 215–240.

_____, 'Family Imagery and Christian Identity in Gal. 5.13–6.10'. In Halvor Moxnes ed., *Constructing Early Christian Families: Family as Social Reality and Metaphor*. London: Routledge, 1997, 121–149.

_____, 'A Social Identity Approach to Paul's Letter to the Galatians: The Examples of Righteousness and the Mosaic Law'. Paper Presented at British New Testament Conference (1998), 1–10.

Fanning, Buist M., *Verbal Aspect in New Testament Greek*. Oxford: Clarendon Press, 1990.

Fee, Gordon, *God's Empowering Presence: The Holy Spirit in the Letters of Paul*. Carlisle: Paternoster Press, 1995.

_____, 'Paul's Conversion as Key to His Understanding of the Spirit'. In R. N. Longenecker ed., *The Road From Damascus: The Impact of Paul's Conversion on His Life, Thought and Ministry*. Grand Rapids: Eerdmans, 1997, 166–183.

Feld, H., 'Christus Diener der Sünde. Zum Auslegung des Streites zwischen Petrus und Paulus'. *TQ* 153 (1973) 119–131.

Feldman, Louis H. and Reinhold, Meyer, eds., *Jewish Life and Thought among Greeks and Romans: Primary Readings*. Edinburgh: T. & T. Clark, 1996.

Fitzmyer, J. A., *To Advance the Gospel*. New York: Crossroad, 1981.

_____, 'Galatians'. In Raymond E. Brown *et al*. eds., *The New Jerome Biblical Commentary*. Englewood Cliffs, N.J.: Prentice-Hall, 1990, 780–790.

_____, *Paul and His Theology*. Englewood Cliffs, NJ: Prentice-Hall, 1989.

Foerster, D., 'Abfassungszeit und Ziel des Galaterbriefes'. In W. Eltester *et al*. ed., *Apophoreta* (E. Haenchen FS). Berlin: Töpelmann, 1964, 135–141.

_____, 'κληρονόμος'. *TDNT* 3:768–785.

Fredriksen, Paula, 'Judaism, the Circumcision of Gentiles, and Apocalyptic Hope: Another Look at Galatians 1 and 2'. *JTS* 42 (1991) 532–564.

Frey, Jörg, 'Die paulinische Antithese von "Fleisch" und "Geist" und die palästinisch-jüdische Weisheitstradition'. *ZNW* 90 (1999) 45–77.

Friedrich, J. H., 'κληρονόμος'. *EDNT* 2:298–299.

Fung, R.Y. K., *The Epistle to the Galatians*. NICNT. Grand Rapids: Eerdmans, 1988.

Funk, R. W., 'The Apostolic Parousia: Form and Significance'. In W. R. Farmer *et al*. eds., *Christian History and Interpretation: Studies Presented to John Knox*. Cambridge: Cambridge University Press, 1967, 249–268.

_____, *Language, Hermeneutic, and the Word of God*. New York: Harper & Row, 1966.
Furnish, Victor, '"He Gave Himself [Was Given] Up": Paul's Use of a Christological Assertion'. In A. J. Malherbe *et al.* eds., *The Future of Christology* (L. Keck FS). Minneapolis: Fortress, 1993, 109–121.
_____, *The Love Command in the New Testament*. Nashville: Abingdon, 1972.
_____, *Theology and Ethics in Paul*. Nashville: Abingdon, 1968.
Gager, John G., 'Functional Diversity in Paul's Use of End-Time Language'. *JBL* 89 (1970) 325–337.
Garrett, Susan R., *The Demise of the Devil: Magic and the Demonic in Luke's Writings*. Minneapolis: Fortress, 1989.
Gaventa, Beverly R., 'Galatians 1 and 2: Autobiography as Paradigm'. *NovT* 28 (1986) 309–326.
_____, 'The Maternity of Paul: An Exegetical Study of Gal 4:19'. In R. T. Fortna *et al.* eds., *The Conversation Continues* (J. Louis Martyn FS). Nashville: Abingdon, 1990, 189–201.
_____, 'The Singularity of the Gospel'. In Jouett M. Bassler ed., *Pauline Theology, Vol 1: Thessalonians, Philippians, Galatians and Philemon*. Minneapolis: Fortress Press, 1991, 147–159.
Geertz, Clifford, *The Interpretation of Cultures*. New York: Basic Books, 1973.
Glasswell, M. E., 'ἀπεκδέχομαι' *EDNT* 1:407.
Goldingay, John, *Approaches to Old Testament Interpretation*. Downers Grove: IVP, 1990.
Goppelt, L., *Typos. The Typological Interpretation of the Old Testament in the New*. Trans. D. H. Madvig. Grand Rapids: Eerdmans, 1982.
Goulder, Michael, 'Already?'. In Thomas E. Schmidt *et al.* eds., *To Tell the Mystery* (Robert H. Gundry FS). JSNTS 100. Sheffield: JSOT Press, 1994, 21–33.
_____, 'The Pauline Epistles'. In Rober Alter *et al.* eds., *The Literary Guide to the Bible*. Cambridge, MA: Harvard University Press, 1987, 479–502.
Grayston, Kenneth, *Dying, We Live: An Enquiry Into the Death of Christ in the New Testament*. Oxford: Oxford University Press, 1990.
Guhrt, J., and Link, H. –G., 'Rule etc.' (κανών). *NIDNTT* 3:399–400.
Gundry, R. H., 'Grace, Works, and Staying Saved in Paul'. *Biblica* 66 (1985) 1–38.
Gundry-Volf, Judith M., *Paul and Perseverance*. WUNT 2. Reihe 37. Tübingen: J. C. B. Mohr, 1990.
Guthrie, Donald, *Galatians*. NCB. London: Oliphants, 1974.
Hagner, Donald, 'Paul and Judaism: The Jewish Matrix of Early Christianity: Issues in the Current Debate'. *BBR* 3 (1993) 111–130.
Hamilton, Neil Q., *The Holy Spirit and Eschatology in Paul*. SJTOP 6. Edinburgh/London: Oliver and Boyd, 1957.
Hammer, P. L., 'A Comparison of *Kleronomia* in Paul and Ephesians'. *JBL* 79 (1960) 267–272.
Hansen, G. Walter, *Abraham in Galatians: Epistolary and Rhetorical Contexts*. JSNTMS 29. Sheffield: Sheffield Academic Press, 1989.
_____, 'A Paradigm of the Apocalypse: the Gospel in the Light of Epistolary Analysis'. L. A. Jervis *et al.* eds., *Gospel in Paul: Studies on Corinthians, Galatians and Romans for Richard N. Longenecker*. JSNTSS 108. Sheffield: Sheffield Academic Press, 1994, 194–209.
_____, 'Paul's Conversion and His Ethic of Freedom in Galatians'. R. N. Longenecker ed., *The Road From Damascus: The Impact of Paul's Conversion on His Life, Thought and Ministry*. Grand Rapids: Eerdmans, 1997, 213–237.
Harnisch, Wolfgang, 'Einübung des Neuen Seins: Paulinische Paränese am Beispiel des Galaterbriefs'. *ZTK* 84 (1987) 279–296.

Hartmann, L., 'Gal 3.15–4.11'. J. Lambrecht ed, *The Truth of the Gospel*. Rome: Benedictina, 1993, 127–172.

Harvey, John D., *Listening to the Text: Oral Patterning in Paul's Letters*. Grand Rapids: Baker Books, 1998.

Haufe, Günter, 'Die Geistmotiv in der paulinischen Ethik'. *ZNW* 85 (1994) 183–191.

_____, 'Reich Gottes bei Paulus und in der Jesustradition'. *NTS* 31 (1985) 467–472.

Hawthorne, G. F., Martin, R. and Reid, D., eds., *Dictionary of Paul and His Letters: A Compendium of Contemporary Biblical Scholarship*. Downers Grove: IVP, 1993.

Hays, Richard, 'Christology and Ethics in Galatians: The Law of Christ'. *CBQ* 49 (1989) 461–476.

_____, *Echoes of Scripture in the Letters of Paul*. New Haven: Yale University Press, 1989.

_____, *The Faith of Jesus Christ*. SBLDS 56. Chico: Scholars Press, 1983.

_____, *The Moral Vision of the New Testament*. Edinburgh: T. & T. Clark, 1996.

_____, 'Review of Galatians by J. L. Martyn'. *JBL* 119 (2000) 373–379.

Hendriksen, William, *Galatians*. Edinburgh: The Banner of Truth Trust, 1968.

Hengel, Martin & Schwemer, Anna Maria, *Paul Between Damascus and Antioch: The Unknown Years*. Trans. John Bowden. London: SCM Press, 1997.

Hester, D. James, 'The "Heir" and Heilsgeschichte: A Study of Gal 4:1ff.' In F. Christ ed., *Oikonomia: Heilsgeschichte als Thema der Theologie* (Oscar Cullman FS). Hamburg-Bergstedt: Reich, 1967, 118–125.

_____, *Paul's Concept of Inheritance: A Contribution to the Understanding of Heilsgeschichte*. SJTOP 14. Edinburgh: Oliver and Boyd, 1968.

Hill, David, *Greek Words and Hebrew Meanings: Studies in the Semantics of Soteriological Terms*. SNTSMS 5. Cambridge: Cambridge University Press, 1967.

Hirsh, Jr., E. D., *Validity of Interpretation*. New Haven and London: Yale University Press, 1967

Hoffmann, E., 'Hope'. *NIDNTT* 2:238–246.

_____, 'Promise'. *NIDNTT* 3:68–74.

Hong, In-Gyu, 'Does Paul Misrepresent the Jewish Law?: Law and Covenant in Gal. 3:1–14'. *NovT* 36 (1994) 164–182.

_____, *The Law in Galatians*. JSNTSS. Sheffield: JSOT Press, 1993.

_____, 'The Perspective of Paul in Galatians'. *Scriptura* 36 (1991) 1–16.

Hooker, Morna D., *From Adam to Christ: Essays on Paul*. Cambridge: Cambridge University Press, 1990.

_____, 'Paul and Covenantal Nomism'. In M.D. Hooker *et al.* eds., *Paul and Paulinism* (C.K. Barrett FS). London: SPCK, 1982, 47–56.

_____, *Pauline Pieces*. London: Epworth, 1979.

Horbury, W., 'Land, Sanctuary and Worship'. In J. Barclay *et al.* eds., *Early Christian Thought in its Jewish Context* (Morna Hooker FS). Cambridge: Cambridge University Press, 1996, 207–224.

Houlden, J. L., *Ethics and the New Testament*. London: Mowbray, 1973.

Howard, George, *Crisis in Galatia²*. Cambridge: Cambridge University Press, 1991.

Hübner, Hans, *Biblische Theologie des Neuen Testaments 2: Theologie des Paulus*. Göttingen: Vandenhoeck, 1993.

_____, *Law in Paul's Thought*. SNTW. Edinburgh: T. & T. Clark, 1984.

_____, 'ἀλήθεια κτλ.' *EDNT* 1:57–60.

Hydahl, Niels, 'Gerechtigkeit durch Gluaben. Historische und theologische Beobachtungen zum Galaterbrief' in *NTS* 46 (2000), 425–444.

Isaacs, Marie E., *The Concept of the Spirit*. HM 1. London: Heythrop College, 1976.

Jeremias, Joachim, *The Central Message of the New Testament*. Philadelphia: Fortress Press, [1965] 1981.

_____, *Jesus' Promise to the Nations*. Trans. S.H. Hooke. London: SCM Press, 1958.

Jervis, L. Ann and Richardson, Peter, eds., *Gospel in Paul: Studies on Corinthians, Galatians and Romans for Richard N. Longenecker*. JSNTSS 108. Sheffield: Sheffield Academic Press, 1994.

Jewett, Robert, 'The Agitators and the Galatian Congregation'. *NTS* 17 (1971) 198–212.

Jobes, Karen H., 'Jerusalem, Our Mother: Metalepsis and Intertextuality in Galatians 4:21–31'. *WTJ* 55 (1993) 299–320.

Johnson, Luke T., *The Writings of the New Testament: An Interpretation*. Philadelphia: Fortress Press, 1986.

Käsemann, Ernst, *Commentary on Romans*. Trans. G. W. Bromiley. Grand Rapids: Eerdmans, 1980.

_____, *New Testament Questions for Today*. Trans. W. J. Montague. London: SCM Press, 1969.

_____, *Perspectives on Paul*. Trans. Margaret Kohl. London: SCM Press, 1971.

Keck, Leander E, 'Justification of the Ungodly'. In J. Friedrich *et al.* eds., *Rechtfertigung* (E. Käsemann FS). Tübingen: Mohr Siebeck, 1976, 199–209.

_____, 'Paul and Apocalyptic Theology'. *Interpretation* 38 (1984) 229–241.

_____, *Paul and His Letters*. Proclamation Commentaries. Philadelphia: Fortress Press, 1988.

_____, 'Paul as Thinker'. *Interpretation* 47 (1993) 27–38.

_____, 'Rethinking New Testament Ethics'. *JBL* 115 (1996) 3–16.

Kern, Philip H., *Rhetoric and Galatians*. SNTSMS 101 Cambridge: Cambridge University Press, 1998.

Kertelge, Karl, 'Zur Deutung des Rechtfertigungsbegriffs im Galaterbrief'. *BZ (Neue Folge)* 12 (1968) 211–222.

_____, 'Gesetz und Freiheit im Galaterbrief'. *NTS* 30 (1984) 382–394.

_____, *'Rechtfertigung' bei Paulus*. Münster: Aschendorff, 1966.

_____, 'δικαιόω'. *EDNT* 1:330–334.

Kim, Seyoon, *The Origin of Paul's Gospel*. WUNT 2. Reihe 4. Tübingen: J. C. B. Mohr (Paul Siebeck), 1984.

_____, *Paul and the New Perspective: Second Thoughts on the Origin of Paul's Gospel*. Grand Rapids: Eerdmans, 2002.

Klein, Günter, 'Gottes Gerechtigkeit als Thema der neuesten Paulus-Forschung'. In *Rekonstruktion und Interpretation bei Paulus. Gesammelte Aufsätze zum Neuen Testament*. München: Kaiser, 1969, 225–236.

_____, 'Individualgeschichte und Weltgeschichte bei Paulus. Eine Interpretation ihres Verhältnisses im Galaterbrief'. In *Rekonstruktion und Interpretation bei Paulus. Gesammelte Aufsätze zum Neuen Testament*. München: Kaiser, 1969, 180–224.

Kremer, J., 'πνεῦμα'. *EDNT* 3:117–122.

Kruse, Coline G., *Paul, the Law and Justification*. Leicester: Apollos, 1996.

Kümmel, W. G., '"Individualgeschichte" und "Weltgeschichte" in Gal 2,15–21'. In *Heilsgeschehen und Geschichte. Band 2*. Marburg: N.G. Elwert, 1978, 130–142.

_____, *Introduction to the New Testament*. Trans. H.C. Kee. London: SCM Press, 1975.

_____, *The New Testament: The History of the Investigation of its Problems*. Trans. S.M. Gilmour and H.C. Kee. London: SCM Press, 1973.

_____, *The Theology of the New Testament*. Trans. John E. Steely. London: SCM Press, 1974.

Kvalbein, Hans, 'The Kingdom of God in the Ethics of Jesus'. *ST* 51 (1997) 60–84.

Laato, T., *Paul and Judaism. An Anthropological Approach*. Atlanta: Scholars Press, 1995.

Ladd, G. E., 'The Holy Spirit in Galatians'. In Gerald F. Hawthorne ed., *Current Issues in Biblical and Patristic Interpretation* (M. Tenney FS). Grand Rapids: Eerdmans, 1975, 211–216.

_____, *A Theology of the New Testament*. Grand Rapids: Eerdmans, 1974.

Lambrecht, Jan, 'Abraham and His Offspring: A Comparison of Galatians 5,1 with 3,13'. *Biblica* 80 (1999) 525–536.

_____, 'Paul's Reasoning in Galatians 2:11-21'. James D. G. Dunn ed., *Paul and the Mosaic Law*. Tübingen: J.C.B. Mohr (Paul Siebeck), 1996, 53–74.

Lategan, B. C., 'Is Paul Developing a Specific Christian Ethics in Galatians?' In D. Balch *et al.* eds., *Greek, Romans, and Christians (A. Malherbe FS)*. Minneapolis: Fortress, 1990, 318–328.

Lattke, M., 'κενός'. *EDNT* 2:281.

Levison, John R., 'Did the Spirit Withdraw From Israel? An Evaluation of the Earliest Jewish Data'. *NTS* 43 (1997) 33–57.

Lietzmann, D. Hans, *An Die Galater⁴*. HNT. Tübingen: J.C.B. Mohr (Paul Siebeck), 1971.

Lightfoot, J. B., *St Paul's Epistle to the Galatians⁶*. London: Macmillan, 1880.

Lincoln, Andrew, *Ephesians*. WBC. Waco, TX: Word, 1990.

_____, *Paradise Now and Not Yet: Studies in the Role of the Heavenly Dimension in Paul's Thought with Special Reference to His Eschatology*. SNTSMS. Cambridge: Cambridge University Press, 1981.

Lohse, Eduard, *Theological Ethics of the New Testament*. Trans. Eugene Boring. Philadelphia: Fortress Press, 1991.

Longenecker, B. W., 'Defining the Faithful Character of the Covenant Community: Galatians 2.15–21 and Beyond'. In J. D. G. Dunn ed., *Paul and the Mosaic Law*. WUNT 89. Tübingen: J. C. B. Mohr (Paul Siebeck), 1996, 75–97.

_____, '"Until Christ Is Formed in You": Suprahuman Forces and Moral Character in Galatians'. *CBQ* 61 (1999) 92–108.

_____, *The Triumph of Abraham's God*. Edinburgh: T. & T. Clark, 1998.

Longenecker, Richard, *Biblical Exegesis in the Apostolic Period*. Grand Rapids: Eerdmans, 1975.

_____, *Galatians*. WBC. Waco, TX: Word, 1990.

Longenecker, R., ed., *The Road from Damascus*. Grand Rapids: Eerdmans, 1997.

Longman III, Tremper, *Literary Approaches to Biblical Interpretation*. FCI 3. Grand Rapids: Zondervan 1987.

Lowe, J., 'An Examination of Attempts to Detect Developments in St Paul's Theology'. *JTS* 42 (1941) 129–142.

Lull, David John, '"The Law Was Our Pedagogue": A Study in Galatians 3:19–25'. *JBL* 105 (1986) 481–498.

_____, *The Spirit in Galatia: Paul's Interpretation of Pneuma as Divine Power*. SBLDS 49. Chico, CA: Scholars Press, 1980.

Luther, Martin, *The Bondage of the Will*. Trans. J. I. Packer et al. Grand Rapids: Fleming H. Revell, 1956.

_____, *Commentary on Galatians*. Middleton Edition. Grand Rapids: Kregel, [1850] 1979.

Luz, Ulich, *Das Geschichtsverständnis des Paulus*. Munich : Kaiser, 1968.

_____, 'βασιλεία'. *EDNT* 1:201–205.

Lyall, F., *Slaves, Citizens, Sons: Legal Metaphors in the Epistles*. Grand Rapids: Zondervan, 1984.

Lyons, George, *Pauline Autobiography: Towards a New Understanding*. SBLDS 73. Atlanta: Scholars Press, 1985.

Lührmann, Dieter, *Galatians*. Minneapolis: Fortress, 1992.

Lütgert, W., *Gesetz und Geist. Eine Untersuchung zur Vorgeschichte des Galaterbriefes.* BFCT 22. Gütersloh: Bertelsmann, 1919.

MacGorman, J. W., 'An Analysis of the Factors which Relate to the Possibility of Tracing Development in Pauline Eschatology'. Ph. D. Dissertation, Duke University, 1965.

Mahoney, R., 'ἐπιτελέω'. *EDNT* 2:42.

Malherbe, Abraham, *Paul and the Thessalonians: The Philosophic Tradition of Pastoral Care.* Philadelphia: Fortress Press, 1987.

_____, 'The Apostle Paul As a Pastor' in *Jesus, Paul and John.* Chuen King Lecture. Hong Kong: Chinese Univerisity of Hong Kong, 1999, 93–138.

Marshall, I. H., 'A New Understanding of the Present and the Future: Paul and Eschatology'. In R.N. Longenecker ed., *The Road from Damascus: The Impact of Paul's Conversion on His Life, Thought and Ministry.* Grand Rapids: Eerdmans, 1997, 43–61.

Martin, Ralph, *New Testament Foundations: A Guide for Christian Students. Vol 2:The Acts, the Letters, the Apocalypse.* Grand Rapids: Eerdmans, 1986.

Martin, Troy, 'Apostasy to Paganism: the Rhetorical Stasis of the Galatians Controversy'. *JBL* 114/3 (1995) 437–461.

_____, 'Whose Flesh? What Temptation? (Galatians 4.13-14)'. *JSNT* 74 (1999) 65–91.

Martyn, J. L., 'The Crucial Event in the History of the Law (Gal 5:14)'. In E. H. Lovering, Jr. *et al.* eds., *Theology and Ethics in Paul and His Modern Interpreters: Essays in Honor of Victor Paul Furnish.* Nashville: Abingdon, 1996, 48–61.

_____, *Galatians.* The Anchor Bible. New York: Doubleday, 1997.

_____, *Theological Issues in the Letters of Paul.* SNTW. Edinburgh: T. & T. Clark, 1997.

_____, 'De-apocalypticizing Paul: An Essay Focused on Paul and the Stoics by Troels Engberg-Pedersen'. *JSNT* 86 (2002) 61–102.

Matera, Frank J., 'The Culmination of Paul's Argument to the Galatians: Gal 5.1–6.17'. *JSNT* 32 (1988) 79–91.

_____, *Galatians.* SP 9. Collegeville, MN: Liturgical Press (Michael Glazier), 1992.

Matlock, Barry, *Unveiling the Apocalyptic Paul: Paul's Interpreters and the Rhetoric of Criticism.* JSNTS 127. Sheffield: Sheffield Academic Press, 1996.

_____, 'Detheologizing the ΠΙΣΤΙΣ ΧΡΙΣΤΟΥ Debate: Cautionary Remarks from a Lexical Semantic Perspective'. *NovT* 42 (2000) 1–23.

Mayer, B., 'ἐλπίς κτλ.' *EDNT* 1:437–441.

McLean, B. H., *The Cursed Christ: Mediterranean Expulsion Rituals and Pauline Soteriology.* JSNTS 126. Sheffield: Sheffield Academic Press, 1996.

Meeks, Wayne A., *The First Urban Christians: The Social World of the Apostle Paul.* New Haven and London: Yale University Press, 1983.

_____, *The Origins of Christian Morality.* New Haven: Yale University Press, 1993.

_____, 'Social Functions of Apocalyptic Language in Pauline Christianity'. In *Apocalypticism in the Mediterranean World and the Near East: Proceedings of the International Colloquium on Apocalypticism, Uppsala, August 12–17, 1979.* Tübingen: J. C. B. Mohr (Paul Siebeck), 1982, 687–705.

Meeks, Wayne A., ed., *The Writings of St. Paul.* Norton Critical Editions. New York/London: W. W. Norton & Company, 1972.

Mell, Ulrich, *Neue Schöpfung: Eine traditionsgeschichtliche und exegetische Studie zu einem soteriologischen Grundsatz paulinischer Theologie.* BZNW 56. Berlin: Walter de Gruyter, 1989.

Merk, Otto, 'Der Beginn der Paränese im Galaterbrief'. *ZNW* 60 (1969) 83–104.

_____, *Handeln aus Glauben: Die Motivierungen der paulinischen Ethik.* Marburg: Elwert, 1968.

Minear, Paul S., 'The Crucified World: The Enigma of Galatians 6,14'. In C. Andersen *et al.* eds., *Theologia Crucis - Signum Crucis* (J. Knox FS). Tübingen: Mohr, 1979, 395–407.

Mitternacht, Dieter, 'Foolish Galatians?-A Recipient-Oriented Assessment of Paul's Letter' in Mark D. Nanos ed., *The Galatians Debate: Contemporary Issues in Rhetorical and Historical Interpretation*. Peabody, MA: Hendricksen, 2002, 408–433.

Moltmann, Jürgen, *Theology of Hope*. Trans. James W. Leitch. Minneapolis: Fortress Press, 1993.

Moo, D. J., '"Law", "Works of the Law", and Legalism'. *WTJ* 45 (1983) 73–100.

_____, 'Paul and the Law in the Last Ten Years'. *SJT* 40 (1987) 287–307.

Moor, R. K., 'δικαιοσύνη and Cognates in Paul: The Semitic Gulf Between Two Major Lexicons (Bauer-Arndt-Gingrich-Danker and Louw-Nida)'. *Colloquium* 30 (1998) 27–43.

Moore, George Foot, *Judaism in the First Centuries of the Christian Era: The Age of Tannaim. 3 Vols.* Peabody, MA: Hendrickson, [1927] 1997.

Moore-Crispin, Derek R., 'Galatians 4:1-9: The Use and Abuse of Parallels'. *EQ* 60 (1989) 203–223.

Morgan, Robert and Barton, John, *Biblical Interpretation*. OBS. Oxford: Oxford University Press, 1988.

Morris, Leon, *The Apostolic Preaching of the Cross: A Study of the Significance of Some New Testament Terms*. Grand Rapids: Eerdmans, 1965.

_____, 'Faith'. *DPHL* 285–291.

Moule, C. F. D., *An Idiom Book of New Testament Greek²*. Cambridge: Cambridge University Press, 1959.

_____, 'Obligation in the Ethic of Paul' C.F.D. Moule *et al.* eds, *Christian History and Interpretation*. Cambridge: Cambridge University Press, 1967, 389–406.

Moulton, J. H., and Milligan, G., *Vocabulary of the Greek New Testament*. Peabody, MA: Hendrickson, 1997. Reprint of 1930 edition by Hodder and Stoughton.

Mulka, A. L., 'Fides Quae Per Caritatem Operantur'. *CBQ* 28 (1966) 174–188.

Mullins, T. Y., 'Formulas in New Testament Epistles'. *JBL* 91 (1972) 380–390.

Munck, Johannes, *Paul and the Salvation of Mankind*. Trans. Frank Clarke. London: SCM Press, 1959.

Murphy-O'Connor, *Paul: A Critical Life*. Oxford: Oxford University Press, 1996.

Mußner, Franz, *Der Galaterbrief*. HTKZNT. Freiburg: Herder, 1981.

Nanos, Mark D., *Irony of Galatians: Paul's Letter in First-Century Context*. Minneapolis, MN: Fortress Press, 2002.

_____, 'The Inter- and Intra-Jewish Political Context of Paul's Letter to the Galatians' in Mark D. Nanos ed., *The Galatians Debate: Contemporary Issues in Rhetorical and Historical Interpretation*. Peabody, MA: Hendricksen, 2002, 396–407.

_____, ed., *The Galatians Debate: Contemporary Issues in Rhetorical and Historical Interpretation*. Peabody, MA: Hendricksen, 2002

Neusner, Jacob, 'Comparing Judaisms' (Review of *Paul and Palestinian Judaism* by E. P. Sanders). *HR* 18 (1978) 177–191.

Neyrey, Jerome H., 'Bewitched in Galatia: Paul and Cultural Anthropology'. *CBQ* 50 (1988) 72–100.

Nikolakopoulos, Konstantin, 'Aspekte der „paulinischen Ironie" am Beispiel des Galaterbriefs'. *BZ* 45 (2001) 193–208.

Nygren, A., *Commentary on Romans*. Trans. C. Rasmussen. Philadelphia: Muhlenberg Press, 1949.

Ornstein, R., *The Psychology of Consciousness*. New York: Penguin Books, 1986.

Ortkemper, Franz-Josef, *Das Kreuz in der Verkündigung des Apostels Paulus: Dargestellt an den Texten der paulinischen Haupbriefe*. SB 24. Stuttgart: Verlag Katholisches Bibelwerk, 1967.

Parsons, Michael, 'Being Precedes Act: Indicative and Imperative in Paul's Writing'. In Brian Rosner ed., *Understanding Paul's Ethics: Twentieth-Century Approach*. Grand Rapids: Eerdmans, 1995 [1988], 217–247.

Patte, Daniel, *Paul's Faith and the Power of the Gospel*. Philadelphia: Fortress Press, 1983.

Paulsen, H., 'ἰσχύω'. *EDNT* 2:208–209.

Perriman, Andrew C., 'The Rhetorical Strategy of Galatians 4:21–5:1'. *EQ* 65 (1993) 27–42.

Pfitzner, Victor C., *Paul and the Agon Motif: Traditional Athletic Imagery in the Pauline Literature*. SNovT. Leiden: E. J. Brill, 1967.

Piage, T., 'Holy Spirit'. *DPHL* 404–413.

Reumann, John, *New Creation: The Past, Present, and Future of God's Creation Activity*. Minneapolis: Augsburg, 1973.

———, *Righthteousness in the New Testament*. Philadelphia/New York: Fortress/Paulist, 1982.

Ridderbos, Herman, *The Epistle of Paul to the Churches of Galatia*. NICNT. Grand Rapids: Eerdmans, 1953.

———, *When the Time Had Fully Come. Studies in New Testament Theology*. Jordan Station, Ontario: Paideia, 1957.

———, *Paul: An Outline of His Theology*. Trans. J. R. de Witt. Grand Rapids: Eerdmans, 1975.

Roetzel, Calvin, *The Letters of Paul. Conversations in Context*. Louisville: Westminster/John Knox Press, 1991.

Ropes, James Hardy, *The Singular Problem of the Epistle to the Galatians*. HTS. Cambridge: Harvard University Press, 1929.

Rosner, Brian S. ed., *Understanding Paul's Ethics: Twentieth-Century Approaches*. Grand Rapids: Eerdmans, 1995.

Rossel, W. H., 'New Testament Adoption – Greco-Roman or Semitic?' *JBL* 71 (1952) 233–234.

Russell, W., 'The Apostle Paul's Redemptive-Historical Argumentation in Galatians 5:13–26'. *WTJ* 57 (1995) 333–357.

Räisänen, Heikki, 'Galatians 2.16 and Paul's Break with Judaism'. *NTS* 31 (1985) 543–553.

———, *Paul and the Law*. Philadelphia: Fortress Press, 1983.

Sampley, J. P., 'From Text to Thought World'. In Jouette Bassler ed., *Pauine Theology, Vol 1: Thessalonians, Philippians, Galatians and Philemon*. Minneapolis: Fortress, 1991, 3–14.

Sand, A., 'ἐπαγγελία κτλ.' *EDNT* 2:13–16.

Sanders, E. P., *Paul*. Past Masters. Oxford: Oxford University Press, 1991.

———, *Paul, the Law, and the Jewish People*. Minneapolis: Fortress Press, 1983.

———, *Paul and Palestinian Judaism*. Minneapolis: Fortress Press, 1977.

Sänger, Dieter, '"Vergeblich bemüht" (Gal 4.11)?: Zur paulinischen A rgumentationsstrategie im Galaterbrief'. *NTS* 48 (2002) 377–399.

Satake, A., 'Apostolat und Gnade bei Paulus'. *NTS* 15 (1968/69) 96–107.

Schlier, Heinrich, *Der Brief an die Galater*. Kritisch-exegetischer Kommentar 7. Göttingen: Vandenhoek & Ruprecht, 1962.

———, 'ἐλευθερία κτλ.' *TDNT* 2:487–502.

———, 'ἀνακεφαλαιόομαι'. *TDNT* 3:681–682.

Schmithals, W., *Paul and the Gnostics*. Trans. J. E. Steely. Nashville: Abingdon, 1972.

_____, 'Judaisten in Galatien?' *ZNW* 74 (1983) 27–58.

Schnabel, Eckhard J., 'How Paul Developed His Ethics'. In B. Rosner ed., *Understanding Paul's Ethics*. Grand Rapids: Eerdmans, 1995, 267–297.

Schnackenburg, Rudolf, *God's Rule and Kingdom*. Edinburgh: Nelson, 1963.

_____, *Der Brief an die Epheser*. EKK X. : Benziger Verlag; Neukirchen-Vluyn: Neukirchener Verlag, 1982.

Schniewind, J. and Friedrich, G., 'ἐπαγγέλλω κτλ.' *TDNT* 2: 576–586.

Schoeps, Hans J., *Paul: The Theology of the Apostle in the Light of Jewish Religious History*. Trans. Harold Knight. London: Lutterworth, 1961.

Schrage, Wolfgang, *The Ethics of the New Testament*. Trans. D.E. Green. Edinburgh: T. &T. Clark, 1988.

Schreiner, Thomas R., *The Law and Its Fulfillment: A Pauline Theology of Law*. Grand Rapids: Baker Books, 1993.

_____, 'Paul and Perfect Obedience to the Law: An Evaluation of the View of E. P. Sanders'. *WTJ* 47 (1985) 245–278.

Schrenk, G., 'δικαιοσύνη κτλ.' *TDNT* 2:192–219.

Schubert, Paul, *Form and Function of the Pauline Thanksgivings*. BZNW 20. Berlin: Töpelmann, 1939.

Schürmann, H., '"Gesetzes des Christus" (Gal 6,2). Jesu Verhalten und Wort als letztgültige sittliche Norm nach Paulus'. In J. Gnilka ed., *Neue Testament und Kirche* (R. Schnackenburg FS). Freiburg: Herder, 1974, 282–300.

Schweitzer, Albert, *The Mysticism of Paul the Apostle*. Trans. William Montgomery. London: The Johns Hopkins University Press, [1931] 1998.

Schweizer, E., 'Gottesgerchtigkeit und Lasterkataloge bei Paulus (inkl. Kol und Eph)'. In J. Friedrich *et al*. eds., *Rechtfertigung* (Käsemann FS). Tübingen: J. C. B. Mohr, 1975, 461–477.

_____, 'πνεῦμα κτλ.' *TDNT* 6:389–455.

Scott, C. A. Anderson, *Christianity According to St Paul*. Cambridge: Cambridge University Press, 1961.

Scott, James M., *Adoption as Sons of God*. WUNT 2. Reihe 48. Tübingen: J. C. B. Mohr (Paul Siebeck), 1992.

_____, '"For as Many as are of Works of the Law are Under Curse" (Galatians 3.10)'. In C. A. Evans et al. eds., *Paul and the Scripture of Israel*. Sheffield: JSOT Press, 1993, 187–221.

Shaw, Graham, *The Cost of Authority*. London: SCM Press, 1983.

Siker, J. S., *Disinheriting the Jew: Abraham in Early Christian Controversy*. Louisville: Westminster/John Knox Press, 1991.

Silva, Moisés, *Biblical Words and Their Meaning: An Introduction to Lexical Semantics*. Grand Rapids: Zondervan, 1983.

_____, 'Eschatological Structures in Galatians'. In Thomas E. Schimdt *et al*. eds., *To Tell the Mystery: Essays on New Testament Eschatology in Honor of Rober H. Gundry*. Sheffield: Sheffield Academic Press, 1994, 140–162.

_____, 'The Law and Christianity: Dunn's New Synthesis'. *WTJ* 53 (1991) 339–353.

_____, *Interpreting Galatians: Explorations in Exegetical Method*. Grand Rapids: Eerdmans, 2001.

Sjöberg, E., 'πνεῦμα κτλ.' *TDNT* 6:375–389.

Sloan, R. B., 'Paul and the Law: Why the Law Cannot Save'. *NovT* 33 (1991) 35–60.

Smail, Tom, *The Forgotten Father: Rediscovering the Heart of the Christian Gospel*. Biblical Classics Library. Carlisle: Paternoster Press, [1980] 1996.

Smiles, Vincent M., *The Gospel and the Law in Galatia: Paul's Response to Jewish-Christian Separatism and the Threat of Galatian Apostasy*. Collegeville, Minnesota: The Liturgical Press, 1998.

Smith, Morton, 'On the History of ΑΠΟΚΑΛΥΠΤΩ and ΑΠΟΚΑΛΥΨΙΣ'. In D. Hellholm ed., *Apocalypticism in the Mediterranean World and the Near East*. Tübingen: J.C.B. Mohr (Paul Siebeck), 1983, 9–20.

Snodgrass, Klyne R., 'Justification by Grace – To the Doers: An Analysis of the Place of Romans 2 in the Theology of Paul'. *NTS* 32 (1986) 72–93.

Soards, Marion L., 'Seeking (ZETEIN) and Sinning (HAMARTOLOS & HARMARTIA) according to Galatians 2.17'. In J. Marcus and M. L. Soards eds., *Apocalyptic and the New Testament* (J. L. Martyn FS). Sheffield: JSOT Press, 1989, 237–254.

Spanje, T. E. van, *Inconsistency in Paul?: A Critique of the Work of Heikki Räisänen*. WUNT 2. Reihe 110 Tübingen: Mohr Siebeck, 1999.

Stählin, G., 'ἐγκόπτειν κτλ.' *TDNT* 3:857–860.

_____, 'νῦν'. *TDNT* 4:1106–1123.

Standhartinger, Angela, '"Zur Freiheit ... befreit"?: Hagar im Galaterbrief'. *ET* 62 (2002) 288–303.

Stanley, Christopher, '"Under a Curse": A Fresh Reading of Galatians 3.10–14'. *NTS* 36 (1990) 481–511.

Stanton, Graham N., 'The Law of Moses and the Law of Christ: Galatians 3:1–6:2'. In J. D. G. Dunn ed., *Paul and the Mosaic Law*. Tübingen: J.C.B. Mohr (Paul Siebeck), 1996, 99–116.

_____, 'Presuppositions in New Testament Interpretation'. In I. H. Marshall ed, *New Testament Interpretation: Essays on Principles and Methods*. Grand Rapids: Eerdmans, 1977, 60–71.

_____, Review of W. Hanson, *Abraham in Galatians*. *JTS* 43 (1992) 614–615.

_____, Review of J. L. Martyn, *Galatians*. *JTS* 51 (2000) 264–270.

Stendahl, Krister, *Paul among Jews and Gentiles*. Philadelphia: Fortress Press, 1976.

Stott, John R. W., *The Message of Galatians*. London: Inter-Varsity Press, 1968.

Stowers, S. K., *Letter Writing in Greco-Roman Antiquity*. Library of Early Christianity. Philadelphia: Westminster, 1986.

Strack, Hermann, and Billerbeck, Paul, *Kommentar zum Neuen Testament aus Talmud und Midrasch*. 4 vols. München: C. H. Beck'sche Verlagsbuchhandlung, 1956–161.

Strecker, Georg, 'Befreiung und Rechtfertigung: Zur Stellung der Rechtfertigungslehre in der Theologie des Paulus'. J. Friedrich *et al.* eds., *Rechtfertigung* (E. Käsemann FS). Tübingen: J. C. B. Mohr, 1975, 479–508.

Stuhlmacher, Peter, *Biblische Theologie des Neuen Testaments 1: Grundlegung von Jesus zu Paulus*. Göttingen: Vandenhoeck & Ruprecht, 1992.

_____, 'Erwägungen zum ontologischen Charakter der *kaine ktisis* bei Paulus'. *ET* 27 (1965) 1–35.

_____, 'Erwägungen zum Problem von Gegenwart und Zukunft in der paulinischen Eschatologie'. *ZTK* 64 (1967) 423–450.

_____, *Gerechtigkeit Gottes bei Paulus*. Göttingen: Vandenhoeck & Ruprecht, 1966.

_____, *Paul's Letter to the Romans. A Commentary*. Trans. S. J. Hafemann. Louisville, KT: Westminster/John Knox Press, 1994.

_____, *Reconciliation, Law, and Righteousness*. Trans. E. R. Kalin. Philadelphia: Fortress Press, 1986.

Styler, G. M., 'The Basis of Obligation in Paul's Christology and Ethics'. In B. Lindars *et al.* eds, *Christ and Spirit in the New Testament* (C.F.D. Moule FS).Cambridge: Cambridge University Press, 1973, 175–187.

Suhl, von Alfred, 'Der Galaterbrief - Situation und Argumentation'. *ANRW* 2.26.2 (1987) 3067–3134.

Tachau, Peter, *"Einst" und "Jetzt" im Neuen Testament: Beobachtungen zu einem urchristlichen Predigtschema in der Neutestamentlichen Briefliteratur und zu seiner Vorgeschichte*. Göttingen: Vandenhoeck & Ruprecht, 1972.

Tannehill, R. C., *Dying and Rising with Christ*. Berlin: Alfred Töpelmann, 1967.

Theissen, Gerd, *Social Reality and the Early Christians: Theology, Ethics, and the World of the New Testament*. Trans. Margaret Kohl. Minneapolis: Fortress, 1992.

Theron, D. J., 'Adoption in Pauline Corpus'. *EQ* 28 (1956) 6–14.

Thielman, Frank, *From Plight to Solution: A Jewish Framework for Understanding Paul's View of the Law in Galatians and Romans*. SNovT 61. Leiden: Brill, 1989.

_____, *Paul and the Law: A Contextual Approach*. Downers Grove: IVP, 1994.

Thiselton, Anthony C., *New Horizons in Hermeneutics: The Theory and Practice of Transforming Biblical Reading*. Grand Rapids: Zondervan, 1992.

Thomson, Ian H., *Chiasmus in the Pauline Letters*. JSNTSS 111. Sheffield: Sheffield Academic Press, 1995.

Thornton, T. C. G., 'Jewish New Moon Festivals, Galatians 4:3–11 and Colossians 2:16'. *JTS* 40 (1989) 97–100.

Tyson, Joseph, 'Paul's Opponents in Galatia'. *NovT* 10 (1968) 241–254.

Vielhauer, Philipp, 'Gesetzesdienst und Stoicheiadienst im Galaterbrief'. In J. Friedrich *et al.* eds., *Rechtfertigung* (E. Käsemann FS). Tübingen: J. C. B. Mohr, 1975, 543–555.

Vos, Geerhardus, 'The Eschatological Aspect of the Pauline Conception of the Spirit'. In *Redemptive History and Biblical Interpretation*. Presbyterian and Reformed Publishing Company, 1980, 91–125.

_____, *Pauline Eschatology*. Presbyterian and Reformed Publishing Company, [1930] 1994.

Vos, Johannes. S., *Traditionsgeschichtliche Untersuchungen zur paulinischen Pneumatologie*. Assen, Niederlande: van Gorcum, 1973.

Watson, Francis, *Paul, Judaism and the Gentiles: A Sociological Approach*. SNTSMS 56. Cambridge: Cambridge University Press, 1989.

_____, *Text, Church and World: Biblical Interpretation in Theological Perspective*. Grand Rapids: Eerdmans, 1994.

Weder, Hans, *Das Kreuz Jesu bei Paulus*. FRLANT 125. Göttingen: Vandenhoeck & Ruprecht, 1981.

Weima, Jeffrey A. D., 'Gal. 6:11–18: A Hermeneutical Key to the Galatian Letter'. *CTJ* 28 (1993) 90–107.

_____, 'What Does Aristotle Have to Do with Paul?' *CTJ* 32 (1997) 458-68.

Wengst, K., *Christologische Formeln und Lieder des Urchristentums*. Gütersloh: Gütersloher, 1972.

Westerholm, Stephen, *Israel's Law and the Church's Faith: Paul and His Recent Interpreters*. Grand Rapids: Eerdmans, 1988.

_____, 'Sinai as Viewed From Damascus: Paul's Reevaluation of the Mosaic Law'. In R. N. Longenecker ed., *The Road From Damascus: The Impact of Paul's Conversion on His Life, Thought and Ministry*. Grand Rapids: Eerdmans, 1997, 147–165.

White, J. L., *The Form and Function of the Body of the Greek Letter: A Study of the Letter-Body in the Non-Literary Papyri and in Paul the Apostle*. Missoula: Scholars Press, 1972.

Wilckens, Ulrich, *Rechtfertigung als Freiheit: Paulusstudien*. Neukirchen-Vluyn: Neukirchen Verlag, 1974.

_____, *Der Brief an die Römer (Röm 1–5)*. EKK VI/1. Zürich, Einsiedeln, Köln: Benziger Verlag; Neukirchen-Vluyn: Neukirchener Verlag, 1978.

_____, 'ὑποκρίνομαι κτλ.' *TDNT* 8:559–571.

Wilcox, M., 'The Promise of the "Seed" in the New Testament and the Targum'. *JSNT* 5 (1979) 2–20.

_____, '"Upon the Tree" – Deut. 21:22–23 in the New Testament'. *JBL* 96 (1977) 85–99.

Wiles, Gordon P., *Paul's Intercessory Prayers: the Significance of the Intercessory Prayer Passages in the Letters of St Paul.* SNTSMS 24. Cambridge: Cambridge University Press, 1974.

Williams, Sam K., *Galatians.* ANTC. Nashville: Abingdon, 1997.

_____, '*Promise* in Galatians: A Reading of Paul's Reading of Scripture'. *JBL* 107 (1988) 709–720.

_____, 'The Hearing of Faith: AKOE PISTEOS in Gal 3'. *NTS* 35 (1989) 82–93.

_____, 'Justification and the Spirit in Galatians'. *JSNT* 29 (1987) 91–100

Wisdom, Jeffrey, *Blessing for the Nations and the Curse of the Law: Paul's Citation of Genesis and Deuteronomy in Galatians 3.8–10.* WUNT 2. Reihe 133. .Tübingen: Mohr Siebeck, 2001.

Witherington III, B., *Grace in Galatia: A Commentary on St Paul's Letter to the Galatians.* Edinburgh: T. & T. Clark, 1998.

Wolter, M., 'Ethos und Identität in paulinischen Gemeinden'. *NTS* 43 (1997) 430–444.

Wrede, W., *Paul.* Trans. E. Lummis. London: Philip Green, 1907.

Wright, N. T., *The Climax of the Covenant.* Edinburgh: T. & T. Clark, 1991.

_____, 'Gospel and Theology in Galatians'. In L. A. Jervis *et al.* eds., *Gospel in Paul: Studies on Corinthians, Galatians and Romans for Richard N. Longenecker.* JSNTSS 108. Sheffield: Sheffield Academic Press, 1994, 222–239.

Yinger, Kent L., *Paul, Judaism, and Judgment according to Deeds.* SNTSMS 105. Cambridge: Cambridge University Press, 1999.

Young, N. H., '*Paidagogos*: The Social Setting of a Pauline Metaphor'. *NovT* 29 (1987) 150–176.

Zerwick, Maximilian, *Biblical Greek.* Trans. Joseph Smith. Rome: E.P.I.B., 1963.

Ziesler, J. A., *The Epistle to the Galatians.* Epworth Commentaries. London: Epworth, 1992.

_____, *The Meaning of Righteousness in Paul.* SNTSMS 20. Cambridge: Cambridge University Press, 1972.

_____, *Pauline Christianity.* OBS. Oxford: Oxford University Press, 1990.

Index of Sources

Old Testament (LXX)

New Testament

Old Testament Apocrypha and Pseudepigrapha

Dead Sea Scrolls

Index of Modern Authors

Index of Subjects

Wissenschaftliche Untersuchungen zum Neuen Testament

Alphabetical Index of the First and Second Series

Bolyki, János: Jesu Tischgemeinschaften. 1997. *Volume II/96.*

Bosman, Philip: Conscience in Philo and Paul. 2003. *Volume II/166.*

Bovon, François: Studies in Early Christianity. 2003. *Volume 161.*

Brocke, Christoph vom: Thessaloniki – Stadt des Kassander und Gemeinde des Paulus. 2001. *Volume II/125.*

Brunson, Andrew: Psalm 118 in the Gospel of John. 2003. *Volume II/158.*

Büchli, Jörg: Der Poimandres – ein paganisiertes Evangelium. 1987. *Volume II/27.*

Bühner, Jan A.: Der Gesandte und sein Weg im 4. Evangelium. 1977. *Volume II/2.*

Burchard, Christoph: Untersuchungen zu Joseph und Aseneth. 1965. *Volume 8.*

– Studien zur Theologie, Sprache und Umwelt des Neuen Testaments. Ed. von D. Sänger. 1998. *Volume 107.*

Burnett, Richard: Karl Barth's Theological Exegesis. 2001. *Volume II/145.*

Byron, John: Slavery Metaphors in Early Judaism and Pauline Christianity. 2003. *Volume II/162.*

Byrskog, Samuel: Story as History – History as Story. 2000. *Volume 123.*

Cancik, Hubert (Ed.): Markus-Philologie. 1984. *Volume 33.*

Capes, David B.: Old Testament Yaweh Texts in Paul's Christology. 1992. *Volume II/47.*

Caragounis, Chrys C.: The Development of Greek and the New Testament. 2004. *Volume 167.*

– The Son of Man. 1986. *Volume 38.*

– see *Fridrichsen, Anton.*

Carleton Paget, James: The Epistle of Barnabas. 1994. *Volume II/64.*

Carson, D.A., O'Brien, Peter T. and *Mark Seifrid* (Ed.): Justification and Variegated Nomism.
Volume 1: The Complexities of Second Temple Judaism. 2001. *Volume II/140.*
Volume 2: The Paradoxes of Paul. 2004. *Volume II/181.*

Ciampa, Roy E.: The Presence and Function of Scripture in Galatians 1 and 2. 1998. *Volume II/102.*

Classen, Carl Joachim: Rhetorical Criticsm of the New Testament. 2000. *Volume 128.*

Colpe, Carsten: Iranier – Aramäer – Hebräer – Hellenen. 2003. *Volume 154.*

Crump, David: Jesus the Intercessor. 1992. *Volume II/49.*

Dahl, Nils Alstrup: Studies in Ephesians. 2000. *Volume 131.*

Deines, Roland: Jüdische Steingefäße und pharisäische Frömmigkeit. 1993. *Volume II/52.*

– Die Pharisäer. 1997. *Volume 101.*

– */ Niebuhr, Karl-Wilhelm (Hrsg.):* Philo und das Neue Testament. 2004. *Volume 172.*

Dettwiler, Andreas and *Jean Zumstein (Ed.):* Kreuzestheologie im Neuen Testament. 2002. *Volume 151.*

Dickson, John P.: Mission-Commitment in Ancient Judaism and in the Pauline Communities. 2003. *Volume II/159.*

Dietzfelbinger, Christian: Der Abschied des Kommenden. 1997. *Volume 95.*

Dobbeler, Axel von: Glaube als Teilhabe. 1987. *Volume II/22.*

Du Toit, David S.: Theios Anthropos. 1997. *Volume II/91*

Dunn, James D.G. (Ed.): Jews and Christians. 1992. *Volume 66.*

– Paul and the Mosaic Law. 1996. *Volume 89.*

Dunn, James D.G., Hans Klein, Ulrich Luz and *Vasile Mihoc* (Ed.): Auslegung der Bibel in orthodoxer und westlicher Perspektive. 2000. *Volume 130.*

Ebel, Eva: Die Attraktivität früher christlicher Gemeinden. 2004. *Volume II/178.*

Ebertz, Michael N.: Das Charisma des Gekreuzigten. 1987. *Volume 45.*

Eckstein, Hans-Joachim: Der Begriff Syneidesis bei Paulus. 1983. *Volume II/10.*

– Verheißung und Gesetz. 1996. *Volume 86.*

Ego, Beate: Im Himmel wie auf Erden. 1989. *Volume II/34*

Ego, Beate and *Lange, Armin* with *Pilhofer, Peter (Ed.):* Gemeinde ohne Tempel – Community without Temple. 1999. *Volume 118.*

Eisen, Ute E.: see *Paulsen, Henning.*

Ellis, E. Earle: Prophecy and Hermeneutic in Early Christianity. 1978. *Volume 18.*

– The Old Testament in Early Christianity. 1991. *Volume 54.*

Endo, Masanobu: Creation and Christology. 2002. *Volume 149.*

Ennulat, Andreas: Die 'Minor Agreements'. 1994. *Volume II/62.*

Ensor, Peter W.: Jesus and His 'Works'. 1996. *Volume II/85.*

Eskola, Timo: Messiah and the Throne. 2001. *Volume II/142.*

– Theodicy and Predestination in Pauline Soteriology. 1998. *Volume II/100.*

Fatehi, Mehrdad: The Spirit's Relation to the Risen Lord in Paul. 2000. *Volume II/128.*

Feldmeier, Reinhard: Die Krisis des Gottessohnes. 1987. *Volume II/21.*

- Die Christen als Fremde. 1992. *Volume 64.*
Feldmeier, Reinhard and *Ulrich Heckel* (Ed.): Die Heiden. 1994. *Volume 70.*
Fletcher-Louis, Crispin H.T.: Luke-Acts: Angels, Christology and Soteriology. 1997. *Volume II/94.*
Förster, Niclas: Marcus Magus. 1999. *Volume 114.*
Forbes, Christopher Brian: Prophecy and Inspired Speech in Early Christianity and its Hellenistic Environment. 1995. *Volume II/75.*
Fornberg, Tord: see *Fridrichsen, Anton.*
Fossum, Jarl E.: The Name of God and the Angel of the Lord. 1985. *Volume 36.*
Foster, Paul: Community, Law and Mission in Matthew's Gospel. *Volume II/177.*
Fotopoulos, John: Food Offered to Idols in Roman Corinth. 2003. *Volume II/151.*
Frenschkowski, Marco: Offenbarung und Epiphanie. Volume 1 1995. *Volume II/79* – Volume 2 1997. *Volume II/80.*
Frey, Jörg: Eugen Drewermann und die biblische Exegese. 1995. *Volume II/71.*
- Die johanneische Eschatologie. Volume I. 1997. *Volume 96.* – Volume II. 1998. *Volume 110.*
- Volume III. 2000. *Volume 117.*
Freyne, Sean: Galilee and Gospel. 2000. *Volume 125.*
Fridrichsen, Anton: Exegetical Writings. Edited by C.C. Caragounis and T. Fornberg. 1994. *Volume 76.*
Garlington, Don B.: 'The Obedience of Faith'. 1991. *Volume II/38.*
- Faith, Obedience, and Perseverance. 1994. *Volume 79.*
Garnet, Paul: Salvation and Atonement in the Qumran Scrolls. 1977. *Volume II/3.*
Gese, Michael: Das Vermächtnis des Apostels. 1997. *Volume II/99.*
Gheorghita, Radu: The Role of the Septuagint in Hebrews. 2003. *Volume II/160.*
Gräbe, Petrus J.: The Power of God in Paul's Letters. 2000. *Volume II/123.*
Gräßer, Erich: Der Alte Bund im Neuen. 1985. *Volume 35.*
- Forschungen zur Apostelgeschichte. 2001. *Volume 137.*
Green, Joel B.: The Death of Jesus. 1988. *Volume II/33.*
Gregory, Andrew: The Reception of Luke and Acts in the Period before Irenaeus. 2003. *Volume II/169.*
Gundry Volf, Judith M.: Paul and Perseverance. 1990. *Volume II/37.*

Hafemann, Scott J.: Suffering and the Spirit. 1986. *Volume II/19.*
- Paul, Moses, and the History of Israel. 1995. *Volume 81.*
Hahn, Johannes (Ed.): Zerstörungen des Jerusalemer Tempels. 2002. *Volume 147.*
Hannah, Darrel D.: Michael and Christ. 1999. *Volume II/109.*
Hamid-Khani, Saeed: Relevation and Concealment of Christ. 2000. *Volume II/120.*
Harrison; James R.: Paul's Language of Grace in Its Graeco-Roman Context. 2003. *Volume II/172.*
Hartman, Lars: Text-Centered New Testament Studies. Ed. von D. Hellholm. 1997. *Volume 102.*
Hartog, Paul: Polycarp and the New Testament. 2001. *Volume II/134.*
Heckel, Theo K.: Der Innere Mensch. 1993. *Volume II/53.*
- Vom Evangelium des Markus zum viergestaltigen Evangelium. 1999. *Volume 120.*
Heckel, Ulrich: Kraft in Schwachheit. 1993. *Volume II/56.*
- Der Segen im Neuen Testament. 2002. *Volume 150.*
- see *Feldmeier, Reinhard.*
- see *Hengel, Martin.*
Heiligenthal, Roman: Werke als Zeichen. 1983. *Volume II/9.*
Hellholm, D.: see *Hartman, Lars.*
Hemer, Colin J.: The Book of Acts in the Setting of Hellenistic History. 1989. *Volume 49.*
Hengel, Martin: Judentum und Hellenismus. 1969, [3]1988. *Volume 10.*
- Die johanneische Frage. 1993. *Volume 67.*
- Judaica et Hellenistica. Kleine Schriften I. 1996. *Volume 90.*
- Judaica, Hellenistica et Christiana. Kleine Schriften II. 1999. *Volume 109.*
- Paulus und Jakobus. Kleine Schriften III. 2002. *Volume 141.*
Hengel, Martin and *Ulrich Heckel* (Ed.): Paulus und das antike Judentum. 1991. *Volume 58.*
Hengel, Martin and *Hermut Löhr* (Ed.): Schriftauslegung im antiken Judentum und im Urchristentum. 1994. *Volume 73.*
Hengel, Martin and *Anna Maria Schwemer:* Paulus zwischen Damaskus und Antiochien. 1998. *Volume 108.*
- Der messianische Anspruch Jesu und die Anfänge der Christologie. 2001. *Volume 138.*
Hengel, Martin and *Anna Maria Schwemer* (Ed.): Königsherrschaft Gottes und himmlischer Kult. 1991. *Volume 55.*

– Die Septuaginta. 1994. *Volume 72.*
Hengel, Martin; Siegfried Mittmann and *Anna Maria Schwemer* (Ed.): La Cité de Dieu / Die Stadt Gottes. 2000. *Volume 129.*
Herrenbrück, Fritz: Jesus und die Zöllner. 1990. *Volume II/41.*
Herzer, Jens: Paulus oder Petrus? 1998. *Volume 103.*
Hoegen-Rohls, Christina: Der nachösterliche Johannes. 1996. *Volume II/84.*
Hofius, Otfried: Katapausis. 1970. *Volume 11.*
– Der Vorhang vor dem Thron Gottes. 1972. *Volume 14.*
– Der Christushymnus Philipper 2,6-11. 1976, ²1991. *Volume 17.*
– Paulusstudien. 1989, ²1994. *Volume 51.*
– Neutestamentliche Studien. 2000. *Volume 132.*
– Paulusstudien II. 2002. *Volume 143.*
Hofius, Otfried and *Hans-Christian Kammler:* Johannesstudien. 1996. *Volume 88.*
Holtz, Traugott: Geschichte und Theologie des Urchristentums. 1991. *Volume 57.*
Hommel, Hildebrecht: Sebasmata. Volume 1 1983. *Volume 31* – Volume 2 1984. *Volume 32.*
Hvalvik, Reidar: The Struggle for Scripture and Covenant. 1996. *Volume II/82.*
Johns, Loren L.: The Lamb Christology of the Apocalypse of John. 2003. *Volume II/167.*
Joubert, Stephan: Paul as Benefactor. 2000. *Volume II/124.*
Jungbauer, Harry: „Ehre Vater und Mutter". 2002. *Volume II/146.*
Kähler, Christoph: Jesu Gleichnisse als Poesie und Therapie. 1995. *Volume 78.*
Kamlah, Ehrhard: Die Form der katalogischen Paränese im Neuen Testament. 1964. *Volume 7.*
Kammler, Hans-Christian: Christologie und Eschatologie. 2000. *Volume 126.*
– Kreuz und Weisheit. 2003. *Volume 159.*
– see *Hofius, Otfried.*
Kelhoffer, James A.: Miracle and Mission. 1999. *Volume II/112.*
Kieffer, René and *Jan Bergman (Ed.):* La Main de Dieu / Die Hand Gottes. 1997. *Volume 94.*
Kim, Seyoon: The Origin of Paul's Gospel. 1981, ²1984. *Volume II/4.*
– "The 'Son of Man'" as the Son of God. 1983. *Volume 30.*
Klauck, Hans-Josef: Religion und Gesellschaft im frühen Christentum. 2003. *Volume 152.*
Klein, Hans: see *Dunn, James D.G..*
Kleinknecht, Karl Th.: Der leidende Gerechtfertigte. 1984, ²1988. *Volume II/13.*
Klinghardt, Matthias: Gesetz und Volk Gottes. 1988. *Volume II/32.*

Koch, Michael: Drachenkampf und Sonnenfrau. 2004. *Volume II/184.*
Koch, Stefan: Rechtliche Regelung von Konflikten im frühen Christentum. 2004. *Volume II/174.*
Köhler, Wolf-Dietrich: Rezeption des Matthäusevangeliums in der Zeit vor Irenäus. 1987. *Volume II/24.*
Köhn, Andreas: Der Neutestamentler Ernst Lohmeyer. 2004. *Band II/180.*
Kooten, George H. van: Cosmic Christology in Paul and the Pauline School. 2003. *Volume II/171.*
Korn, Manfred: Die Geschichte Jesu in veränderter Zeit. 1993. *Volume II/51.*
Koskenniemi, Erkki: Apollonios von Tyana in der neutestamentlichen Exegese. 1994. *Volume II/61.*
Kraus, Thomas J.: Sprache, Stil und historischer Ort des zweiten Petrusbriefes. 2001. *Volume II/136.*
Kraus, Wolfgang: Das Volk Gottes. 1996. *Volume 85.*
– and *Karl-Wilhelm Niebuhr* (Ed.): Frühjudentum und Neues Testament im Horizont Biblischer Theologie. 2003. *Volume 162.*
– see *Walter, Nikolaus.*
Kreplin, Matthias: Das Selbstverständnis Jesu. 2001. *Volume II/141.*
Kuhn, Karl G.: Achtzehngebet und Vaterunser und der Reim. 1950. *Volume 1.*
Kvalbein, Hans: see *Ådna, Jostein.*
Kwon, Yon-Gyong: Eschatology in Galatians. 2004. *Volume II/183.*
Laansma, Jon: I Will Give You Rest. 1997. *Volume II/98.*
Labahn, Michael: Offenbarung in Zeichen und Wort. 2000. *Volume II/117.*
Lambers-Petry, Doris: see *Tomson, Peter J.*
Lange, Armin: see *Ego, Beate.*
Lampe, Peter: Die stadtrömischen Christen in den ersten beiden Jahrhunderten. 1987, ²1989. *Volume II/18.*
Landmesser, Christof: Wahrheit als Grundbegriff neutestamentlicher Wissenschaft. 1999. *Volume 113.*
– Jüngerberufung und Zuwendung zu Gott. 2000. *Volume 133.*
Lau, Andrew: Manifest in Flesh. 1996. *Volume II/86.*
Lawrence, Louise: An Ethnography of the Gospel of Matthew. 2003. *Volume II/165.*
Lee, Pilchan: The New Jerusalem in the Book of Relevation. 2000. *Volume II/129.*

Lichtenberger, Hermann: see *Avemarie, Friedrich.*

Lichtenberger, Hermann: Das Ich Adams und das Ich der Menschheit. 2004. *Volume 164.*

Lierman, John: The New Testament Moses. 2004. *Volume II/173.*

Lieu, Samuel N.C.: Manichaeism in the Later Roman Empire and Medieval China. ²1992. *Volume 63.*

Loader, William R.G.: Jesus' Attitude Towards the Law. 1997. *Volume II/97.*

Löhr, Gebhard: Verherrlichung Gottes durch Philosophie. 1997. *Volume 97.*

Löhr, Hermut: Studien zum frühchristlichen und frühjüdischen Gebet. 2003. *Volume160.*

– *:* see *Hengel, Martin.*

Löhr, Winrich Alfried: Basilides und seine Schule. 1995. *Volume 83.*

Luomanen, Petri: Entering the Kingdom of Heaven. 1998. *Volume II/101.*

Luz, Ulrich: see *Dunn, James D.G.*

Mackay, Ian D.: John's Raltionship with Mark. 2004. *Volume II/182.*

Maier, Gerhard: Mensch und freier Wille. 1971. *Volume 12.*

– Die Johannesoffenbarung und die Kirche. 1981. *Volume 25.*

Markschies, Christoph: Valentinus Gnosticus? 1992. *Volume 65.*

Marshall, Peter: Enmity in Corinth: Social Conventions in Paul's Relations with the Corinthians. 1987. *Volume II/23.*

Mayer, Annemarie: Sprache der Einheit im Epheserbrief und in der Ökumene. 2002. *Volume II/150.*

McDonough, Sean M.: YHWH at Patmos: Rev. 1:4 in its Hellenistic and Early Jewish Setting. 1999. *Volume II/107.*

McGlynn, Moyna: Divine Judgement and Divine Benevolence in the Book of Wisdom. 2001. *Volume II/139.*

Meade, David G.: Pseudonymity and Canon. 1986. *Volume 39.*

Meadors, Edward P.: Jesus the Messianic Herald of Salvation. 1995. *Volume II/72.*

Meißner, Stefan: Die Heimholung des Ketzers. 1996. *Volume II/87.*

Mell, Ulrich: Die „anderen" Winzer. 1994. *Volume 77.*

Mengel, Berthold: Studien zum Philipperbrief. 1982. *Volume II/8.*

Merkel, Helmut: Die Widersprüche zwischen den Evangelien. 1971. *Volume 13.*

Merklein, Helmut: Studien zu Jesus und Paulus. Volume 1 1987. *Volume 43.* – Volume 2 1998. *Volume 105.*

Metzdorf, Christina: Die Tempelaktion Jesu. 2003. *Volume II/168.*

Metzler, Karin: Der griechische Begriff des Verzeihens. 1991. *Volume II/44.*

Metzner, Rainer: Die Rezeption des Matthäus-evangeliums im 1. Petrusbrief. 1995. *Volume II/74.*

– Das Verständnis der Sünde im Johannesevan-gelium. 2000. *Volume 122.*

Mihoc, Vasile: see *Dunn, James D.G..*

Mineshige, Kiyoshi: Besitzverzicht und Almosen bei Lukas. 2003. *Volume II/163.*

Mittmann, Siegfried: see *Hengel, Martin.*

Mittmann-Richert, Ulrike: Magnifikat und Benediktus. 1996. *Volume II/90.*

Mußner, Franz: Jesus von Nazareth im Umfeld Israels und der Urkirche. Ed. von M. Theobald. 1998. *Volume 111.*

Niebuhr, Karl-Wilhelm: Gesetz und Paränese. 1987. *Volume II/28.*

– Heidenapostel aus Israel. 1992. *Volume 62.*

– see *Deines, Roland*

– see *Kraus, Wolfgang*

Nielsen, Anders E.: "Until it is Fullfilled". 2000. *Volume II/126.*

Nissen, Andreas: Gott und der Nächste im antiken Judentum. 1974. *Volume 15.*

Noack, Christian: Gottesbewußtsein. 2000. *Volume II/116.*

Noormann, Rolf: Irenäus als Paulusinterpret. 1994. *Volume II/66.*

Novakovic, Lidija: Messiah, the Healer of the Sick. 2003. *Volume II/170.*

Obermann, Andreas: Die christologische Erfüllung der Schrift im Johannesevangeli-um. 1996. *Volume II/83.*

Öhler, Markus: Barnabas. 2003. *Volume 156.*

Okure, Teresa: The Johannine Approach to Mission. 1988. *Volume II/31.*

Onuki, Takashi: Heil und Erlösung. 2004. *Volume 165.*

Oropeza, B. J.: Paul and Apostasy. 2000. *Volume II/115.*

Ostmeyer, Karl-Heinrich: Taufe und Typos. 2000. *Volume II/118.*

Paulsen, Henning: Studien zur Literatur und Geschichte des frühen Christentums. Ed. von Ute E. Eisen. 1997. *Volume 99.*

Pao, David W.: Acts and the Isaianic New Exodus. 2000. *Volume II/130.*

Park, Eung Chun: The Mission Discourse in Matthew's Interpretation. 1995. *Volume II/81.*

Park, Joseph S.: Conceptions of Afterlife in Jewish Insriptions. 2000. *Volume II/121.*

Pate, C. Marvin: The Reverse of the Curse. 2000. *Volume II/114.*

Peres, Imre: Griechische Grabinschriften und neutestamentliche Eschatologie. 2003. *Volume 157.*

Philonenko, Marc (Ed.): Le Trône de Dieu. 1993. *Volume 69.*

Pilhofer, Peter: Presbyteron Kreitton. 1990. *Volume II/39.*

– Philippi. Volume 1 1995. *Volume 87.* – Volume 2 2000. *Volume 119.*

– Die frühen Christen und ihre Welt. 2002. *Volume 145.*

– see *Ego, Beate.*

Plümacher, Eckhard: Geschichte und Geschichten. Aufsätze zur Apostelgeschichte und zu den Johannesakten. Herausgegeben von Jens Schröter und Ralph Brucker. 2004. *Volume 170.*

Pöhlmann, Wolfgang: Der Verlorene Sohn und das Haus. 1993. *Volume 68.*

Pokorný, Petr and *Josef B. Souček:* Bibelauslegung als Theologie. 1997. *Volume 100.*

Pokorný, Petr and *Jan Roskovec* (Ed.): Philosophical Hermeneutics and Biblical Exegesis. 2002. *Volume 153.*

Porter, Stanley E.: The Paul of Acts. 1999. *Volume 115.*

Prieur, Alexander: Die Verkündigung der Gottesherrschaft. 1996. *Volume II/89.*

Probst, Hermann: Paulus und der Brief. 1991. *Volume II/45.*

Räisänen, Heikki: Paul and the Law. 1983, ²1987. *Volume 29.*

Rehkopf, Friedrich: Die lukanische Sonderquelle. 1959. *Volume 5.*

Rein, Matthias: Die Heilung des Blindgeborenen (Joh 9). 1995. *Volume II/73.*

Reinmuth, Eckart: Pseudo-Philo und Lukas. 1994. *Volume 74.*

Reiser, Marius: Syntax und Stil des Markusevangeliums. 1984. *Volume II/11.*

Richards, E. Randolph: The Secretary in the Letters of Paul. 1991. *Volume II/42.*

Riesner, Rainer: Jesus als Lehrer. 1981, ³1988. *Volume II/7.*

– Die Frühzeit des Apostels Paulus. 1994. *Volume 71.*

Rissi, Mathias: Die Theologie des Hebräerbriefs. 1987. *Volume 41.*

Roskovec, Jan: see *Pokorný, Petr.*

Röhser, Günter: Metaphorik und Personifikation der Sünde. 1987. *Volume II/25.*

Rose, Christian: Die Wolke der Zeugen. 1994. *Volume II/60.*

Rothschild, Clare K.: Luke Acts and the Rhetoric of History. 2004. *Volume II/175.*

Rüegger, Hans-Ulrich: Verstehen, was Markus erzählt. 2002. *Volume II/155.*

Rüger, Hans Peter: Die Weisheitsschrift aus der Kairoer Geniza. 1991. *Volume 53.*

Sänger, Dieter: Antikes Judentum und die Mysterien. 1980. *Volume II/5.*

– Die Verkündigung des Gekreuzigten und Israel. 1994. *Volume 75.*

– see *Burchard, Christoph*

Salier, Willis Hedley: The Rhetorical Impact of the Sēmeia in the Gospel of John. 2004. *Volume II/186.*

Salzmann, Jorg Christian: Lehren und Ermahnen. 1994. *Volume II/59.*

Sandnes, Karl Olav: Paul – One of the Prophets? 1991. *Volume II/43.*

Sato, Migaku: Q und Prophetie. 1988. *Volume II/29.*

Schäfer, Ruth: Paulus bis zum Apostelkonzil. 2004. *Volume II/179.*

Schaper, Joachim: Eschatology in the Greek Psalter. 1995. *Volume II/76.*

Schimanowski, Gottfried: Die himmlische Liturgie in der Apokalypse des Johannes. 2002. *Volume II/154.*

– Weisheit und Messias. 1985. *Volume II/17.*

Schlichting, Günter: Ein jüdisches Leben Jesu. 1982. *Volume 24.*

Schnabel, Eckhard J.: Law and Wisdom from Ben Sira to Paul. 1985. *Volume II/16.*

Schutter, William L.: Hermeneutic and Composition in I Peter. 1989. *Volume II/30.*

Schwartz, Daniel R.: Studies in the Jewish Background of Christianity. 1992. *Volume 60.*

Schwemer, Anna Maria: see *Hengel, Martin*

Scott, James M.: Adoption as Sons of God. 1992. *Volume II/48.*

– Paul and the Nations. 1995. *Volume 84.*

Shum, Shiu-Lun: Paul's Use of Isaiah in Romans. 2002. *Volume II/156.*

Siegert, Folker: Drei hellenistisch-jüdische Predigten. Teil I 1980. *Volume 20* – Teil II 1992. *Volume 61.*

– Nag-Hammadi-Register. 1982. *Volume 26.*

– Argumentation bei Paulus. 1985. *Volume 34.*

– Philon von Alexandrien. 1988. *Volume 46.*

Simon, Marcel: Le christianisme antique et son contexte religieux I/II. 1981. *Volume 23.*

Snodgrass, Klyne: The Parable of the Wicked Tenants. 1983. *Volume 27.*

Söding, Thomas: Das Wort vom Kreuz. 1997. *Volume 93.*

– see *Thüsing, Wilhelm.*
Sommer, Urs: Die Passionsgeschichte des Markusevangeliums. 1993. *Volume II/58.*
Souček, Josef B.: see *Pokorný, Petr.*
Spangenberg, Volker: Herrlichkeit des Neuen Bundes. 1993. *Volume II/55.*
Spanje, T.E. van: Inconsistency in Paul? 1999. *Volume II/110.*
Speyer, Wolfgang: Frühes Christentum im antiken Strahlungsfeld. Volume I: 1989. *Volume 50.*
– Volume II: 1999. *Volume 116.*
Stadelmann, Helge: Ben Sira als Schriftgelehrter. 1980. *Volume II/6.*
Stenschke, Christoph W.: Luke's Portrait of Gentiles Prior to Their Coming to Faith. *Volume II/108.*
Sterck-Degueldre, Jean-Pierre: Eine Frau namens Lydia. 2004. *Volume II/176.*
Stettler, Christian: Der Kolosserhymnus. 2000. *Volume II/131.*
Stettler, Hanna: Die Christologie der Pastoralbriefe. 1998. *Volume II/105.*
Stökl Ben Ezra, Daniel: The Impact of Yom Kippur on Early Christianity. 2003. *Volume 163.*
Strobel, August: Die Stunde der Wahrheit. 1980. *Volume 21.*
Stroumsa, Guy G.: Barbarian Philosophy. 1999. *Volume 112.*
Stuckenbruck, Loren T.: Angel Veneration and Christology. 1995. *Volume II/70.*
Stuhlmacher, Peter (Ed.): Das Evangelium und die Evangelien. 1983. *Volume 28.*
– Biblische Theologie und Evangelium. 2002. *Volume 146.*
Sung, Chong-Hyon: Vergebung der Sünden. 1993. *Volume II/57.*
Tajra, Harry W.: The Trial of St. Paul. 1989. *Volume II/35.*
– The Martyrdom of St.Paul. 1994. *Volume II/67.*
Theißen, Gerd: Studien zur Soziologie des Urchristentums. 1979, ³1989. *Volume 19.*
Theobald, Michael: Studien zum Römerbrief. 2001. *Volume 136.*
Theobald, Michael: see *Mußner, Franz.*
Thornton, Claus-Jürgen: Der Zeuge des Zeugen. 1991. *Volume 56.*
Thüsing, Wilhelm: Studien zur neutestamentlichen Theologie. Ed. von Thomas Söding. 1995. *Volume 82.*
Thurén, Lauri: Derhethorizing Paul. 2000. *Volume 124.*

Tomson, Peter J. and *Doris Lambers-Petry* (Ed.): The Image of the Judaeo-Christians in Ancient Jewish and Christian Literature. 2003. *Volume 158.*
Trebilco, Paul: The Early Christians in Ephesus from Paul to Ignatius. 2004. *Volume 166.*
Treloar, Geoffrey R.: Lightfoot the Historian. 1998. *Volume II/103.*
Tsuji, Manabu: Glaube zwischen Vollkommenheit und Verweltlichung. 1997. *Volume II/93*
Twelftree, Graham H.: Jesus the Exorcist. 1993. *Volume II/54.*
Urban, Christina: Das Menschenbild nach dem Johannesevangelium. 2001. *Volume II/137.*
Visotzky, Burton L.: Fathers of the World. 1995. *Volume 80.*
Vollenweider, Samuel: Horizonte neutestamentlicher Christologie. 2002. *Volume 144.*
Vos, Johan S.: Die Kunst der Argumentation bei Paulus. 2002. *Volume 149.*
Wagener, Ulrike: Die Ordnung des „Hauses Gottes". 1994. *Volume II/65.*
Walker, Donald D.: Paul's Offer of Leniency (2 Cor 10:1). 2002. *Volume II/152.*
Walter, Nikolaus: Praeparatio Evangelica. Ed. von Wolfgang Kraus und Florian Wilk. 1997. *Volume 98.*
Wander, Bernd: Gottesfürchtige und Sympathisanten. 1998. *Volume 104.*
Watts, Rikki: Isaiah's New Exodus and Mark. 1997. *Volume II/88.*
Wedderburn, A.J.M.: Baptism and Resurrection. 1987. *Volume 44.*
Wegner, Uwe: Der Hauptmann von Kafarnaum. 1985. *Volume II/14.*
Weissenrieder, Annette: Images of Illness in the Gospel of Luke. 2003. Volume II/164.
Welck, Christian: Erzählte ,Zeichen'. 1994. *Volume II/69.*
Wiarda, Timothy: Peter in the Gospels . 2000. *Volume II/127.*
Wilk, Florian: see *Walter, Nikolaus.*
Williams, Catrin H.: I am He. 2000. *Volume II/113.*
Wilson, Walter T.: Love without Pretense. 1991. *Volume II/46.*
Wischmeyer, Oda: Von Ben Sira zu Paulus. 2004. *Volume 178.*
Wisdom, Jeffrey: Blessing for the Nations and the Curse of the Law. 2001. *Volume II/133.*
Wucherpfennig, Ansgar: Heracleon Philologus. 2002. *Volume 142.*
Yeung, Maureen: Faith in Jesus and Paul. 2002. *Volume II/147.*

Zimmermann, Alfred E.: Die urchristlichen
  Lehrer. 1984, ²1988. *Volume II/12.*
Zimmermann, Johannes: Messianische Texte
  aus Qumran. 1998. *Volume II/104.*
Zimmermann, Ruben: Christologie der Bilder im
  Johannesevangelium. 2004. *Volume 171.*

– Geschlechtermetaphorik und Gottes-
  verhältnis. 2001. *Volume II/122.*
Zumstein, Jean: see *Dettwiler, Andreas*
Zwiep, Arie W.: Judas and the Choice of
  Matthias. 2004. *Volume II/187.*

For a complete catalogue please write to the publisher
Mohr Siebeck • P.O. Box 2030 • D–72010 Tübingen/Germany
Up-to-date information on the internet at www.mohr.de